An understanding of the origins of earnings distributions is of central importance for any public policy which has the aim of combating economic inequality. The aim of this book is to provide a satisfactory theoretical foundation which could serve as the rational basis for such policies. The approach, strongly influenced by human capital theory, is especially novel in that it permits individual analyses at three interconnecting levels of aggregation using the same basic microeconomic model: the level of earnings distribution within age groups; the level of the overall earnings distribution across all age groups; and the distribution of lifetime earnings. The analysis demonstrates the interdependence between age composition, inequality and public distribution policy. It also addresses the question of how differences between individuals are transformed into income differences.

A theory of earnings distribution

A theory of earnings distribution

ROBERT K. von WEIZSÄCKER
University of Bonn and University of Halle-Wittenberg

CAMBRIDGE
UNIVERSITY PRESS

Published by the Press Syndicate of the University of Cambridge
The Pitt Building, Trumpington Street, Cambridge CB2 1RP
40 West 20th Street, New York, NY 10011-4211, USA
10 Stamford Road, Oakleigh, Victoria 3166, Australia

Originally published in German as *Theorie der Verteilung der Arbeitseinkommen* by J. C. B. Mohr (Paul Siebeck) 1986 and

First published in English by Cambridge University Press 1993 as *A theory of earnings distribution*

Printed in Great Britain at the University Press, Cambridge

A catalogue record for this book is available from the British Library

Library of Congress cataloguing in publication data

Weizsäcker, Robert K. von.
[Theorie der Verteilung der Arbeitseinkommen. English]
A theory of earnings distribution / Robert K. von Weizsäcker.
p. cm.
Includes bibliographical references and index.
ISBN 0 521 34294 5 (hard)
1. Income distribution. I. Title
HB523.W4413 1993
339.2–dc20 93–19777 CIP

ISBN 0 521 34294 5 hardback

VN

Contents

Preface

I wish to thank Professor Anthony B. Atkinson of the London School of Economics under whose critical eye this study came into being. Without his prompting I would not have chanced upon the topic that is the subject matter of this book, nor would the study have taken this form. His invaluable and expert advice and his constant encouragement over the past four years were crucial to the completion of my work. I should also like to thank Professor Dieter Bös of Bonn University. His detailed comments were an invaluable aid. Finally I must thank Dr Richard N. Vaughan of Cambridge University for many fruitful discussions.

Bonn, November 1984 Robert K. von Weizsäcker

Preface

Introduction: presentation of problem and overview

The distribution of income is one of the main features of any social system. David Ricardo, the classical economist *par excellence*, regarded the determination of income distribution as the most important task facing economics. This view is no longer widely held in the face of today's problems (unemployment, inflation).[1] Nevertheless, the stagnation in economic growth in virtually all modern industrialised societies, which has become the subject of public debate recently, has meant increasing pressure for more attention to be paid to the *distribution* of the national cake, now that this seems to have reached a maximum for the time being.

Whereas Ricardo's statement was related to the rewards to aggregate factors of production such as labour, capital and land (i.e. to the distribution of factor incomes), today's distributional debate is increasingly concerned with disaggregated considerations. The distribution of factor incomes, which was the central object of research in distribution theory in the eighteenth and nineteenth centuries, has been replaced by, for example, the institutional, structural, sectoral or sociological distribution of income. There can be no doubt, however, that the focal point of interest is the distribution of *personal* income. This is the aspect which lies at the root of modern distribution policy controversies, not least because the conventional classifications have little normative significance for the social problem of *inequality of income*. A distributional policy which seeks to address this issue does, however, require a rational foundation, i.e. a *theory* of personal income distribution. Whatever normative ideas the economic policymaker may have, and however he defines 'just' and 'unjust', he cannot put his ideas into practice without the knowledge of how his instruments work.

Theoretical successes in the field of personal income distribution are still

[1] Although, of course, unemployment, inflation and income distribution are ultimately interconnected.

modest. Although this field, which has only recently emerged from limbo in economic theory, has now produced a plethora of approaches,[2] none of the existing theories are entirely satisfactory. Tinbergen's statement would seem to be still valid: 'The fairly satisfactory state of affairs with respect to the statistical description of income distribution contrasts with an unsatisfactory state in the area of economic interpretation' (Tinbergen, 1956, p. 156).

What is particularly needed is a theory of the *distribution of earnings*. Earnings (wages and salaries) provide by far the most important source of income for most people, so that not only does the individual's position on the income scale depend essentially on the size of earnings received, but also the inequality of earnings generally accounts for by far the greatest share of inequality in income as a whole. In recognition of this, Alan Blinder concludes: 'It is clear that there is much more work, both empirical and theoretical, to be done on explaining the dispersion in *wage rates*. So far, it must be admitted, economists have not travelled very far along this path. The simulation results reported here suggest that the payoff to such research, in terms of increasing our understanding of the income distribution, may be quite high indeed' (Blinder, 1974, pp. 140–1). Despite this encouragement and despite the obvious urgency, the current state of the theory of earnings distribution is still unsatisfactory. The present work is my contribution towards an attempt to revive this neglected field.

A theory of the distribution of earnings must achieve two things: firstly, it must explain the empirical facts; secondly, it must be in a position to assess the effects of distribution policy measures. It must be able to generate alternative forecasts for distribution policy. The theoretical approach developed in the present study accordingly concerns itself with the question of how the distribution of earnings arises (or might arise), and how it can be influenced as a result. The aim is to develop a model which can be solved in closed form and which will permit explicit analytical treatment of this question.

The general structure of the model is developed in Chapter 1. This structure was motivated by the study of stochastic theories of personal income distribution, which are theoretically capable of elegantly generating (at least approximately) the distribution observed empirically. The initial fascination of these was, however, rapidly superseded by lasting disenchantment, since this elegance is sterile in economic terms. Pure stochastic

[2] There is a comprehensive review in Sahota (1978). Other good general outlines can be found in Mincer (1970), Blinder (1974, pp. 3–16), Lydall (1976) and Osberg (1981, ch. 6–9).

theories are void of economic content, since they only describe whilst explaining nothing.

What is needed here, in order to identify the possible *economic* determinants of individual earnings and (in the neoclassical sense) integrate them usefully, is an exact *structural* model. A model of this kind is developed and solved in Chapter 2. This forms the economic foundation for all subsequent analyses of distribution.

The theoretical distribution models derived in Chapters 3, 4 and 5 follow the familiar dual goals of supplying possible explanations for empirical phenomena and making possible specific predictions on the consequences of measures motivated by distributional considerations. The analysis is carried out at three different levels: firstly, in terms of the distribution of earnings within a given age group (Chapter 3); secondly, in terms of the total distribution over all age groups (Chapter 4); and finally in terms of the distribution of lifetime earnings (Chapter 5). By explicitly distinguishing these three levels it is possible *inter alia* to demonstrate the links between *age structure*, *inequality* and *public pricing policy* – links which have been dealt with inadequately (if at all) in the theoretical literature to date.

In addition, the individual chapters offer possible answers to the following questions, *inter alia*:

Chapter 2

- How is the length of basic education affected by subsequent opportunities for further education and training?
- 'The major stylized fact of observed life-earnings patterns [is] that earnings rise at a decreasing rate with years of experience in the market' (Rosen, 1977, p. 22). Why is this so, and what does it depend on?
- The recent availability of panel data has contributed significantly to the fact that academic interest in the *intertemporal* aspects of income has increased considerably of late. The individual lifetime earnings path is of particular significance, especially in the currently much-debated reform of social security schemes (e.g. pension schemes). The nature of the measures adopted will depend to a very great extent on the expected earnings profile during the period of employment.[3] But how do these profiles look as a function of individual and structural features, and how do they shift as a result of intervention in the interests of distribution policy?

Chapter 3

- How can the repeatedly observed positive skewness of the distribution of earnings within age groups be explained?

[3] See, for example, Schmähl and Göbel (1983).

- How is the inequality of earnings within age groups determined by the assumed rational behaviour (→ optimisation behaviour) of the individual?
- Why is there a tendency for the empirically observed age profile of inequality to be U-shaped? What are the factors determining this shape?
- What *dynamic* effects on inequality within age groups result from the economic policy instrumental parameters associated with the model?
- Why does correlation between earnings and measured IQ increase over the working life?

Chapter 4
- How does an increase in the price of education affect the inequality of earnings within an economy?
- Why are the social goals of higher per capita income and lower inequality of income generally incompatible?
- To what extent can a significant part of the existing inequality of earnings be regarded as 'self-generated'?
- What lies behind the model prediction that the inequality in earnings within an economy will increase if the birth rate declines? What are the implications of this for distribution policy?

Chapter 5
- In the current model, inequality of lifetime earnings declines as the rate of interest rises. Why?
- Empirical data on the inequality of earnings is generally only available for the current distribution (→ Chapter 4), not for the lifetime earnings distribution. Distribution policy measures must therefore generally be adopted on the basis of the overall distribution of earnings as observed at a particular moment, although (as argued in Chapters 4 and 5, i.e. given the type of model described here), a lifetime concept of inequality would be more appropriate for evaluating the effects of these measures.

  The key question then is this: are the policy decisions taken on the basis of the current distribution *generally compatible* with those which would be taken on the basis of the lifetime distribution of income? To come straight to the point: they are not. Why is this the case? Does it apply to all instrumental parameters of economic policymakers associated with the model?
- There is a widely accepted view that inequality of lifetime earnings is always smaller than inequality of earnings in current periods. Is there a theoretical foundation for this view? Not necessarily, as we shall see.
- In line with the model used here, the inequality of lifetime earnings can be broken down into an initial component and a growth component. The

latter covers the factors altering income which are relevant to growth in individual earnings, the former those factors which determine individual basic productivity at the start of the planning period. What proportion of the inequality in lifetime earnings is explained by the initial component and what proportion by the growth component? If it were possible to find a solution to this question, it would have major implications for social and distributional policy.

- What role does the assumed intertemporal optimisation behaviour of the individuals play in determining the shape of the distribution of lifetime earnings?
- What can be said about the quantitative implications of the effects of distributional policies by using the model? Which instruments of economic policy are accordingly the most effective in combating inequality of lifetime earnings?

Technical note: The chapters in this book are structured in a systematic manner and cannot be read in isolation.

1 The general structure of the model

1.1 Stochastic models of personal income distribution: the general random walk approach

A large number of empirical studies of the distribution of earnings, i.e. individual earnings within a given economic system over a specific period (generally one year), have shown that the observed distribution can be represented by a *log-normal curve* as a first approximation.

Note: This is particularly true for the range of more frequently occurring earnings, i.e. the central portion of the distribution. The log-normal distribution generally provides a less satisfactory fit for the less frequent highest and lowest incomes. The upper end of the distribution, for example, is often more adequately described by Pareto's law.[1]

Generally speaking, the literature encounters so many problems in fitting a functional form to the observed distribution that there are fundamental problems in drawing firm conclusions on the form of the distribution. These problems are partly due to the inadequate correlation between the observed data and theoretical constructions, and partly to the statistical techniques themselves.[2]

All observed earnings distributions have certain qualitative features in common, in that they are typically:

- unimodal
- positively skewed
- showing positive kurtosis

and the log-normal distribution has all of these properties.

[1] The standard references are Aitchison and Brown (1957, ch. 11.6), Lydall (1968, ch. 3.4), Thatcher (1968, pp. 151–9) and Phelps Brown (1977, ch. 9.1).

[2] Cf. McDonald and Ransom (1979). On the problem of fitting (remembering that the existing literature generally relates to income and not earnings), see also Dagum (1977) and the references cited therein, Vartia and Vartia (1980), Harrison (1981) and McDonald (1984).

The further striking stability of this form of distribution has led to speculation on possible ways in which it may have come about.

One main approach employs the techniques and results of *probability theory*, for which reason such models are also described as *stochastic*.[3] Heuristically, this approach can be characterised as follows:

- income changes are stochastic;
- however, the stochastic process which generates them is defined to permit derivation of the probability distribution of future income.
- If this process applies independently to a large number of individuals, it can be used to make predictions on income distribution.

A stochastic model is seen as a possible explanation of the observed relative frequency distribution if the observed relative frequencies correspond approximately to the equilibrium probabilities generated by the model. This naturally gives rise to the question of how such a stochastic process could be defined. Phelps Brown comments on this: 'We know ways in which distributions of various forms can be simulated, and it seems probable that the forces generating any distribution of like form in the real world will be acting in similar ways. These ways therefore provide a framework or template for the impact of the forces that we have reason to believe act upon personal earnings, and for the combination of their impacts' (Phelps Brown, 1977, p. 290).

One of these ways is based on the law of proportionate effect, which states that: 'A variate subject to a process of change is said to obey the law of proportionate effect if the change in the variate at any step of the process is a random proportion of the previous value of the variate' (Aitchison and Brown, 1957, p. 22). If the probability distribution of proportional income changes is independent of the current level of income, or, to put it another way, if the relative rate of growth of income is a random variable (with a given distribution), then changes in income will follow the law of proportionate effect.

In formal terms:

$$\frac{\tilde{Y}_{t+1}^{j} - \tilde{Y}_{t}^{j}}{\tilde{Y}_{t}^{j}} = \tilde{\varepsilon}_{t}^{j}, \qquad (1)$$

where:

$\tilde{Y}_t^j$ represents the earnings of individual j in period t and $\tilde{}$ generally indicates a random variable;

$\{\tilde{\varepsilon}_t^j\}$ are random variables independent of one another and of the variables $\{\tilde{Y}_t^j\}$.

[3] There is a useful survey of the literature in Brown (1976). See also Champernowne (1978).

Assuming a given (i.e. deterministic) initial income Y_0^j, (1) yields the following:

$$\tilde{Y}_{t+1}^j = \tilde{Y}_t^j(1 + \tilde{\varepsilon}_t^j) = Y_0^j \prod_{i=0}^{t} (1 + \tilde{\varepsilon}_i^j).$$

If we further assume that Y_0^j and $\{(1 + \tilde{\varepsilon}_i^j)\}$ are positive variables, taking the logarithm gives

$$\tilde{X}_{t+1}^j = \tilde{X}_t^j + \tilde{Z}_t^j = X_0^j + \sum_{i=0}^{t} \tilde{Z}_i^j. \qquad (2)$$

where $\tilde{X}_t^j := \log \tilde{Y}_t^j$ and $\tilde{Z}_t^j := \log(1 + \tilde{\varepsilon}_t^j)$. This equation defines a general unrestricted one-dimensional random walk in discrete time.

In the simplest case, the $\tilde{Z}_i^j$ are independent random variables with an identical distribution and $E(\tilde{Z}_i^j) = \mu_Z$ and $\operatorname{var}(\tilde{Z}_i^j) = \sigma_Z^2(<\infty)$, so that by applying the Central Limit Theorem we have:

$$\tilde{X}_t^j \sim \text{asy}\, N(X_0^j + t\mu_Z, t\sigma_Z^2). \qquad (3)$$

Accordingly, for sufficiently large t, $\log \tilde{Y}_t^j$ is approximately normally distributed, i.e. $\tilde{Y}_t^j$ has an approximately log-normal distribution. In the context of the distribution of earnings, this result reveals the real point to the law of proportionate effect.

The ideas behind this concept can be traced back to Galton (1879), McAlister (1879) and Kapteyn (1903), although it was Gibrat (1930, 1931) who first formulated the '*loi de l'effet proportionnel*'. In economic terms it is clear that the changes resulting from the stochastic shocks tend to be proportional to the level of earnings rather than having an absolute even impact on income independent of the level. Nevertheless, the law of proportionate effect remains to some extent an *ad hoc* assumption, so that the random walk described by (2) could equally serve as a starting point.[4]

> *Note*: There are generally major conceptual problems involved in demonstrating empirically the invalidity of the assumption of the law of proportionate effect. The reason is that a stochastic model of the form shown in (2) involves at least three assumptions:
>
> – the assumption of the law of proportionate effect ($\tilde{Z}_t^j$ is stochastically independent of $\tilde{X}_t^j$)
> – the Markov assumption ($\tilde{Z}_t^j$ is stochastically independent of $\tilde{Z}_{t+1}^j$ $\forall i \neq 0$), and

[4] The law of proportionate effect is *the* central feature of all the stochastic models generating skewed distributions. The only exception is Mandelbrot (1961). In the context of the theory of the firm, the law of proportionate effect corresponds to the case of constant returns to scale (see Ijiri and Simon, 1977, p. 141).

- the assumption of time homogeneity ($\tilde{Z}_t^j$ are identically distributed with respect to t).

If the empirical evidence contradicts the model, then it is generally impossible to distinguish the assumptions which were violated. See Shorrocks (1976a) and Creedy (1978).

It should further be noted that the above derivation applies to a single individual. Generating the probability distribution for an individual's income does not *per se* permit any statements regarding the distribution of income within a group of individuals (or within an economy as a whole). This would require further assumptions – a point which is frequently overlooked in the literature.[5] If, for example, all the individuals in a group began with the same initial income Y_0^j and the stochastic processes generating the individual incomes were identical and independent of one another, then equation (3) would indeed give the (asymptotic) distribution within the group. I shall be considering the problems arising here in detail in the subsequent development.

Note: The above formulation of a stochastic process with a *continuous* state space and *discrete* time is realistic and appropriate in the current context of *income*. Naturally, a Markov process with a continuous state space and discrete time would be a more general form than the process of equation (2); however, the theory for this is virtually non-existent.[6]

1.2 Criticisms

The above approach leading to (3) is open to criticism for many reasons. Major assumptions include the stochastic independence of $\tilde{Z}_i^j$ over time (i.e. with respect to i) and the stochastic independence of $\tilde{Z}_i^j$ over individuals (i.e. with respect to j). If individual variation in initial income is permitted (a realistic assumption) an additional problem of stochastic dependence arises between $\tilde{Z}_i^j$ and $\tilde{X}_0$ (based on equation (2)). The constant increase in variance implied by (3) is also generally inconsistent with empirical results. Finally, approaches of the above nature are vulnerable to the criticism that, strictly speaking, they are devoid of economic content.

1.2.1 The variance problem

In order to reconcile the model with empirical findings, a *stability condition* has to be imposed to prevent the trend towards a diffusion in the relative dispersion of incomes.[7]

[5] Notable exceptions are Vaughan (1975, ch. 2) and Atkinson and Harrison (1978, ch. 8).
[6] See Cox and Miller (1965, pp. 133–5).
[7] Empirical studies generally show constant dispersion. See Thatcher (1968, pp. 163–5), Göseke and Bedau (1974, section 5 (specifically p. 95)) and Blinder (1980, section 6.4).

The approaches deriving from Gibrat can be directly distinguished by the type and interpretation of the chosen stability condition. Kalecki (1945) introduced the condition of negative correlation between $\tilde{Z}_t^j$ and $\tilde{X}_t^j$, which naturally sacrifices the law of proportionate effect. This condition is to some extent imposed on the model *ad hoc* in order to generate constant relative dispersion of income (or constant dispersion of the logarithm of income), since $\mathrm{var}(\tilde{X}_{t+1}^j) = \mathrm{var}(\tilde{X}_t^j)$ together with $\mathrm{var}(\tilde{X}_{t+1}^j) \stackrel{!}{=} \mathrm{var}(\tilde{X}_t^j + \tilde{Z}_t^j)$ instantly yields $2\mathrm{cov}(\tilde{X}_t^j + \tilde{Z}_t^j) = -\sigma_Z^2$; this prompts Kalecki's assumption:

$$\tilde{Z}_t^j = -\alpha \tilde{X}_t^j + \tilde{u}_t^j; \quad 0 < \alpha < 1, \tag{4}$$

where $\tilde{u}_t^j$ is a random variable independent of $\tilde{X}_t^j$; the $\tilde{u}_t^j$ are independent and identically distributed (iid) and $\mathrm{var}(\tilde{u}_t^j) = \sigma_u^2 (< \infty)$. This means that:

$$\tilde{X}_{t+1}^j = (1 - \alpha)\tilde{X}_t^j + \tilde{u}_t^j, \tag{5}$$

corresponding to the specification of a *regression towards the mean* where $0 < 1 - \alpha < 1$. Recursive substitution in (5) yields:

$$\tilde{X}_{t+1}^j = (1 - \alpha)^{t+1} X_0^j + \sum_{i=0}^{t} (1 - \alpha)^{t-i} \tilde{u}_i^j, \tag{6}$$

so that

$$\mathrm{var}(\tilde{X}_{t+1}^j) = \sum_{i=0}^{t} (1 - \alpha)^{2(t-i)} \sigma_u^2,$$

which converges towards the constant value $\sigma_u^2/[1 - (1 - \alpha)^2]$ as $t \to \infty$.

Note: Kalecki's application of the Central Limit Theorem to (5) and (6) is incorrect (cf. Vaughan, 1975, pp. 49–51); his approach is only permissible if $\tilde{u}_t^j$ is assumed from the start to be *normally distributed*.

The other stabilisation approach developed in the context of income distribution which calls for a brief review here is that of Rutherford (1955). This is much less arbitrary than Kalecki's, and is based on the following idea.

The unrestricted random walk model (2) is not designed to apply for the population as a whole, but only for the individual age groups of which the population is comprised; t accordingly refers to age rather than a calendar period. This is a very plausible assumption, since the time parameter in (2) must be the same for all the individuals under observation. The overall distribution derived from the aggregation of all age group distributions is subject to the continuous arrival of new wage earners and departure of old earners (through birth and death). Although the dispersion of incomes within an age group increases monotonically with age, there is a steady decrease in the number of survivors within an age group of older members, so that the growing dispersion within the age group has less and less effect on the overall distribution: in aggregate, there is a monotonic decrease in the weight of this effect. The stability of the overall dispersion is then guaranteed by the stability of the model's demographic parameters.[8]

There are two other stabilisation approaches in the context of stochastic theories of personal income distribution, namely those of Champernowne (1953, 1973) and Mandelbrot (1960, 1961). These, however, depart from the random walk approach and employ entirely different techniques which are irrelevant for the purposes of the model developed in the present work. Champernowne uses the theory of Markov chains (he also uses a discrete state space), while Mandelbrot uses techniques based on properties of the class of so-called stable distributions (→ Pareto–Lévy stable laws).[9]

1.2.2 The problem of intertemporal stochastic dependence

Stochastic independence of $\tilde{Z}_i^j$ over time is a critical assumption, and one which is ultimately necessary for application of the Central Limit Theorem (in view of (3)).

Although some elements of dependence (e.g. within specific time periods) are permissible, depending on which version of the Limit Theorem is used, stochastic independence is nevertheless still required between these periods.[10] These ideas based on periodisation are further only admissible where sufficiently long periods are examined (including a correspondingly long aggregate time period for observations). This, however, produces its own dilemma. (3) involves an *asymptotic* characteristic. Strictly speaking, $\tilde{X}_t^j$ (the logarithm of income of individual j in period t) therefore has to be broken down into an infinite number of stochastically independent parts. In order to satisfy this condition at least as an approximation, the logical response is to observe periods which are as short as possible (in order to accumulate sufficient partial units).[11] The closer, however, the $\tilde{Z}_i^j$ are together, the more likely it is that the assumption of independence will be

[8] In its essence this idea forms the basis underlying many stochastic models (none of them concerned with earnings). I shall also make use of this idea (cf. particularly Section 4.2).

[9] In concluding this section, it is surprising that the prediction yielded by (3),

$$E(\tilde{X}_i^j) = X_0^j + t\mu_Z \to \infty \quad \text{as} \quad t \to \infty \quad (\text{and } \mu_Z > 0),$$

has never attracted special attention. Theoretically, it could of course be noted that the model does not rule out $\mu_Z = 0$ as a possibility.

[10] See, for example, Schönfeld (1971).

[11] Note that $\tilde{X}_t^j$ relates to the *individual* j (and not for example to dynasty j or some similar entity). It should also be remembered that the limit theorem argument in the present context (cf. (2)) must be applied to a dynamic process over time.

violated. $\tilde{X}_t^j$ would then no longer necessarily have the limiting property (3).

Apart from this basic dilemma, there is yet another objection to the assumption of independence. Within the framework of the approach described in Section 1.1, $\tilde{Z}_i^j$ corresponds to the relative rate of growth of individual income ('relative' because these are logarithms): $\tilde{Z}_i^j = \tilde{X}_{i+1}^j - \tilde{X}_i^j$. Since, however, those factors which determine these growth rates are for the most part related to *individuals*, the assumption of the independence of relative changes (over time) becomes extremely dubious.

Note: In fact, an empirical study by Osberg (1977) showed a high level of correlation across i in $\tilde{Z}_i^j$.

There is another problem with the application of the Central Limit Theorem in this context which needs to be considered. If the Government or any other institution ensures that an individual's income is always above a certain minimum level, i.e. $\tilde{Y}_t^j > y_0$ where y_0 is the poverty level or some similar concept, then the probability distribution of percentage changes is naturally no longer independent of the actual level of income. The law of proportionate effect would then be violated and instead of an unrestricted random walk (2) one would have a random walk with a so-called reflecting barrier.[12] Under these circumstances, the Central Limit Theorem is no longer applicable. Where $y_0 = 0$, however, this problem does not arise in (2): the logarithmic transformation $\tilde{X}_t^j = \log \tilde{Y}_t^j$ is only defined for positive $\tilde{Y}_t^j$ (and thus satisfies the barrier condition $\tilde{Y}_t^j > y_0 = 0$) and also ensures that $\tilde{X}_t^j$ is unrestricted.[13] Generally, however, y_0 is likely to be positive. (2) and (3) would then benefit from a generalisation via $\tilde{X}_t^j := \log(\tilde{Y}_t^j - y_0)$. I shall, however, ignore the case where $y_0 > 0$.

It should also be noted that the typical assumption of *time homogeneity* of the process $\{\tilde{Z}_t^j\}_{i \in \mathrm{N}}$ does not give rise to such major limit theory problems. There are versions of the Central Limit Theorem which permit this assumption to be relaxed, subject to certain conditions and thus do not require the assumption of identically distributed $\tilde{Z}_t^j$.[14]

In concluding this section, I should like to point out that I shall not be overly emphasising the Central Limit Theorem in the course of this study, since I do not attach great importance to the ultimate (asymptotic) 'equilibrium distribution' which features in the philosophy of stochastic models of distribution (cf. p. 7); for my purposes, the initial distribution thus plays an important role.

[12] This is essentially the concept behind Champernowne (1953).
[13] If $\tilde{Y}_t^j$ represents the total income of individual j, the assumption of positive values is harder to justify than when $\tilde{Y}_t^j$ represents the earnings of individual j (as in my model).
[14] See, for example, Fisz (1976, pp. 241, 245) and Gnedenko and Kolmogorow (1968).

Note: The philosophy of stochastic modelling also uses the term *equilibrium* to mean a macroscopic or statistical equilibrium (as in Feller (1968, pp. 394–5)). This is not an equilibrium as is usually understood by the term. Although the ultimate distribution is stable, the individuals of which it is composed, are not; it is a state of macroscopic equilibrium maintained by a very large number of transitions in opposite directions. It should be noted that this view of equilibrium can already be found in Marshall. The notion was originally developed by physicists working in the field of *statistical mechanics*. It should also be remembered in this context that the 'equilibrium' based on the Central Limit Theorem has a peculiar feature. Although the *form* of the distribution approximates the normal distribution asymptotically, the parameters of the distribution (or the moments) are not constant. In the context of the model presented in Section 1.1, this naturally reflects the fact that the generalised random walk is a *non-stationary* process.

1.2.3 The lack of economic content

Let me say right away that this criticism applies not only to the random walk model under discussion but to stochastic models generally.

While the stochastic properties of equation (2) do lead (subject to the conditions shown) to (3), equation (2) itself does not contain any *structural* information at all on the generation and distribution of individual incomes. As long as the stochastic model of Section 1.1 fails to identify the economic parameters underlying the generation and development of individual incomes, it remains a purely descriptive model which thus lacks *any economic explanatory value*. Thus, the non-homogeneous linear stochastic difference equation (2) is an inadequate model of the evolution of individual incomes and of individual behaviour. It is possible to justify models of this kind with the argument that individual incomes are subject to so many complex and interrelated factors that any attempt at explicit theoretical modelling would only be either hopelessly complicated or unrealistically oversimplified.[15] This view can, however, only be accepted if the sole or primary objective is to arrive at the functional limiting form of the distribution under conditions which are as general as possible. Otherwise, I regard this position as not only purist (and in a certain sense destructive) but also indefensible, since empirical research has shown that there are a few significant parameters which determine income along with a very large number of individually insignificant factors; the isolated systematic factors should certainly be reflected in the individual accumulation equations (→ economic endogenisation of the stochastic process (2)).

[15] Cf. Champernowne (1973, p. 246).

The stochastic model in the form of equation (2) neither offers insights into the economic causes of the observed distribution nor is able to predict the effects of specific policy measures on income distribution and thus income inequality. These, however, are the very points of interest to the Government and economic policymakers. It is the task of economic theory (in the absence of a '*ceteris paribus* test laboratory') to identify, at least to a first approximation, the complex economic mechanism underlying the observed income distribution in order to provide possible answers to questions on how we can influence the distribution of income and the effects this would have. This work is an attempt to do just this.[16]

The lack of economic content in stochastic approaches was also the motivation for Mincer's work (under the heading 'human capital theory').[17] Mincer, however, went to the other extreme. He also did not come up with any distribution theory in the sense of the model developed in the present work. Nevertheless, he has a certain copyright on the criticism based on lack of economic content. At the same time it should be noted that Mincer – like many other critics – seems not to have properly understood the role of stochastic models, since he equates stochastic processes like (2) with equations familiar from econometrics (systematic component and unexplained residual).[18] Although such a division of stochastic equations is convenient for empirical purposes, it is still far from clear why economic factors should operate in this manner – in other words, why the systematic component of a stochastic equation should be identifiable.[19]

There is another point which needs to be made here. In contrast to deterministic models of income concerned with the 'representative individual', stochastic models are concerned with the distribution over all individuals. Accordingly, realism impels us to abandon the assumption of a homogeneous population. The admission for example of individual differences in initial income is handled by treating initial income as a random variable $\tilde{Y}_0$. This, however, results (as already indicated on pp. 9–10) in further problems of stochastic dependence, particularly in connection with the argument that many factors affecting income are linked to individuals (i.e. personal, non-market factors). I shall return to this issue in due course.

[16] The criticism of lack of economic content was – together with Champernowne's book of 1973 – the inspiration for my work. See also p. 3.
[17] See Mincer (1958, 1970, 1974).
[18] See Mincer (1970, p. 4).
[19] See, on this, Shorrocks (1976b, p. 92) and Steindl (1965, ch. 1).

1.3 A more sophisticated model

1.3.1 *Structural formulation*

To counter the criticisms to the approach outlined in Section 1.1, the following structure is proposed.

To begin with, (1) is related to the number of years in the labour force (working age) n rather than calendar period t, with $n = 0$ the point of entry into the labour force (= period of monetary earning) and $n = N$ the point of exit.[20]

Next, the growth factor $(1 + \tilde{\varepsilon}_n^j)$ is broken down as follows into an expected individual growth factor $(1 + \tau_n^j)$ and a random residual growth factor $(1 + \tilde{e}_n^j)$:

$$(1 + \tilde{\varepsilon}_n^j) := (1 + \tau_n^j)(1 + \tilde{e}_n^j),$$

with $\tau_n^j = E(\tilde{\varepsilon}_n^j)$, $E(\tilde{e}_n^j) = 0$ and $\operatorname{var}(\tilde{e}_n^j) = \sigma_e^2$, where $\tilde{e}_n^j$ would be stochastically independent over working age n and individuals j; these assumptions will be discussed further below.

This gives instead of (1)

$$\frac{\tilde{Y}_{n+1}^j - \tilde{Y}_n^j(1 + \tau_n^j)}{\tilde{Y}_n^j(1 + \tau_n^j)} = \tilde{e}_n^j, \quad n = 0, \ldots, N - 1; \tag{7}$$

where $\tilde{e}_n^j \sim \operatorname{iid}(0, \sigma_e^2)$ and $\{\tilde{e}_n^j\}$ are stochastically independent of $\{\tilde{Y}_n^j\}$.

Again, assuming a deterministic initial income Y_0^j from (7), we arrive at:

$$\tilde{Y}_{n+1}^j = \tilde{Y}_n^j(1 + \tau_n^j)(1 + \tilde{e}_n^j) = Y_0^j \prod_{i=0}^{n} (1 + \tau_i^j) \prod_{i=0}^{n} (1 + \tilde{e}_i^j). \tag{8}$$

Note: In formal terms, (8) is distantly related to Aitchison and Brown (1957, p. 109) (and consequently also to Fase (1970, ch. 2)).

Since

$$E(\tilde{Y}_{n+1}^j) = E(\tilde{Y}_n^j)(1 + \tau_n^j) = Y_0^j \prod_{i=0}^{n} (1 + \tau_i^j),$$

we can substitute $E(\tilde{Y}_{n+1}^j) =: A_{n+1}^j$ in (8) to yield:

$$\tilde{Y}_{n+1}^j = A_{n+1}^j \prod_{i=0}^{n} (1 + \tilde{e}_i^j),$$

or

[20] For more on this, see Chapter 2.

$$\tilde{Y}_n^j = A_n^j \prod_{i=0}^{n-1} (1 + \tilde{e}_i^j); \quad n = 0, \ldots, N.^{21} \tag{9}$$

Under the condition (which can generally be taken as satisfied) that the variables A_n^j and $\{(1 + \tilde{e}_i^j)\}$ are positive, (9) can be transformed logarithmically to yield $[\tilde{u}_i^j := \log(1 + \tilde{e}_i^j)]$:

$$\tilde{X}_n^j := \log \tilde{Y}_n^j = \log A_n^j + \sum_{i=0}^{n-1} \tilde{u}_i^j. \tag{10}$$

The logarithm of earnings of individual j accordingly describes an unrestricted general random walk around the expected level $\log A_n^j$.

Note: The random walk component $\Sigma_i \tilde{u}_i^j$ should not be confused with pure white noise. It is important here to note the distinction referred to above (p. 14). From (8) we obtain:

$$\tilde{X}_{n+1}^j = \tilde{X}_n^j + \log(1 + \tau_n^j) + \tilde{u}_n^j. \tag{8a}$$

Here, the term $\tilde{u}_n^j$ is not a disturbance component (as, for example, in regression analysis): $\tilde{u}_n^j$ is *not* an unexplained residual; rather it describes individual variation in income.

With $\tilde{u}_i^j \sim \text{iid}(\mu_u, \sigma_u^2(<\infty))$, applying the Central Limit Theorem yields:

$$\tilde{X}_n^j \sim \text{asy}\, N(\log A_n^j + n\mu_u, n\sigma_u^2), \tag{11}$$

or

$$\tilde{Y}_n^j \sim \text{asy}\, \Lambda(\log A_n^j + n\mu_u, n\sigma_u^2).^{22,23} \tag{11a}$$

1.3.2 *Interpretation and derivation of distribution*

If we denote the product in (9), resulting from n random shocks occurring in working periods 0 to $n - 1$ and having a joint effect on the earnings at working age n, by $\tilde{C}_n^j$, we arrive at:

$$\tilde{Y}_n^j = A_n^j \tilde{C}_n^j; \quad n = 0, \ldots, N. \tag{9a}$$

21 With the standard (if vague) convention that $\Pi_{i=0}^{-1}(1 + \tilde{e}_i^j) \equiv 1$ for $n = 0$.

22 The approach developed here could naturally be extended, for example by permitting a regression towards the mean (in the manner of Kalecki) and serial correlation in $\tilde{u}_n^j$. I do not propose to pursue this further here although this does not mean that extension along these lines would not merit consideration. Explicit theoretical development of an empirically defensible stochastic residual structure would go beyond the aims of this chapter; cf. the panel studies by Lillard *et al.* (1978, 1979).

23 In conclusion, there is a possible connection here between the literature on *capital market efficiency* and the random walk model discussed above (earnings viewed as a price; '*labour market efficiency*'). The theoretical justifications of the random walk hypothesis in this literature can be traced to Samuelson (1965). There is no analogous theoretical foundation for corresponding changes in income.

This can be interpreted as follows.

A_n^j is the expected value of the random variable $\tilde{Y}_n^j$. Following a loose analogy with Friedman (1957, pp. 21–2), this component covers the *permanent* income factors, including both those of initial income and those of changes in income, by virtue of:

$$A_n^j = Y_0^j \prod_{i=0}^{n-1} (1 + \tau_i^j).$$

The component $\tilde{C}_n^j$ can then be regarded as incorporating the *transitory* income change factors.

The systematic factors determining the initial value of and changes in the expected earnings of individual j, A_n^j, will be considered in subsequent chapters. For the present, however, the question arises whether these factors may share a common theoretical structure, and whether an economic model can be developed for A_n^j. An attempt will be made to do this below (see Chapter 2).

The $\tilde{C}_n^j = \Pi_{i=0}^{n-1} (1 + \tilde{e}_i^j)$ cover both individual random factors (illness and accident) and random changes in market conditions. In the most general terms, these are factors which are not anticipated by individual j and which are random in terms of the individual's perception.[24]

The term 'transitory' may be somewhat misleading in this context. It is important to distinguish between the cause of a stochastic shock $(1 + \tilde{e}_i^j)$ and the effect. The shock is caused by random income change factors; these are assumed to be transitory (that is, the cause of the shock varies continuously). The effect of the shock, on the other hand, is not limited to a single period; as (9) makes clear, $\tilde{Y}_n^j$ is a function of all preceding stochastic shocks. The fact that the shock process nevertheless has an overall 'transitory' character is expressed in $E(\tilde{C}_n^j) = 1$,[25] so that the stochastic shocks do not have a 'permanent' effect on expected income levels.

For a given A_n^j, according to (9a), the probability distribution of $\tilde{Y}_n^j$ is derived from the law of distribution of the random variables $\tilde{C}_n^j$. Moving from the individual j to the consideration of the complete set of all individuals, we must assume that individuals will have different expected income levels A_n^j. This variability is taken into account by interpreting expected individual earnings as a random variable $\tilde{A}_n$ (where it is generally assumed that A_n^j is continuously distributed over individuals; this requires a

[24] The inclusion of these factors is supported by a wealth of empirical studies. Nowadays it is regarded as an empirically established fact that 'there is a large influence of random, and probably unanticipated, events on the actual earnings experience of an individual' (Griliches, 1977a, p. 13). [25] This is ensured by $\tilde{e}_i^j \sim \text{iid}(0, \sigma_e^2)$.

sufficiently large number of individuals). Assuming furthermore, that all individuals are subject *ex ante* to the same transitory process ($\rightarrow \tilde{C}_n$; assumption of homogeneity in relation to residual changes $(1 + \tilde{e}_i^j)$) and that the individual transitory processes are stochastically independent (for more on this, see Section 1.4.2 below), the following equation provides a basis for deriving the *ex ante* probability distribution:[26]

$$\tilde{Y}_n = \tilde{A}_n \tilde{C}_n, \quad n = 0, \ldots, N. \tag{12}$$

Given the above composition as regards contents, it is logical to require independence between the *permanent* component, $\tilde{A}_n$, and the *transitory* component, $\tilde{C}_n$.[27]

This yields the theoretical distribution function of $\tilde{Y}_n$:[28]

$$F_{Y_n}(y_n) = \int_{-\infty}^{y_n} \int_{-\infty}^{\infty} \frac{1}{|a_n|} f_{A_n}(a_n) f_{C_n}\left(\frac{y_n}{a_n}\right) da_n \, dy_n. \tag{13}$$

Under the foregoing assumptions, F_{Y_n} corresponds to the theoretical distribution function of the characteristic $\tilde{Y}_n$ for the observed population. By applying the *law of large numbers*, we are able to move from this *ex ante* probability distribution to the *ex post* distribution across all individuals – which is exactly what we are interested in, ultimately.

If it is given a basic population in which the characteristic $\tilde{Y}_n$ of the elements ($\hat{=}$ individuals) making up the population, has the theoretical distribution function F_{Y_n}. From this basic population, a simple random sample is drawn of size m ($\hat{=}$ size of population or, in the present case, size of age group n): $\tilde{Y}_n^\zeta, \zeta = 1, \ldots, m$; the $\tilde{Y}_n^\zeta$ are by construction independent and identically distributed (with F_{Y_n}).[29] The empirical distribution function of this sample, $S_n^m(y_n)$ [$S_n^m(y_n) :=$ (number of $\tilde{Y}_n^1, \ldots, \tilde{Y}_n^m \leqslant y_n)/m$; $y_n \in \mathbf{R}$] together with the strong law of large numbers results in $\{S_n^m(y_n)\}_{m \in \mathbf{N}}$ converging with probability one to $F_{Y_n}(y_n)$ as $m \rightarrow \infty$ ($\forall y_n \in \mathbf{R}$) (according to Glivenko's theorem, convergence is uniform for $y_n (y_n \in \mathbf{R})$; cf. for example Fisz (1976, pp. 456–9)).

This transition also requires an adequately large population or age

[26] This naturally requires that the earnings of each individual j are generated by (9a).

[27] Friedman is in fact directly relevant here: 'This assumption seems very mild and highly plausible. Indeed, it can almost be regarded as simply complementing or translating the definitions of transitory and permanent components; the qualitative notion that the transitory component is intended to embody is of an accidental and transient addition to or subtraction from income, which is almost equivalent to saying an addition or subtraction that is not correlated with the rest of income' (Friedman, 1957, pp. 26–7). One could say the $\tilde{A}_n$ represents the 'random individual' and $\tilde{C}_n$ the 'purely random' component of the random variable $\tilde{Y}_n$.

[28] Cf. for example Fisz (1976, p. 84). y_n and a_n denote the values of the variables $\tilde{Y}_n$ and $\tilde{A}_n$.

[29] Note therefore that $\tilde{y}_n^\zeta \neq \tilde{Y}_n^j$.

group. Since in reality $m < \infty$, F_{Y_n} must strictly speaking be described as the *expected* distribution of earnings within age group *n*.

> *Note*: In the same way, the probability density function f_{Y_n} corresponding to (13) (with $\tilde{Y}_n$ understood as a continuous variable) can be reinterpreted analogously: in this case f_{y_n} is described as the *expected* relative frequency function.

This is an appropriate point for a brief preview of the structure of the remaining chapters:

- equation (12) forms the focal point of Chapter 3, consolidating the economic model developed in Chapter 2
- Chapter 4 deals with the *distribution aggregation* $f_Y = \Sigma_n h(n) f_{Y_n}$ ($h(n)$ = age distribution) or with the first moments of the $\tilde{Y}$-distribution, where f_{Y_n} is the density function associated with (13)
- Chapter 5 deals with the *income component aggregation* $\tilde{W} = (1+r)^{-S}\Sigma_n \tilde{A}_n (1+r)^{-n}$ where $\tilde{A}_n$ is taken from (12). For more details, see Chapters 2 and 5.

1.4 Discussion

1.4.1 Advantages compared with conventional structures

What can be gained from the approach outlined in Section 1.3 compared with the conventional approach (Section 1.1)?

(I) The variance problem can now be solved, since the random walk model now relates to the *working age* and not calendar time (→ attribution to constant demographic parameters on the lines of Rutherford's concept). In addition, the monotonic rise in individual income variation within *age* groups predicted by (11a) is not irreconcilable with empirical findings (cf. Chapter 3).

(II) Furthermore, in contrast to the conventional approach, the Central Limit Theorem is now only applied to the total of the *transitory* income change components. Bearing in mind that these components represent solely the effects of random and transient events, it is clear that the assumption of stochastic independence over time (see 1.2.2) is much easier to justify here than in (2). The current approach no longer assumes the summands $\tilde{Z}_i^j$ to be stochastically independent over *i*. The individual nature of many of the factors determining income is no longer an issue: permanent factors linked to individuals are now incorporated in $\tilde{A}_n$ and not in $\tilde{C}_n$.[30]

[30] Although it is now far easier to justify the assumption of stochastic independence over time, I shall not rely too often on the Central Limit Theorem during the remainder of this study, not least because *n* cannot become large arbitrarily (more on this in Chapter 3).

(III) The interpretation in Section 1.3.2 justifies the assumption of stochastic independence of the two components $\tilde{A}_n$ and $\tilde{C}_n$. Application of the law of proportionate effect (and consequently the Central Limit Theorem) is now unaffected by the problems arising in the conventional approach of stochastic dependence between $\tilde{Z}_i$ and $\tilde{X}_0$ (after permitting individual variation across $\tilde{Z}_i^j$ and X_0^j). The law of proportionate effect in the present approach applies solely to random *residual* changes, since the permanent element in income changes has been isolated (cf. (7)).

(IV) Finally, the new approach disarms one of the basic criticisms of stochastic models, namely the absence of economic content. The random walk structure can now be explicitly combined with economic variables. In fact, $\tilde{A}_n$ is explicitly generated by the economic models developed in Chapters 2 and 3.

This economic endogenisation of the random walk approach means that the stochastic model no longer merely describes the mechanism of the evolution of individual income and the generation and evolution of income distribution but also explains them (at least to some extent).

1.4.2 Interpersonal stochastic dependence: an unsolved problem

One problem remains unresolved even with the new approach, namely, that of the stochastic dependence over j of the $\tilde{Z}_i^j$ (alternatively the $\tilde{\varepsilon}_i^j$, or in the present context the $\tilde{u}_i^j$ (or $\tilde{e}_i^j$)). This problem is common to all individual-based stochastic models, and the literature not only fails to deal with it in principle but in general ignores it (cf. footnote 5, p. 9).

First, what is actually meant by stochastic dependence between individuals? As already noted in Section 1.3.2, there are two categories of *transitory* components $\tilde{C}_n^j$ in the income equation for individual j. Firstly, there is the group of those transitory income change factors which only affect individual j (for example, illness). These factors do not result in stochastic dependence between individuals. Secondly, there are the transitory factors which affect several (or all) individuals simultaneously and relate to an entire market or the economy as a whole. These factors can be grouped under the heading 'macroeconomic noise'. If these stochastic macroeconomic fluctuations are described by $\tilde{v}$ and are the only cause of stochastic variations in $\tilde{e}_i^j$ (in other words, if factors in the first group are ignored), then $\tilde{e}_i^j = e_i^j(\tilde{v})\, \forall j \in \mathbf{J}$ (= index set). The determining factor of the stochastic shock $\tilde{e}_i^j$ is the same for all j in an affected set $\mathbf{J}$, *and* this factor is a random variable. This naturally leads to mutual correlation between all the individual equations (9) for the population.

An illustrative example of the second group of factors is provided in the case of *farmers*. Their income depends *inter alia* on the quality of their soil, their individual skills and their technical equipment, but it also depends on weather conditions, and particularly on rainfall. Since it typically rains on a whole series of fields simultaneously rather than on just one field, 'rãin' as a factor determining income, when interpreted as a random variable, results in stochastic interdependence between individual farmers' incomes.

Vaughan (1975, ch. 2) has pointed out that the assumption of stochastic independence between the stochastic mechanisms generating individual incomes (which, as we have just seen, is violated if these mechanisms depend jointly on a factor which is in itself a random variable) is also difficult to reconcile with the existence of fixed aggregated macroeconomic parameters. In fact, a (deterministic) aggregate can result in stochastic dependence between individuals. Consider, for example, *environmental pollution*: cases can arise where the key factor is the density of particles in the air, rather than the neighbour's chimney. Another example is *market demand*: the price something reaches depends on total production (and not just on the neighbour's output).

Generally, the individual stochastic processes are invariably *no longer* independent where individual income levels depend on macroeconomic parameters. *Government budget constraints*, for example, similarly create stochastic interdependence between individuals. Consider, for instance, the following redistributive tax:

$$\tilde{Y}^j_{\text{net}} = \Theta(\tilde{Y}^j_{\text{gross}})^{\Psi}; \quad \Theta > 1, 0 < \Psi < 1;$$

Ψ represents the degree of progression (the smaller Ψ, the more progressive the tax); Θ is the instrument through which the Government returns tax revenue to the economy. The Government accordingly collects the tax in a progressive manner and spends the revenue proportionately. Taxes here are raised purely for redistributive purposes, so that the Government budget constraint is described by 'Government expenditure $\stackrel{!}{=}$ tax revenue'. As a result of this constraint, the net income of individual j naturally depends on the moments of the distribution of $\tilde{Y}_{\text{gross}}$.[31,32]

The *central question* now is, in general terms, how is interpersonal stochastic dependence reflected in the theoretical distribution function F_{Y_n}, i.e. in the distribution over all $\tilde{Y}^j_n$ in the population, $j \in \mathbf{J}$? In the case of the

[31] This is because these moments determine the size of Θ for a given Ψ. 'Stochastic' dependences occur here incidentally because Θ is a function of total revenue for a given Ψ, making it a function of all individual income levels, which are *ex ante* ('before random sampling') random variables; as a result, Θ is also a random variable as a function of the random sample.

[32] The empirical literature *explicitly* treats stochastic interdependence between individuals only in the context of studies on twins and siblings (see, for example, Griliches (1979) and the references cited there) and work on spatial autocorrelation (see, for example, Cliff and Ord (1973)).

farmers, it is for example intuitively obvious that increasing positive correlation between farmers resulting from rainfall will reduce the degree of skewness in the distribution of their incomes. Naturally, however, stochastic interdependence resulting from rain need not increase in this direction. Although the variable $\tilde{v}$ ($\hat{=}$ rainfall) enters the income equation for every farmer *j*, it need not carry the same weight for every individual. Some farmers may possibly benefit more from the rain than others: rain may be more important for one farmer's produce than for another's. It is even possible that rain may be beneficial for one farmer but damaging for another (→ negative individual correlation). The greater the differences in weighting in the individual equations in the population, the greater the additional contribution resulting from rain (the 'macroeconomic noise') to skewness in the income distribution for all *j*.

On the other hand, if all the individual equations (9) had identical weighting, $\tilde{v}$ would have no effect on the (relative) skewness of the distribution for all *j*, since the relative income positions would not change as a result. There would be no distributive effects either, if the individual stochastic processes $\{\tilde{e}_i^j\}_{i \in \mathrm{N}}$ (and thus the individual $\tilde{Y}_n^j$) were stochastically independent (i.e. rain did not have any joint effect on farmers' fields).

The two extreme cases just described (complete positive correlation between all individual equations in the theoretical population, and stochastic independence between individuals) are *compatible* with my specification of the transitory component $\tilde{C}_n$ in (12). In my model, each individual *j* is assumed *ex ante* to be subject to the same transitory process; the probability distribution of the effects of these unforeseen events is both given and identical for all individuals; the stochastic properties of the $\tilde{e}_i^j$ are determined without comment (cf. p. 15). The probability distribution of $\tilde{C}_n^j$ is accordingly independent of *j* (hence the notation '$\tilde{C}_n$'). Implicitly, my model embraces both extreme cases, depending on the interpretation. In addition, however, no allowance is made in the aggregate for any effects on the $\tilde{C}_n^j$ due to interdependence (such as increased skewness or the like). If the elements in the population, i.e. the individuals *j*, were stochastically dependent, then F_{Y_n} as constructed would not correspond to the theoretical distribution function of the characteristic $\tilde{Y}_n$ in this population (except, of course, in the extreme case of perfect positive correlation). The difficult cases are accordingly those which lie *between* these two extremes.

Conceptually, this type of stochastic dependence would have to be taken into account in forming (12), since any correlation between $\tilde{Y}_n^j$ and $\tilde{Y}_n^k$ appears in the properties of the distribution function of $\tilde{Y}_n^j$. Stochastic dependence between $\tilde{Y}_n^j$ and $\tilde{Y}_n^k$ manifests itself as we have seen through the $\tilde{e}_i^j$, but how can we determine the distribution of $\tilde{C}_n = \Pi_{i=0}^{n-1}(1 + \tilde{e}_i)$? This problem cannot in my view be reduced to a single dimension, and requires knowledge of the joint probability density function of $\{\tilde{C}_n^j = \Pi_{i=0}^{n-1}(1 + \tilde{e}_i^j)\}_{j \in J}$.

An explicit inclusion of interpersonal stochastic interdependences and an analysis of the associated problems would accordingly require a *multi-dimensional* approach. Modelling the joint density would, however, not only be difficult but would also to some extent be an arbitrary exercise. I cannot imagine any *a priori* theoretical structure which would explicitly specify the effect of these stochastic interdependences on the distribution of earnings.[33]

[33] If it should further prove impossible to find a mapping back to the one-dimensional distribution function F_{Y_n}, this would create difficulties for the transformation from the joint probability density function to an (expected) relative frequency function (cf. p. 18) because of the conceptual problems with the associated random experiment (how to construct the random sample). The random sample of size m in the discussion so far would effectively be replaced by a random sample 'of size one' (the multivariate approach requires all individuals to be drawn simultaneously).

2 A life-cycle model of individual earnings

Following the development in Chapter 1 of a general structure for the distribution model, I intend in the present chapter to lay the *economic* foundation for the distribution analysis in Chapters 3, 4 and 5. To use the terminology of the first chapter, what would a possible economic model for A_n^j look like?

A sensible economic theory of earnings distribution must start with a model of the formation of individual incomes, and Sections 2.1 and 2.2 are devoted to this topic. Section 2.3 consolidates this work of answering the questions posed in the Introduction on the life-cycle profile of individual earnings and also provides results of great importance for understanding in economic terms the subsequent inequality analysis.

> *Notes*: (i) In the present work, 'income' is always synonymous with 'earnings', and 'age' will be used consistently to mean 'years in the labour force'.
> (ii) Since the present chapter is concerned exclusively with *one* individual, the superscript j, indicating individual j, will be omitted for the sake of clarity; it will reappear from Chapter 3 onwards.

2.1 A life-cycle model of optimal human capital investment

The wages of labour vary with the easiness and cheapness, or the difficulty and expence of learning the business. When any expensive machinery is erected, the extraordinary work to be performed by it before it is worn out, it must be expected, will replace the capital laid out upon it, with at least the ordinary profits. A man educated at the expence of much labour and time to any of those employments which require extraordinary dexterity and skill, may be compared to one of those expensive machines. The work which he learns to perform, it must be expected, over and above the usual wages of common labour, will replace to him the whole expence of his education, with at least the ordinary profits of an equally valuable capital. It must do this too in a reasonable time, regard being had to the very uncertain duration of human life, in the same manner as to the more certain duration of the machine. The difference between the wages of skilled labour and those of common labour, is founded upon this principle. (Adam Smith, 1776, book I, ch. X, part I).

The model constructed in the present work is based on an idea which in its essentials goes back more than two hundred years, namely the neoclassical refinement of Adam Smith's principle: the *theory of human capital.*

This theory is not only one of the best developed and most widely disseminated theories of individual earnings[1] but also seems to me the most suitable for the present purposes, particularly because it can be used to develop a *structural* approach (something which has been neglected in the literature) which permits explicit treatment of the questions raised in the introduction. Naturally, the human capital theory is not the only attempt: there are a number of other approaches which attempt to explain the formation of and changes in individual earnings. My aim here, however, is not to review the basic advantages and disadvantages of the various schools of thought – this has already been done elsewhere.[2] Whether these other economic approaches are capable of matching the results of the human capital theory approach adopted in the present work, however, still remains to be seen.

2.1.1 Outline and discussion

In order to give precise answers to the questions posed in the introduction, several specific assumptions are essential, since precise answers presuppose a precise structure. As always in such cases, one is confronted with a dilemma: 'In devising a theoretical model there is an inevitable trade-off between elegance and generality on the one hand and concrete results on the other' (Blinder, 1974, p. 23). In the present work I am giving priority to concrete results. Naturally, the reader can only decide at the end how far an abstract neoclassical micro-model of the type developed below is able to satisfy the criteria listed in the introduction. It should be said immediately

[1] See the pioneering works of Becker (1975) and Mincer (1974); on the empirical side, see Rosen (1977).

[2] See the comprehensive *Journal of Economic Literature* article by Sahota (1978) and Osberg (1981, chapters 6–9). For a critical view of the human capital theory, see specifically Sahota (1978, pp. 14–19) and Thurow (1970). Sahota (1978, p. 19) concludes: 'As a theory and methodology the human capital theory remains unscathed from multidirectional attacks' – an opinion I fully agree with.

Besides the human capital theory, other approaches typically cited are:
'screening' models
hierarchical wage system models
contract models.

Recent works are Riley (1976, 1979) on the first group, Waldman (1984) and the references cited therein on the second group, and Harris and Holmström (1982) on the third group. For a general critical survey, see Sahota (1978).

that even an abstract economic system composed of the 'model individuals' described here is capable of generating many of the features which have actually been observed and which have remained unexplained so far. The tools of economic theory used are also serviceable in terms of the predictive power of the model, since the present approach succeeds in identifying economic interdependencies which have escaped attention to date.

The following sections present and discuss the basic assumptions of the model.

(1) Leisure is not included in the analysis (the work–leisure choice is ignored). Consequently, the time spent in the labour market is fixed and constant for all working-periods; this applies uniformly to all individuals.[3]

(2) An individual's *human capital stock* reflects the individual's productive economic skills, talents and knowledge, i.e. it is a measure of the individual's *productive capacity*. This human capital stock is *homogeneous* and there is, accordingly, only one type of human capital: individual stocks differ only in size and not in composition.[4]

(3) The human capital stock does not impinge upon the individual utility function, i.e. human capital itself does not affect the utility associated with any given consumption plan. Intangible benefits of accumulating human capital are accordingly ignored.

(4) There is a *perfect capital market* (for human capital investment); at any time, unrestricted funds are available for lending and borrowing at a constant rate of interest r (>0). This assumption permits, e.g. comparison between an income stream and both other income streams and incomes accumulated at different times.[5]

The assumptions so far allow the individual decision to be separated conceptually into two elements:

(a) the individual solves the maximisation problem as formulated below;

[3] It is debatable how significant is the omission of life-cycle decisions on labour supply, particularly in view of the observation that the great majority of wage and salary earners do not have any freedom of choice in this respect. On attempts to include the work–leisure choice, see Heckman (1976), Blinder and Weiss (1976), Ryder, Stafford and Stephan (1976), McCabe (1983). Note, however, that these approaches do not establish any connection at all with income *distribution*.

[4] The human capital stock represents a measure of 'labour' in homogeneous efficiency units; more on this, later. This assumed homogeneity has been confirmed empirically, most recently by Carliner (1982, pp. 28, 31).

[5] For a relaxation of this assumption, see Wallace and Ihnen (1975) and (in a rather different context) Lee (1981).

The existence of a capital market of this kind also naturally provides a foundation later for calculating present values.

(b) given an optimal time path for disposable earnings, the individual then chooses a time path for consumption (say, to maximise his lifetime utility).[6]

This approach is based on Irving Fisher's *separation theorem*.[7] Under these assumptions the model developed below is an *income* maximisation model and not a utility maximisation model.

(5) The prices in the model (human capital price R, educational goods price P and interest rate r) are constant, *exogenous*, market-determined factor prices; individuals act as price-takers in all markets.[8]

The human capital market in the present model constitutes a general aggregate labour market in which all individuals are involved. The price set in this market for hiring the services of a unit of human capital for one period is R.[9] Each individual j can hire out any amount of human capital K^j at a fixed price R per unit of human capital. Each individual thus possesses only a small fraction of the total stock of homogeneous human capital in the economy, and his market share is so small that the other participants in the market do not generally take his actions into account (perfect competition). To put it another way, demand for the individual human capital stock K^j is completely elastic, i.e. the price elasticity of demand for K^j is infinite.[10]

Underlying this, of course, is the idea of a homogeneous human capital stock as a measure of labour in *homogeneous units of efficiency* (one unit of human capital corresponds to one efficiency unit of labour; cf. assumption 2).

If we take the view (Mincer 1958, 1970, 1974) that labour cannot be measured in such standard units – in other words, human capital must be regarded as heterogeneous (→ 'specific' human capital),[11] this rapidly leads to problems with statements on *distribution*;[12] no further progress

[6] (b) is typically the starting point for lifetime consumption theories; the consumption plan is explained as a function of an *exogenous* income stream.

[7] According to this theorem, the assumptions make it possible to analyse investment decisions independently of consumption decisions. See Fisher (1930); cf. also Hirshleifer (1970).

[8] The assumption that prices R, P and r are exogenous clearly also means that any distribution effects are neglected; R, P and r are treated as independent of the distribution of earnings.

[9] On the demand side, this means that companies can arbitrage fully between the labour markets (assuming there are more than one), so that there is only *one* efficiency-price for labour. Companies are concerned only with the *total* human capital employed, independent of its distribution between individuals. This is also appropriate in terms of assumption (2).

[10] This does not mean that the *aggregate* demand curve for human capital is horizontal; it could very well be downward-sloping, for example because of decreasing marginal productivity within the company's production process.

[11] See, for example, Lichtenberg (1981). See also the criticisms expressed in Sattinger (1980, pp. 20–1). [12] See, for example, Rosen (1977, pp. 9–13) or Sattinger (1980, pp. 14–15).

would be possible without an explicit model for the demand side. With the aid of the efficiency-units assumption, however, the distribution of earnings can ultimately be derived from the distribution of individual characteristics, since the number of productivity units corresponding to the 'labour' of an individual is a feature of the individual himself which is invariant under any changes in the economic system.

My approach assumes a competitive and perfectly operating labour market which is in equilibrium, with all individuals with *identical* qualifications (i.e. identical productivity) receiving the *same* earnings.

There are naturally a number of possible reasons for disequilibrium to arise in the labour market, resulting in individuals with identical supply characteristics receiving different earnings, e.g.[13]

incomplete information on the part of the companies
very slow adjustment processes
government intervention
institutional barriers
discrimination
trade unions
internal labour markets.

An explicit treatment of these and other demand-side features must, however, be left to later projects.[14]

(6) Human capital acts purely as a 'time-augmenting' factor, in the manner of *Harrod-neutral* endogenous technological progress.

As far as its effect on productivity is concerned, human capital as an *integral feature of the individual* is unaffected by the use made of it; a larger stock of human capital enhances the individual's productivity equally in both current earnings and the (explicit) production of additional human capital. This is an important analytical assumption of the model.

(7) The individuals are *risk-neutral* (with respect to random influences) and have identical certain, *ex post undistorted* expectations regarding the future.

This brings the optimisation behaviour described below into line with the general stochastic framework developed in Chapter 1. The term 'income' corresponds to 'expected income' in the present economic model, so that the approach developed below relates to *permanent* earnings (on the lines of the interpretation in Section 1.3.2).

Note: In this context it is certainly attractive to consider the consequences for behaviour of an explicit inclusion of stochastic elements in the

[13] See Atkinson (1975, ch. 6), Beach, Card and Flatters (1981, ch. 3), Osberg (1981, ch. 8), Phelps Brown (1977, chapters 5, 8) and Wood (1978). On 'internal labour markets', see specifically Abraham and Medoff (1983) and Thurow (1975).

[14] An exception is Section 2.3.5, which explicitly deals with certain aspects of demand.

economic model itself.[15] If, for example, random individual circumstances are taken into account in the system equation (see Section 2.1.2) by way of an additive disturbance term (with expected value = 0) and random changes in the economy through $\tilde{R}$ (with $E(\tilde{R}) = R$), it emerges that the present structure is surprisingly robust with respect to modifications of this type; as long as assumption (7) is upheld, the certainty equivalence principle can be employed.[16]

Basically, however, this type of introduction of uncertainty represents a *more direct* bridging between the human capital theory and the stochastic theories of personal income distribution than the one developed in the present model. This would methodically lead into the area of *stochastic control theory*, which is, however, beyond the objectives of this study.

(8) The individuals have perfect knowledge about themselves.[17]

Now I turn to the *structure* of the economic model; in other words, the exact description of the individual's formation of income.

The (expected) length of working life amounts to $N + 1$ periods. The length of a single period thereby defines the relevant time unit for the model (in general it is based on annual units). As is already known from Chapter 1, the working age of the individual is n ($n = 0, \ldots, N$; $n, N \in \mathbf{N}$); $n = 0$ marks the entry into the working life, i.e. the phase of earning money; $n = N$ marks the exit.[18]

At the beginning of his working life the individual is endowed with an initial stock of human capital amounting to $K_0 (>0)$. As the wage rate for the services made available from a human capital unit for one period amounts to R, the *potential* (maximum possible) earnings of the individual in the initial period are RK_0 (cf. assumptions (2) and (5)).

It is assumed that the level of the individual human capital stock is not fixed for all time; rather that the individual has the possibility of increasing his human capital stock in two ways: firstly, by the reinvestment of his human capital stock and, secondly, by purchasing market goods (particularly educational goods).

Since the view of the model in the present section (2.1) refers to the working life of the individual, i.e. to his earnings phase ($n = 0$ defines the beginning of positive earnings received), it follows at once that only a part of the disposable human capital stock is used for investment purposes, since, if the individual exhausted his stock completely, he would have nothing left to offer to the labour market and consequently would not earn

15 For an initial general attempt, see Levhari and Weiss (1974). See also Eden (1980).

16 However, there would be effects on the investment decisions if, for example, the objective function were quadratic (see Section 2.1.2).

17 A certain relaxation of this assumption occurs in Section 2.3.5.

18 The latter can also be expressed thus: $R = 0$, $\forall n \geqslant N + 1$.

any income; therefore he would be dropped from the current consideration.[19] If the fraction of the existing human capital stock, K_0, which is diverted for investment purposes in earnings period 0, is represented by s_0, then the earnings *actually realised* in the period 0 amount to:

$$R(K_0 - s_0 K_0) = RK_0(1 - s_0)[>0].$$

If the direct[20] education costs are PD_0, where D_0 stands for the collection of goods and services purchased in period 0 and P designates the price per unit of D, then the *disposable* earnings of the individual in working period 0 are $RK_0(1 - s_0) - PD_0$. It is this variable which forms the basis of the economic model. In the overall context, therefore: $RK_0(1 - s_0) - PD_0 \equiv A_0$ (cf. Chapter 1; note also the omission of the personal index j). The disposable earnings of the individual generated by the present economic model with assumption (7) actually correspond to the *expected* disposable earnings of the overall framework; the term 'expected' will not be included from now on.

The definitions thus far naturally apply to the same extent for all periods, so that in general one has the following equation for the disposable earnings of the individual:

$$A_n \equiv RK_n(1 - s_n) - PD_n;$$

$$s_n \in [0, 1),\ D_n \in [0, \infty),\ R > 0,\ P > 0; \quad n = 0, \ldots, N.^{21} \qquad (14)$$

How does the individual human capital stock alter from period to period? What effect do the individual investment measures have?

Let us describe the individual investment effect by an 'internalised' *human capital production function* Q_n incorporated into the individual at the beginning of his working life.[22]

A problem which was discussed at the beginning of this chapter (p. 25) emerges again here. If one is interested in concrete results and consequently in explicit analytical solutions, then one cannot avoid specifying the functional form of Q_n in a concrete manner. It was emphasised in the

[19] There is an expanded consideration in Section 2.2.

[20] 'Direct' as opposed to the opportunity costs Rs_0K_0.

[21] In contrast to the earnings *received* $RK_n(1 - s_n)$, the *disposable* earnings A_n can thus be negative. This is discussed later (Section 2.3).

[22] In connection with this, the crucial difference between *human* capital and *physical* capital must be pointed out. This difference consists of an 'input-fixity' problem which occurs as a result of the fact that the individual cannot simply 'purchase' additional human capital but has to produce this himself. If the marginal value product of one human capital unit exceeds the price R, then the individual can only bring those factors to coincidence by the process of additional human capital production. A company, on the other hand, could remove any 'fixity' of the capital input in a similar case (under the same model conditions) by its access to the capital market.

introduction that the objective is a closed soluble model. If the theoretical model is to satisfy the criterion, in particular, of providing possible explanations for empirically established facts, then it must be able to generate something which is comparable with the observed phenomena. In relation to the present model, this means that a theoretical income path here would have to be derived which can be compared with the one observed. Haley (1973, p. 929) has the following remark to make: 'In general, this cannot be done. To produce an income stream from theory has been an intractable mathematical problem.' Indeed, it has only been in a very few number of special cases, that solutions to a life-cycle model of the type developed in this chapter have been obtained in a closed form (these cases are contained as special cases in the analytical solutions derived in Section 2.1.2 below). The second criterion given in the introduction, i.e. that of making specific policy prognoses possible, also requires an analytically tractable model.

The present approach assumes a Cobb–Douglas production function:

$$Q_n = b_0 (s_n K_n)^{b_1} D_n^{b_2};$$
$$b_0 > 0,\ b_1 > 0,\ b_2 > 0,\ b_1 + b_2 < 1; \quad n = 0, \ldots, N. \tag{15}$$

The parameters and form of this function reflect the opportunities and abilities of the individual, to increase his productive capacity. A closer economic interpretation of the parameters b_0, b_1 and b_2 will take place below in a separate paragraph (with the interpretation of the remaining model parameters).

Yoram Ben-Porath, the originator of the structural human capital accumulation models has this to say:

> The technology which the individual faces when he makes decisions about investing in himself is a complicated system of technical and institutional relationships ... By writing down a simple production function of the sort used here we are attempting, not to reproduce this system, but only to provide a framework within which some of the possible characteristics of the technology can be considered and their implications studied (Ben-Porath, 1967, p. 359).

There is no need to expand on this.[23]

The inequality listed in (15), $b_1 + b_2 < 1$, implies diminishing returns to scale in human capital production. This assumption has not only been empirically substantiated but it can also be supported with the aid of the results in the literature on learning curves.[24]

[23] Ben-Porath also employs a Cobb-Douglas production function. His discussion of this function (1967, pp. 359–62) is very instructive.

[24] On the former, see Haley (1976, pp. 1233–5); on the latter, Hartog (1976, pp. 71–2) and the literature quoted therein.

The chosen Q_n specification also reflects assumption (6). The variable s_n can be interpreted in terms of time as follows:

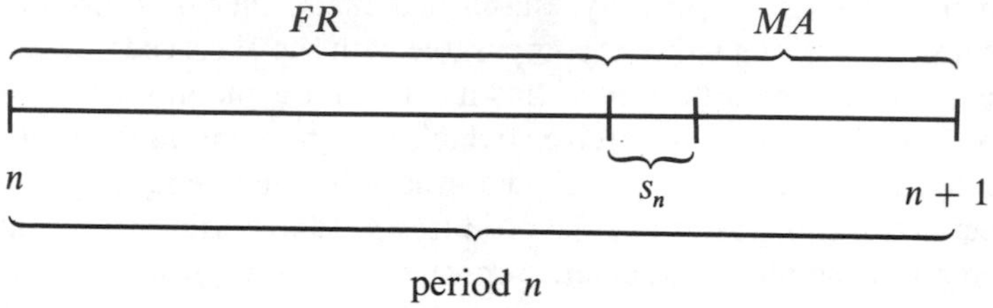

FR = leisure part of period n
MA = market or working share of period n, 'earnings period n', 'working period' n.

s_n can be defined as the fraction of the fixed given market time MA (cf. assumption (1)) which is employed in period n explicitly for the production of additional human capital. The pure money-earning activity is then restricted to the remaining fraction of the market time; if one takes the norm as $MA = 1$, for the purposes of this study, this is $1 - s_n$.[25] This interpretation clarifies the neutrality assumption (6) embedded in (14) and (15).

It must be remembered that the qualitative characteristics of the optimal earnings path derived below do not derive from the Cobb-Douglas production function *as such*, but purely from the fact that Q_n is a *homogeneous* production function with decreasing returns to scale. If, for example, a quadratic production function is assumed, i.e. a production function with increasing returns to scale, then totally different results are obtained. However this type of function is neither empirically substantiated nor supported as regards the content and will thus not be pursued any further.

An explicit specification of Q_n cannot be avoided for the present analytical objectives. Other types as well which have the same type of qualitative characteristics as (15) (for example, CES production functions), would be worthy of consideration; the only question is how far would one get? Would it still be possible to obtain the results in a *closed* form? That would be crucial, as the majority of the questions affecting this study (see the Introduction) could not be resolved in any other manner. The development of this type of model, like the one in Chapters 3, 4 and 5 requires a closed soluble structure.

The amount of human capital Q_n produced with the aid of the two inputs $s_n K_n$ and D_n in the working period is not necessarily the only reason for

[25] As only subperiods of the working period (and, hence, only subperiods of MA) are discussed in the present model, this norm will be adopted subsequently.

changes in the individual human capital stock. There are also two other reasons. Firstly, the human capital stock is subject to a constant exogenous *rate of depreciation* δ, $0 < \delta < 1$ (see below for more detailed economic interpretation). Secondly, the human capital stock profits from the '*learning-by-doing*' phenomenon. The present approach, encouraged *inter alia* by the criticism of Eckaus (1963), explicitly takes into account this effect of practical job experience in contrast, in particular, to the Ben-Porath model. The accumulation of practical job experience taking place within the earnings period, and therefore within the section $1 - s_n$ of the working period n, leads to an automatic increase in the productive capacity of the individual.

This 'implicit' human capital production (in contrast to the 'explicit' production Q_n) is integrated into the state equation of the individual human capital stock by the inclusion of the expression: $c(1 - s_n)K_n$, $c > 0$. The human capital implicitly produced in the working period n is therefore directly proportional to the time span $1 - s_n$ and to the productive capacity accumulated thus far $(= K_n)$.[26] The latter for example reflects the idea that the higher the human capital stock, the better equipped one is to learn from experience. At the same time, this specification satisfies the neutrality assumption (6). The parameter c reflects the efficiency with which the activity in the working life can be transformed into an increase in the productive capacity. Alternatively, one could take c as a measure of the inevitable minimum learning-by-doing rate as well, in the sense of Eckaus (1963) and Psacharopoulos and Layard (1979, pp. 489–90).[27]

All the components of a change in productivity have now been introduced. The following accumulation equation for the individual human capital stock summarises this as follows:

$$K_{n+1} = K_n + Q_n + c(1 - s_n)K_n - \delta K_n, \quad n = 0, \ldots, N - 1.$$
$$K_0 > 0 \text{ given.} \tag{16}$$

The individual's objective is to choose his investment inputs s_n and D_n with consideration of equation (16), so that the present value of his disposable earnings V is maximised:

$$V := \sum_{n=0}^{N} A_n(1 + r)^{-n}, \tag{17}$$

26 Cf., in general, Arrow (1962, p. 155). In a somewhat different context, see also Killingsworth (1982, pp. 266–7).

27 Of course, other, more complex specifications of the learning-by-doing effect are also accessible. Anyone is free to experiment with them (on whatever theoretical basis). Overcomplication would not, however, have any effect on the integration of the learning-by-doing effect as such, and this is what I am concerned with in this context. Moreover, one would in general be risking the analytical solubility of the model.

with A_n defined by (14).[28] Basically, the model just described is a neoclassical life-cycle model of efficient human capital investment.

Note: The fact that an accumulation mechanism of the type described above, generating the individual earnings profile, is an *empirically significant phenomenon* has been confirmed repeatedly.[29]

Before this model is explicitly solved in Section 2.1.2, a more detailed *economic interpretation* of the parameters introduced will be carried out.

The parameter 'c' has already been mentioned. Parameter 'δ', the (geometric) depreciation rate of the human capital stock can be associated with a wide variety of income determination factors. These range from individual factors, such as failing health, failing resilience, failing mental agility (for example, bad short-term memory) – in short ageing; to factors such as forced change of job; and finally to more global aspects such as technological change.[30] As, within the framework of this study, δ is understood as a fixed structural factor in the observed economy, i.e. a factor which is the same for all individuals (more on this later), it primarily reflects the ageing of the human capital stock due to technological change.

Notes: (i) $0 < \delta < 1$. $\delta = 1$ would mean that one cannot use any productive capacity in the future which one has acquired in the past; one would only have in the future what is added today: $K_{n+1} = Q_n + c(1 - s_n)K_n$. This is certainly unrealistic. (ii) (16) can be reformulated as follows:

$$K_{n+1} - K_n = Q_n - [\delta - c(1 - s_n)]K_n. \tag{16a}$$

The expression in square brackets can be interpreted as the *net depreciation rate* of the human capital stock. In contrast to the ageing rate δ the net ageing rate defined thus is a *variable* which is dependent on the working time $1 - s_n$, i.e. on the part of the working period n used for earning money. This net specification obtained as a result of the explicit integration of the learning-by-doing effect does in fact

[28] Cf. in this connection the basic assumptions (1)–(8) again (in particular assumption (4)). Incidentally, the individual must be *free* to make his own intertemporal investment decisions; he must be able to choose what is the optimum in accordance with his goal. The basic question as to what extent the actions of the individual in reality can actually be interpreted as 'optimising' will not be discussed in any greater detail at this point. It refers to microeconomic theory as a whole nowadays. See, for example, Becker (1976). Typically, the argument is supported as follows: that which one observes in reality is compatible with the idea that the individual behaves in accordance with his optimising approach (without necessarily assuming that the individual actually calculates this approach explicitly). The question is then how far does one proceed with this type of hypothesis?

[29] See Lillard and Weiss (1979), Hause (1980), Klevmarken (1981), Bourguignon and Morrisson (1982) and Barge and Payen (1982). The fact that this literature has been brought out so recently is because the *panel* data required for this type of analysis has only been available in the last few years.

[30] All these factors also appear in the study by Carliner (1982), the most recent and best study on human capital depreciation rates known to me.

correspond to more recent (and so far little explained) empirical findings, according to which human capital depreciation varies with the working time: see Mincer and Ofek (1982).

(iii) The present theoretical approach is not committed to $\delta > c$ or $c > \delta$, but assumes that $r + \delta > c$. This assumption is not only empirically motivated (cf. the explanations on the 'standard parameter set' below) but also reflects the plausible idea in economic terms that the effect of practical job experience (via c) in isolation would not be sufficient to prevent the diminution of human capital (where 'diminution' describes both the depreciation effect (via δ) and the discounting effect (via r)).

The parameters b_0, b_1 and b_2 of the production function Q_n can be interpreted as follows. Firstly, consider b_1 and b_2. b_1 gives the *production elasticity* of the factor $s_n K_n$ and b_2 provides the same for factor D_n.[31] b_1 and b_2 also reflect the *scale elasticity* ($= b_1 + b_2$) in human capital production; where $b_1 + b_2 < 1$ there are decreasing returns to scale (cf. p. 31). By assumption, the individuals do not differ in b_1 and b_2 within the framework of the distribution models in Chapters 3, 4 and 5. Rather, b_1 and b_2 are fixed given structural factors of the observed economy.

This implies the same 'technical knowledge' for all individuals with regard to human capital production methods. This assumption is less serious than it seems at first, as later an explicit individual variation in b_0 will be allowed. A given percentage increase in the investment inputs for all individuals would thereby result in the same percentage increase in the output volume Q_n; however not all individuals who use the same input volume produce the same output. From a given prior knowledge of the techniques of human capital production, individuals with a higher b_0 can profit more than those with a lower level.

Before this central parameter b_0 is discussed in any more detail, one brief remark must be made on the other two structural factors (c and δ). One should not be bothered here either; c is indeed the same size for all individuals as a fixed structural factor of the observed economy; yet, the amount of human capital produced 'on the side' by the learning-by-doing effect is not the same for all individuals, since: $c(1 - s_n^j)K_n^j$. The same applies for the human capital depreciation δK_n^j (j denotes the individual j); this is discussed further in Section 2.2.

'b_0' can generally be interpreted as a factor-neutral (if you like, Hicks-neutral) parameter of *production efficiency*. It reflects, in a wider sense, the 'ability' of the individual to increase his productive capacity

31 $s_n K_n$ is the amount of human capital diverted from the existing stock K_n in working period n for Q_n production; or (if you like) the fraction of working period n 'time-augmented' by K_n which is used for Q_n-production (cf. assumption (6)). D_n is the amount of goods and services purchased in working period n for Q_n-production.

during the course of his working life. What factors is this ability primarily dependent on? In other words, what factors beyond the learning-by-doing effect and the ageing effect determine the individual human capital accumulation and consequently the individual *increase* in income?

The empirical literature has identified a wide variety of personal characteristics, which can be considered as permanent income growth factors.[32] Which of these determining factors are appropriate for an explicit inclusion in the efficiency parameter b_0? A comprehensive study of that literature ultimately produces the following group of factors:

$$b_0 = b_0[\overset{+}{LA}(G, HO, CU); \overset{+}{DF}(HO, CU);$$

$$\overset{+}{QPC}(\underline{a}, \underline{b}, \underline{c}); \overset{+}{CR}; \overset{+}{SQ}]. \qquad (18)$$

LA denotes the learning ability of the individual, i.e. the capability to acquire new methods of thinking and apply them. Indicators of this cognitive ability (such as, for example, the measured *IQ*) are part of the main determining factors of the growth rates of individual earnings.[33] The plus sign above *LA* marks the assumed sign of the partial derivative $\partial b_0 / \partial LA$. The learning ability of the individual for its part is dependent on three clusters of factors: the genetic endowment (*G*), the family background (*HO*) and the cultural influences (*CU*). *LA* is therefore not an ability which is exclusively inherited, but the result of parental upbringing, nutrition, finances and cultural milieu, to name but a few of the factors.[34]

[32] Cf. assumption (5): this is the reason for the concentration on personal characteristics. See p. 17 on 'permanent'.

[33] The empirical significance of the *LA* effect has been proved by the following, *inter alia*: Conlisk (1971), Taubman and Wales (1974), Hanushek and Quigley (1978) and Willis and Rosen (1979). Cf. also Sahota (1978, section II) and Osberg (1981, ch. 6.3). Cf. in a different context Cornford (1980).

[34] Individually, the *G* cluster also includes physical characteristics, such as strength, resilience, health, sight, hearing, etc., as well as the cognitive genetic factors affecting the learning ability. See, for example, Carter (1976). Psychologists generally appear to agree that the genetic component *G* affecting the learning ability is composed of many individual factors, and not, as for the colour of the eye, affected by just one pair of genes. However, attempts to isolate these individual factors and evaluate them individually are contentious.

As regards the *HO* cluster, the following apply *inter alia*: level of education of the parents, job status of the father and/or mother, parental income, parental wealth, attitude of parents towards their children, personalities of parents, parental values and practical upbringing, family size, connections of parents, personal and social contacts (cf. here, in particular, Granovetter (1974)) – to name just the most important individual factors. Cf., for example, Meade (1973), Gustafsson (1980), Atkinson, Maynard and Trinder (1983, pp. 134–58). In the *CU* cluster, cultural influences include national, social, religious and racial influences and those gleaned from schools and other social institutions; cf., for example, Bowles (1972) and Lydall (1976).

w that all the parameters of the human capital accumulation equation have been discussed, a brief remark must be added on the prices R, P r occurring in (17) (or (14)).

Vithin the framework of the present model, the effect of Government isures on the distribution of earnings is analysed via these three ameters, as the human capital price R, the price of educational goods P the rate of interest r are the parameters of the model which the state can uence *most directly*; R and P by way of tax and spending measures, r by of the central bank (or monetary measures in general). Public rvention is certainly also possible on other model parameters; however, e of the factors discussed above can be influenced so directly by the state the central bank) as R, P or r. Therefore the phrase 'instrumental ameters of the economic policymaker' is often mentioned in the text ow, where these prices are being discussed.

Notes: (i) Strictly speaking, one can of course only talk of *indirect* instrumental parameters of the economic policymaker since, in accordance with assumption (5), R, P and r denote factor prices determined by the market. That assumption is naturally primarily aimed at the justification of the 'price-taker' characteristic of individuals and with the idea that R, P and r are instruments of the state is that compatible.
(ii) The present model neglects *macroeconomic* aspects (such as economic growth, inflation, unemployment, etc.) in order to concentrate totally on microeconomic optimising behaviour of the individuals. At the same time, an integration of certain macroeconomic aspects is possible with a specification of '$R(.)$', '$P(.)$' and/or '$r(.)$'; this is not however going to be pursued any further here.

A reference specification: the standard parameter set

sequently, in the course of the study, numerical calculations are loyed now and again for illustrative purposes. In order to obtain a istic picture in terms of size, one should revert to *empirically supported* ameter values as far as possible.

he following 'standard parameter set' fulfils this condition:

$$\{R = 1;\ P = 1;\ r = 0.06;\ c = 0.02;\ \delta = 0.04;\ b_1 = 0.4;\ b_2 = 0.2;\ N = 45\};$$
$$\{K_0 = 15\,000;\ b_0 = 10;\ a_0 = 3\,000;\ a_1 = 1\,400\}. \qquad (19)$$

first group contains the parameters which, by assumption, are the same ll individuals: the *prices* R, P, r and the *structural parameters* c, δ, b_1, b_2 the working *lifespan* N. The second group includes the so-called *vidual parameters*, i.e. those factors which can vary, in line with the mption, from individual to individual: K_0, b_0, a_0 and a_1. This division,

Note: The fact that the G, HO and CU factors ar determining factors for individual learning ability, The question which is the subject of lively debate weight applies to each cluster of factors. So far t methodological problems associated with the sepa the individual clusters from one another within statistical analysis; cf. the Taubman (1976)–Gold The usefulness for economic policy of this type of does not incidentally seem to be above criticism in a (1979)).

DF stands for Lydall's D-factor (hereafter DF-factor in confusion with the input variable D_n). This non-cog influenced by HO and CU factors, includes personal ch motivation, energy, initiative, ambition, staying pow aggression, charm, toughness, nerve, dynamics, ind pline.[35]

$QPC(\underline{a}, \underline{b}, \underline{c})$ denotes other traits of personality and the empirical literature, such as leadership qualities abilities ($\underline{a}$), willingness to take risks ($\underline{b}$) and abilit assume responsibility ($\underline{c}$).[36]

CR stands for 'class-rank' variables, for example,

Finally, SQ means school quality. This factor als individual income growth rates – in the present conte individual to accumulate human capital during his

Notes: (i) $QPC(\underline{a}, \underline{b}, \underline{c})$, CR and SQ are to be co factors (beyond any possible correlation with G arises from the results of Wise (1975).

(ii) The reader may possibly miss an integration (18), in order to take into account the effect of pro with age. However, this ageing effect has alread the parameter δ in the accumulation equation (

[35] Cf. Lydall (1976, pp. 25–30), Meade (1973, pp. 363–4), but also components also play a role in relation to the DF factor; cor factors, however, this is a very insignificant one. This is the reas the present (at any rate stylised) specification. The same H(indeed applied to the present specifications of LA and DF, but type of integration has to be the same.

[36] On $\underline{a}$ and $\underline{b}$, cf., for example, Wise (1975), but also Ghiselli (1 126–7) concerning $\underline{c}$.

[37] Cf. in particular, Wise (1975, pp. 358–62) and Weisbrod and

[38] The significance of SQ is supported in the following studies, *int* and Wachtel (1975), Wachtel (1975), Taubman (1975, ch. 3. Rizzuto and Wachtel (1980). Note also Behrman and Birdsa

and the parameters a_0 and a_1 specified here are considered further later (see Section 2.2).

The *theoretical* parameter restrictions of the present model will be summarised before any explanation of the above reference specification is carried out (incidentally none of these contradict the existing empirical findings):

$$R > 0, P > 0, r > 0;$$
$$c > 0, 0 < \delta < 1; r + \delta > c; b_1 > 0, b_2 > 0, b_1 + b_2 < 1;$$
$$b_0 > 0; a_0 > 0, a_1 > 0.$$

For the purposes of the present study, R has been normalised at 1. This refers to a real price (just as with the prices P and r). The monetary unit can be chosen at will; I generally employ '\$'. P has also been set to 1, in order to give the price ratio R/P (which is the most decisive as we will see later) the unit value of 1. This is certainly arbitrary, but it simplifies the general evaluation of the many analytical relations occurring later and also enables the units of measurement of the inputs $s_n K_n$ and D_n to be compared. However, $P \neq 1$ is also employed experimentally in a series of calculations.

The reference specification assumes a period length of one year. The (discrete) discounting rate r therefore denotes an annual rate of interest. A real interest rate on capital of 6% seems to be a plausible average value, if we work out the average by taking the term structure of all interest rates as the basis, and if we assume no risk of default. If you consider the interest trend in Great Britain or in the USA, then considerably higher values are possible; some calculations therefore assume a rate of 10% or more.

> *Note*: Note, in this connection, the dual role which the interest rate r has to play because of the assumption of a perfect capital market.

The chosen δ value is based on the results of Johnson and Hebein (1974), Haley (1976), Rosen (1976) and van Reijn and Theeuwes (1981). Equipped with this δ specification, the value for c was derived indirectly from the estimated results of Carliner (1982) on human capital *net* depreciation rates.[39] The parameters b_1 and b_2 were determined such that their sum was 0.6. This value was taken from Haley (1976, pp. 1233, 1235).[40] The higher

[39] Cf. note (ii), p. 34. The inference has been simplified by the fact that the estimates by Carliner relate to the *end* of the working life. For high values of n, s_n approaches 0 (as one will see from Section 2.1.2). The present net depreciation rate thereby approximates the difference $\delta - c$. This fact has been exploited in the determination of c.

[40] The study by Haley (1976) provides the most comprehensive attempt so far to estimate a model of optimum human capital investments *directly*. This is why the present reference specification refers back particularly to the results of Haley. His approach ignores the input variable D_n (and of course the learning-by-doing effect – as with all conventional human

value of b_1 assumes that 'own' inputs can be applied more efficiently, comparatively speaking, than those purchased.

N (to be more precise, $N + 1$) represents the length of working life in years (if you like, life working time). Naturally, other N values apart from $N = 45$ are plausible. However, it is not dependent on the exact figure, but only on the size of the factor in question.

The same applies for the individual parameters K_0, b_0, a_0 and a_1. With $R = 1$, K_0 gives the potential starting annual earnings of the individual. This amounts to 15,000 monetary units (DM, \$, £ or something similar – here, there are no boundaries; but, in general, the figures are expressed in \$).

The parameters a_0 and a_1 are introduced and interpreted in Section 2.2. The reference values of a_0 and a_1 reproduce the K_0 value exactly. There is no direct empirical information on either a_1 or b_0 (nor on a_0). However, as those parameters occur in different model stages and the overall structure of the model is recursive (more on this later), a_1 and b_0 do not have to be determined simultaneously. On the basis of the basic model (Section 2.1), b_0 was chosen for given reference values of the remaining parameters applied there, such that the values of the theoretically generated income path are compatible with the empirically observed progressions in terms of size. This results in the reference value $b_0 = 10$. A realistic size of a_1 could thereby be obtained indirectly in the expanded model (Section 2.2). A reproduction of the K_0 value would then finally produce a_0.

2.1.2 *Solution*

The life-cycle model created in the previous section assumes the form of a *control problem*. This is summarised in the following statement:

$$\underset{\{s_n \in [0,1), D_n \in [0,\infty)\}}{\text{Max}} \quad V = \sum_{n=0}^{N-1} L_n(K_n; s_n, D_n) + L_N(K_N),$$

under the constraint that:

$$K_{n+1} = g(K_n; s_n, D_n), \quad n = 0, \ldots, N-1;$$
$$\text{given } K_0 > 0$$

where

capital accumulation models). Haley shows however (p. 1235) that the scale parameter estimated by him is an unbiased estimator of the sum $b_1 + b_2$. The values of his scale parameter all come to 0.6. If one assumes a value like that here, and this does not only apply for b_1 and b_2, then one must of course be aware that there are two different models, especially with $c \neq 0$; therefore it is not, strictly speaking, acceptable to take any of those estimated values literally.

$$
\begin{aligned}
L_n(K_n; s_n, D_n) &:= A_n(1+r)^{-n} \\
&= [RK_n(1-s_n) - PD_n](1+r)^{-n}, \\
n &= 0, \ldots, N-1; \\
L_N(K_N) &:= A_N(1+r)^{-N} = RK_N(1+r)^{-N}; \\
g(K_n; s_n, D_n) &:= b_0(s_n K_n)^{b_1} D_n^{b_2} \\
&\quad + [1 + c(1-s_n) - \delta]K_n, \\
n &= 0, \ldots, N-1.
\end{aligned}
$$

Note: The split formulation of the objective function V corresponds to the standard notation in the literature on control theory. Since the system equation $K_{n+1} = g(K_n; s_n, D_n)$ is forward-looking there are, of course, no investments of any kind in the final period, $n = N$, for these would only begin to take effect from $N + 1$. However, according to the assumption, the human capital stock of the individual after $N + 1$ no longer has any market value at all (to recap: $R = 0, \forall n \geqslant N + 1$). Consequently, $s_N = D_N = 0$ (we are concerned with the maximisation of income) and the above split is obtained.

The present control problem reveals a *non-linear* objective function (because of the product of the variables s_n and K_n) and a *non-linear* system equation. Normally, no analytical solution can be expected in such a case. In the comparison of the two principal techniques which have been developed for solving control problems,[41] Intriligator (1971, p. 357) comes to the conclusion that, 'For an analytical solution the maximum principle approach is generally more useful than the dynamic programming approach.' In fact, it is possible with the aid of the maximum principle approach to achieve the desired analytical objective despite the awkward non-linearities.

Notes: (i) Note that the concern below is with a *discrete* version of the maximum principle.[42]
(ii) Economists typically apply the maximum principle, for which they have apparently developed a preference. The control theorists themselves employ this principle far less frequently. The dynamic programming approach dominates, particularly in cases where discrete problems are concerned.

A solution to the present control problem designed on that principle first requires the definition of a sequence H_n (this is the discrete equivalent to the continuous formulations of the Hamiltonian function):[43]

[41] These are the *maximum principle* approach referred to by Pontryagin and the *dynamic programming* approach from Bellman.
[42] Cf., for example, Bryson and Ho (1969, ch. 2).
[43] Cf., for what follows, in particular, Bryson and Ho (1969, ch. 2.2).

$$H_n(K_n; s_n, D_n; \lambda_{n+1}) := L_n(K_n; s_n, D_n) + \lambda_{n+1} g(K_n; s_n, D_n),$$
$$n = 0, \ldots, N-1,$$

where λ_{n+1} is called an *adjoint variable* (co-state variable); the economic significance of this variable will be discussed in more detail at a later stage. If interior solutions are assumed (thus: $s_n^* \in (0,1)$ and $D_n^* \in (0, \infty)$, $n = 0, \ldots, N-1$), then the required conditions for a (local) maximum of V are represented as follows:

$$\frac{\partial H_n}{\partial s_n} = 0, \quad \frac{\partial H_n}{\partial D_n} = 0; \quad n = 0, .., N-1; \tag{20}$$

$$K_{n+1} = g(K_n; s_n, D_n), \quad n = 0, \ldots, N-1; \tag{21}$$

K_0 given;

$$\lambda_n = \frac{\partial L_n}{\partial K_n} + \lambda_{n+1} \frac{\partial g}{\partial K_n}, \quad n = 0, \ldots, N-1;$$
$$\lambda_N = \frac{dL_N}{dK_N}. \tag{22}$$

Note: If the optimum values for s_n^* and D_n^* subsequently derived are applied to the (discrete) Hamiltonian function H_n, it can be seen that the maximised Hamiltonian function $H_n(K_n; s_n^*, D_n^*; \lambda_{n+1}) =: H_n^0(K_n, \lambda_{n+1})$ is a linear function of the state variables K_n, $n = 0, \ldots, N-1$. According to a theorem proved by Arrow, the optimality conditions listed in (20), (21) and (22) are thereby not only necessary but also sufficient.[44]

If the 'marginal value product = factor price' equations resulting from the stationary conditions (20) are solved for the control variables, the following is obtained:

$$s_n^* = \frac{1}{K_n} \left[\frac{b_0 b_1}{R(1+r)}\right]^{\frac{1-b_2}{a}} \left[\frac{b_0 b_2}{P(1+r)}\right]^{\frac{b_2}{a}} \psi_{n+1}^{1/a}$$
$$\cdot \left(1 + \frac{c}{R(1+r)} \psi_{n+1}\right)^{\frac{b_2-1}{a}}, \quad n = 0, \ldots, N-1; \tag{23}$$
$$D_n^* = \left[\frac{b_0 b_1}{R(1+r)}\right]^{\frac{b_1}{a}} \left[\frac{b_0 b_2}{P(1+r)}\right]^{\frac{1-b_1}{a}} \psi_{n+1}^{1/a}$$

[44] Cf. Kamien and Schwartz (1981, part II, section 15) and the references quoted therein (p. 211).

Note that H_n is a strictly concave fucntion of s_n and D_n, $n = 0, \ldots, N-1$, as $0 < b_1 < 1$ and $0 < b_2 < 1$. Note also the peculiarities of discrete problems occurring in connection with this as well (cf., for example, Bryson and Ho (1969, pp. 208–11).

Now that all the parameters of the human capital accumulation equation (16) have been discussed, a brief remark must be added on the prices R, P and r occurring in (17) (or (14)).

Within the framework of the present model, the effect of Government measures on the distribution of earnings is analysed via these three parameters, as the human capital price R, the price of educational goods P and the rate of interest r are the parameters of the model which the state can influence *most directly*; R and P by way of tax and spending measures, r by way of the central bank (or monetary measures in general). Public intervention is certainly also possible on other model parameters; however, none of the factors discussed above can be influenced so directly by the state (or the central bank) as R, P or r. Therefore the phrase 'instrumental parameters of the economic policymaker' is often mentioned in the text below, where these prices are being discussed.

Notes: (i) Strictly speaking, one can of course only talk of *indirect* instrumental parameters of the economic policymaker since, in accordance with assumption (5), R, P and r denote factor prices determined by the market. That assumption is naturally primarily aimed at the justification of the 'price-taker' characteristic of individuals and with the idea that R, P and r are instruments of the state is that compatible.
(ii) The present model neglects *macroeconomic* aspects (such as economic growth, inflation, unemployment, etc.) in order to concentrate totally on microeconomic optimising behaviour of the individuals. At the same time, an integration of certain macroeconomic aspects is possible with a specification of '$R(.)$', '$P(.)$' and/or '$r(.)$'; this is not however going to be pursued any further here.

A reference specification: the standard parameter set

Subsequently, in the course of the study, numerical calculations are employed now and again for illustrative purposes. In order to obtain a realistic picture in terms of size, one should revert to *empirically supported* parameter values as far as possible.

The following 'standard parameter set' fulfils this condition:

$$\{R = 1;\ P = 1;\ r = 0.06;\ c = 0.02;\ \delta = 0.04;\ b_1 = 0.4;\ b_2 = 0.2;\ N = 45\};$$
$$\{K_0 = 15\,000;\ b_0 = 10;\ a_0 = 3\,000;\ a_1 = 1\,400\}. \qquad (19)$$

The first group contains the parameters which, by assumption, are the same for all individuals: the *prices* R, P, r and the *structural parameters* c, δ, b_1, b_2 and the working *lifespan* N. The second group includes the so-called *individual parameters*, i.e. those factors which can vary, in line with the assumption, from individual to individual: K_0, b_0, a_0 and a_1. This division,

Note: The fact that the *G*, *HO* and *CU* factors are the most important determining factors for individual learning ability, is not in contention. The question which is the subject of lively debate concerns how much weight applies to each cluster of factors. So far there have been great methodological problems associated with the separation of the effects of the individual clusters from one another within the framework of a statistical analysis; cf. the Taubman (1976)–Goldberger (1978) debate. The usefulness for economic policy of this type of attempt at separation does not incidentally seem to be above criticism in all cases (cf. Goldberger (1979)).

DF stands for Lydall's *D*-factor (hereafter *DF*-factor in order to prevent any confusion with the input variable D_n). This non-cognitive factor, mainly influenced by *HO* and *CU* factors, includes personal characteristics, such as motivation, energy, initiative, ambition, staying power, will power, drive, aggression, charm, toughness, nerve, dynamics, industry and self discipline.[35]

$QPC(\underline{a}, \underline{b}, \underline{c})$ denotes other traits of personality and character isolated in the empirical literature, such as leadership qualities and organisational abilities ($\underline{a}$), willingness to take risks ($\underline{b}$) and ability and willingness to assume responsibility ($\underline{c}$).[36]

CR stands for 'class-rank' variables, for example, for 'grades'.[37]

Finally, *SQ* means school quality. This factor also significantly affects individual income growth rates – in the present context, the 'ability' of the individual to accumulate human capital during his working life.[38]

Notes: (i) $QPC(\underline{a}, \underline{b}, \underline{c})$, *CR* and *SQ* are to be considered as *independent* factors (beyond any possible correlation with *G*, *HO* and/or *CU*); this arises from the results of Wise (1975).

(ii) The reader may possibly miss an integration of the working age *n* in (18), in order to take into account the effect of production efficiency falling with age. However, this ageing effect has already been accounted for via the parameter δ in the accumulation equation (16).

[35] Cf. Lydall (1976, pp. 25–30), Meade (1973, pp. 363–4), but also Seiler (1982). Of course, *G* components also play a role in relation to the *DF* factor; compared to the *HO* and *CU* factors, however, this is a very insignificant one. This is the reason why it does not figure in the present (at any rate stylised) specification. The same *HO* and *CU* components are indeed applied to the present specifications of *L A* and *DF*, but this does not mean that the type of integration has to be the same.

[36] On $\underline{a}$ and $\underline{b}$, cf., for example, Wise (1975), but also Ghiselli (1969). See Lydall (1968, pp. 126–7) concerning $\underline{c}$.

[37] Cf. in particular, Wise (1975, pp. 358–62) and Weisbrod and Karpoff (1968).

[38] The significance of *SQ* is supported in the following studies, *inter alia*: Wise (1975), Solmon and Wachtel (1975), Wachtel (1975), Taubman (1975, ch. 3.3 and 6.4), Solmon (1975), Rizzuto and Wachtel (1980). Note also Behrman and Birdsall (1983).

and the parameters a_0 and a_1 specified here are considered further later (see Section 2.2).

The *theoretical* parameter restrictions of the present model will be summarised before any explanation of the above reference specification is carried out (incidentally none of these contradict the existing empirical findings):

$$R > 0, P > 0, r > 0;$$
$$c > 0, 0 < \delta < 1; r + \delta > c; b_1 > 0, b_2 > 0, b_1 + b_2 < 1;$$
$$b_0 > 0; a_0 > 0, a_1 > 0.$$

For the purposes of the present study, R has been normalised at 1. This refers to a real price (just as with the prices P and r). The monetary unit can be chosen at will; I generally employ '\$'. P has also been set to 1, in order to give the price ratio R/P (which is the most decisive as we will see later) the unit value of 1. This is certainly arbitrary, but it simplifies the general evaluation of the many analytical relations occurring later and also enables the units of measurement of the inputs $s_n K_n$ and D_n to be compared. However, $P \neq 1$ is also employed experimentally in a series of calculations.

The reference specification assumes a period length of one year. The (discrete) discounting rate r therefore denotes an annual rate of interest. A real interest rate on capital of 6% seems to be a plausible average value, if we work out the average by taking the term structure of all interest rates as the basis, and if we assume no risk of default. If you consider the interest trend in Great Britain or in the USA, then considerably higher values are possible; some calculations therefore assume a rate of 10% or more.

Note: Note, in this connection, the dual role which the interest rate r has to play because of the assumption of a perfect capital market.

The chosen δ value is based on the results of Johnson and Hebein (1974), Haley (1976), Rosen (1976) and van Reijn and Theeuwes (1981). Equipped with this δ specification, the value for c was derived indirectly from the estimated results of Carliner (1982) on human capital *net* depreciation rates.[39] The parameters b_1 and b_2 were determined such that their sum was 0.6. This value was taken from Haley (1976, pp. 1233, 1235).[40] The higher

[39] Cf. note (ii), p. 34. The inference has been simplified by the fact that the estimates by Carliner relate to the *end* of the working life. For high values of n, s_n approaches 0 (as one will see from Section 2.1.2). The present net depreciation rate thereby approximates the difference $\delta - c$. This fact has been exploited in the determination of c.

[40] The study by Haley (1976) provides the most comprehensive attempt so far to estimate a model of optimum human capital investments *directly*. This is why the present reference specification refers back particularly to the results of Haley. His approach ignores the input variable D_n (and of course the learning-by-doing effect – as with all conventional human

value of b_1 assumes that 'own' inputs can be applied more efficiently, comparatively speaking, than those purchased.

N (to be more precise, $N+1$) represents the length of working life in years (if you like, life working time). Naturally, other N values apart from $N = 45$ are plausible. However, it is not dependent on the exact figure, but only on the size of the factor in question.

The same applies for the individual parameters K_0, b_0, a_0 and a_1. With $R = 1$, K_0 gives the potential starting annual earnings of the individual. This amounts to 15,000 monetary units (DM, \$, £ or something similar – here, there are no boundaries; but, in general, the figures are expressed in \$).

The parameters a_0 and a_1 are introduced and interpreted in Section 2.2. The reference values of a_0 and a_1 reproduce the K_0 value exactly. There is no direct empirical information on either a_1 or b_0 (nor on a_0). However, as those parameters occur in different model stages and the overall structure of the model is recursive (more on this later), a_1 and b_0 do not have to be determined simultaneously. On the basis of the basic model (Section 2.1), b_0 was chosen for given reference values of the remaining parameters applied there, such that the values of the theoretically generated income path are compatible with the empirically observed progressions in terms of size. This results in the reference value $b_0 = 10$. A realistic size of a_1 could thereby be obtained indirectly in the expanded model (Section 2.2). A reproduction of the K_0 value would then finally produce a_0.

2.1.2 *Solution*

The life-cycle model created in the previous section assumes the form of a *control problem*. This is summarised in the following statement:

$$\underset{\{s_n \in [0,1), D_n \in [0,\infty)\}}{\text{Max}} \quad V = \sum_{n=0}^{N-1} L_n(K_n; s_n, D_n) + L_N(K_N),$$

under the constraint that:

$$K_{n+1} = g(K_n; s_n, D_n), \quad n = 0, \ldots, N-1;$$
$$\text{given } K_0 > 0$$

where

capital accumulation models). Haley shows however (p. 1235) that the scale parameter estimated by him is an unbiased estimator of the sum $b_1 + b_2$. The values of his scale parameter all come to 0.6. If one assumes a value like that here, and this does not only apply for b_1 and b_2, then one must of course be aware that there are two different models, especially with $c \neq 0$; therefore it is not, strictly speaking, acceptable to take any of those estimated values literally.

$$
\begin{aligned}
L_n(K_n; s_n, D_n) &:= A_n(1+r)^{-n} \\
&= [RK_n(1-s_n) - PD_n](1+r)^{-n}, \\
n &= 0, \ldots, N-1; \\
L_N(K_N) &:= A_N(1+r)^{-N} = RK_N(1+r)^{-N}; \\
g(K_n; s_n, D_n) &:= b_0(s_n K_n)^{b_1} D_n^{b_2} \\
&\quad + [1 + c(1-s_n) - \delta]K_n, \\
n &= 0, \ldots, N-1.
\end{aligned}
$$

Note: The split formulation of the objective function V corresponds to the standard notation in the literature on control theory. Since the system equation $K_{n+1} = g(K_n; s_n, D_n)$ is forward-looking there are, of course, no investments of any kind in the final period, $n = N$, for these would only begin to take effect from $N + 1$. However, according to the assumption, the human capital stock of the individual after $N + 1$ no longer has any market value at all (to recap: $R = 0, \forall n \geqslant N + 1$). Consequently, $s_N = D_N = 0$ (we are concerned with the maximisation of income) and the above split is obtained.

The present control problem reveals a *non-linear* objective function (because of the product of the variables s_n and K_n) and a *non-linear* system equation. Normally, no analytical solution can be expected in such a case. In the comparison of the two principal techniques which have been developed for solving control problems,[41] Intriligator (1971, p. 357) comes to the conclusion that, 'For an analytical solution the maximum principle approach is generally more useful than the dynamic programming approach.' In fact, it is possible with the aid of the maximum principle approach to achieve the desired analytical objective despite the awkward non-linearities.

Notes: (i) Note that the concern below is with a *discrete* version of the maximum principle.[42]
(ii) Economists typically apply the maximum principle, for which they have apparently developed a preference. The control theorists themselves employ this principle far less frequently. The dynamic programming approach dominates, particularly in cases where discrete problems are concerned.

A solution to the present control problem designed on that principle first requires the definition of a sequence H_n (this is the discrete equivalent to the continuous formulations of the Hamiltonian function):[43]

[41] These are the *maximum principle* approach referred to by Pontryagin and the *dynamic programming* approach from Bellman.
[42] Cf., for example, Bryson and Ho (1969, ch. 2).
[43] Cf., for what follows, in particular, Bryson and Ho (1969, ch. 2.2).

$$H_n(K_n; s_n, D_n; \lambda_{n+1}) := L_n(K_n; s_n, D_n) + \lambda_{n+1} g(K_n; s_n, D_n),$$
$$n = 0, \ldots, N-1,$$

where λ_{n+1} is called an *adjoint variable* (co-state variable); the economic significance of this variable will be discussed in more detail at a later stage. If interior solutions are assumed (thus: $s_n^* \in (0,1)$ and $D_n^* \in (0, \infty)$, $n = 0, \ldots, N-1$), then the required conditions for a (local) maximum of V are represented as follows:

$$\frac{\partial H_n}{\partial s_n} = 0, \quad \frac{\partial H_n}{\partial D_n} = 0; \quad n = 0, .., N-1; \tag{20}$$

$$K_{n+1} = g(K_n; s_n, D_n), \quad n = 0, \ldots, N-1; \tag{21}$$

K_0 given;

$$\left.\begin{aligned} \lambda_n &= \frac{\partial L_n}{\partial K_n} + \lambda_{n+1} \frac{\partial g}{\partial K_n}, \quad n = 0, \ldots, N-1; \\ \lambda_N &= \frac{dL_N}{dK_N}. \end{aligned}\right. \tag{22}$$

Note: If the optimum values for s_n^* and D_n^* subsequently derived are applied to the (discrete) Hamiltonian function H_n, it can be seen that the maximised Hamiltonian function $H_n(K_n; s_n^*, D_n^*; \lambda_{n+1}) =: H_n^0(K_n, \lambda_{n+1})$ is a linear function of the state variables K_n, $n = 0, \ldots, N-1$. According to a theorem proved by Arrow, the optimality conditions listed in (20), (21) and (22) are thereby not only necessary but also sufficient.[44]

If the 'marginal value product = factor price' equations resulting from the stationary conditions (20) are solved for the control variables, the following is obtained:

$$s_n^* = \frac{1}{K_n} \left[\frac{b_0 b_1}{R(1+r)} \right]^{\frac{1-b_2}{a}} \left[\frac{b_0 b_2}{P(1+r)} \right]^{\frac{b_2}{a}} \psi_{n+1}^{1/a}$$
$$\cdot \left(1 + \frac{c}{R(1+r)} \psi_{n+1} \right)^{\frac{b_2 - 1}{a}}, \quad n = 0, \ldots, N-1; \tag{23}$$

$$D_n^* = \left[\frac{b_0 b_1}{R(1+r)} \right]^{\frac{b_1}{a}} \left[\frac{b_0 b_2}{P(1+r)} \right]^{\frac{1-b_1}{a}} \psi_{n+1}^{1/a}$$

[44] Cf. Kamien and Schwartz (1981, part II, section 15) and the references quoted therein (p. 211).
Note that H_n is a strictly concave fucntion of s_n and D_n, $n = 0, \ldots, N-1$, as $0 < b_1 < 1$ and $0 < b_2 < 1$. Note also the peculiarities of discrete problems occurring in connection with this as well (cf., for example, Bryson and Ho (1969, pp. 208–11).

$$\cdot\left(1+\frac{c}{R(1+r)}\psi_{n+1}\right)^{-\frac{b_1}{a}}, \quad n=0,\ldots,N-1; \qquad (24)$$

where $a := 1 - b_1 - b_2$ and $\psi_{n+1} := \lambda_{n+1}(1+r)^{n+1}$.[45]

After the optimal investment values $s_n^* K_n$ and D_n^* have been obtained by way of this step as functions of the model parameters and the adjoint variable, the question naturally arises of the dependency on n. To that end, the time path of ψ_{n+1} must be found. Normally, this requires the explicit solution of a formidable two-point boundary value problem, namely the solution of the difference equations (21) and (22). Note, that these equations are connected to one another by way of (23) and (24) and that the difference equation for the state variable is designed with an initial boundary condition and the one for the adjoint variable with a terminal boundary condition. In the present case, there is, however, a simpler way to achieve the objective.[46] If one applies the optimal values from (23) and (24) to (22) (on consideration of the definitions of L_n and g), then, after some algebraic manipulation, the following equation is obtained:

$$\psi_n = R + \frac{1-\delta+c}{1+r}\psi_{n+1}; \quad n=0,\ldots,N-1.$$

For the terminal boundary condition $\psi_N = R$ is produced. Consequently, one is faced with a non-homogeneous linear first-order difference equation with constant coefficients, for which that particular solution is being sought which fulfils the condition $\psi_N = R$. With $r+\delta > c$ (cf. Section 2.1.1) $(1-\delta+c)/(1+r) \neq 1$ is ensured so that the following equation is obtained for the desired time path:

$$\psi_n = \frac{R(1+r)}{r+\delta-c}\left[1-\left(\frac{1-\delta+c}{1+r}\right)^{N+1-n}\right]; \quad n=0,\ldots,N. \qquad (25)$$

This now permits an explicit analytical solution of the model in combination with (23) and (24).

However, firstly the variable ψ_n must be observed more closely, for it contains some interesting economic information. ψ_n reveals by how much the *maximum* attainable value of V would change if the human capital stock in period n were increased by one unit. This change in value is expressed in terms of period n. As V is the present value of disposable earnings, this figure for the change in value corresponds to the income *flow* discounted to period n which is caused by the additional human capital unit available

[45] The adjoint variable λ_{n+1} (or ψ_{n+1}) should strictly speaking be denoted with a '*'. However, this is not common practice in the literature and will therefore be omitted.

[46] This is not least because of the neutrality assumption (assumption (6)).

from period n onwards, with the assumption of a constant human capital rate of decay, δ, and a constant learning-by-doing rate, c. In fact, an additional human capital unit in period n causes a potential increase in income amounting to R (in period n); in $n + 1$ one equivalent to $R(1 - \delta + c)/(1 + r)$ (viewed from period n); in $n + 2$ one equivalent to $[R(1 - \delta + c)](1 - \delta + c)/(1 + r)^2$ (viewed from period n), ...; and in N one equivalent to $R(1 - \delta + c)^{N-n}/(1 + r)^{N-n}$ (viewed from period n).[47] If these increases in income are added together the result is exactly ψ_n (cf. (25)).

The explicit production of an additional unit of human capital requires the employment of the scarce factors sK and D; consequently, one can ascribe a shadow price to this production. If the previous derivation is taken into account, then it becomes clear that those costs which the individual is prepared to take on as the maximum, run along ψ_n exactly; any slight decrease in costs would leave him with a positive net gain. In this natural sense, ψ_n represents the (optimal) shadow price of an additional human capital unit produced in period $n - 1$ and thus additionally available from period n (note the system equation of the control problem is looking forward).[48]

> *Notes*: (i) $\psi_n > 0$, $n = 0, \ldots, N$; $\psi_n = 0 \,\forall n \geqslant N + 1$, as there $R = 0$. A human capital unit additionally produced in period N, and thereby additionally available from period $N + 1$ onwards, would not achieve anything as, according to the assumption, the individual retires from his earning life at the end of the period N. Consequently, $\psi_{N+1} = 0$ ($\Rightarrow s_N^* = D_N^* = 0$, cf. (23) and (24)). This applies in the same way for all human capital production taking place after $n = N$.
> (ii) With the previous considerations the difference equation for the adjoint variable derived above become clearer. If one understands ψ_n and ψ_{n+1} as sums of the increases in income explained above, then the immediate consequence is that these two sums differ in terms of the period n by exactly the first summand in ψ_n, thus by R; this amount is missing in $[(1 - \delta + c)/(1 + r)]\psi_{n+1}$ because the remaining working life is shortened by one period.

47 If one assumes the relation $\delta > c$ at the outset (suggested by the results of empirical studies (see Section 2.1.1)), the additional human capital unit in each period $i > n$ only contributes a part $(1 - \delta + c)^{i-n}$ of a whole unit. In theory, it is perfectly plausible for the effect of practical job experience to compensate for the ageing process of productive abilities and knowledge, so that net decline in human capital stock is prevented entirely. In such a case, the contributions of the human capital unit would remain constant or even increase; $(1 - \delta + c)^{i-n}$ would then be $\geqslant 1$ $(i > n)$. If these contributions are evaluated in terms of the period n, then they are to be discounted to this period (cf. again assumption (4)). In $N + 1$ and all further periods an additional human capital unit no longer, of course, provides an increase in income, as $R = 0 \,\forall n \geqslant N + 1$.

48 It thereby becomes clear why ψ_{n+1} (and not ψ_n) enters the equations for the optima, (23) and (24).

Consequently the shadow price of an additional unit of human capital decreases (in terms of period n) from period n to period $n+1$ by the amount R. This decreasing effect caused by the remaining period becoming shorter (end-of-horizon effect) can be represented as follows:

$$\psi_{n+1} - \psi_n = -R\left(\frac{1-\delta+c}{1+r}\right)^{N-n} < 0; \quad n = 0, \ldots, N-1.$$

Now that the time path of the adjoint variable has been determined explicitly, a complete solution of the model is possible.

First of all, the following closed-form expressions are obtained for the optimum investment trajectories $\{s_n^*\}_{n=0}^{N-1}$ and $\{D_n^*\}_{n=0}^{N-1}$:

$$s_n^* = \frac{1}{K_n}\left(\frac{b_0 b_1}{r+\delta-c}\right)^{\frac{1}{a}}\left(\frac{b_2 R}{b_1 P}\right)^{\frac{b_2}{a}}\left[1-\left(\frac{1-\delta+c}{1+r}\right)^{N-n}\right]^{\frac{1}{a}}$$

$$\cdot\left(1+\frac{c}{r+\delta-c}\left[1-\left(\frac{1-\delta+c}{1+r}\right)^{N-n}\right]\right)^{\frac{b_2-1}{a}};$$

$$n = 0, \ldots, N-1. \quad (26)$$

$$D_n^* = \left(\frac{b_0 b_1}{r+\delta-c}\right)^{\frac{1}{a}}\left(\frac{b_2 R}{b_1 P}\right)^{\frac{1-b_1}{a}}\left[1-\left(\frac{1-\delta+c}{1+r}\right)^{N-n}\right]^{\frac{1}{a}}$$

$$\cdot\left(1+\frac{c}{r+\delta-c}\left[1-\left(\frac{1-\delta+c}{1+r}\right)^{N-n}\right]\right)^{-\frac{b_1}{a}};$$

$$n = 0, \ldots, N-1.^{49} \quad (27)$$

Note: Where $c = 0$ in (26) and (27) one is faced with discrete versions of the optimal input equations implicitly included in the Ben-Porath model (1967). A detailed discussion of the present generalisation will take place within the framework of an expanded model in Section 2.3. See also the graphic and numerical illustrations at the end of this section.

[49] It must be remembered that this approach is based on *internal* solutions. (26) and (27) are the optimum equations obtained under this condition. One can immediately see from (27) that, in fact, $D_n^* \in (0, \infty)$; $n = 0, \ldots, N-1$ (note the parameter restrictions explained in Section 2.1.1). It is immediately clear from (26) that $s_n^* > 0$, $n = 0, \ldots, N-1$; (26), however, leaves it open as to whether $s_n^* < 1, n = 0, \ldots, N-1$. The assumption which can always be made in this case is that of a sufficiently large human capital stock K_n and, thereby, that of a sufficiently large initial stock K_0, which is given in the present control problem (see also the accounting equation developed below for K_n (29)). In addition, there are also certain possible checks which can be effected by applying relevant economic parameter values to (26). This actually results in $s_n^* < 1, n = 0, \ldots, N-1$ – as originally required (cf. the comments on the standard parameter set (19); K_n (and/or K_n^*) is obtained from the accounting equation of human capital stock (29)).

One thing can already be recognised from the present demand functions (26) and (27): the explicit integration of the learning-by-doing effect into the accumulation equation for individual human capital stock results in the human capital factor $s_n^* K_n$ for the Q_n^* production becoming less efficient in proportion to the quantity used of the goods purchased D_n^*; the proportion of the marginal products of both production factors shifts in favour of the factor purchased, D_n^* (this can be derived from (20)). In the present model, therefore, the amount $s_n^* K_n$ used in Q_n^* is smaller, relatively speaking, than in the Ben-Porath model, *ceteris paribus*:

$$\frac{s_n^* K_n}{D_n^*}(c > 0) < \frac{s_n^* K_n}{D_n^*}(c = 0).$$

If (26) and (27) are applied to (15), the time path of the optimal production values is obtained:

$$Q_n^* = b_0 \left(\frac{b_0 b_1}{r + \delta - c}\right)^{\frac{b_1 + b_2}{a}} \left(\frac{b_2 R}{b_1 P}\right)^{\frac{b_2}{a}} \left[1 - \left(\frac{1 - \delta + c}{1 + r}\right)^{N-n}\right]^{\frac{b_1 + b_2}{a}}$$
$$\cdot \left(1 + \frac{c}{r + \delta - c}\left[1 - \left(\frac{1 - \delta + c}{1 + r}\right)^{N-n}\right]\right)^{-\frac{b_1}{a}};$$
$$n = 0, \ldots, N - 1. \quad (28)$$

Through recursive application, the following accounting equation of the human capital stock is obtained for a given K_0 from the system equation $K_{n+1} = g(K_n; s_n, D_n)$:

$$K_n = K_0(1 - \delta + c)^n + \sum_{i=0}^{n-1} (Q_i - cs_i K_i)(1 - \delta + c)^{n-1-i};$$
$$n = 0, \ldots, N.^{50} \quad (29)$$

If (28) and (26) are applied to this equation, then the optimal human capital path $\{K_n^*\}_{n=0}^N$ is obtained (with a given K_0).

Now, if one recalls the definition equation of disposable earnings presented in Section 2.1.1:

$$A_n = RK_n(1 - s_n) - PD_n, \quad n = 0, \ldots, N - 1,$$
$$A_N = RK_N$$

(cf. note on p. 41(top) and note (i), p. 44)

the following closed-form expression for the desired optimal trajectory of disposable earnings is eventually obtained by applying the optimal variable values:

[50] In this instance and subsequently, the common (if vague) convention is assumed, that for $n = 0$ the sum expression '$\Sigma_{i=0}^{n-1} \ldots$' disappears, therefore that '$\Sigma_{i=0}^{-1} \ldots$' $\equiv 0$.

$$A_n^* = RK_0(1-\delta+c)^n + (b_0 b_1)^{\frac{1}{a}}\left(\frac{b_2}{P}\right)^{\frac{b_2}{a}}\left(\frac{R}{b_1}\right)^{\frac{1-b_1}{a}}$$

$$\cdot\left[\sum_{i=0}^{n-1} q_i^{1/a}(1+cq_i)^{\frac{b_2-1}{a}}[q_i^{-1}+c(1-b_1)](1-\delta+c)^{n-1-i}\right.$$

$$\left. - q_n^{1/a}(1+cq_n)^{\frac{b_2-1}{a}}[b_1+b_2(1+cq_n)]\right],$$

$$n = 0,\ldots,N; \quad (30)$$

where:

$$q_i := \frac{1}{r+\delta-c}\left[1-\left(\frac{1-\delta+c}{1+r}\right)^{N-i}\right] \quad \text{and} \quad a := 1-b_1-b_2;$$

$K_0 > 0$ given.

Notes: (i) $q_i = \psi_{i+1}/R(1+r)$.
(ii) I will frequently be referring to the abbreviated form $A_n^* = RK_0(1-\delta+c)^n + M_n$ below, where M_n denotes the second main term of the sum in (30).

$$M_n := A_n^* - RK_0(1-\delta+c)^n$$
$$= R\sum_{i=0}^{n-1}(Q_i^* - cs_i^* K_i)(1-\delta+c)^{n-1-i} - I_n^*;$$

M_n therefore corresponds to the sum of the weighted net increases in income of previous periods minus the current investment costs, $I_n^* (:= Rs_n^* K_n + PD_n^*)$.

An explicit analytical study of this theoretical income path will follow within the context of an expanded model in Section 2.3. However, in order at this stage to give the reader an idea of the nature of the solution, several graphical (Figs. 1–6) and numerical (Table 1) illustrations are shown (based on the standard parameter set (19)).[51]

Note: The optimal trajectories (26), (27), (28) and (30) contain the trajectories derived both from Haley and from the Ben-Porath model as special cases. Where $b_2 = 0$, $c = 0$ and $b_1 = \frac{1}{2}$, discrete versions of the earnings phase results of Haley (1973) are obtained, whose economic discussion of this case is, incidentally, well worth reading. Where $b_2 = 0$ and $c = 0$, discrete versions from Haley (1976) follow and, where $c = 0$, the optimal trajectories (in discrete time) implicitly contained in the Ben-Porath model (1967) are obtained.

[51] The curves are drawn smoothly, which is not strictly speaking admissible, as n is discrete and not continuous. This stylisation will be adhered to in all diagrams in this study. Those readers who find this disturbing, should imagine the graphs being evaluated at the discrete points n.

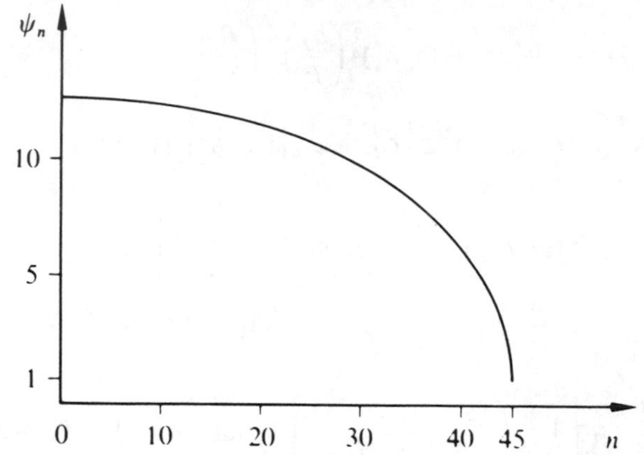

Fig. 1. The shadow price path (equation (25)) (ψ_n in \$; n = working age in years)

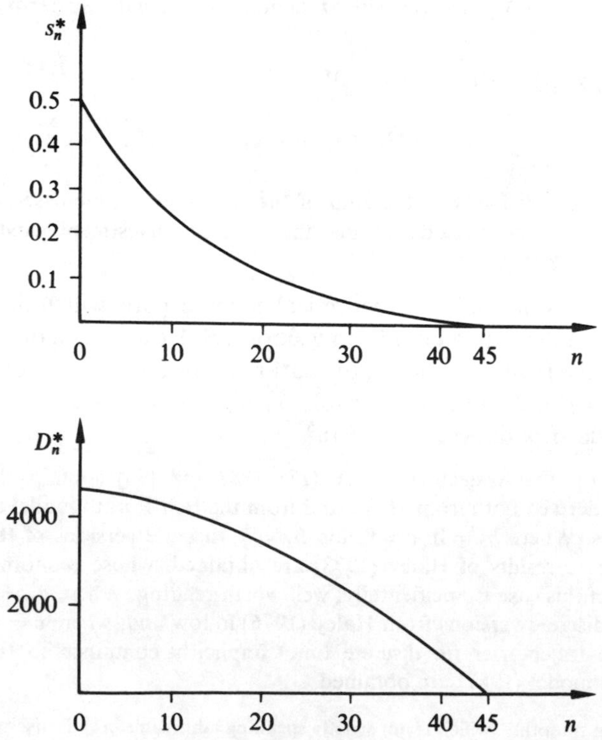

Fig. 2. The optimal investment plans (equations (26) and (27))

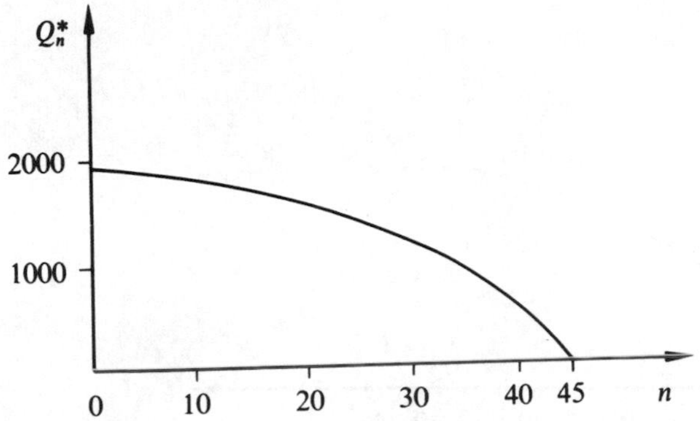

Fig. 3. The time path of optimal human capital production (equation (28)) (Q_n^* in human capital units)

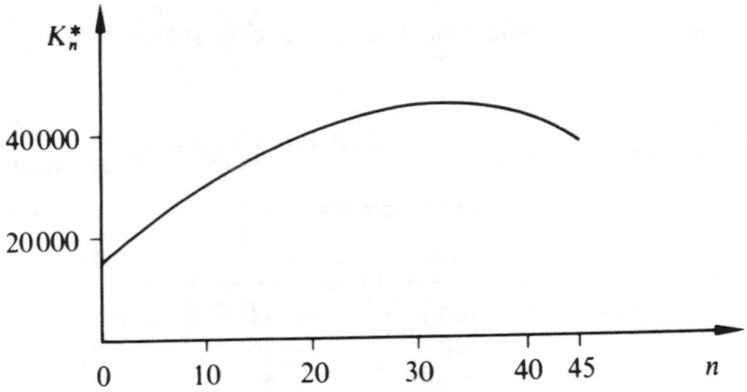

Fig. 4. The optimal human capital path (K_n^* in human capital units)

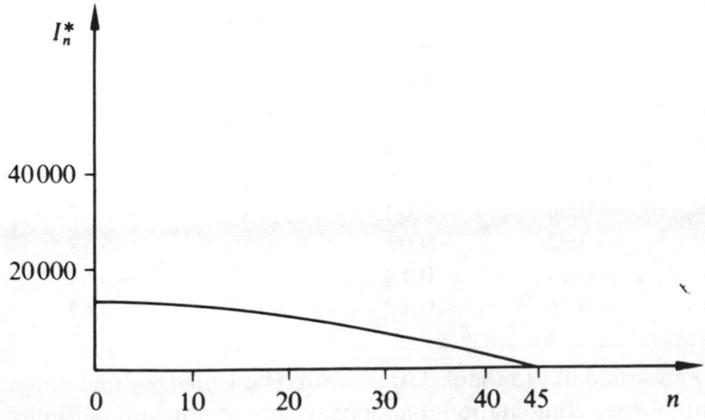

Fig. 5. The investment cost profile ($I_n^* := Rs_n^* K_n + PD_n^*$) ($I_n^*$ in \$)

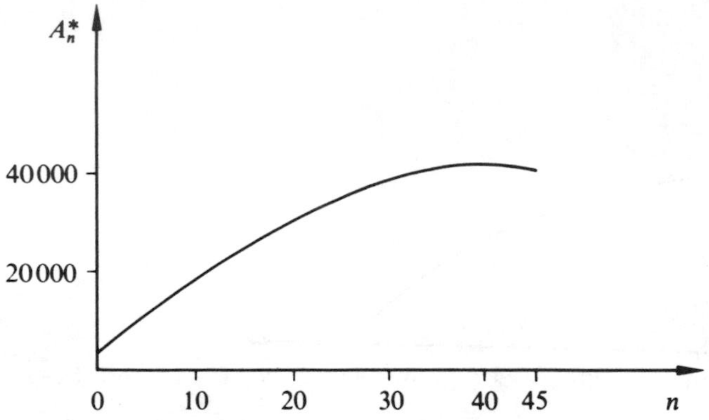

Fig. 6. The optimal path of disposable earnings (equation (30)) (A_n^* in \$)
Note: $A_n^* = RK_n^* - I_n^*$

Table 1. *Quantiative comparative dynamics: the dependence of the solution (30) on the model parameters*[a]

$$\left(\text{Elasticities: } \varepsilon_{A_n^*,x} := \frac{\partial A_n^*}{\partial x}\frac{x}{A_n^*},\ n = 0,\ldots,N;\ x \in \{R, P, r, c, \delta, b_1, b_2, N;\ b_0, K_0\}\right)$$

n	$\varepsilon_{A_n^*,R}$	$\varepsilon_{A_n^*,P}$	$\varepsilon_{A_n^*,r}$	$\varepsilon_{A_n^*,c}$	$\varepsilon_{A_n^*,\delta}$
0	−1.18	2.15	6.30	−0.74	4.18
1	−0.20	1.18	3.69	−0.39	2.31
2	0.27	0.72	2.46	−0.22	1.41
3	0.54	0.46	1.74	−0.12	0.89
4	0.71	0.28	1.28	−0.05	0.54
5	0.84	0.16	0.95	0.00	0.29
6	0.93	0.07	0.70	0.04	0.10
7	1.00	0.00	0.51	0.07	−0.06
8	1.06	−0.05	0.36	0.10	−0.18
9	1.10	−0.10	0.24	0.12	−0.29
10	1.14	−0.14	0.14	0.15	−0.37
11	1.17	−0.17	0.05	0.17	−0.45
12	1.20	−0.20	−0.02	0.18	−0.52
13	1.22	−0.22	−0.09	0.20	−0.58
14	1.24	−0.24	−0.14	0.22	−0.64
15	1.26	−0.26	−0.19	0.23	−0.69

[a] I am indebted to and would like to thank Dipl.-Math. Hans-Georg Zimmermann (University of Bonn) for his computational support in the production of Tables 1 and 2 (Section 5.6).

Table 1 (*continued*)

n	$\varepsilon_{A_n^*,R}$	$\varepsilon_{A_n^*,P}$	$\varepsilon_{A_n^*,r}$	$\varepsilon_{A_n^*,c}$	$\varepsilon_{A_n^*,\delta}$
16	1.28	−0.27	−0.23	0.24	−0.73
17	1.29	−0.29	−0.27	0.26	−0.78
18	1.31	−0.30	−0.31	0.27	−0.82
19	1.32	−0.31	−0.34	0.28	−0.85
20	1.33	−0.32	−0.36	0.29	−0.89
21	1.34	−0.33	−0.39	0.30	−0.92
22	1.35	−0.34	−0.41	0.31	−0.95
23	1.35	−0.35	−0.43	0.32	−0.98
24	1.36	−0.36	−0.45	0.33	−1.00
25	1.37	−0.36	−0.46	0.34	−1.03
26	1.37	−0.37	−0.48	0.35	−1.05
27	1.38	−0.37	−0.49	0.36	−1.07
28	1.39	−0.38	−0.50	0.36	−1.09
29	1.39	−0.38	−0.51	0.37	−1.11
30	1.39	−0.39	−0.52	0.38	−1.13
31	1.40	−0.39	−0.53	0.39	−1.15
32	1.40	−0.40	−0.53	0.39	−1.17
33	1.41	−0.40	−0.54	0.40	−1.18
34	1.41	−0.40	−0.54	0.41	−1.20
35	1.41	−0.41	−0.54	0.42	−1.21
36	1.42	−0.41	−0.54	0.42	−1.23
37	1.42	−0.41	−0.54	0.43	−1.25
38	1.42	−0.41	−0.54	0.44	−1.26
39	1.42	−0.42	−0.54	0.45	−1.28
40	1.42	−0.42	−0.53	0.46	−1.30
41	1.43	−0.42	−0.53	0.47	−1.32
42	1.43	−0.42	−0.53	0.48	−1.34
43	1.43	−0.42	−0.52	0.50	−1.37
44	1.43	−0.42	−0.52	0.52	−1.40
45	1.43	−0.42	−0.52	0.54	−1.44

Table 1 (*continued*)

n	$\varepsilon_{A_n^*,b_1}$	$\varepsilon_{A_n^*,b_2}$	$\varepsilon_{A_n^*,N}$	$\varepsilon_{A_n^*,b_0}$	$\varepsilon_{A_n^*,K_0}$
0	−48.61	−22.80	−0.97	−10.90	5.33
1	−26.98	−12.67	−0.62	−5.98	3.38
2	−16.80	−7.90	−0.46	−3.67	2.46
3	−10.88	−5.13	−0.37	−2.32	1.92
4	−7.01	−3.31	−0.31	−1.44	1.57
5	−4.28	−2.04	−0.26	−0.82	1.33

Table 1 (*continued*)

n	$\varepsilon_{A_n^*,b_1}$	$\varepsilon_{A_n^*,b_2}$	$\varepsilon_{A_n^*,N}$	$\varepsilon_{A_n^*,b_0}$	$\varepsilon_{A_n^*,K_0}$
6	−2.26	−1.09	−0.23	−0.36	1.14
7	−0.69	−0.36	−0.21	−0.01	1.00
8	0.55	0.23	−0.19	0.28	0.89
9	1.56	0.70	−0.17	0.51	0.80
10	2.40	1.09	−0.16	0.70	0.72
11	3.11	1.43	−0.15	0.86	0.66
12	3.72	1.71	−0.14	1.00	0.60
13	4.24	1.95	−0.13	1.11	0.56
14	4.69	2.17	−0.12	1.22	0.52
15	5.09	2.35	−0.12	1.31	0.48
16	5.45	2.52	−0.11	1.39	0.45
17	5.77	2.67	−0.10	1.46	0.42
18	6.05	2.80	−0.10	1.53	0.39
19	6.30	2.92	−0.09	1.58	0.37
20	6.54	3.03	−0.09	1.64	0.35
21	6.75	3.13	−0.08	1.68	0.33
22	6.94	3.22	−0.07	1.73	0.31
23	7.11	3.30	−0.06	1.77	0.30
24	7.27	3.37	−0.05	1.81	0.28
25	7.42	3.44	−0.04	1.84	0.27
26	7.55	3.50	−0.03	1.87	0.26
27	7.67	3.56	−0.01	1.90	0.25
28	7.79	3.61	0.00	1.93	0.24
29	7.89	3.66	0.02	1.95	0.23
30	7.98	3.70	0.05	1.97	0.22
31	8.07	3.74	0.07	1.99	0.21
32	8.14	3.78	0.10	2.01	0.20
33	8.21	3.81	0.14	2.03	0.19
34	8.27	3.83	0.19	2.05	0.19
35	8.32	3.86	0.24	2.06	0.18
36	8.37	3.88	0.30	2.08	0.17
37	8.40	3.89	0.37	2.09	0.17
38	8.43	3.90	0.45	2.10	0.17
39	8.45	3.91	0.55	2.11	0.16
40	8.46	3.91	0.67	2.12	0.16
41	8.46	3.91	0.81	2.13	0.16
42	8.45	3.91	0.96	2.13	0.15
43	8.44	3.90	1.14	2.14	0.15
44	8.43	3.90	1.33	2.14	0.15
45	8.42	3.89	1.51	2.14	0.15

Numerical basis: The standard parameter set (19). (Note, incidentally, that $N \in \mathbf{N}$; difference quotients occur in place of derivatives).

2.2 Expanded model: The optimal length of basic education

The life-cycle model developed in Section 2.1 was based on an exogenously given basic productive capacity K_0. With this basic stock, the individual entered the labour market and began his earnings life. The assumption of an exogenously given K_0 is without doubt unrealistic. At least a part of the initial capacity K_0 would have to be generated endogenously; therefore it must result from education and/or human capital investment decisions which occur *before* entry into working life.

In the terminology of the model created in Section 2.1, the education period before entry into the working life can be interpreted as a phase in which the individual reinvests his entire human capital stock for educational purposes; the fraction diverted from the available human capital stock is then equal to 1 and the realised earnings are consequently equal to 0 (cf. p. 29). In other words, this is the phase in which the individual places the total time resources available to him into human capital production (cf. p. 32). This phase is generally termed the *basic education phase* or the period of 'full-time schooling' phase. Now, the vital question arises as to whether an economic model can be created for K_0, or whether the education decisions occurring prior to $n = 0$ can be integrated into the model as well.

Because of the recursive nature of the problem, this is, in fact, possible in a relatively simple manner. For Ishikawa (1975, cf. special proposition 3, p. 640) has shown for a wide range of models including the model in question, that the phase of 'full-time schooling' in which the individual remains completely separated from the labour market, if it occurs at all, does so at the very beginning of economic life;[52] the full-time schooling phase optimally takes place prior to the earnings phase characterised in Section 2.1. Thus a backwards induction can be applied. If the argument is confined to the length of full-time schooling, S, and if $K_0 = K_0(S)$, then the maximisation of V (the sum of the disposable earnings discounted for the period $n = 0$) for any given $K_0(S)$, and thereby for any predetermined value of S, follows (cf. Section 2.1.2). The optimal trajectory of disposable earnings (30) ultimately obtained and thus the optimal value V^* are made a function of S in this manner. The primary objective then is to find the S which would create, so to speak, the best of all optimal trajectories for the individual. This is possible with the aid of elementary methods, as will be seen shortly. If you like, the solution is consequently obtained by working from back to front.[53]

[52] 'Economic' life denotes life which begins with the first education decision ($\triangleq$ 'economic birth') and ends with the withdrawal from working life ($\triangleq$ 'economic death'). Cf. also the general view of the model, p. 56.

[53] A typical characteristic of dynamic programming based on the Bellman optimality principle.

Therefore, if $K_0 = K_0(S)$ and $S =$ any freely chosen length of full-time schooling

$$S \in [0, \infty); \text{ where } K_0(0) > 0 \quad \text{and} \quad dK_0/dS > 0.$$

$K_0(0) > 0$ expresses the fact that untrained individuals (unskilled workers, etc.) can also achieve positive earnings, and $dK_0/dS > 0$ is necessary as otherwise any education prior to $n = 0$ would be unproductive.[54] Thus $A_n^* = A_n^*(S)$; $n = 0, \ldots, N$. The aim of the individual again would be to maximise the present value (at the time of planning) of his disposable earnings. The control problem solved in Section 2.1.2 provides the value:

$$V^* = \sum_{n=0}^{N} A_n^*(S)(1+r)^{-n} = V^*(S); \tag{31}$$

therefore, the task is now to maximise this value with respect to S, discounted to the time of the choice of S.[55]

If one ignores the direct costs of full-time schooling,[56] the maximisation problem is represented as follows:

$$\underset{S \in [0,\infty)}{\text{Max}} \; W = V^*(S)(1+r)^{-S},$$

whereby W denotes the value of the future disposable earnings discounted at the point of economic birth.[57]

> *Notes*: (i) Note that W is dependent exclusively on the variable S as all other decision variables have been 'optimised out' by way of the procedure described in Section 2.1.2. This underlines the recursive structure of the overall model.
> (ii) It is very possible that basic education does not only increase the productive initial capacity but also positively influences the learning

[54] Both together imply a positive K_0 for all $S \in [0, \infty)$ – as required in Section 2.1.

[55] Note in particular in connection with this, assumptions (3) (education as such does not contain any elements of consumption) and (4) (perfect capital market).

[56] In principle, of course, the introduction of direct costs is perfectly reasonable. However, in contrast to the direct costs in the further education phase, the term direct costs in the full-time schooling phase is vague. The 'full-time schooling phase', in general, means the phase of attending school; in many countries (for example, Germany) schooling is free (the funding is provided by the state) and general upkeep costs can hardly be counted as direct schooling costs (because you have to eat and drink, even when you are not being educated). As, in addition to this, there are no conclusive empirical findings on the subject of 'full-time schooling costs', their association with the model is being omitted.

[57] As described in Section 2.1, the length of the individual periods n determines the relevant time unit for the model. This must also be taken into account in this case (S is thus to be expressed in the same time unit as r, etc.). It should be noted that all the assumptions made in Section 2.1 also apply for the present Section 2.2; 2.2 is concerned with an *expanded* model and not an entirely new one.

ability *as such*. As a result of basic education, one would then not only start at a higher level, but also be better equipped for future human capital accumulation.[58] In the context of the present model it would, for example, certainly be interesting to analyse the effects of $b_0 = b_0(S)$. One would have assumed a complementary relationship instead of the substitutional relationship implied by $K_0 = K_0(S)$ between human capital investments in the full-time schooling phase and the earnings phase (that is, between S and $\{s_n, D_n\}$). This would, however, cancel out the neutrality assumption (assumption (6))[59] and result in analytical intractabilities. The consequences of $b_0 = b_0(S)$ are too complex to be discussed explicitly within the framework of the model in question.

Before solving the maximisation problem above, it would perhaps be quite useful to provide a *general outline of the structure* of the whole model; cf. Fig. 7 with respect to this. In terms of the expanded model, the economic planning horizon of the individual extends from 0 to $N + S$. According to the assumption, the individual acts as if he wanted to maximise the present value (based at the planning point (i.e., based on 0)) of his disposable earnings. With respect to this, he has a *two-stage optimisation problem* to solve when exploiting the *recursive* model structure. The first stage, described in Section 2.1, generates the optimal trajectory $\{A_n^*[K_0(S)]\}$ for any given $K_0(S)$; whereas the second stage, which is the object of the present section, ultimately provides the optimal trajectory of disposable earnings with explicit consideration being given to the basic education decision as well: $A_n^*(S^*) =: A_n^{**}$; $n = 0, \ldots, N$. The optimal income path obtained in this way, $\{A_n^{**}\}$, creates the economic key to the distribution models formulated in the subsequent chapters 3, 4 and 5.

Now the 'Max W' problem can be considered again. If one assumes the existence of an internal solution, i.e., $S^* \in (0, \infty)$, then one obtains the following simple equation for the desired optimal length of basic education from the necessary condition for a (local) maximum of W, $dW/dS = 0$:[60]

$$\frac{dV^*}{dS}(S^*) = \ln(1 + r)V^*(S^*). \tag{32}$$

[58] Cf. in this instance Welch (1970) in particular. Cf. also Welch (1975), Lazear (1976) and Psacharopoulos and Layard (1979).

[59] For now the marginal costs of production of an additional unit of human capital in the further education phase (cf. Section 2.1) would be a function of previous investment (namely, a function of S). Cf., in connection with this, the discussion in Ben-Porath (1967, p. 360) as well.

[60] In order to ensure that the optimal S^* resulting from (32) is a *maximum* (and not a minimum), it is known that $d^2W(S^*)/dS^2 < 0$ is required (with the requirement that W is twice differentiable). It depends on the characteristics of the function $K_0(S)$, which has so far not been explicitly specified, whether this sufficient condition for a (local) maximum of

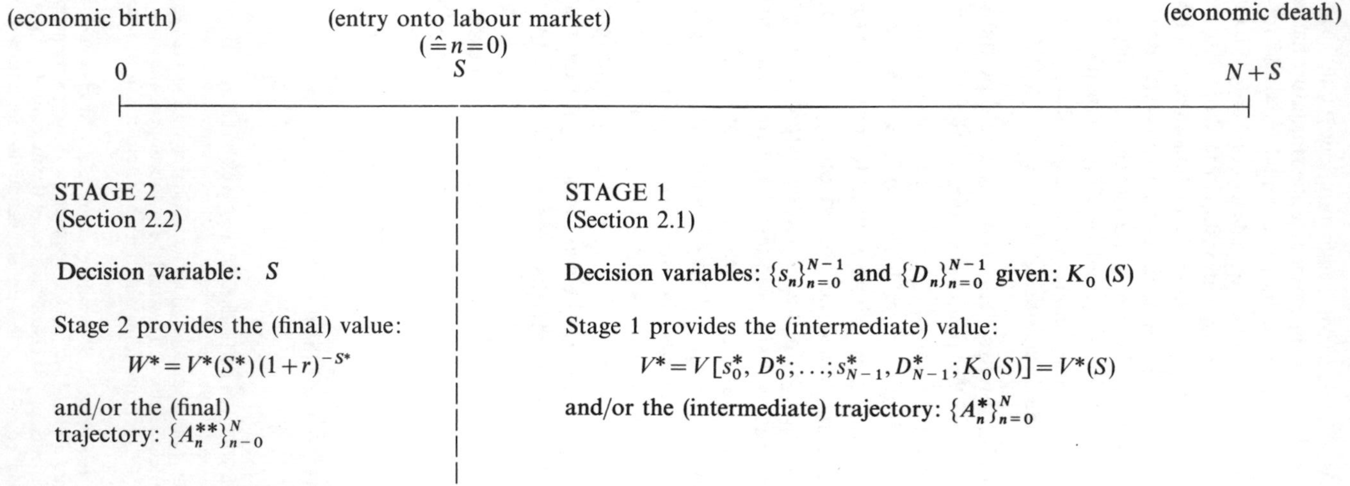

STAGE 2
(Section 2.2)

Decision variable: S

Stage 2 provides the (final) value:

$$W^* = V^*(S^*)(1+r)^{-S^*}$$

and/or the (final) trajectory: $\{A_n^{**}\}_{n-0}^{N}$

STAGE 1
(Section 2.1)

Decision variables: $\{s_n\}_{n=0}^{N-1}$ and $\{D_n\}_{n=0}^{N-1}$ given: $K_0\ (S)$

Stage 1 provides the (intermediate) value:

$$V^* = V[s_0^*, D_0^*; \ldots; s_{N-1}^*, D_{N-1}^*; K_0(S)] = V^*(S)$$

and/or the (intermediate) trajectory: $\{A_n^*\}_{n=0}^{N}$

Fig. 7. Overview of the model

Therefore, the period of full-time schooling is extended until the marginal gain of a marginal increase in S, dV^*/dS corresponds to the marginal opportunity costs $\ln(1+r)V^*$, arising from the delayed start of the income flow.[61] Decision rules of this type have been familiar to economists at least since Jevons (1871).

How does the S^* in question differ from the one in a 'pure schooling' model (where $s_n = D_n = 0\,\forall n$)? According to (30) and (31), (32) can be rewritten in the following manner:

$$\left[\frac{dK_0}{dS}(S^*) - \ln(1+r)K_0(S^*)\right] R \sum_{n=0}^{N}\left(\frac{1-\delta+c}{1+r}\right)^n = \ln(1+r)\sum_{n=0}^{N} M_n(1+r)^{-n}.$$

In a pure full-time schooling model, the following would apply:

$$\frac{dK_0}{dS}(S^*) = \ln(1+r)K_0(S^*)$$

as in that case $M_n = 0\,\forall n$ (cf. the definition of M_n, p. 47). In the present case, one has, however, $dK_0(S^*)/dS > \ln(1+r)K_0(S^*)$, as the right-hand side of

W is in fact fulfilled. For example, if this function satisfies the condition that $d^2K_0(S^*)/dS^2 \leqslant 0$, then the required sufficient condition is fulfilled in any case.
Proof:

$$\frac{d^2W}{dS^2} = (1+r)^{-S}\left[\frac{d^2V^*}{dS^2} - 2\ln(1+r)\frac{dV^*}{dS} + [\ln(1+r)]^2V^*\right];$$

The following applies in line with (32):

$$\frac{d^2W}{dS^2}(S^*) = (1+r)^{-S^*}\left[\frac{d^2V^*}{dS^2}(S^*) - [\ln(1+r)]^2V^*(S^*)\right].$$

Where $K_0(S) > 0\,\forall S \in [0,\infty)$ – cf. footnote 54, p. 54 – V^* is always positive so that the second derivative of W is then negative in any case at the point $S = S^*$, if $d^2V^*(S^*)/dS^2 \leqslant 0$ (which states that non-increasing marginal revenues in basic education occur at the point $S = S^*$). The following is sufficient for the inequality just mentioned: $d^2A_n^*(S^*)/dS^2 \leqslant 0$, $n = 0,\ldots,N$; where $A_n^* = A_n^*[K_0(S)]$. Thus:

$$\frac{d^2A_n^*}{dK_0^2}\left(\frac{dK_0}{dS}\right)^2 + \frac{dA_n^*}{dK_0}\frac{d^2K_0}{dS^2} \leqslant 0, \quad \text{at the point } S = S^*\ (n = 0,\ldots,N).$$

This condition is reduced to the following when applied to (30):

$$\frac{d^2K_0}{dS^2}(S^*) \leqslant 0 \quad (\text{where } R(1-\delta+c)^n > 0\,\forall n).$$

The specification of $K_0(S)$ introduced below will in fact satisfy this condition.

61 If you like, the marginal costs are noted in this instance in terms of flows (→ interest outgoings).

the equation above is positive.[62] The immediate consequence of this is that the S^* here is *smaller*. In a 'pure schooling' model the S would continue to be increased until the marginal revenue relating to the productive capacity K_0 corresponded exactly to the marginal costs. In the present framework, the possibility of human capital investments even after the basic education phase is explicitly included so that this productive capacity now only represents the *initial* capacity. An extension of the full-time schooling phase would increase K_0 and at the same time delay the start of the working phase; this applies to the same extent for both models. However, because of the opportunities for further education now existing during the working phase, this postponement in the present case has a far greater opportunity cost value. Hidden behind this is, of course, the implicitly assumed *substitutional* relationship between S and $\{s_n, D_n\}$.

The inclusion of the discounted sum of the potential income net increases M_n resulting from further education, distinguishes this choice of S specifically from the one in the conventional 'pure schooling' models;[63] the now greater marginal opportunity costs (with otherwise unchanged conditions regarding marginal revenue) necessarily lead to a comparatively smaller value of S^*.

In order to be able to solve this expanded model in closed form and therefore in order to be able to obtain an explicit value for S^* and/or $K_0^* = K_0(S^*)$ with the aid of (32) – and thereby via (30) an explicit A_n^{**} path as the final result of the two-stage maximisation problem – it is inevitable that the function $K_0(S)$ must be specified explicitly. It must be emphasised yet again that an analytical A_n^{**} solution is an indispensable condition for the objectives of the present study formulated in the introduction.

The following relationship is assumed:

$$K_0(S) = a_0 + a_1 S; \quad a_0 > 0, a_1 > 0; \quad S \in [0, \infty). \tag{33}$$

This simple specification proves perfectly satisfactory for the present purposes. In addition, it does not only fulfil the conditions required above, $K_0(0) > 0$ and $dK_0/dS > 0$, but it also ensures that $d^2W(S^*)/dS^2 < 0$, as with $d^2K_0/dS^2 = 0$, $\forall S \in [0, \infty)$ it satisfies the condition developed in

[62] It is true that $M_0 < 0$, and in certain cases the same applies for M_1 and M_2; yet this is compensated for by the remaining positive M_n. This logically has to be the case, as the M_n are ultimately obtained from an approach, the objective of which was the *maximisation* of V. With the standard parameter set (19), for example, the value ($) 7252.6 follows for the right-hand side. Within the framework of Section 2.3.1 the positivity is also proved analytically.

[63] The fact that present values of the type considered in this case actually do play a part in full-time education decisions has recently been empirically confirmed by Willis and Rosen (1979), Pissarides (1982) and Fuller, Manski and Wise (1982).

footnote 60. Moreover the specification put forward also seems to be substantiated, in my view, as far as the content is concerned:[64] the functional dependence between productivity and length of education familiar from the literature on learning curves is ultimately strictly concave because it reaches saturation limits (as regards the absorption capabilities and retention abilities, for example); however, if one assumes that, in the basic education phase (and this is what concerns us here), those limits are not yet being achieved, then the learning curve in this initial phase can be approximated by way of a linear function. The decline in the learning curve which is, however, to be expected later on in the further education phase (→ Section 2.1) is considered explicitly, i.e., the production function Q_n shows decreasing marginal products.

Note: Note, that the present approach (in contrast to previous approaches) does not demand the same human capital production function for both phases (basic education and further education) but permits *different* production functions.[65]

The parameters occurring in (33) can be interpreted in the following manner. 'a_0' represents the *basic stock* of human capital at the beginning of the economic planning horizon: $a_0 = K_0(0)$. This basic productive capacity of the individual is chiefly characterised by the inherited characteristics, the family background and the cultural influences which the individual is subjected to – according to the unanimous view of the empirical literature. With the notation introduced in Section 2.1.1, one therefore has:

$$a_0 = a_0(G, HO, CU). \tag{34}$$

See footnote 34 (p. 36) for the individual components of the three factors G, HO and CU.

'a_1' (as with b_0) can be interpreted as a parameter of *production efficiency*. It describes the individual learning efficiency during the basic education phase. Significant determining factors for this efficiency are (according to the empirical literature) the learning ability and the DF factor so that one can approximately assume:

$$a_1 = a_1[\overset{+}{LA}(G, HO, CU);\ \overset{+}{DF}(HO, CU)] \tag{35}$$

(cf. pp. 36–7, on LA and DF as well as the associated references).

Notes: (i) This specification of a_1 is to be interpreted as a working hypothesis and not an exhaustive tract on a_1.

64 Quite apart from the fact that (33) would be difficult to disprove empirically owing to the generally fairly short period of pure full-time schooling.

65 Which is at least basically taking account of the criticism by Griliches (1977b, pp. 618–19).

(ii) If one compares the specification of a_1 with that of b_0, then one may miss the factors CR and SQ (the QPC group only comes into effect in the working phase owing to the content). Yet, according to the empirical results of Wise (1975, p. 356) and Wachtel (1975) the productive initial capacity K_0 remains virtually unaffected by these two factors.

The distinction between a *full-time schooling* production parameter a_1 and an *earnings phase* production parameter b_0 underlines in a broad sense the difference between a 'theorist' and a 'practitioner'. As will be seen later in Section 2.3.4, practice-related human capital accumulation abilities ($QPC(\underline{a}, \underline{b}, \underline{c})$) have completely different effects on the income profile than, for example, the general ('theoretical') characteristics LA and DF.

(iii) Bowles (1972, pp. S233–5; 1973), Taubman (1975, pp. 156–62, 185–92) and Atkinson, Maynard and Trinder (1983, pp. 134–6, 181) have discovered that the HO bundle influences the individual earnings both in a direct and an indirect manner. This branching effect is also included in the present specification: the direct HO effect is captured by $a_0 = a_0(HO)$ and the indirect one by $a_1 = a_1\ (LA(HO); DF(HO))$ (just as with b_0).

Now all the model parameters have been introduced. If one recaps briefly the details of Section 2.1.1, the individual j is faced with a group of *exogenous* economic factors and a group of '*inner restrictions*'. The first group includes the prices R, P and r, the structural parameters c, δ, b_1 and b_2 and the horizon parameter N. The second group contains the individual parameters a_0^j, a_1^j and b_0^j.

Note: The parameters a_0 and a_1 introduced in this section thus belong to those factors, which by assumption can vary from individual to individual. Of course, it would be more general to allow the fixed parameters c, δ, b_1, b_2 and N to vary among the individuals too, as an individual relation to these factors is perfectly plausible. This has not, however, been pursued for two reasons.

Firstly, the analytical objectives of the present study would have to be abandoned. The distribution analysis in the subsequent chapters would have to be based on the joint distribution of the variables $\tilde{a}_0$, $\tilde{a}_1$, $\tilde{b}_0$, $\tilde{c}$, $\tilde{\delta}$, $\tilde{b}_1$, $\tilde{b}_2$ and $\tilde{N}$ (thus on an *eight*-dimensional distribution) – which would be a hopeless exercise in analytical terms. One would have to resort to numerical simulations in that case.[66] It would no longer be possible to develop a precise inequality analysis of the type created below.

Secondly, in the present context, with the variable 'individual' para-

[66] And even this type of simulation would be based on fairly shaky ground, as there are neither theoretical *a priori* derivations nor empirical information on that joint distribution. Typically, multidimensional normal distributions are assumed in practice, where the mean values (as far as possible) are determined with the aid of empirical sources, the variance-covariance matrix, however, generally has to be set 'freehand', cf. e.g. Blinder (1974, ch. 4).

meters a_0^j, a_1^j and b_0^j, we are concerned with *central* parameters of the model, which not only enable almost all the personal factors determining income isolated in the empirical literature to be incorporated, but also permit an individualisation of the structural effects.[67] Therefore, it is debatable to what extent it would be sensible to allow other variable parameters within the framework of the present approach.

There is clearly one consideration not to be overlooked. Owing to the admission of individual variations in a_0^j, a_1^j and b_0^j, the optimal length of the basic education naturally becomes a variable as well: $S^{j*} = S^*(a_0^j, a_1^j, b_0^j)$. The consequence of this is that individuals with a larger value of S^{j*} have a longer economic life (thus retire later) than individuals with a smaller S^{j*}, as N is supposed to be the same for all individuals (cf. Fig. 7). To a certain extent this really is the case, as the empirical results by Mincer (1974, p. 8) show. Beyond that (according to Mincer differences up to five years occur) the assumption of a fixed N can no longer be empirically substantiated. A variable N will have to remain a project for the future.[68]

After this explanation regarding the contents, I now return to the technical problem of solving explicitly the expanded model in question. If (33) is applied to (30) then the following closed-form expression is obtained for the desired optimal length of full-time schooling from (32) (on consideration of (31)):

$$S^* = \frac{1}{\ln(1+r)} - \frac{a_0}{a_1} - \frac{1}{a_1 R \Pi_N} \sum_{n=0}^{N} M_n (1+r)^{-n}, \tag{36}$$

where:

$$\Pi_N := \sum_{n=0}^{N} \left(\frac{1 - \delta + c}{1 + r} \right)^n .^{69}$$

Notes: (i) The substitutional relationship between human capital investment in the full-time schooling phase and in the earnings phase implied by

[67] On the last point mentioned, see p. 35 and pp. 45–7, from which it becomes clear that with a_0^j, a_1^j and b_0^j, the four factors and s_n^*, D_n^*, Q_n^* and K_n^* are dependent on j and therefore can be individually different.

[68] However, I do not believe that this type of extension would encourage new findings on the inequality of earnings.

[69] It must be remembered that at the beginning (p. 55) the existence of an inner solution was assumed. It can indeed clearly be seen (in accordance with the parameter restrictions discussed) from (36) that $S^* < \infty$; however, it remains open as to whether S^* is positive. The assumption should be made here that the basic stock of human capital a_0 is still small enough to make a phase of full-time schooling profitable. No one should have such a great amount of productivity available from the very beginning that it would not be worth their while attending school. The exact condition for a positive value of S^* is the following:

$$(0 <) a_0 < \frac{a_1}{\ln(1+r)} - \frac{1}{R \Pi_N} \sum_{n=0}^{N} M_n (1+r)^{-n}.$$

$K_0 = K_0(S)$ is revealed explicitly in (36) by the *deduction* of the discounted sum of the potential net increases in productivity resulting from the further education measures.

(ii) $R\Pi_N = \psi_0$ (cf. (25)).

If one observes the considerable theoretical and empirical interest in the topic of 'full-time schooling' (in particular, in the context of the discussion on inequality),[70] there are sufficient grounds for dedicating a separate chapter to an analysis of the decision equation (36) generated by way of the above structural approach. The reduced form (36) does not only provide a specification basis for empirical studies, but also reveals (in consideration of (18), (34) and (35)) a series of theoretical discoveries, which in part are in contradiction to previous discoveries. Within the framework of the present study, the equation (36) is, however, only treated as a by-product. Some results of comparative statics can be found in Appendix 1 (they come into play in parts of Section 2.3 and Chapter 5). With (36) the optimal starting stock K_0^* (and therefore the optimal productive capacity with which the individual enters the labour market) is obtained from (33):

$$K_0^* = a_0 + a_1 S^* \quad (>0)$$

$$= \frac{a_1}{\ln(1+r)} - \frac{1}{R\Pi_N} \sum_{n=0}^{N} M_n (1+r)^{-n}. \tag{37}$$

Note: The fact that a_0 is omitted here is a consequence of the assumption of linearity in (33). The reader should not allow this to irritate him. The aim of the individual is, of course to maximise the present value W. If the parameter a_0 is omitted from K_0^* and thereby from A_n^{**}, $n = 0, \ldots, N$ and/or V^{**}, it reappears in $(1+r)^{-S^*}$. It can easily be shown that $\partial W^*/\partial a_0 > 0$ (see also Appendix 6); therefore, a greater basic stock of human capital is advantageous to the individual in any case.

Equation (37) applied to (30) provides the desired final result.

Last but not least, as the result of the two-stage optimisation problem, the following closed-form expression is obtained for the *optimal trajectory of disposable earnings with explicit consideration of full-time schooling*:

$$A_n^{**} := A_n^*(S^*) = R(a_0 + a_1 S^*)(1 - \delta + c)^n + M_n$$

$$= w_{1n} a_1 + w_{2n} b_0^{1/a}, \quad n = 0, \ldots, N; \tag{38}$$

where:

$$w_{1n} := \frac{R(1-\delta+c)^n}{\ln(1+r)};$$

$$w_{2n} := \hat{M}_n - \frac{(1-\delta+c)^n}{\Pi_N} \sum_{k=0}^{N} \hat{M}_k (1+r)^{-k},$$

[70] See, for example, Wallace and Ihnen (1975) and Griliches (1977a) and the literature referenced therein.

with:

$$\hat{M}_k := b_1^{1/a}\left(\frac{b_2}{P}\right)^{\frac{b_2}{a}}\left(\frac{R}{b_1}\right)^{\frac{1-b_1}{a}}\left[\sum_{i=0}^{k-1} q_i^{1/a}(1+cq_i)^{\frac{b_2-1}{a}}\right.$$

$$\cdot[q_i^{-1}+c(1-b_1)](1-\delta+c)^{k-1-i}$$

$$\left.-\,q_k^{1/a}(1+cq_k)^{\frac{b_2-1}{a}}[b_1+b_2(1+cq_k)]\right],$$

$$q_i := \frac{1}{r+\delta-c}\left[1-\left(\frac{1-\delta+c}{1+r}\right)^{N-i}\right],$$

$$a := 1-b_1-b_2,$$

$$\Pi_N := \sum_{k=0}^{N}\left(\frac{1-\delta+c}{1+r}\right)^k.$$

Note: With (38), the objective of an explicit analytical A_n^{**} path has been achieved. Note the advantage of the present approach compared to those methods which incorporate the choice of S as a corner solution of the control problem ($\rightarrow s_n^* = 1$); this is a much more complex procedure.[71] The present approach exploits two things: firstly, the fact that the control variable s_n does not jump around its corner value, and secondly, the sequential nature of education decisions.

The economic foundation has been laid for the distribution analysis which is to follow in the subsequent chapters by way of the derivation of the earnings equation (38) from the structural human capital approach developed in Sections 2.1 and 2.2. This equation for the optimal (or, more transparently, *planned*) disposable earnings clarifies *which* factors in the context of the present model determine the distribution of disposable earnings.[72] These are:

- the prices R, P and r;
- the structural parameters c, δ, b_1 and b_2 and the horizon parameter N;
- the joint distribution of the parameters of individual production efficiency a_1 and b_0;
- the age distribution within the observed population (therefore, the distribution over n, $n = 0, \ldots, N$; cf. Chapter 4).

[71] Cf., for example, Haley (1973), Wallace and Ihnen (1975) or Ryder, Stafford and Stephan(1976).

[72] Strictly speaking one ought to refer to the *stationary* distribution of earnings, as the calendar time t does not occur in (38). It must be stressed at this point that the later distribution derivations and inequality analyses as such are *independent* of whether a stationary economic situation exists or not. In fact, it would be simple to incorporate calendar effects into the model explicitly by specification of $R(t)$, $P(t)$ and/or $r(t)$. This complication will not be pursued any further here.

At the same time it can now be seen (and this is absolutely vital) in what way they do this and therefore, *how* the different factors enter the final form (38). This is an explicit result of the maximisation process.[73]

At this point a key position in the present study is making its presence felt. In the subsequent inequality analyses, the inequality of earnings will not be attributed to the individual factors as such, but summarised as the result of the optimisation behaviour of the individuals described in Sections 2.1 and 2.2, which, for its part, is in turn dependent on the individual factors. The often-asked question as to what extent inequality is a consequence of individual decisions or of individual basic stocks and abilities, does not seem particularly sensible. *Both react together* and the equation (38) is the explicit expression of this interaction. It would be more reasonable to pose the question of how the picture of inequality created here differs from a situation in which the individuals do not optimise. This is considered further later.

2.3 The optimal earnings path

What does the optimal plan $\{A_n^{**}\}$ look like exactly? What properties does it have? What life-cycle pattern does it show? And how does it react to parameter variations? These and other intertemporal questions are the object of the economic evaluation of the final form (38) which follows in this section. As has already been mentioned in the introduction, life-cycle aspects are occupying the centre-stage of the discussion on theoretical and political distribution more and more, not least because of the recent availability of panel data. If the following analyses also seem to be of rather a technical nature, they are, nevertheless, *fundamental* for the economic comprehension of the results on the inequality of earnings derived in Chapters 3, 4 and 5. Moreover, they gain an individual significance because of the provision of a structural basis for empirical longitudinal analyses (for which there is a lack of theoretical foundation).

2.3.1 Creation of an approximation

We must never forget that, in applications of mathematics, exact hypotheses are usually only approximations to the real situations and that other approximations may be as good, or even better, as those we first made (John W. Tukey, 1958, TR 10, p. II-3).

[73] And apart from that, of course, it is thanks to the situation that the A_n^{**} profile can be represented in a closed form.

An analytical treatment of (38) would be faced with insurmountable problems with the determination of the sign of the derivatives – quite apart from the difficulties of obtaining the derivatives as such. Neither the creation of first differences ($A^{**}_{n+1} - A^{**}_n$), nor variations of a parameter with the simultaneous 'compensatory' variation of another (free) parameter (with the idea, thereby, of being able to consider as constant certain recurring blocks in (38)) are of any further help in this case.

Expression (38) has to be approximated in some way by a simpler one; otherwise an analytical evaluation of the optimal earnings trajectory would be unworkable. This approximation must at the same time be fashioned in such a way as to reflect as well as possible all the qualitative characteristics of the original equation, and – as far as feasible – represent a satisfactory quantitative adaptation.

The complex equation (38) can, in fact, be approximated by a simpler equation which satisfies these criteria. The assumption required here is that of a sufficiently large N, i.e. that of a *sufficiently long working life*. This method is as follows. If N is sufficiently large, then q_i, the expression occurring in w_{2n}, can be approximated where $r + \delta > c$ (see Section 2.1.1) by way of $q := 1/(r + \delta - c)$.[74] The following expression is thereby obtained for the complicated M_n ($= b_0^{1/a} \hat{M}_n$):

$$\underline{M}_n := M_n(q) = (b_0 b_1)^{\frac{1}{a}} \left(\frac{b_2}{P}\right)^{\frac{b_2}{a}} \left(\frac{R}{b_1}\right)^{\frac{1-b_1}{a}} q^{\frac{b_2}{a}} (r+\delta)^{\frac{b_2-1}{a}}$$

$$\cdot \left[(r + \delta - cb_1) \sum_{i=0}^{n-1} (1 - \delta + c)^{n-1-i} - b_1 - b_2(1 + cq) \right].$$

Note: The concern here is with *approximations* and *not* with the model case of an infinite horizon. The latter would occur as a result of a control problem with an infinite horizon – a different control approach from that on pp. 40–1, which apart from this, would also demand quite different solution techniques (cf., e.g. (in a continuous context) Kamien and Schwartz (1981, part II, section 9)).

What *economic* significance does a fixed q have? Now, with note (i) p. 47, a fixed q has the same significance as a fixed ψ and therefore as a fixed shadow

[74] For with $r + \delta > c$, $(1 - \delta + c)/(1 + r) < 1$; thus it follows (*ceteris paribus*):

$$\lim_{N \to \infty} \left(\frac{1 - \delta + c}{1 + r}\right)^{N-i} = 0.$$

A precise technical definition of the word 'sufficiently' has been omitted, as this is dependent on criteria which affect matching aspects and an explicit discussion of such criteria in this case would be taking matters too far. However, it is easy to recognise that the question is aimed at how rapidly $[(1 - \delta + c)/(1 + r)]^N$ moves towards zero with increasing N, and thus how clearly r exceeds the difference $c - \delta$ (or how large $r + \delta - c$ is).

price of an additional unit of human capital. This implies the neglect of the 'end-of-horizon' effect discussed in Section 2.1.2 with the consequence of now constant optimal investments $(sK)^*$ and D^*. $\underline{M}_n$ can be expressed thus:

$$\underline{M}_n = [Q^* - c(sK)^*]R \sum_{i=0}^{n-1} (1 - \delta + c)^{n-1-i} - I^*.$$

Although, in this case, an explicit reference to time (and/or working age) only occurs via the net depreciation weights $(1 - \delta + c)^{n-1-i}$, the approximation formula $\underline{M}_n$ proves to be quite precise. This may be surprising at first, but the reason for this is the following. Both the optimal production quantities Q_i^* and the optimal input volumes $s_i^* K_i$ decrease due to the falling shadow price with i during the course of working life; both are ignored in $\underline{M}_n$, whereby a certain compensation for the errors does occur. In addition, diminishing increases in net earnings (this can be derived from (26) and (28)) work against falling investment costs (i.e., '$-I_n^*$' increases). This also induces an error compensating effect in $\underline{M}_n$, as there a constant human capital net production rate is assumed and, consequently, so are constant investment costs. The overall profile of the sum of the weighted net increases in earnings in previous periods reduced by the current investment costs, $\{M_n\}$, can, therefore, be summarised relatively precisely by the approximation $\{\underline{M}_n\}$. Substantial deviations, if they appear, only do so towards the end of the working life, i.e., the appearance of the 'end-of-horizon' effect.

Even in *quantitative* terms, the adaptation is surprisingly good. See, in connection with this, Fig. 8a and 8b. Fig. 8a is based on the standard parameter set (19); three-quarters of the trajectory $\{\underline{M}_n\}_{n=0}^{N=45}$ deviates less than 10% from $\{M_n\}_{n=0}^{N=45}$; the average relative deviation amounts to 10%. As is easy to perceive from the formula for q_i, the more clearly r exceeds the difference $c - \delta$, the more exact is the approximation. If the calculations are, for example, based on $r = 0.1$ and $c = 0.01$ and the remaining values of the standard parameter set are retained, the result is Fig. 8b (an interest rate of 10% and a net $(\delta - c)$ depreciation rate of 4% − 1% = 3% can both be empirically substantiated); there 94% of the $\underline{M}_n$ profile deviates by less than 10% from the M_n path; the average relative deviation amounts to 2.5%.

With the approximation $\underline{\hat{M}}_n$ $(=: b_0^{1/a} \underline{M}_n)$, the complicated expression $1/\Pi_N \Sigma_{k=0}^N \hat{M}_k (1 + r)^{-k}$ (in w_{2n}) can be substituted for a simpler one, if N is assumed to be sufficiently large. The approximation error which occurs is limited, since for large k ('end-of-horizon' effect) the gap between the trajectories $\{\underline{\hat{M}}_k\}$ and $\{\hat{M}_k\}$ is scarcely significant, given that r is not negligibly small; at the same time $[(1 - \delta + c)/(1 + r)]^{N+1}$ (cf. the

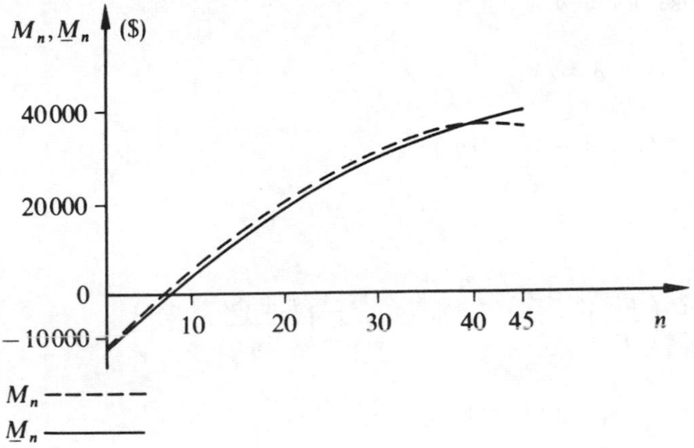

Fig. 8a.

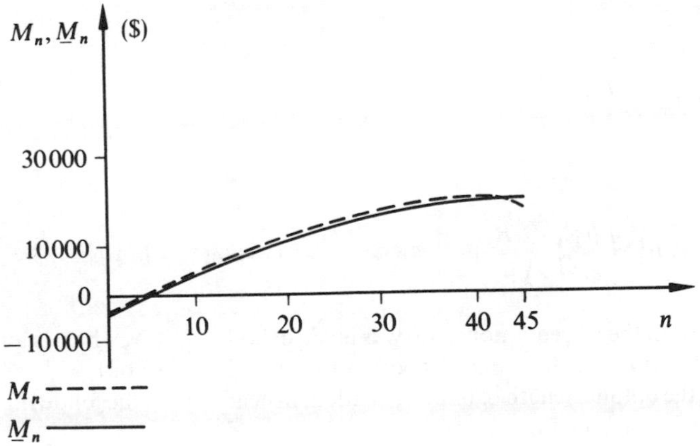

Fig. 8b.

definition of Π_N) where $r + \delta > c$ for large N is almost zero. The following approximation formula is eventually obtained:

$$b_1^{1/a}\left(q\frac{b_2}{P}\right)^{\frac{b_2}{a}}\left(\frac{R}{b_1}\right)^{\frac{1-b_1}{a}}(r+\delta)^{-\frac{b_1}{a}}\frac{a}{r} \quad (>0).$$

The following approximation formula for the optimal profile of disposable earnings is thus obtained after some algebraic reformulation:

$$\underline{A}_n^{**} := \underline{w}_{1n}a_1 + \underline{w}_{2n}b_0^{1/a}, \quad n = 0, \ldots, N; \tag{39}$$

where, in the case of $c \neq \delta$:

$$\underline{w}_{1n} := \frac{R}{r}(1-\delta+c)^n,$$

$$\underline{w}_{2n} := \pi_w \frac{(1-\delta+c)^n - rq}{c-\delta},$$

with:

$$\pi_w := b_1^{1/a}\left(\frac{qb_2}{P}\right)^{\frac{b_2}{a}}\left(\frac{R}{b_1}\right)^{\frac{1-b_1}{a}}(r+\delta)^{\frac{b_2-1}{a}}\left(\frac{r+\delta a}{rq}+cb_2\right),$$

$$q := \frac{1}{r+\delta-c} \quad \text{and} \quad a := 1-b_1-b_2;$$

and in the case where $c = \delta$:

$$\underline{w}_{1n} := \frac{R}{r},$$

$$\underline{w}_{2n} := \pi_{w,c=\delta}\left(n-\frac{1}{r}\right),$$

with:

$$\pi_{w,c=\delta} := b_1^{1/a}\left(\frac{b_2}{rP}\right)^{\frac{b_2}{a}}\left(\frac{R}{b_1}\right)^{\frac{1-b_1}{a}}(r+c)^{\frac{b_2-1}{a}}[r+c(1-b_1)].$$

Notes: (i) In the $\underline{w}_{1n}$ equations, use was made of $\ln(1+r) \cong r$, which is an approximation which can be supported for realistic values of r.
(ii) For the optimal length of basic education, instead of (36), the following approximation equation is obtained:

$$\underline{S}^* := \frac{1}{r} - \frac{a_0}{a_1} - \frac{a(r+\delta)}{a_1 b_1 r}T, \tag{40}$$

where:

$$T := (b_0 b_1)^{\frac{1}{a}}\left(q\frac{b_2 R}{b_1 P}\right)^{\frac{b_2}{a}}(r+\delta)^{\frac{b_2-1}{a}}.$$ [75]

[75] The condition for the existence of an internal solution is therefore the following:

$$a_0 < \frac{a_1}{r} - \frac{a(r+\delta)}{b_1 r}T$$ (cf. footnote 69, p. 61).

Incidentally $T = (sK)^*$, cf. (23) with $\psi_{n+1} = \psi = R(1+r)q$.
(iii) $\underline{A}_n^{**} = R(a_0 + a_1\underline{S}^*)(1-\delta+c)^n + \underline{M}_n$.
(iv) All qualitative results obtained analytically in the following sections of this chapter on the basis of (39) have been *confirmed* by a numerical analysis of (38).

2.3.2 *The life-cycle profile of earnings: general characteristics*

Before the *comparative dynamic* analysis of the optimal earnings profile begins in Section 2.3.3, the solution finally developed, (39), still has to undergo a test. It is a recognised empirical fact that individual earnings increase during the course of working life, but that the rate of increase during the life cycle falls.[76] Does the optimal plan $\{\underline{A}_n^{**}\}$ show these characteristics?

The graphic and numerical illustrations in Section 2.1.2 based on the standard parameter set show good correspondence; yet it is only possible to provide clear analytical answers now that the approximation formula (39) has been developed for the expanded model.

To begin with, it must be noted that given the empirical results of Carliner (1982), one must assume that $\delta > c$ (cf. the explanations on the standard parameter set (19)). If first differences are calculated, the following *growth equation* of planned disposable earnings results:

$$\underline{A}_{n+1}^{**} - \underline{A}_n^{**} = R\left[(c-\delta)\frac{a_1}{r} + \left(\frac{r+\delta a}{rq} + cb_2\right)\frac{T}{b_1}\right](1-\delta+c)^n; \quad n = 0,\ldots,N-1. \quad (41)$$

It depends on the sign of the constant '[ ]' whether this difference is positive or negative. From the above formulation, this can not yet be established, as with $\delta > c$ the first main term of the sum in the square brackets is negative; but the second main term in the sum is always positive (note the theoretical restrictions on the model parameters as detailed in Section 2.1.1 (overview on p. 39)). The question of the sign remains purely an empirical one in this form; a_1 which cannot be observed directly, can be bypassed with the aid of (40) and $\underline{K}_0^* = a_0 + a_1\underline{S}^*$, and the following condition is obtained:

$$\text{'[ ]'} > 0 \Leftrightarrow R\underline{K}_0^* < \frac{r+\delta-cb_1}{\delta-c}\frac{R}{b_1}T.$$

[76] To use the words of Rosen (1977, p. 22), 'The major stylized fact of observed life-earnings patterns [is] that earnings rise at a decreasing rate with years of experience in the market.' There are empirical confirmations in amongst others: Thatcher (1968), Lillard (1977a, 1977b), Moss (1978), Creedy and Hart (1979), Klevmarken (1981), Baudelot (1983) and Mayer and Papastefanou (1983). Note that in this case only *panel studies* permit a valid conclusion to be drawn. Cross-sectional analyses are inadequate.

As long as the potential initial income $R\underline{K}_0^*$ satisfies this requirement, $\underline{A}_n^{**}$ increases monotonically during the course of working life. If the values in the empirically based reference specification (19) are applied, the condition obtained is as follows:

potential initial annual earnings < \$92,000.

Although this condition must certainly have been achieved empirically (I am not aware of any contradictory examples from the salary and wage statistics), it would be still more satisfactory if there were a theoretical reason for the positive nature of (41). This is, in fact, possible. In accordance with the definition equation, $\underline{A}_n^{**} = R\underline{K}_n^{**} - I^*$, where $\underline{K}_n^{**} := \underline{K}_n^*\ (\underline{K}_0^*)$, and the human capital accumulation equation (16), the following is found:

$$\underline{A}_{n+1}^{**} - \underline{A}_n^{**} = R([Q^* - c(sK)^*] - (\delta - c)\underline{K}_n^{**}).$$

From this, $\underline{A}_n^{**}$ increases with n, if the human capital net production exceeds the net depreciation loss in period n. Is this type of requirement feasible? At any rate, it is plausible that the human capital stock is ultimately so large, that the depreciation loss is dominant (note that Q^* and $(sK)^*$ are independent of $\underline{K}_n^{**}$). This form of the difference equation (41) is too vague and may therefore not be satisfactory.

With the accounting equation of the human capital stock:

$$\underline{K}_n^{**} = \underline{K}_0^*(1 - \delta + c)^n + [Q^* - c(sK)^*] \sum_{i=0}^{n-1} (1 - \delta + c)^{n-1-i},$$

however, it follows that:

$$\underline{A}_{n+1}^{**} - \underline{A}_n^{**} = R[[Q^* - c(sK)^*] - (\delta - c)\underline{K}_0^*](1 - \delta + c)^n,$$

$$n = 0, \ldots, N - 1; \quad (42)$$

this produces a weaker condition and one which is independent of n. In line with (42), the planned (or rather optimal) disposable earnings of the individual are a monotonically increasing function of n, if the human capital net production rate $(Q^* - c(sK)^*)$ overcompensates for the loss from the net depreciation of the *initial* capacity. This is now an acceptable theoretical requirement.

Note: The human capital net production rate is always positive, as:

$$Q^* - c(sK)^* = (r + \delta - cb_1)\frac{T}{b_1} > 0.$$

(Note the theoretical parameter restrictions p. 39.)

With the positivity of the constant '[ ]' and $\delta > c$, the characteristics of the profile of the optimal trajectory $\{\underline{A}_n^{**}\}_{n=0}^N$ can be summarised as follows:

$$\underline{A}^{**}_{n+1} - \underline{A}^{**}_{n} > 0, \quad n = 0, \ldots, N-1; \tag{43a}$$

$$(\underline{A}^{**}_{n+2} - \underline{A}^{**}_{n+1}) - (\underline{A}^{**}_{n+1} - \underline{A}^{**}_{n}) = R[\ ](c-\delta)(1-\delta+c)^n < 0,$$
$$n = 0, \ldots, N-2. \tag{43b}$$

(43a) and (43b) imply a *concave* $\underline{A}^{**}_n$ profile.[77]

The trajectory approximation derived from the present structural human capital approach would, therefore, pass the test quoted at the beginning of this section, and therefore could offer a possible interpretation of that empirical fact. The main difference between $\{\underline{A}^{**}_n\}$ and $\{A^{**}_n\}$ is that the approximation $\{\underline{A}^{**}_n\}$ ignores the end-of-horizon effect. The original A^{**}_n profile is a logical consequence of the investment behaviour adapted in accordance with 'Max V' (and/or 'Max W') during the working phase. This investment behaviour is dictated in intertemporal terms from the (optimal) shadow price trajectory $\{\psi_n\}$ which in turn is mainly influenced by the end-of-horizon effect (cf. the discussion in Section 2.1.2). Typically then, the interpretation of the observed concave nature of the age–income profile is based on the monotonic decrease of the optimal production inputs s^*_n and D^*_n brought about by that effect.[78] This argument loses strength, however, in the approximation context; the shadow price is now constant and the life-cycle characteristics of the income path are exclusively a consequence of the interaction between the learning-by-doing rate c and the rate of depreciation δ; the concave effect is induced by the empirically substantiated relation $\delta > c$ and the theoretical condition $Q^* - c(sK)^* > (\delta - c)\underline{K}^*_0$. The fact that any investment behaviour which is based on a constant shadow price (→ constant optimal investment quantities $(sK)^*$ and D^*) in connection with that interaction represents a sufficient hypothesis for the generation of the path characteristics (43a) and (43b), is not least due to the compensation effects mentioned on p. 66.

2.3.3 Life-cycle effects of public policy measures: variations in R, P and r

Politically motivated distribution measures by the public sector are analysed within the framework of the present model by way of the human capital price R, the price for education goods P and the interest rate r (cf. the statements in Section 2.1.1). How is the solution (39) dependent on these model parameters? Thus, how does the optimal plan $\{\underline{A}^{**}_n\}^N_{n=0}$ change as

77 'Concave' in the sense that the function values joined at intervals from A^{**}_n, $n = 0, \ldots, N$ form a concave function.

78 Cf., for example, Ben-Porath (1967, pp. 356–7). It is worth noting in connection with this, of course, that the relation $b_1 + b_2 < 1$ implies increasing marginal costs of producing an additional human capital unit.

the result of a (marginal) variation in R, P or r? As the solution of that optimal plan is available in a closed form, this question can be answered in the form of an explicit *comparative dynamic analysis*. The technical character of this type of analysis would tire the reader rather than motivate him, however, so the analytical details have been placed in Appendix 2.

The results derived there are of two kinds. Firstly, they describe the relation between the model parameters x (in the present case R, P and r are included) and the *level* of earnings at a certain age (or earnings period); under the assumption of a sufficiently 'smooth' structure (differentiability assumptions) and on the condition of internal solutions for all endogenous variables, both before and after the parameter change, the optimal solutions to the control problem in each case will be set out in comparison with one another for each period n ($n = 0, \ldots, N$) as follows:

$$\lim_{(x_1 - x_0) \to 0} \frac{\underline{A}_n^{**}(x_1) - \underline{A}_n^{**}(x_0)}{x_1 - x_0} =: \frac{\partial \underline{A}_n^{**}}{\partial x}.$$

On the other hand they also describe the relation between the model parameters x and the increase in the age–income profile:

$$\frac{\partial(\underline{A}_{n+1}^{**} - \underline{A}_n^{**})}{\partial x}; \quad n = 0, \ldots, N-1.$$

The results obtained are summarised in the subsequent illustrations.

Notes: (i) A change in x corresponds to a variation in the initial *conditions* of the (two-stage) optimisation problem.
(ii) In principle, in the evaluation of the results, the case distinctions $\delta > c$, $\delta = c$ and $\delta < c$ should be made in all cases. However, as only $\delta > c$ can be empirically substantiated, the following interpretations and graphic representations are limited to this case. For the sake of theoretical interest, however, the case $c \geqslant \delta$ is observed in great detail at several points in Appendix 2; it is, at any rate, perfectly feasible for the rate of experience c to exceed the ageing rate δ and thus the net decline in human capital stock is prevented completely.
(iii) In general, possible deviations from the diagram curves can be seen in Appendix 2.
(iv) Even if it does not occur in the following diagrams, which are based on the reference specification (19): optimal disposable earnings can also assume negative values, of course, in the starting periods (there is the possibility of getting into debt (assumption 4)). This is considered in the analyses of Appendix 2. The pattern shifts as such remain unaltered.
(v) Another reminder here of note (iv) p. 69.

A purely technical derivation of the life-cycle effects on the basis of (39) is still not satisfactory, as it does not reveal any direct economic information.

Ultimately, we are not only interested in the how, but also the *why*. At this point the following unresolved formulation is helpful (cf. note (iii) p. 69; also note that $\delta > c$):

$$\underline{A}_n^{**} = R(a_0 + a_1\underline{S}^*)\underbrace{(1 - \delta + c)^n}_{\text{decreases with } n}$$

$$+ R[Q^* - c(sK)^*]\underbrace{\frac{1 - (1 - \delta + c)^n}{\delta - c}}_{\text{increases with } n} - I^*, \quad n = 0, \ldots, N; \tag{44}$$

where (to recap):

$\underline{S}^*$ from (40),

$Q^* = b_0(sK)^{*b_1}D^{*b_2}$,

$I^* = R(sK)^* + PD^*$;

the optimal investment quantities $(sK)^*$ and D^* are obtained from (23) and (24) with $\psi_{n+1} = \psi = R(1 + r)/(r + \delta - c)$ (cf. Section 2.3.1):

$$(sK)^* = (b_0 b_1)^{\frac{1}{a}}\left(\frac{b_2 R}{b_1 P}\right)^{\frac{b_2}{a}}(r + \delta - c)^{-\frac{b_2}{a}}(r + \delta)^{\frac{b_2 - 1}{a}}; \tag{45}$$

$$D^* = (b_0 b_1)^{\frac{1}{a}}\left(\frac{b_2 R}{b_1 P}\right)^{\frac{1 - b_1}{a}}(r + \delta - c)^{\frac{b_1 - 1}{a}}(r + \delta)^{-\frac{b_1}{a}}. \tag{46}$$

For the planned disposable initial earnings, there is the following special case:

$$\underline{A}_0^{**} = R(a_0 + a_1\underline{S}^*) - I^*. \tag{47}$$

The adaptation reactions of the individual to the modified framework conditions of his two-stage maximisation problem are hidden within the trajectory shifts illustrated below (and obtained analytically in the Appendix). These reactions are explicit consequences of the optimising behaviour adapted to the assumed final objective, 'Max W', which is manifested in the decision equations (40), (45) and (46). An economic explanation of the pattern change illustrated is therefore mainly substantiated by these equations.

Let us observe in Fig. 9 the effect of a (marginal) increase in the price for educational goods P. In line with this tax and/or contributory policy measures which have an increase in P as the consequence, an increase is induced in the planned (read 'optimal') disposable earnings at the

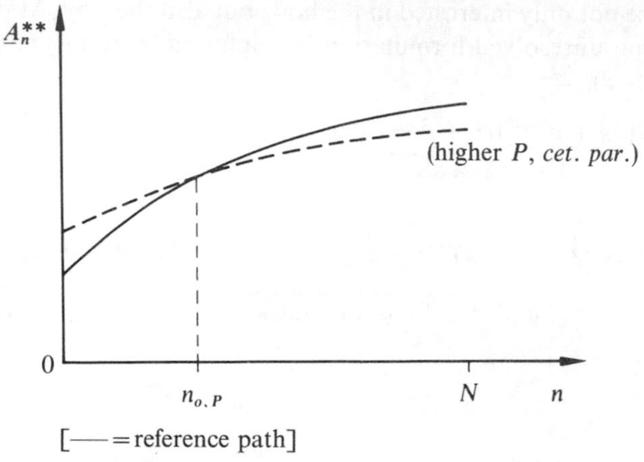

Fig. 9.

beginning of the working life; this rise levels off more and more during the course of working life and finally turns into a decrease below the reference path.

> *Note*: The turning point of the curve can be determined precisely; it is found by:
>
> $$n_{0,P} = \frac{\log r - \log(r + \delta - c)}{\log(1 - \delta + c)},$$
>
> which (in accordance with $r + \delta > c$) increases with r and c and decreases with δ. With the values of the standard parameter set $n_{0,P} = 14.2$; therefore the turning point occurs in this case after approximately one-third of the earnings phase.

A higher value of P increases the cost of investment in further education. Consequently, the individual places a larger part of his investment than before in the basic education phase; firstly, because there are no direct education costs in that case (P only occurs in the earnings phase)[79] and secondly, there is a substitutional relation between investment in basic and further education based on the assumed $K_0 = K_0(S)$. In fact, one can recognise from the 'marginal revenue product = factor price' equations (45) and (46), that a higher value of P (*ceteris paribus*) leads to a reduction in the optimal further education inputs. Simultaneously, the basic education phase is extended: $\partial \underline{S}^*/\partial P > 0$ (cf. Appendix 1). These reactions, which

[79] Cf. footnote 56, p. 54.

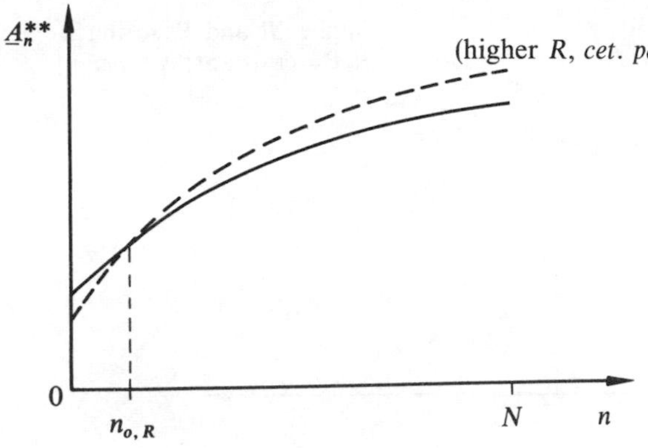

Fig. 10.

follow the logic of maximisation behaviour, imply a higher initial stock $\underline{K}_0^*$ and lower investment costs I^* than in the reference situation and thereby a higher disposable initial income $\underline{A}_0^{**}$ (cf. (47)). Moreover, the reduction in investment in further education, signifies that the earnings phase increase in the human capital stock slows down (this also applies for net values; the human capital net production $Q^* - c(sK)^*$ falls with increasing P – see note p. 00): thus the present $\underline{A}_n^{**}$ profile has a flatter curve. From $n_{0,P}$ the negative effect caused by less human capital accumulation in the earnings phase dominates (with $\delta > c$ the $\underline{K}_0^*$ influence decreases more and more – cf. (44)): the trajectory falls below the reference trajectory.

In a similar way, the shift effect of a higher price for human capital R (Fig. 10) can be interpreted in economic terms with the aid of the decision equations (40), (45) and (46), in accordance with (47) and (44).

> *Note*: Incidentally, one finds that $n_{0,R} < n_{0,P}$. The reason for this is the following. P occurs within the framework of the control problem formulated in Section 2.1.2 purely as a cost factor. R, on the other hand, appears both as wage and (opportunity) cost factor. A higher P increases the marginal costs of the earnings phase production of an additional unit of human capital, but does not affect the marginal gain ψ. A higher R increases not only the marginal costs but also the marginal gain of human capital production (the latter increase is incidentally more extreme than that of marginal costs). The overall effect on the optimum disposable initial income (47) is relatively more subdued, in comparison with that of an increase in P, because of this two-way reaction (in absolute terms, thus without considering the different directions of the effects); on the precise conditions, see Appendix 2. Simultaneously (and this is the essential

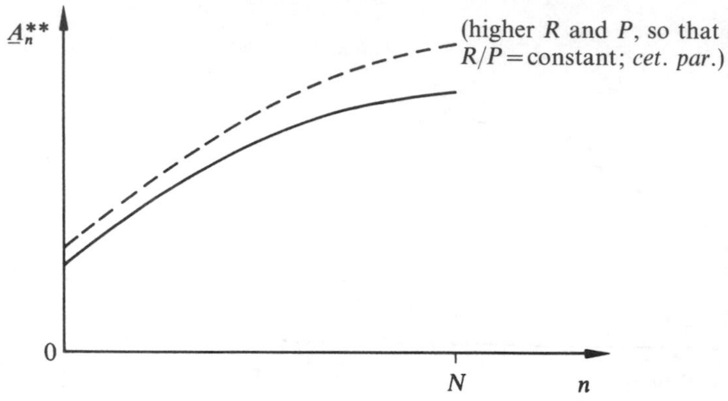

Fig. 11.

thing), the growth effect of the increased net production in the earnings phase is strengthened (cf. (44); note that the effect on I^* is already incorporated by (47)). This implies an earlier crossover point than in Fig. 9.

Assuming that certain public sector (or even macroeconomic – cf. note (ii) p. 38) influences made for a *joint* increase in the prices R and P, what would be the consequence for the optimal plan $\{\underline{A}_n^{**}\}$? An answer to this question would require several cases to be distinguished; the reader will find precise details in Appendix 2. Fig. 11 shows, for example, the effect of an increase in the two prices by the same percentage. Here is a brief explanation of this: an increase of R and P by the same percentage means that the price ratio R/P remains unaffected. An inspection of the optimal investment plans (40), (45) and (46) reveals that this type of increase would not affect the actions of the individual. The effect of a higher human capital reward now remains: a higher starting point (cf. (47), or: $\underline{A}_0^{**} = R[\underline{K}_0^* - (sK)^* - D^*P/R]$) and a sharper progression (cf. (42)).

Last but not least, Fig. 12 reflects the life-cycle effect of the third instrumental parameter of the economic policymaker, the interest rate r. The given trajectory shift scarcely differs visually from the one in Fig. 9: yet the basic underlying mechanism is more complex in this instance, and in contrast to Fig. 9, a series of exceptions are possible in the present case.

As with all the other figures, Fig. 12 is based on the reference specification. The direction of the path shift as a result of a higher price for education goods P (therefore the sign of $\partial\underline{A}_n^{**}/\partial P$; $n = 0, \ldots, N$), given the theoretical restrictions of the model parameters, depends purely on δ, c and r; on the other hand, the shift represented in Fig. 12 (i.e., $\partial\underline{A}_n^{**}/\partial r$; $n = 0, \ldots, N$) is dependent on all model parameters (see Appendix 2).

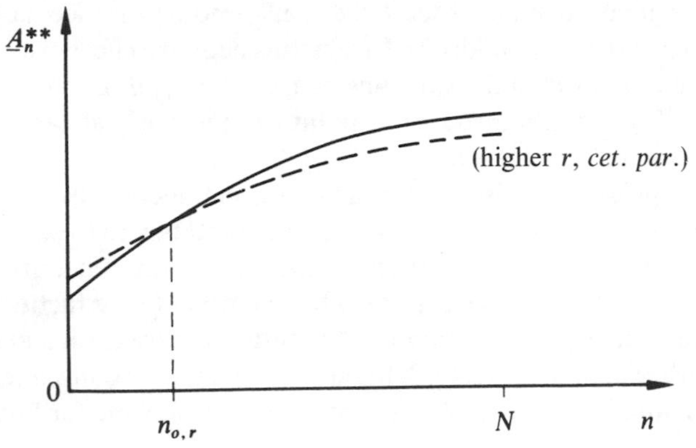

Fig. 12.

The complication in comparison with the case of a higher P (but also in comparison with the case of a higher human capital price R) emerges from the formulation of the expanded 'Max W' model and the determining rule for the optimal length of basic education resulting from this. As can be deduced from the 'marginal revenue product = factor price' equations, (45) and (46), the individual is encouraged to reduce his optimal investments $(sK)^*$ and D^* by a higher rate of interest. Because of the substitutional relationship between human capital investment in the full-time schooling phase and the earnings phase, this has a positive effect on the length of basic education $\underline{S}^*$. On the other hand, a higher rate of interest, *ceteris paribus*, results in a reduction of the discounting weight and thereby in a reduction in the present value W, which, as a consequence, has a negative effect on $\underline{S}^*$ (this is reflected in the first term of (40)). This two-way reaction between the interest rate and the optimum length of basic education, and thereby the potential initial income $R\underline{K}_0^*$, is expressed in the conditions derived in Appendix 1. If $\partial \underline{S}^*/\partial r > 0$, then the optimal disposable initial income, $\underline{A}_0^{**}$, in the new situation is situated above the one in the reference situation in any case. However, even with $\partial \underline{S}^*/\partial r < 0$, a higher disposable initial income can occur, and this would be the case when the reduction in investment costs caused by the higher rate of interest overcompensates for the drop in the potential initial income. For the precise conditions, see Appendix 2. On the basis of the reference path, precisely this type of situation is achieved; the planned disposable initial income *increases* in this instance following an increase in the interest rate. This upward shift does not necessarily follow for the overall optimal trajectory. The lower level of human capital investment in the earnings phase results in a lower rate of increase in the human capital stock; the net production decreases: $\partial[Q^* - c(sK)^*]/\partial r < 0$ (cf. Appendix 2). In fact, this negative effect of lower human capital accumulation in the earnings phase after $n_{0,r}$ dominates the positive effect $((-I^*)\uparrow)$, so that from that point on, the optimal earnings profile lies *below* the reference path.

In other words, the opportunity of earning additional income by way of investment (read 'loans' – assumption 4) of the income stream in the capital market, which is now more profitable owing to the interest rate, encourages the individual to become more active in the labour market ($\hat{=}$ reduction in $(sK)^*$) and reduce his acquisition of goods D^* in order to have capital at his disposal much earlier than previously. A higher rate of interest consequently causes the individual's willingness to sacrifice current income for future income to diminish.

> *Note*: The individual behaves, if you like, as if his working life had become shorter; the 'quasi-reduced' earnings phase caused by the higher rate of interest makes human capital investment less worthwhile, and one dedicates oneself earlier to the money market than otherwise.

As a result of this reaction, the new optimal earnings path begins above the reference profile (this is the case for situations which can be empirically substantiated; however, there are exceptions – see below). This upward shift effect is, however, limited in length, as the investment quantities $(sK)^*$ and D^* have been reduced, causing a fall in the rate of accumulation of human capital; this is the price which has to be paid for more income earlier. The slower rate of increase in the human capital stock ultimately results in a fall in the new trajectory below the original one. If one follows this line of argument, then one would expect that a higher rate of interest would induce a decrease in the optimal length of basic education in all cases. For, with a higher discount rate r, the significance of distant future income falls and the value of income in the near future increases. Thus, the individual should feel obliged to shorten the length of basic education in order to be able to enter the earnings phase earlier. However, in this case, there are two aspects to be noted; firstly, the assumed substitutional relationship between human capital investment in the full-time schooling phase and that in the earnings phase; and, secondly, the assumption that the length of working life remains unaffected by the decision concerning basic education. Both speak in favour of a shift in investment towards the basic education phase in order to enter the labour market directly with a comparatively high human capital stock. The exact conditions when each of the identified effects dominates, can be seen from Appendix 1. Clearly, if an earlier entry into the earnings life, and therefore a reduction in the length of basic education, is worthwhile when the initial stock in the reference situation is already a 'profitable investment' (for example, because of a high a_1); a higher rate of interest causes the reference initial stock to appear too large in comparison and, as regards the logic of the maximising behaviour directed to the final objective 'Max W', the individual corrects this by a reduction in $\underline{S}^*$.

Note: If the starting stock (or the initial disposable income $\underline{A}_0^{**}$) of the reference path lies above a critical limit (cf. Appendix 2), then a higher rate of interest induces such an extreme fall in $\underline{S}^*$ that the reduction caused by this in the initial potential income overcompensates the positive effect $\partial(-I^*)/\partial r$ from the very beginning. The new optimal trajectory $\{\underline{A}_0^{**}\}$ therefore keeps below the reference path throughout its length.

A very high initial disposable income $\underline{A}_0^{**}$ has the same significance as a very high initial potential income $R\underline{K}_0^*$ or very low investment costs I^*. The attraction of achieving an earlier greater gain, caused by a rise in the rate of interest, can scarcely be realised by a reduction in I^* in such a case, as the earnings phase inputs $(sK)^*$ and D^* should be extremely small anyway. The initial stock $\underline{K}_0^*$ appears, on the contrary, to be too large; in order to be able to cover marginal revenues and marginal costs in the new situation as well, the length of the basic education $\underline{S}^*$ must be cut drastically. Therefore, correspondingly, one can turn to earning money that much earlier (in other words, the acquisition of capital). $R\underline{K}_0^*$ falls more extremely than I^*; $\underline{A}_0^{**}$ already lies *below* the optimum initial disposable income of the reference path.

2.3.4 *Further results: variations in structural and individual parameters*

In what way is the optimum plan $\{\underline{A}_n^{**}\}_{n=0}^N$ dependent on the remaining model parameters? What additional comparative dynamic information is contained within (39)? The following diagrams provide the answer to this question. Analytical details can be found in Appendix 2. The trajectory shifts illustrated are the result of the optimising reactions of the individual and can be interpreted in economic terms as such, in the same way as those in the previous section. The decision equations (40), (45) and (46) play a central role in this again. In order not to tire the reader with repetition, the present section sometimes does without detailed economic discussion and confines itself to a brief graphic presentation of the results.

Fig. 13 reflects the effect of a higher learning-by-doing rate c; Fig. 14 reflects that of a higher human capital depreciation rate δ. In both cases it must be noted that a variation in these parameters affects the human capital net depreciation rate and thereby the terms dependent on n in (39) and (44) as well.

Fig. 15 refers to an economy in which the opportunity reflected by c of increasing productive capacity by the acquisition of practical job experience, is just as great as the ageing rate δ.[80] If c and δ increase in such a way in this type of situation such that, as before, $\delta = c$, then the optimum earnings profile shifts as represented in Fig. 15. The δ effect consequently overrides the c effect, if you like (cf. Figs. 13 and 14). Roughly speaking, the reason for this is as follows. A higher c, *ceteris paribus*, slows down the human capital rate of decline and thereby gives an incentive for production, as newly produced human capital units (via Q) are preserved for a longer length of time; the marginal revenue ψ increases. On the other hand, a higher learning-by-doing rate induces more human capital to be accumulated than before in an 'implicit' manner (thus through practical job experience) and induces the explicit production Q to be driven down. If a higher c is accompanied by a higher δ, in such a way that $\delta = c$ in all cases, then the incentive to production resulting from an increase purely in c is lost as there are then no longer any effects of any kind on the decay in human capital. The negative effect on the Q production previously discussed remains, and thereby remains for the inputs sK and D – an effect which corresponds to that of an increase in δ alone.[81]

Figs. 16 and 17 contain the pattern shifts for the case of higher human capital production elasticities b_1, *ceteris paribus*, and b_2, *ceteris paribus*. They were obtained through numerical differentiation of (39).

The results obtained thus far on the policy and structural parameters of the model refer to a so-called 'typical' individual, as, according to the assumption, prices and structural factors are the same for all individuals. The results do not permit any description of a *cross-section* of individuals with different incomes at identical ages. This is only possible with the comparative dynamic analysis of 'individual' parameter variations (in this case, therefore, of a_1 and b_0).[82]

Although the two parameters a_1 and b_0 are parameters of production efficiency, they have quite different effects on the optimal earnings profile. Fig. 18 reflects the effect of a higher full-time schooling accumulation efficiency a_1. Fig. 19 reflects that of a higher earnings-phase accumulation efficiency b_0. Whereas the former induces an upward initial shift and a

[80] Fig. 15 is based on (39) where $\delta = c$; this is the reason for the linear trend. Equation (38) would, on the other hand, generate an income path with decreasing growth rates for $\delta = c$ because of the end-of-horizon effect; cf. the discussion in Section 2.3.1. '$\delta = c$' is incidentally a purely theoretical construct; only the case $\delta > c$ is known to be empirically substantiated.

[81] Cf. Appendixes 1 and 2 on precise analytical derivations. In connection with this, notice should be taken of note (ii) p. 34; $\delta = c$ does not therefore mean that the net depreciation rate of the human capital stock would disappear totally.

[82] For the leaving out of a_0, see the note on p. 62.

flattening out of the optimal profile, the latter results in a downward initial shift and a steeper income curve.

A higher a_1, *ceteris paribus*, leads to a higher initial stock; $\underline{K}_0^* = \underline{K}_0^*(a_1)$ is the only channel through which the accumulation efficiency a_1 affects the planned disposable earnings. If c is now not large enough to prevent the decline in human capital, then the influence of a_1 is reduced over time, for the simple reason that, because of the depreciation effect, less and less remains left over from the initial stock (cf. (39) or (44)). The effect of a higher a_1 is therefore at its greatest for $n = 0$ and falls monotonically during the course of the working life.[83]

Notes: (i) One finds, incidentally, that:

$$\frac{\partial}{\partial r}\underbrace{\left(\frac{\partial \underline{A}_n^{**}}{\partial a_1}\right)}_{>0} < 0, \quad n = 0, \ldots, N,$$

i.e. with a rising rate of interest the effect of a higher learning efficiency a_1 on the disposable earnings decreases. In his fundamental study on human capital theory, Becker (1975, pp. 94–144) differentiates between ability ($\hat{=}\, a_1$) and opportunity ($\hat{=}\, r$). The model developed in this study, with the above result, provides an example for why such a distinction is not necessarily helpful; ability and opportunity effects work hand in hand.[84]
(ii) On further interaction between the prices R, P and r and the human capital accumulation abilities a_1 and b_0, see Appendix 2.

A higher b_0, *ceteris paribus*, on the other hand, results in a shortening of the basic education phase since human capital accumulation in the earnings phase, as a consequence of higher production efficiency in that case, is more profitable in comparison. With the shift of investment into the earnings phase, the investment costs I^* also increase of course. Both imply a decrease in the disposable initial income $\underline{A}_0^{**}$ (cf. (47)). The growth in human capital stock accelerated by the increased investment activity in the earnings phase, however, soon allows this initial loss to be recouped; from $n_{0,bo}$ the earnings path is above the reference trajectory so $n_{0,bo}$ marks the so-called point of 'overtaking'.

With (18), it follows, for example, that individuals with greater leadership and organisational abilities, with a greater willingness to take risks and assume responsibility, and a qualitatively better school education

[83] In the case where $c > \delta$ it would be exactly the opposite. Yet, this case of 'overcompensation of the human capital ageing process by practical job experience' cannot be empirically substantiated.

[84] Similar aspects can be found for the ability parameter b_0 (see Appendix 2 for the analytical details). Cf. Weiss (1971) as well in this context.

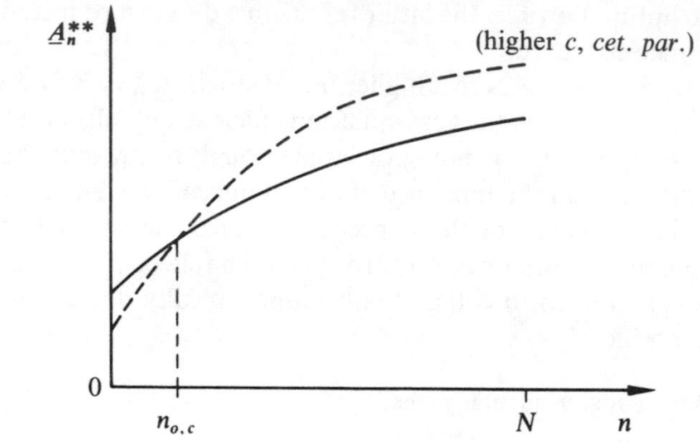

Fig. 13.

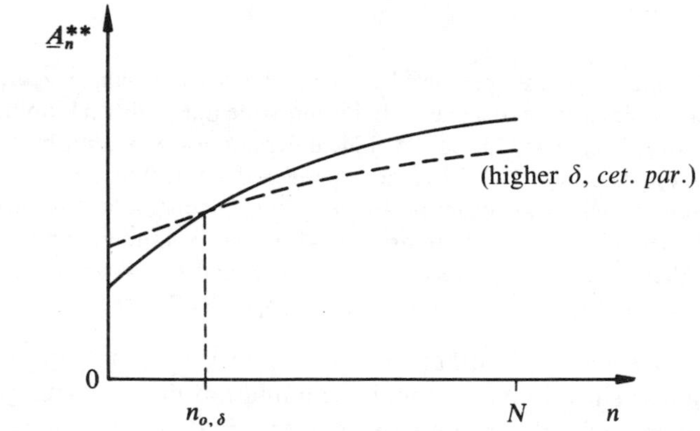

Fig. 14.

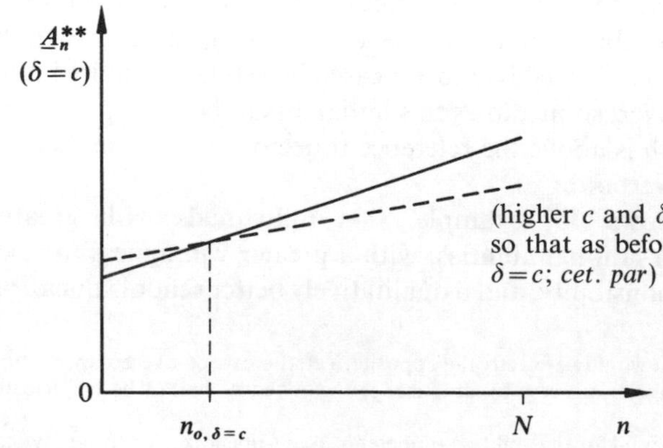

Fig. 15.

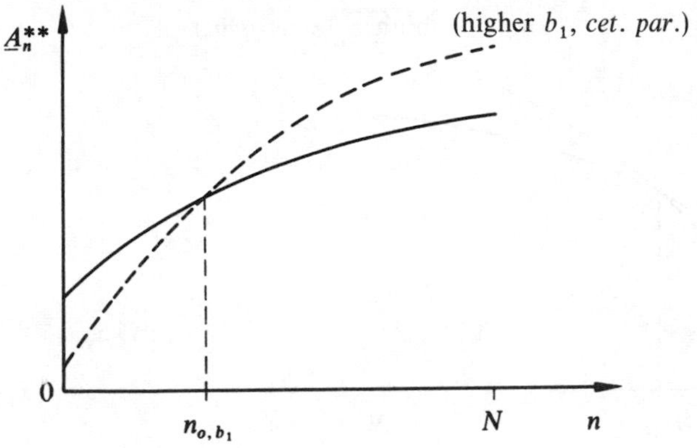

Fig. 16.

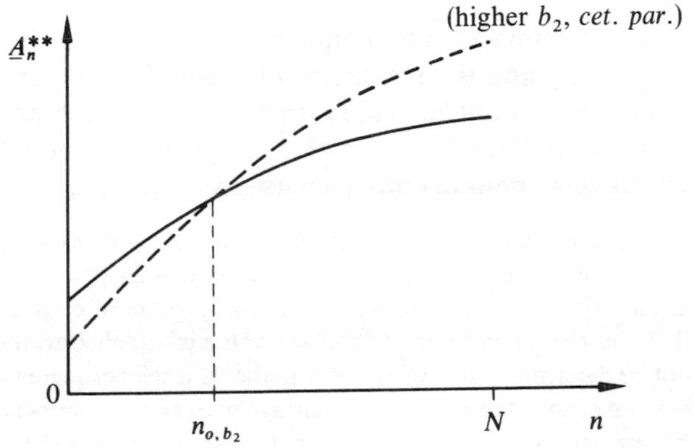

Fig. 17.

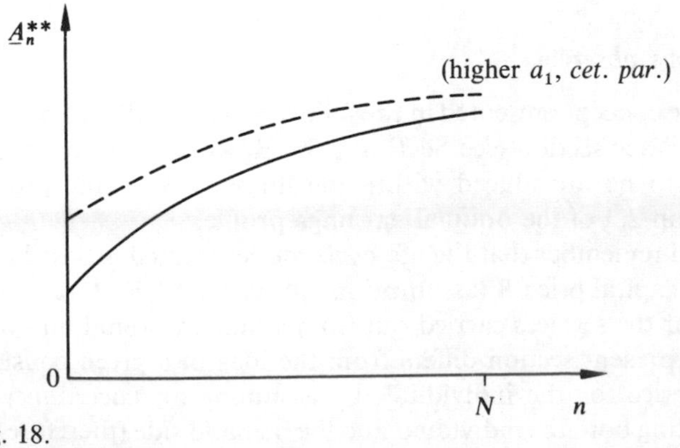

Fig. 18.

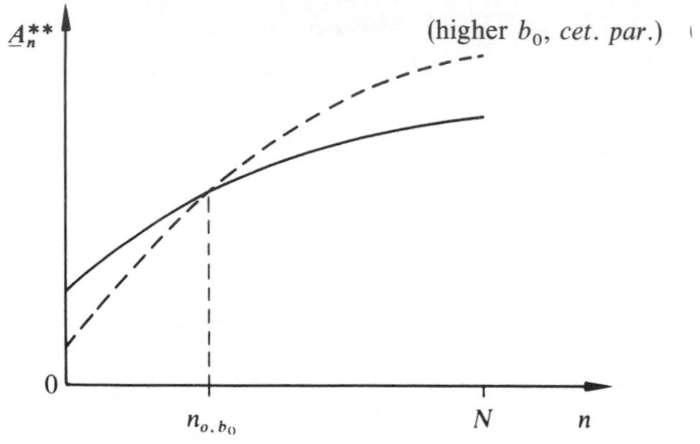

Fig. 19.

show steeper earnings trajectory curves, comparatively speaking. If one observes the learning ability and the *DF* factor of the individual, on the other hand, such a statement cannot be made with certainty as these factors are both integrated into b_0 and a_1 (cf. (18) and (35)). Appendix 2 should be consulted on the effects of a simultaneous increase in b_0 and a_1.

> *Note*: When one considers Fig. 19, then the question could occur as to whether a higher accumulation efficiency b_0 in the earnings phase would be useful at all. Ultimately, it concerns the present value of disposable earnings (the later the incomes occur, the less value is attached to them) and it cannot be determined from Fig. 19, whether the steeper increase in the trajectory can absorb the initial disadvantage or even overcompensate for it. As the analysis in Chapter 5 will show, the latter is in fact the case, i.e. $\partial W^*/\partial b_0 > 0$. Nothing else would correspond to the logic of the maximising behaviour.

2.3.5 Learning by observing

The essence of the concept presented in the following pages will not become apparent until a later section (see Section 3.3). However, the concept as such is suitable to be introduced within the framework of the present analysis in Section 2.3 of the optimal earnings profile.

The reader will remember that the life-cycle model created is based on a constant human capital price *R* (assumption 5, Section 2.1.1); *R* represented the reward for the services carried out from a human capital unit over one period. The present section differs from the idea of a given constant human capital price for the individual, by assuming an *uncertainty of information* affecting both the individual and the demand side (therefore the firms). Neither the single individual nor the demand side would be aware from the very beginning of the productivity of the individual: the 'true' productivity of a human capital unit would thus be unknown to both sides of the market at first.[85] For this reason, the freely determined market price for the services made available for one period from one unit of human capital would initially be situated *below* R, which is the price which corresponds to the 'true' productivity of a human capital unit in line with the assumption. In this case the assumption is based on those on the demand side who are averse to risk and who insure against this uncertainty of information by way of a *risk premium*. The greatest uncertainty on the demand side is at the very beginning of the individual working life, that is in the initial period ($\hat{=} n = 0$). However, the longer the individual is active in the production process of the company, the smaller this uncertainty becomes: 'learning-by-observing' is the slogan and with the increasing recognition of the productivity resulting from this, the risk premium falls. Provided that there is a competitive and perfectly functioning labour market (assumption 5), the risk premium then drops towards zero during the course of the working life.

This process of recognition on the part of the companies can, according to the present concept, be promoted by the individual: the greater his ability to probe into his own productivity and then to communicate this as precisely and conscientiously as possible, the less uncertainty of information on the part of those in demand; the reduction in the risk premium resulting from this causes the price paid per human capital unit from the very beginning to deviate *less* from R in comparison.

> *Note*: In line with the assumption, the price per human capital unit for all individuals amounts to R, *as long as* there is no uncertainty of information of any kind and the risk premium is the only reason for deviation. As a result of the assumed homogeneous nature of human capital (assumption 2, Section 2.1.1), the human capital stocks of the individuals only differ in level and not in their composition. Therefore, recognition of one's own productivity means the correct evaluation of the *level* of one's own human capital stock. It is therefore not significant whether this stock is large or small for the correct evaluation on the market, as the evaluation occurs per human capital unit.
>
> For the firms, it is important to discover the 'true' level of that human capital stock. Only when this has succeeded, does each unit of the individual human capital stock learn of its just reward R.

Ultimately, the decreasing uncertainty of information with an increasing recognition of productivity does not only have the consequence of a

[85] A reminder is given of assumption 2. Assumption 8 is omitted.

reduction in the risk premium, but also that of a better worker–jobs adaptation. The latter allows for a more efficient production and thereby, *ceteris paribus*, an increase in output. The greater such *on-the-job-sorting* possibilities are on the demand side,[86] the *more rapidly* the 'true' productivity of the individual can be done justice to and the faster the market price, established for the services from a human capital unit, approaches the price R, the 'true' marginal value product of human capital.

In order to integrate the concept of learning-by-observing thus created into the life-cycle model already developed, some formalisation is required. The market price, which is determined on the basis of the phenomena discussed, for the services provided for one period from a human capital unit would have the following functional form:

$$R_n(v) := R[1 - vb_3^n]; \quad 0 < v, b_3 < 1. \tag{48}$$

In this expression, v denotes the inability of the individual to recognise his own capabilities; $1/v$ thereby stands for the ability discussed of the individual to establish his own productivity and then to communicate this as precisely and conscientiously as possible to the demand side.[87] b_3 is a parameter which is the same for all individuals, which reflects characteristics of the demand side $1/b_3$; can serve approximately as a yardstick for the on-the-job-sorting possibilities mentioned.

In line with (48), the reward per human capital unit in each working age group n, $n = 0, \ldots, N$, is the higher in each case, the smaller the individual v and therefore the greater the self-recognition and communication abilities $1/v$ of the individual. In addition, the smaller b_3 is, the better the on-the-job-sorting possibilities on the demand side, and the more rapidly the approach towards the appropriate price R of the 'true' productivity of a human capital unit is made.

'Learning-by-observing' generally leads to a continuous reduction in the difference $R - R_n(v)$ $(= Rvb_3^n > 0;\ Rvb_3^{n+1} < Rvb_3^n$ as $0 < b_3 < 1)$.[88]

[86] A series of writers from the 'screening' school have drawn attention to possibilities of this type. See, for example, Ross, Taubman and Wachter (1981). References can also be found in the classic paper by Stigler (1962).

[87] v is thus a parameter relating to the individual and should therefore strictly speaking be identified with the index j. But you are in this case reminded of note (ii) p. 24.

[88] The type of modified exponential function used in (48) was chosen for its analytical simplicity. Of course, the logistic function, for example, is a more suitable 'learning curve' (e.g. in contrast to (48), the logistic function has a point of inflexion). The present concept of 'learning-by-observing' can, however, be represented just as adequately by the simpler function (48).

The reader will have perceived that $R_n(v)$ approaches the value R only asymptotically ('$n \to \infty$'). This does, however, make sense when one considers that, generally speaking, one will never fully establish the overall 'true' productivity and, even if this were known, it is

It is tempting to substitute (48) in the final solution (38) in place of R and to examine the consequences for the optimal path of individual earnings. However, in this case, one is confronted with a *conceptual* problem. The model developed in this chapter of individual earnings is known to be based on the assumption of life-cycle planning. This type of process is no longer possible without further consideration, as the individual at the time of planning (i.e., at the time of his economic birth) cannot be familiar with the detailed human capital price path $\{R_n\}_{n=0}^{N}$ which is determined as a result of the learning phenomena described. An R_n profile which is unknown at the time of planning necessarily requires a different solution technique to the one which was applied in Section 2.1.2: instead of life-cycle planning there must be *sequential* planning; the indicated technique would then be *closed loop* control and no longer *open loop* control. Such a complication of the model would, however, be taking the matter too far.

There is one other simpler possibility, which could neatly integrate the concept created in this section into the life-cycle model. For this, it is necessary to omit the input variable D_n (= the amount of goods and services purchased in working period n for the production of Q_n). For then, the personal human capital stock is the only input resource and a change in the human capital price alters the marginal revenues and marginal costs by exactly the same amount (this applies for all n), so that optimal human capital production is independent of the level of the human capital price. In fact, it can be seen from the equations (26), (28) and (36) that, in the case of a lack of purchased input, thus for the case where $b_2 = 0$, the optimal plans $\{s_n^* K_n\}$, $\{Q_n^*\}$ and S^* (and consequently also K_0^*) are *independent* of R.[89] This permits life-cycle planning to be preserved (and thus the approach created in Sections 2.1 and 2.2), despite the explicit introduction of an R_n profile of which the precise progression is not known to the individual.[90]

doubtful whether it could ever be fully covered by job characteristics and thereby be fully recognised. This is because the level of the reward R would not then be justified until that point (in line with the present concept).

Finally, it should be mentioned that possible counter-arguments, from the area of new contract literature, against the risk premium concept presented above have been ignored. Reference is made in connection with this, however, to the contract study by J. N. Brown (1980) whose results are compatible with the $R_n(v)$ formulation (48). His study also contains an empirical confirmation of the approximation to R last mentioned: 'The main empirical finding is that of short-term divergence, but long-term equality between wages and marginal value products' (J. N. Brown, 1980, p. I).

89 As far as (36) is concerned, the reader is reminded that M_n denotes the second principal terms of the sum in (30). Additionally, it should be noted that the individual is risk-neutral in line with the assumption.

90 It is immaterial how high the average price anticipated by the individual for the services from one human capital unit at the time of planning turns out to be; his decisions remain unaffected by this.

This method is to be applied here.

Where $b_2 = 0$, one now has the following:

$$A_n^{**} = R\left[K_0^*(1-\delta+c)^n + \sum_{i=0}^{n-1}(Q_i^* - cs_i^* K_i)(1-\delta+c)^{n-1-i} - s_n^* K_n\right], \quad n = 0, \ldots, N,$$

where all the terms in the square brackets are independent of R; the human capital price appears purely as a proportional factor in front of the square brackets. Of course, this simplifies matters – both technically and conceptually. If $R_n(v)$ from (48) is substituted into it instead of R, the result for the desired path is as follows:

$$A_n^{**}(v) := (1 - vb_3^n)A_n^{**}, \quad n = 0, \ldots, N; \tag{49}$$

with A_n^{**} from (38) (taking into account $b_2 = 0$).

The uncertainty of information described hence induces an income penalty (assuming a positive A_n^{**}) which is higher, the greater the optimal disposable earnings achieved with certainty, A_n^{**}, the smaller the self-recognition and communication ability $1/v$ and the worse the on-the-job-sorting possibilities on the demand side, measured by $1/b_3$:

$$A_n^{**} - A_n^{**}(v) = vb_3^n A_n^{**}.$$

Furthermore, one can recognise the ultimate approximation to $\{A_n^{**}\}$ through the learning-by-observing of the $A_n^{**}(v)$ path since:

$$\lim_{n\to\infty}(1 - vb_3^n) = 1.$$

How the level of the income loss changes over the working life, can be seen from:

$$[A_{n+1}^{**} - A_{n+1}^{**}(v)] - [A_n^{**} - A_n^{**}(v)] < 0 \Leftrightarrow A_n^{**} > b_3 A_{n+1}^{**}.$$

The fact that this loss does not necessarily fall monotonically with n, is due to its connection with A_n^{**}.

Last but not least, reference is made to Fig. 20.[91] There the previously described reference trajectory and two examples on the present concept of 'learning-by-observing' are given: here the pattern shifts for the case of different self-recognition and communication abilities v, *ceteris paribus*, can

[91] For reasons of uniformity this figure refers to (39) (just as the figures of the two previous sections did); thus it is:

$$\underline{A}_n^{**}(v) := (1 - vb_3^n)\underline{A}_n^{**}; \quad n = 0, \ldots, N.$$

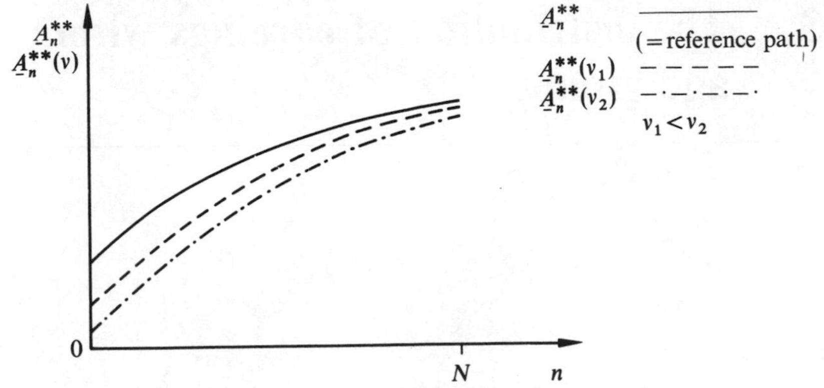

Fig. 20.

be seen. In general:

$$\frac{\partial \underline{A}_n^{**}(v)}{\partial v} = -b_3^n \underline{A}_n^{**}, \quad n = 0, \ldots, N;$$

and:

$$\frac{\partial[\underline{A}_{n+1}^{**}(v) - \underline{A}_n^{**}(v)]}{\partial v} = -b_3^n(b_3 \underline{A}_{n+1}^{**} - \underline{A}_n^{**}), \ n = 0, \ldots, N-1.$$

3 The distribution of earnings within age groups

> The great idea of examining the relationship between wage differences and differences in ability opens up huge new perspectives to us. The new path is steep and stony, but it must be trod.
>
> Joseph Schumpeter (1916, p. 68).

Equipped with the economic foundation of Chapter 2 and the general structure of Chapter 1, it is now time to move on to the actual distribution analysis. The subject of this chapter is the distribution of earnings within a group of individuals of the same working age: the *distribution within age groups*.

This is the first of the three distribution levels discussed in the introduction. In order to clarify the general view, it must be remembered that the chapters of this study are systematically built on one another; the approach developed in Chapters 1 and 2 is created precisely to enable a separate treatment of three interconnected distribution levels on the basis of one and the same basic model: that of the distribution within age groups (the present chapter), that of the overall distribution among all age groups (Chapter 4) and that of the distribution of lifetime earnings (Chapter 5).

Now, what does a structural model of the type developed in Chapter 2 imply for the distribution of earnings within an age group, following the inclusion of individual variations across a_1^j and b_0^j (cf. (38)) and following the embedding in the random walk structure of Section 1.3? Preliminary responses are provided in Sections 3.1 and 3.2.

The functional form of the distribution as such is indeed of theoretical interest; in terms of distribution policy, it is, however, only of secondary importance. First and foremost, the first two central moments of the distribution are relevant and/or a yardstick of the relative variation (roughly speaking, the 'inequality') of earnings, which is why a large part of the study concentrates on precisely this point. What does the inequality within age groups look like on the above basis? How does it develop from age group to age group? And what interpretations does the model contribute to this? Section 3.3 will be dedicated to these questions. In what way do the inequalities obtained there depend on the instrumental parameters of the economic policymakers which are associated with the model? Therefore, how are the inequalities between age groups modified by variations in R, P or r? These key questions are pursued in Section 3.4. The answers discovered are based on a fairly complex interaction between the basic distributions of the individual parameters and the adaptation reactions of optimising individuals. This mechanism will also play an active role in the following chapters, 4 and 5. As has already been emphasised in the introduction, one of the main objectives of this study is to derive tractable analytical relations between the distribution (or the inequality) of earnings and public policy parameters, in order to obtain precise statements on the consequences of politically motivated intervention in distributions. With the results in Section 3.4, this aim has been achieved for the first of the three distribution levels discussed.

Interest in longitudinal (or profile) analyses has increased sharply recently, not least because of the recent availability of panel data. This empirical literature has produced a series of interesting results which have, however, only permitted partial interpretation in economic terms so far. The present model framework allows both for the economic interpretation of the widely discussed life-cycle development of the correlation between abilities and earnings (Section 3.5) and the derivation of an endogenous variance–covariance structure of earnings (Section 3.6).

3.1 The basic structure of the age group model

If the person index j suppressed in Chapter 2 is reintroduced, the final equation of the economic model developed in Chapter 2 is as follows:

$$A_n^{j**} = w_{1n}a_1^j + w_{2n}b^j; \quad n = 0, \ldots, N. \tag{50}$$

Here, we only renamed $b_0^{j^{1/a}} =: b^j$; cf. (38) (or (39), if N is sufficiently large). b^j denotes the *modified* production efficiency of the individual j in the working phase. Note that the notation in (38) (or (39)) has already been focused on the individual parameters.

In the overall context, A_n^{j**} corresponds to the *expected* optimum disposable earnings of the individual j in the working period n (or at working age n).[1] This was discussed in detail in Chapter 2. If the examination is extended to encompass all individuals, then the variation

[1] Cf. Section 1.3 and Section 2.1.1.

among the individual human capital production efficiency parameters a_1^j and b_0^j (or b^j) must be taken into account and thereby the fact that the individuals can differentiate in their planning A_n^{j**}. This heterogeneous character of the population is symbolised by '$\tilde{a}_1$' and '$\tilde{b}$', i.e. the individual efficiency parameters are regarded as random variables (cf. Section 1.3.2).

If the economic component $\tilde{A}_n^{**}$ obtained thus, is integrated into the general income equation (12) from Chapter 1, the basic equation of this age group model is obtained:

$$\tilde{Y}_n^{**} = \tilde{A}_n^{**}\tilde{C}_n$$

$$= (w_{1n}\tilde{a}_1 + w_{2n}\tilde{b}) \prod_{i=0}^{n-1} (1 + \tilde{e}_i), \quad n = 0, \ldots, N; \tag{51}$$

where:

$$\tilde{b} := \tilde{b}_0^{1/a}; \quad w_{1n} \text{ and } w_{2n} \text{ from (38).}^2$$

Notes: (i) For a sufficiently large value of N, instead of w_{1n} and w_{2n} in (51), the coefficients $\underline{w}_{1n}$ and $\underline{w}_{2n}$ appear from (39) and one writes:

$$\underline{\tilde{Y}}_n^{**} := \underline{\tilde{A}}_n^{**}\tilde{C}_n.$$

(ii) The term *age group* refers to a *working age group* in this study. By an age group n is meant a group of individuals of working age n. The members of an age group are classified by the fact that they are all of the same working age.

(iii) $\tilde{a}_1$ and $\tilde{b}_0$ (and thereby also $\tilde{b}$) are positive variables.

If you like, (51) reflects the connection between a *stochastic* theory and a *multifactor* theory of the earnings distribution on the basis of a *human capital* theory approach.

In line with this fundamental equation, the distribution of the disposable earnings within an age group n is derived from the distribution of the product of two variables, namely, $\tilde{A}_n^{**}$, of which the density function describes the variation in the planned (or expected optimal) disposable earnings within age group n, and $\tilde{C}_n$, of which the density function reflects the variation in the randomly occurring income components within age group n. On consideration of the stochastic independence of the *permanent* component $\tilde{A}_n^{**}$ and the *transitory* component $\tilde{C}_n$ (cf. Section 1.3.2), the general formula for the density function of $\tilde{Y}_n^{**}$ is as follows:

$$f_{Y_n^{**}}(y_n) = \int_{-\infty}^{\infty} \frac{1}{|a_n|} f_{A_n^{**}}(a_n) f_{C_n}\left(\frac{y_n}{a_n}\right) da_n, \tag{52}$$

[2] Here a reminder of the conventions in footnote 21 of Chapter 1 (p. 16) and footnote 50 of Chapter 2 (p. 46) is in order.

where y_n and a_n denote the realisations of the variables $\tilde{Y}_n^{**}$ and $\tilde{A}_n^{**}$.[3] With the conditions formulated in Section 1.3.2, $f_{Y_n^{**}}$ can then be interpreted as the (expected) relative frequency distribution of disposable earnings within age group n.

The analytical solvability of the expression (52) is dependent on the characteristics of the density functions $f_{A_n^{**}}$ and f_{C_n}. Generally speaking, it is difficult or even impossible to derive $f_{Y_n^{**}}$ in a closed form.[4] Typically, one has to rely on the determination of approximate forms. As the technical effort required for this would be enormous and, in contrast, the significance in theoretical and policy terms of the functional form of the earnings distribution within age groups is minimal, this method will not be pursued. However, the form of the lifetime earnings distribution is of considerable interest, particularly since the theoretical literature in connection with this has had little to say on the subject so far. There, the effort involved seems more justified and the reader can familiarise himself with Section 5.5 as to how something like this can be put into operation. The approximation process implemented there could be applied in the same way to the present case of the distribution within age groups.

There is, however, a special case (the origin of which lies in the structure of the fundamental equation (51)) which permits an explicit derivation of the exact density function of $\tilde{Y}_n^{**}$. If indeed both the permanent component $\tilde{A}_n^{**}$ and the transitory component $\tilde{C}_n$ were *log-normally* distributed variables, then $\tilde{Y}_n^{**}$ would also satisfy the requirements for a log-normal distribution. In fact, it follows from $\tilde{A}_n^{**} \sim \Lambda(\mu_{\log A_n^{**}} + \sigma^2_{\log A_n^{**}})$ and $\tilde{C}_n \sim \Lambda(\mu_{\log C_n} + \sigma^2_{\log C_n})$ and the stochastic independence of $\tilde{A}_n^{**}$ and $\tilde{C}_n$ that:

$$\tilde{Y}_n^{**} \sim \Lambda(\mu_{\log A_n^{**}} + \mu_{\log C_n}, \sigma^2_{\log A_n^{**}} + \sigma^2_{\log C_n}).^5$$

The solution of (52) is thus obtained in closed form:

$$f_{Y_n^{**}}(y_n) = \frac{1}{y_n\sqrt{2\pi}\,\sigma_{\log Y_n^{**}}} \exp\left\{-\frac{1}{2\sigma^2_{\log Y_n^{**}}}(\log y_n - \mu_{\log Y_n^{**}})^2\right\},$$

$$0 < y_n < \infty;$$

with:

$$\mu_{\log Y_n^{**}} = \mu_{\log A_n^{**}} + \mu_{\log C_n},$$

$$\sigma^2_{\log Y_n^{**}} = \sigma^2_{\log A_n^{**}} + \sigma^2_{\log C_n}.$$

[3] The integrand is continuous for $a_n = 0$.
[4] Cf., in connection with this, Lomnicki (1967) and Springer (1979).
[5] Cf. Theorem 2.2 in Aitchison and Brown (1957, p. 11).

Notes: (i) As will be seen in Section 3.2.1, the assumption of a log-normally distributed $\tilde{C}_n$ can be supported by a multiplicative version of the Central Limit Theorem.
(ii) On the other hand, the distribution law of $\tilde{A}_n^{**}$ is less clear. With the results of Section 3.2.2 one could, in fact, assume that the efficiency variables $\tilde{a}_1$ and $\tilde{b}$ are jointly log-normally distributed; this, however, would not necessarily imply that $\tilde{A}_n^{**}$ too is log-normally distributed. Of course, this type of distribution would clearly not be out of the question.
(iii) The assumption of a log-normally distributed $\tilde{A}_n^{**}$ and thereby the relevance of the above-mentioned exception as well can however be motivated as follows. Empirical examinations have shown that the distribution of earnings within age groups can in fact be described relatively well by a log-normal distribution.[6] Applied to the fundamental equation (51), the information that $\tilde{Y}_n^{**}$ is log-normally distributed means that $\tilde{A}_n^{**}$ (just like $\tilde{C}_n$) also possesses a log-normal distribution, if $\tilde{A}_n^{**}$ and $\tilde{C}_n$ are stochastically independent, positive variables.[7] And indeed $\tilde{A}_n^{**}$ and $\tilde{C}_n$ are stochastically independent and, as a rule, positive variables.[8]

If the above-mentioned case does occur, the disposable earnings within an age group n are log-normally distributed; this then naturally implies that the $\tilde{Y}_n^{**}$ distribution is positively skewed and has positive kurtosis:[9]

$$\gamma_1(\tilde{Y}_n^{**}) := \frac{E[(\tilde{Y}_n^{**} - \mu_{Y_n^{**}})^3]}{\sigma_{Y_n^{**}}^3} > 0$$

and

$$\gamma_2(\tilde{Y}_n^{**}) := \frac{E[(\tilde{Y}_n^{**} - \mu_{Y_n^{**}})^4]}{\sigma_{Y_n^{**}}^4} - 3 > 0.$$

The positive skewness characteristic of the distribution within age groups is not incidentally tied to the log-normal distribution of the two components $\tilde{A}_n^{**}$ and $\tilde{C}_n$. As long as the distribution of $\tilde{A}_n^{**}$ and $\tilde{C}_n$ *are positively skewed (Section* 3.2 *will clarify that one can indeed assume this), the* $\tilde{Y}_n^{**}$ distribution also reveals a positive skewness.[10] Even if planned disposable

[6] The most recent evidence known to me is situated in v. Reijn and Theeuwes (1981, pp. 20–1). Further confirmations are supplied by Thatcher (1976, pp. 227–8), Phelps Brown (1977, pp. 285–9), Osberg (1977, p. 209) and Creedy and Hart (1979, p. 286).
[7] Cf. Theorem 2.5 in Aitchison and Brown (1957, p. 12).
[8] A *positive* variable is a variable whose density function is defined on $\mathbf{R}_+$. For $\tilde{C}_n$ the requirement for being a positive variable is unproblematic. This is also true for $\tilde{A}_n^{**}$ in general, even though the economic model of Chapter 2 permits negative $\tilde{A}_n^{**}$ values. This case should be excluded here.
[9] Cf. e.g. Aitchison and Brown (1957, pp. 8–9).
The notation is:

$$\mu_{Y_n^{**}} := E(\tilde{Y}_n^{**}); \ \sigma_{Y_n^{**}}^2 := \text{var}(\tilde{Y}_n^{**}).$$

[10] Cf. in general Springer (1979, ch. 4).

earnings within an age group n and the stochastic income component are distributed *symmetrically*, the distribution within age groups of disposable earnings can be *positively skewed*. If $\tilde{A}_n^{**}$ and $\tilde{C}_n$ are normally distributed variables, then it follows for the positive skewness of the $\tilde{Y}_n^{**}$ distribution (on consideration of the stochastic independence of $\tilde{A}_n^{**}$ and $\tilde{C}_n$) that:[11]

$$\gamma_1(\tilde{Y}_n^{**}) = \frac{6V_{A_n^{**}}^2 V_{C_n}^2}{(V_{A_n^{**}}^2 + V_{C_n}^2 + V_{A_n^{**}}^2 V_{C_n}^2)^{3/2}} > 0 \quad \forall_n \geq 1,$$

where V^2 denotes the squared coefficient of variation of the respective variables.[12]

Note: A positive skewness only occurs in this case from $n = 1$ as, in line with the assumption, the random-walk process starting at $n = 0$ only affects the disposable earnings from $n = 1$ ((7) or (8) are forward lagged). The model framework formulated in Section 1.3.1 assumes a given initial disposable income ($\tilde{C}_0 \equiv 1$), so that for a symmetrically distributed $\tilde{A}_0^{**}$, the result must, of course, be $\gamma_1(\tilde{Y}_0^{**}) = 0$.

The multiplicative basic structure (51) thus not only permits the *reproductive characteristics* of the (two-parameter) log-normal distribution to be exploited, but also induces a *trend towards a positive skewness* as such in the distribution within age groups. In the face of the empirical discoveries on the earnings distribution within age groups, this is an encouraging preliminary finding.[13]

As has already been mentioned in the introductory section to this chapter, the aspects just treated play only a subordinate role in terms of distribution *policy*. There, the income inequality as such is of more interest than the functional form of the frequency distribution. Therefore, the difficulty connected with an analytical determination of (52) is regrettable, but not necessarily of any great consequence. Even the positive skewness characteristic should preferably be seen as a test to be passed by the age group model; for political economists interested in 'income inequality', statements on the asymmetry of the distribution are irrelevant to some extent.[14] The yardstick most frequently employed in the statistical literature for the measurement of income disparity is the variance $\sigma_{\tilde{Y}_n^{**}}^2$.

[11] This formula can be derived with the aid of the results in Haldane (1942, p. 234).

[12] This notation is so common in the literature that it is also retained in this study. (The squared coefficient of variation of a variable $\tilde{X}$, V_X^2 must not be confused with the present value V defined in (17); there is, however, no great danger of such an error, as the reader will certainly confirm at the end of this study.)

[13] Cf. the references in footnote 6, p. 94, and Lydall (1968). In particular, the positive skewness characteristic is to be considered as one of the empirical facts which is best substantiated according to this.

[14] As Cowell (1977, p. 31) puts it: '[Measures of skewness] do not appear to capture the essential ideas of inequality measurement.'

However, this measure has the characteristic of being mean-dependent (in other words, if all individual incomes were doubled, $\sigma^2_{Y_n^{**}}$ would be quadrupled). Therefore, it is only of limited value as a measure of inequality. What is needed is a measure for the *relative* dispersion of income. One such measure is obtained by the standardisation: $\sigma^2_{Y_n^{**}}/\mu^2_{Y_n^{**}}$; this is the *squared coefficient of variation* of $\tilde{Y}_n^{**}$, one of the most frequently used inequality measures anywhere. As the present study will make full use of this measure, some remarks are in order on the suitability of the squared coefficient of variation, V^2, as a *measure of inequality*:

Disadvantage: V^2 does not attach a greater weight to what occurs at the bottom end of the income scale; the V^2 decrease is the same whether there is a transfer payment of 1 DM from a person with 10,100 DM to a person with 10,000 DM or a transfer payment of 1 DM from a person with 500 DM to a person with 400 DM. V^2 therefore acts, so to speak, as a 'top-sensitive' measure of inequality.

Advantage: V^2 is a member of the *generalised entropy family* and thus has the following favourable characteristics, amongst others:

(i) V^2 is invariant in terms of the same proportional change at all levels of income, i.e. V^2 is mean-independent; V^2 is dimensionless. In other words, the coefficient of variation is a dispersion measure with the expected value (or mean value) as a unit; in this instance, the basically arbitrary value of the variance (σ^2) arising from its dependence on the unit of measurement is removed. V^2 measures the *relative* dispersion of income.

(ii) V^2 fulfils the Dalton-Pigou criterion (which can be regarded as a minimum normative requirement of an inequality measurement).

(iii) V^2 is additively decomposable. This will be useful, particularly in Chapter 4.[15]

> *Notes*: (i) There is a significant practical advantage within the present framework in that $V^2_{Y_n^{**}}$ can be built up from the first two moments of $\tilde{Y}_n^{**}$, irrespective of any *specific* distribution assumptions (in contrast, for example, to the inequality measures of Gini, Theil or Atkinson).
> (ii) V^2 is primarily employed for illustrative purposes. The objective of this study is to provide information on the basis of *positive* analysis; income inequality is considered without explicit reference to welfare theory (which would impinge on the territory of normative analysis). Purists may employ the term 'relative dispersion' in each case in place for the word 'inequality'.

[15] See Shorrocks (1980, 1982) for further characteristics.

Now what does the basic structure of the present age group model imply for the squared coefficient of variation of $\tilde{Y}_n^{**}$?

Taking consideration of the stochastic independence of $\tilde{A}_n^{**}$ and $\tilde{C}_n$, the following expression is obtained:

$$V_{Y_n^{**}}^2 := \frac{\sigma_{Y_n^{**}}^2}{\mu_{Y_n^{**}}^2} = V_{A_n^{**}}^2 + V_{C_n}^2 + V_{A_n^{**}}^2 V_{C_n}^2$$
$$= (1+\sigma_e^2)^n V_{A_n^{**}}^2 + V_{C_n}^2; \quad n = 0, \ldots, N. \qquad (53)$$

Therein:

$$V_{A_n^{**}}^2 := \frac{\sigma_{A_n^{**}}^2}{\mu_{A_n^{**}}^2} = \alpha_n^2 V_{a_1}^2 + (1-\alpha_n)^2 V_b^2 + 2\alpha_n(1-\alpha_n) V_{a_1} V_b \rho_{a_1 b}, \qquad (54)$$

with:

$$\alpha_n := \frac{w_{1n}\mu_{a_1}}{\mu_{A_n^{**}}}, \quad \mu_{A_n^{**}} = w_{1n}\mu_{a_1} + w_{2n}\mu_b;$$

$$\rho_{a_1 b} := \frac{\operatorname{cov}(\tilde{a}_1, \tilde{b})}{\sigma_{a_1}\sigma_b};$$

and:

$$V_{C_n}^2 := \frac{\sigma_{C_n}^2}{\mu_{C_n}^2} = (1+\sigma_e^2)^n - 1, \qquad (55)$$

as, according to the assumption: $\tilde{e}_i \sim \text{iid}(0, \sigma_e^2)$.[16]

The inequality in disposable earnings within an age group n is greater, according to (53), the greater the within-group variation in planned disposable earnings and the greater the income inequality caused by the stochastic shocks. $V_{A_n^{**}}^2$ corresponds, so to speak, to the planned *ex ante* inequality (or *permanent* inequality), $V_{C_n}^2$ to the *transitory* inequality and $V_{Y_n^{**}}^2$ to the *realised ex post* inequality.

σ_e^2 can be interpreted as a measurement of the *uncertainty of income*, which occurs as a result of the transitory income change factors (cf. Section 1.3.2). The greater this uncertainty within the observed economy, i.e., the greater the bandwidth of the possible income values established as a result

[16] Cf. Section 1.3.
$V_{C_0}^2 = 0$ corresponds to $\tilde{C}_0 \equiv 1$.
Another word on notation: μ and σ^2 denote in each case the expected value and the variance of the variable shown – or (with the aid of the Law of Large Numbers; cf. also Section 1.3.2) the mean and the dispersion of the individual variable values. This customary notation is adhered to throughout the entire study.

of the accumulation of shocks, and the greater the inequality of disposable earnings: $\partial V^2_{Y_n^{**}}/\partial \sigma_e^2 > 0, \forall n \geqslant 1$.

The statement that the inequality of disposable earnings increases with the inequality of *planned* disposable earnings is hardly surprising in formal terms. Yet it expresses the position that income inequality is not to be ascribed to the basic distributions of the individually varying factors as such, but must be considered as the result of the *optimising behaviour* of the individual which is influenced in turn by those individual factors. Equation (54) contains all the answers to the *key question* of how differences between individuals on the basis of a dynamic optimisation model of the type developed in Chapter 2 are transformed into differences in income. Therefore it will play a crucial part in the further course of this study. Without going into too much detail at this stage, two optimisation effects are apparent. In line with (54), the inequality of planned disposable earnings within an age group n is dependent on the inequalities in $\tilde{a}_1$ and $\tilde{b}$, the correlation between those efficiency parameters and the share value a_n. The influence of the optimisation behaviour of the individuals on the inequality within age groups becomes clear in two respects. Firstly, it is not the inequality of the efficiency parameter $\tilde{b}_0$ itself, but that of the *modified* human capital production efficiency parameter $\tilde{b}_0^{1/a}$ $(=:\tilde{b})$ which is integrated into (54). This modification reflects the interaction of the parameters of the human capital production function considered within the framework of the optimisation process. As the latter function shows decreasing returns to scale and consequently $1/a > 1$, the inequality of the modified parameter is greater than that of the original one.

> *Note*: For a log-normally distributed $\tilde{b}_0$, which can be assumed for approximation purposes (see Section 3.2.2), the following is, for example, directly obtained:
>
> $$V^2_{b_0} = e^{\sigma^2_{\log b_0}} - 1 < e^{\frac{1}{a^2}\sigma^2_{\log b_0}} - 1 = V^2_{b_0^{1/a}} = V^2_b.$$

'Mechanical' models which ignore the reactions of individuals to their individual circumstances (in this case, therefore, to their capabilities to use their own and purchased factor inputs efficiently), thereby *underestimate* the inequality effect resulting from a variation in $\tilde{b}_0$.

Secondly, the fractional value α_n also occurs as a result of the maximisation process. It affects how great the inequality effect on $V^2_{A_n^{**}}$ resulting from $\tilde{a}_1$ and $\tilde{b}$ is in each period n. Therefore, not only the time and/or age dependence of these influences as such (influences which incidentally are not taken into account in conventional models) are generated *endogenously* here (more later in connection with this; see Section 3.5), but also the type of development of this dependence is generated *endogenously* in this case. This point is also dropped with 'mechanically descriptive' models which are not based on optimising individuals, and where the relative cohort-variation in (expected) earnings is given by:

$$V_A^2 = \alpha^2 V_{a_1}^2 + (1-\alpha)^2 V_{b_0}^2 + 2\alpha(1-\alpha) V_{a_1} V_{b_0} \rho_{a_1 b_0},$$

with:

$$\alpha := \mu_{a_1}/(\mu_{a_1} + \mu_{b_0}).$$

It will be explained in Section 3.3 in what way the influence of the (as such, constant) inequalities in $\tilde{a}_1$ and $\tilde{b}$ on $V_{A_n^{**}}^2$ varies from age group to age group.

Equation (54) also contains all the answers to the question of how the inequality within age groups of disposable earnings reacts to the pricing policy (or taxation or transfer policies) of the public sector; for the following is obtained for the model-related integrated public policy parameters x, $x \in \{R, P, r\}$:

$$\frac{\partial V_{Y_n^{**}}^2}{\partial x} = (1+\sigma_e^2)^n \frac{\partial V_{A_n^{**}}^2}{\partial x} \gtreqless 0 \Leftrightarrow \frac{\partial V_{A_n^{**}}^2}{\partial x} \gtreqless 0; \quad n = 0, \ldots, N. \tag{56}$$

Section 3.4 contains a detailed examination of this question.[17]

Finally, it should be *fundamentally* pointed out (and this does not only apply for this chapter, but also for the two subsequent ones) that it is part of the nature of the interdependences between basic distributions, optimising behaviour and stochastic shocks that the inequality of earnings is neither determined purely by choices (a hypothesis of the 'conservatives'), nor defined by the initial distributions and subsequently unchanged (a hypothesis of the 'fatalists'). Income inequality results, in my view, rather from a *simultaneous interaction* of the given factors. Ability distributions,

[17] For the case of a *log-normally* distributed $\tilde{Y}_n^{**}$ (cf. the discussion above) the $V_{A_n^{**}}^2$ analysis can also, incidentally, be transcribed directly to the *positive skewness* and the kurtosis of the distribution within age groups. As γ_1 and γ_2 are monotonically increasing functions of $\sigma_{\log Y_n^{**}}^2$ (see Aitchison and Brown, 1957, pp. 8–9) and, for the variance of the logarithm of disposable earnings within an age group n, one finds (note Theorem 2.5 and equation (2.9) in Aitchison and Brown, 1957, pp. 12 and 8):

$$\sigma_{\log Y_n^{**}}^2 = \sigma_{\log A_n^{**}}^2 + \sigma_{\log C_n}^2 = \log(1 + V_{A_n^{**}}^2) + n \log(1 + \sigma_e^2),$$

i.e. $\sigma_{\log Y_n^{**}}^2$ is in turn a monotonically increasing function of $V_{A_n^{**}}^2$.

For a similar reason, the $V_{A_n^{**}}^2$ analysis in the log-normal distribution case can be transcribed over to a series of *other* (other than $V_{A_n^{**}}^2$) inequality measures; the Gini coefficient, the Lorenz measure of concentration, the Theil entropy index and the Atkinson index (to name but a few) are then all monotonically increasing functions of $\sigma_{\log Y_n^{**}}^2$ (see, e.g., Cowell, 1977, pp. 152–5).

economic structures, life-cycle decisions and random shocks work hand-in-hand and (53) (together with (54) and (55)) is an explicit expression of this interaction. The aim of such a draft of a model is not least to better understand the nature and causes of individual income differences in order to provide a more rational basis for the public policy distribution measures.

3.2 Two special cases

3.2.1 *Identical individuals*

If individuals do not differ in their individual parameters, then they do not differ in their optimal plans, and one has $A_n^{j**} = A_n^{**}, \forall j$. $\tilde{A}_n^{**}$ is to be considered in this case as a degenerated variable with a one-point distribution; instead of (51) one has:

$$\tilde{Y}_n^{**} = A_n^{**}\tilde{C}_n = A_n^{**}\prod_{i=0}^{n-1}(1+\tilde{e}_i), \quad n = 0,\ldots,N, \tag{57}$$

i.e. the distribution of disposable earnings within one age group n is purely determined by the distribution of the *randomly conditioned* income component $\tilde{C}_n$.[18] With the help of (57), the following is obtained directly ($A_n^{**} \neq 0$):

$$V_{Y_n^{**}}^2 = V_{C_n}^2 \tag{58}$$

and

$$\gamma_1(\tilde{Y}_n^{**}) = \gamma_1(\tilde{C}_n), \quad \gamma_2(\tilde{Y}_n^{**}) = \gamma_2(\tilde{C}_n). \tag{59}$$

With (55), it follows from (58) that the inequality within age groups increases from age group to age group ($V_{Y_n^{**}}^2$ is a strictly monotonically increasing function of n) and that it can only be reduced for a given n by a reduction in the general uncertainty of income σ_e^2.

For the skewness measure, γ_1, the following expression is obtained on consideration of (59) and $\tilde{e}_i \sim \text{iid}(0, \sigma_e^2)$:

$$\gamma_1(\tilde{Y}_n^{**}) = \frac{(1+3\sigma_e^2+m_{3,e})^n - 3(1+\sigma_e^2)^n + 2}{[(1+\sigma_e^2)^n - 1]^{3/2}}, \; n \geqslant 1; \tag{60}$$

where:

$$m_{3,e} := E(\tilde{e}_i^3).$$

[18] If one wanted to explain the empirical findings on this basis, then the component $\tilde{C}_n$ should contain all the typical characteristics of the distribution within age groups hidden within (which, of course, it does not, as will be seen in particular in Section 3.3).

(60) provides an interesting result: even if the randomly conditioned income growth rates $\tilde{e}_i$ are symmetrically distributed, a *positive skewness* is introduced into the distribution within age groups from $n = 2$.[19] Of course, then the same applies for a positively skewed $\tilde{e}_i$ distribution ($\rightarrow m_{3,e} > 0$). As is clear from (60), even a negatively skewed $\tilde{e}_i$ distribution ($\rightarrow m_{3,e} < 0$) can induce a positive skewness in the distribution within age groups, as long as n is sufficiently large (more on this shortly). In a similar manner, it can be established by way of γ_2 from (59) that the distribution within age groups for positively skewed or symmetrically distributed growth rates $\tilde{e}_i$ from $n = 2$ displays a *positive* kurtosis.[20]

Several other more *specialised* predictions are also possible apart from these general statements based on the multiplicative structure of the transitory component $\tilde{C}_n$. In line with the random walk approach developed in Section 1.3, the remaining random growth factors $(1 + \tilde{e}_i)$ are identically distributed and stochastically independent variables. In the event that these factors satisfy a log-normal distribution, the reproductive characteristic familiar from Section 3.1 of this type of distribution will come into play such that $\tilde{C}_n$ and consequently also $\tilde{Y}_n^{**}$ will be log-normally distributed too.[21]

This form of the distribution within age groups can be approached in another way as well. If, apart from $\tilde{e}_i \sim \text{iid}(0, \sigma_e^2)$, the stochastic shocks $(1 + \tilde{e}_i)$ are positive variables, so that the influence of the transitory income change factors does not result in the income disappearing altogether (i.e., the realisations of $\tilde{e}_i$ are $\leqslant -1$), then $\tilde{C}_n$ is *asymptotically log-normally distributed* according to a multiplicative version of the Central Limit Theorem[22] (a result which has already been repeatedly applied in Chapter 1).

[19] If the $\tilde{e}_i$ are *symmetrically* distributed, then it follows with $\tilde{e}_i \sim \text{iid}(0, \sigma_e^2)$ that $m_{3,e} = 0$. It can be proved by way of complete induction that:

$$(1 + 3\sigma_e^2)^n - 3(1 + \sigma_e^2)^n + 2 > 0 \quad \forall n \geqslant 2.$$

As the denominator of (60) for $n \geqslant 1$ is positive, the assertion thereby follows.

In connection with this, a reminder must be given that the random income change factors only have an effect on earnings from $n = 1$ as a result of the forward formulation of the random walk model (cf. Section 1.3.1). Clearly, for the case of identical individuals in $n = 0$, the skewness is equal to zero. In $n = 1$, in accordance with (57): $\tilde{Y}_1^{**} = A_1^{**}\tilde{C}_1 = A_1^{**}(1 + \tilde{e}_0)$; here with a symmetrically distributed $\tilde{e}_0$, the skewness is zero as well. From $n = 2$, the positive skewness effect explained above in the multiplicative structure of the transitory component $\tilde{C}_n$ comes into play.

[20] If the $\tilde{e}_i$ are *normally distributed* variables (an assumption frequently made in statistical practice), then the results of Haldane (1942, pp. 231–2, 238) can be applied to (57). Then a positive skewness is produced in the distribution within age groups as well as a positive kurtosis if the random shocks $\tilde{e}_i$ are not identically normally distributed or are positively correlated. [21] Cf. Theorem 2.3 in Aitchison and Brown (1957, p. 11).

[22] Cf. Theorem 2.8 in Aitchison and Brown (1957, p. 13). Under certain conditions it also applies when shocks are not identically distributed ($\rightarrow$ multiplicative analogue to the

With $\tilde{C}_n \sim \text{asy}\,\Lambda(\mu_{\log C_n} + \sigma^2_{\log C_n})$ and $A_n^{**} > 0$:

$$\tilde{Y}_n^{**} \sim \text{asy}\,\Lambda(\log A_n^{**} + \mu_{\log C_n}, \sigma^2_{\log C_n}). \tag{61}$$

It has to be emphasised that this result does not depend on whether the $\tilde{e}_i$ have positively skewed symmetrical or negatively skewed distributions. Nevertheless, it follows from the asymptotic log-normal distribution of $\tilde{C}_n$ that the distribution within age groups is ultimately positively skewed (and has a positive kurtosis). In fact, for the log-normal case, the following relationships apply (note (59)):[23]

$$\gamma_1(\tilde{Y}_n^{**}) = V_{C_n}^3 + 3V_{C_n}$$

and

$$\gamma_2(\tilde{Y}_n^{**}) = V_{C_n}^8 + 6V_{C_n}^6 + 15V_{C_n}^4 + 16V_{C_n}^2,$$

whereby with $V_{C_n}^2$ from (55) the further result is obtained that, in this case, the positive skewness and kurtosis will *increase* from age group to age group (and therefore are monotonically increasing functions of n).

Of course, for smaller n, it is no longer possible to work with the Central Limit Theorem and in that case it is generally extremely difficult to derive an explicit derivation of the functional form of the distribution within age groups.[24] Without more detailed information on the formation mechanism of the random rates of increase in income, it is impossible to progress any further. This type of information is typically not available. If one is interested in the exact analytical form of the frequency distribution over and above the more general characteristics obtained above, then one is forced to make concrete assumptions about the type of distribution of $\tilde{e}_i$.

One point must be stressed; the transitory shock process affecting any earnings, *observed in isolation*, already results in asymmetry; the distribution of the disposable earnings within an age group consisting of *identical* individuals is *positively skewed*.

3.2.2 *Exclusion of chance*

Consider the case where the individual earnings are not subject to any random influences. This would mean: $\tilde{e}_i = 0, \forall i$ and therefore also $\tilde{C}_n = 1$, $\forall n$, so that:

theorems of Ljapunoff and Lindeberg-Feller; cf. Theorem 2.9 in Aitchison and Brown (1957, p. 14), Fisz (1976, pp. 241–5) and Gnedenko and Kolmogorow (1968)). Also the assumption of stochastic independence can be relaxed (see Eicker (1964) and Schönfeld (1971)). [23] Cf. Aitchison and Brown (1957, p. 8).

[24] Incidentally, whatever the special distribution type one assumes for the $\tilde{e}_i$ (or $(1 + \tilde{e}_i)$), the most successful technical aid for the derivation of the distribution is the *Mellin Transformation*. Cf. Lomnicki (1967) and Springer (1979, chs. 4, 6 and 7).

$$\tilde{Y}_n^{**} = \tilde{A}_n^{**} = w_{1n}\tilde{a}_1 + w_{2n}\tilde{b}_0^{1/a}, \quad n = 0, \ldots, N; \tag{62}$$

the distribution of disposable earnings within an age group n would therefore be identical with the distribution of *planned* disposable earnings. What does the latter look like? How are the human capital accumulation abilities $\tilde{a}_1$ and $\tilde{b}_0$ distributed among the individuals? And in what way is the $\tilde{A}_n^{**}$ distribution characterised by these basic distributions (given the equation structure (62) resulting from the optimising behaviour of the individuals)?

The question concerning the distributions of $\tilde{a}_1$ and $\tilde{b}_0$ can, in the end, only be answered empirically, of course (although it is not at all clear that this would indeed be possible). However, in theoretical terms, several points can be made on the basis of (35) and (18).

The efficiency, with which the individual increases his productive capacity in the full-time schooling phase, depends on his ability to learn and his *DF* factor in accordance with (35). The $\tilde{a}_1$ distribution itself thus depends on how these factors vary among the individuals.

Firstly, the learning ability must be considered. As explained in Section 2.1.1, three groups of factors play a role: the genetic endowment (G), the home background (HO) and the cultural influences (CU). Accordingly the distributions and the type of interaction of the individual components of each of the three groups determine the distribution law of $\tilde{LA}$.

In general one has:

$$\begin{aligned}\tilde{LA} &= LA(\tilde{G}, \tilde{HO}, \tilde{CU}) \\ &= LA(\tilde{G}_1, \tilde{G}_2, \ldots, \tilde{HO}_1, \tilde{HO}_2, \ldots, \tilde{CU}_1, \tilde{CU}_2, \ldots).\end{aligned} \tag{63}$$

References to the $\tilde{LA}$ distribution from empirical sources must be approached with a great deal of caution. Typically, one tries to establish those characteristics which (by assumption) determine the learning ability of an individual, by way of certain intelligence tests. This, however, results in considerable problems of measurement.[25] In fact, almost any $\tilde{LA}$ distribution can be generated depending on the construction of the test. If it is asserted (and it often is) that the abilities are normally distributed, this is principally a statement on the *measurement* of ability and only secondly a statement on the ability *distribution*. If the individual components in (63) are independent and identically distributed variables, which are incorporated *additively* into $\tilde{LA}$, either directly as a sum or as a linear transformation of this sum, then $\tilde{LA}$ would in fact be approximately normally distributed in accordance with the Central Limit Theorem. If those

[25] See, for example, Tyler (1965), Ryan (1972) or Block and Dworkin (1976).

components could also be rendered as fractional sums and a version of the Central Limit Theorem applied in each case to the fractional sums, $\widetilde{LA}$ would also have a normal distribution if the fractional sums were correlated.[26] But, even if one could arrive at the point where the conditions for certain diluted versions of the Central Limit Theorem could be seen to be approximately fulfilled, the assumption of an *additive* effect would still have to be justified.

With a lot of the relevant *G*, *HO* and *CU* dimensions (cf. footnote 34, p. 36) it does not seem to me to be a question of 'either–or', but rather a question of 'both–and'. Therefore, this means that these factors are not combined additively, but *multiplicatively* in $\widetilde{LA}$; their effects are therefore of a proportional nature.[27] If all the individual components influencing the learning ability were independent of one another and identically distributed and if these had a multiplicative effect on $\widetilde{LA}$, $\widetilde{LA}$ would be the product of a variety of simultaneously acting, independent and identically distributed variables, then, with an increasing number of factors, the distribution of $\widetilde{LA}$ would converge to a log-normal distribution.[28] If this product could be divided up into fractional products, so that these fractional products fulfilled the conditions of certain variants of the Central Limit Theorem, then $\widetilde{LA}$, as a product of (asymptotically) log-normally distributed variables would still (asymptotically) converge to a log-normal distribution, even if the fractional products were not independent of one another.[29] On the other hand in case of stochastic dependencies between the individual components, the conditions of the Central Limit Theorem can often be satisfied by summarising the individual factors into groups, such that these groups are not causally connected to one another, so that there is stochastic independence between these groups. But whether an exact log-normal distribution occurs as a result or not, the $\widetilde{LA}$ distribution is *positively skewed* in any case and displays a *positive kurtosis* as a result of the assumed basic multiplicative structure with a sufficiently large number of factors (this is also the case if the individual components and/or the factor blocks are symmetrically distributed).[30] The latter characteristics of the

[26] Cf. Hogg and Craig (1978, p. 409).

[27] This type of thought is found in Boissevain (1939); see also Burt (1943) and Roy (1950). Apart from the proportional factor integration considered here, other types of interaction of the individual components are plausible, e.g.:

$$LA^j = LA[\min(G_1^j, G_2^j, \ldots)] \quad \text{or} \quad LA^j = LA[\max(G_1^j, G_2^j, \ldots)];$$

the latter corresponds to a formulation which is based on the *comparative advantage* of the individual *j* – see in connection with this, Houthakker (1974) or Sattinger (1980).

[28] See, in connection with this, the literature quoted in footnote 22, p. 101 from which it can be established to what extent the conditions of independence and identical distribution can be relaxed. [29] Cf. Aitchison and Brown (1957, pp. 11–12).

[30] We have already come across this point in Sections 3.1 and 3.2.1 (although it was in different contexts in each case).

learning ability distribution are reinforced by the fact that a whole series of individual components integrated in (63) are positively correlated with one another.[31] What has been said so far with regard to $\tilde{LA}$ can be applied similarly to the second determining factor of $\tilde{a}_1$, the DF factor:

$$\tilde{DF} = DF(\tilde{HO}, \tilde{CU}) = DF(\tilde{HO}_1, \tilde{HO}_2, \ldots, \tilde{CU}_1, \tilde{CU}_2, \ldots). \quad (64)$$

If we return to the underlying specification (35), another stipulation for the efficacy of $\tilde{LA}$ and $\tilde{DF}$ is required in order to be able to make distributional statements on the human capital accumulation ability $\tilde{a}_1$. A high level of production efficiency is only brought about, in my view, when the individual has a high learning ability *and* the relevant motivation (to name but one of the DF components). Boissevain (1939, p. 50) wrote that, 'A man of great intelligence, but at the same time extremely lazy is unlikely to accomplish anything worthwhile, and the same is true of the man of great energy but of low intelligence'. This means that learning ability and the DF factor are integrated into $\tilde{a}_1$ in the form of a *product*: $\tilde{a}_1 = a_1(\tilde{LA} \cdot \tilde{DF})$.

As from the preceding discussion both $\tilde{LA}$ and $\tilde{DF}$ are not symmetrically distributed, but are positively skewed, this applies all the more for the $\tilde{a}_1$ distribution due to the multiplicative interaction. This tendency is reinforced further by the fact that $\tilde{LA}$ and $\tilde{DF}$ are partially dependent on the same basic factors often with the same direction of effect, which induces a positive correlation between $\tilde{LA}$ and $\tilde{DF}$. The same applies for the positive kurtosis.

> *Note*: More specific statements on the $\tilde{a}_1$ distribution require, as always, a more precise characterisation of the distributions of $\tilde{LA}$ and $\tilde{DF}$ and a more detailed specification of the $a_1(\cdot)$ function. The assumption of (asymptotically) log-normally distributed $\tilde{LA}$ and $\tilde{DF}$ and the application of Theorem 2.4 in Aitchison and Brown (1957, p. 12) would seem quite appropriate. However, apart from one exception in Chapter 5 (Section 5.5), the present study restricts itself to the first two moments – for reasons which were discussed in Section 3.1 – and therefore excludes any detailed distribution hypotheses.

The second parameter of human capital production efficiency $\tilde{b}_0$ is also dependent on $\tilde{LA}$ and $\tilde{DF}$, the factors which have just been discussed. In accordance with (18), three further determining factors accompany these factors; namely, the personality characteritics summarised in $\tilde{QPC}$, examination grades ($\tilde{CR}$) and an indicator for the quality of schooling ($\tilde{SQ}$). In line with this, the following is obtained for the parameter $\tilde{b}_0$ which, in contrast to $\tilde{a}_1$, refers to the earnings phase:

[31] Compare the factor list in footnote 34, p. 36 again, and, e.g., Meade (1973, pp. 364–73) and Phelps Brown (1977, pp. 220–9).

$$\tilde{b}_0 = b_0[\widetilde{LA}; \widetilde{DF}; QPC(\underline{\tilde{a}}, \underline{\tilde{b}}, \underline{\tilde{c}}); \widetilde{CR}; \widetilde{SQ}], \tag{18a}$$

with:

$\widetilde{LA}$ from (63) and $\widetilde{DF}$ from (64).

An analysis similar to that relating to $\tilde{a}_1$ can be applied to this.

The distribution of $\tilde{b}_0$ therefore also exhibits a positive skewness and a positive kurtosis. Since the earnings phase production efficiency $\tilde{b}_0$ is dependent on a larger number of factors than the full-time schooling production efficiency $\tilde{a}_1$ and since the type of interaction of the additional determining factors $\widetilde{QPC}$, $\widetilde{CR}$ and $\widetilde{SQ}$ (mutually as well as in relation to $\widetilde{LA}$ and $\widetilde{DF}$) and its effect on $\tilde{b}_0$ in my opinion is also subject to the 'both–and' principle above, we can expect that:

$$V_{b_0}^2 > V_{a_1}^2, \quad \gamma_1(\tilde{b}_0) > \gamma_1(\tilde{a}_1) > 0 \quad \text{and} \quad \gamma_2(\tilde{b}_0) > \gamma_2(\tilde{a}_1) > 0.$$ [32]

Any further characterisation of the $\tilde{b}_0$ distribution will be omitted at this point. As has been emphasised several times already, the exact analytical shape of the frequency distribution of $\tilde{b}_0$ is not crucial for the intended analyses. The above qualitative description is perfectly adequate.[33]

If one summarises the discoveries made previously on the distributions of the human capital accumulation abilities $\tilde{a}_1$ and $\tilde{b}_0$, then one can not only assume that those distributions are *positively skewed* and have a *positive kurtosis*, but also that there is a distinct dependence between the variables $\tilde{a}_1$ and $\tilde{b}_0$. In fact, $\tilde{a}_1$ and $\tilde{b}_0$ are *positively correlated* on the basis of the specifications (35) and (18), since the determining factors of $\tilde{a}_1$ (namely, $\widetilde{LA}$ and $\widetilde{DF}$) are integrated with effectively the same sign in $\tilde{b}_0$ as well.[34]

[32] See, in connection with this, Appendix 3 as well.

[33] The only exception is Section 5.5. There, a log-normally distributed $\tilde{b}_0$ is assumed – a tenable assumption according to the theoretical explanations in this section. In connection with this, note the generation of the distribution in Phelps Brown (1977, pp. 298–305), which comes to a similar conclusion (concerning the tenability of the log-normal distribution hypothesis).

[34] These characteristics of $\tilde{a}_1$ and $\tilde{b}_0$ could be given a precise analytical form by assuming a *joint log-normal distribution*. The implied log-normality of the marginal distributions would, at any rate, be compatible (at least asymptotically) with the theoretical considerations of the present section. As $\tilde{b}_0^{1/a}$ would also have this type of distribution given a log-normal $\tilde{b}_0$ (Theorem 2.1 in Aitchison and Brown, 1957, p. 11), then the frequency distribution of planned disposable earnings within an age group n in line with (62) would represent the frequency distribution of a difference or sum (w_{1n} is positive for all n; w_{2n} is negative at the beginning of working life, but then becomes positive – cf. also Appendix 4) of two non-identically log-normally distributed dependent variables. A more exact determination of the resulting distribution has been omitted at this stage because it is not relevant (see the explanations on p. 93).

According to a well-known theorem in probability theory, $\tilde{A}_n^{**}$ from (62) would incidentally be normally distributed if the vector $(\tilde{a}_1, \tilde{b}_0^{1/a})$ would suffice a two dimensional normal distribution (see Hogg and Craig, 1978, p. 409). As all marginal distributions of a normally distributed random vector are normal, then both $\tilde{a}_1$ and $\tilde{b}_0^{1/a}$ $(=:\tilde{b})$ must also be

Now the distribution of planned disposable earnings within an age group n is not characterised by the basic distributions in themselves, but by the analytical final form (62), which is the result of the maximisation process described in Chapter 2. The consequence of this is that, even in the case of a symmetrically distributed $\tilde{b}_0$, this efficiency factor would cause a tendency to positive skewness since it appears as $\tilde{b}_0^{1/a}$ in (62) and $1/a > 1$.[35] As the assumption of a human capital production function with decreasing returns to scale is not only theoretically, but also empirically well founded (Section 2.1.1), the sum of the production elasticities b_1 and b_2 should therefore be less than one and thus $1/a > 1$ cannot be questioned (recall that $a := 1 - b_1 - b_2$). This provides the fourth reason for a *positive skewness in the* $\tilde{A}_n^{**}$ *distribution*:

(i) $\tilde{a}_1$ distribution positively skewed;
(ii) $\tilde{b}_0$ distribution positively skewed;
(iii) $\tilde{a}_1$ and $\tilde{b}_0$ positively correlated;
(iv) $1/a > 1$.

> *Note*: The additional tendency to positive skewness caused by $1/a > 1$ increases with increasing $1/a$. Therefore, the closer the scale elasticity in human capital production ($= b_1 + b_2$) is to 1, the stronger this tendency becomes.

A similar chain of argument can be set up for the *positive kurtosis of the* $\tilde{A}_n^{**}$ *distribution*.[36]

The analysis of the permanent component $\tilde{A}_n^{**}$ has been completed here. Further results, in particular with regard to the age profile and the policy effects, can be found in the following sections.

3.3 The age profile of earnings inequality

According to (53), inequality within age groups $V_{Y_n^{**}}^2$ is characterised by the permanent inequality $V_{A_n^{**}}^2$ and the transitory inequality $V_{C_n}^2$. The latter can be dealt with quickly. As a result of the accumulation of shocks period by period, the bandwidth of possible income realisations becomes larger and larger; the random walk approach formulated in Section 1.3 implies a monotonic increase in the inequality $V_{C_n}^2$ caused by transitory income change factors. In fact, the following are obtained from (55):

normally distributed. This implies a symmetrical distribution for $\tilde{a}_1$ and a negatively skewed distribution for $\tilde{b}_0$ (as $\tilde{b}_0 = \tilde{b}^a$ with $\tilde{b} \sim N(\cdot,\cdot)$ and $0 < a < 1$). The assumption of a symmetrical $\tilde{a}_1$ distribution is not, however, tenable and that of a negatively skewed $\tilde{b}_0$ distribution is out of the question too (as seen above).

35 See also, in connection with this, Becker (1975, pp. 138–40).

36 For technical details, see, in general, Springer (1979), in particular chs. 3 and 4.

$$V^2_{C_{n+1}} - V^2_{C_n} = \sigma^2_e (1+\sigma^2_e)^n > 0 \quad \forall n; \tag{65}$$

$$(V^2_{C_{n+2}} - V^2_{C_{n+1}}) - (V^2_{C_{n+1}} - V^2_{C_n}) = \sigma^4_e (1+\sigma^2_e)^n > 0 \quad \forall n. \tag{66}$$

These show that $V^2_{C_n}$ is a strictly monotonically increasing function of n and has a rising rate of increase.

Clearly it depends on the age profile of the permanent inequality whether the realised *ex post* inequality $V^2_{Y^{**}_n}$ has this trend as well. The permanent profile resulting from the optimising behaviour of the individuals is considerably more complicated than that of the transitory inequality. It is chiefly determined by the age pattern of the weight α_n, which denotes the fraction of mean disposable earnings within the age group n which falls to the weighted, average basic education efficiency.

> *Note*: $\mu_{Y^{**}_n} = \mu_{A^{**}_n}; n = 0, \ldots, N$, since $\tilde{A}^{**}_n$ and $\tilde{C}_n$ (cf. (51)) are stochastically independent and μ_{C_n} is equal to one (for all n) because $\tilde{e}_i \sim \text{iid}(0, \sigma^2_e)$.

If one assumes that within each of these age groups n the disposable average income $\mu_{A^{**}_n}$ is positive (the case of $\mu_{A^{**}_n} < 0$ will be treated separately below), then, with the aid of the formulas developed in Section 2.3.1, it is immediately clear that α_n is a strictly monotonically decreasing function of n (Fig. 21). This incidentally also applies when one incorporates the end-of-horizon effect and is also independent of the ratio between c and δ. Moreover, one can see that α_n only assumes positive values, and is greater than 1 (since w_{2n} is negative there) at the beginning of the working life (i.e. for small values of n). From these characteristics, the trends of the functions of the weight α_n occurring in (54) can be obtained; they indicate the influence profile of the $\tilde{a}_1$ – and $\tilde{b}$ $(:= \tilde{b}_0^{1/a})$ – inequalities on $V^2_{A^{**}_n}$. The analytics do not contain any complications and the reader can take the patterns of those proportionality factors from Figs. 22, 23 and 24 (which are based quantitatively on the standard parameter set (19)[37]).

If one ignores the correlation effect (the third summand in (54)), differences in the individual full-time schooling accumulation abilities $V^2_{a_1}$ affect the inequality of planned disposable earnings at the beginning of the working life to a greater extent. However, this increased effect becomes weaker and weaker during the course of the working life and is finally transformed into an under-proportional effect (α^2_n becomes smaller than 1; cf. Fig. 22). What is the cause of this monotonic decrease in the effect of the $\tilde{a}_1$ inequality on the permanent inequality $V^2_{A^{**}_n}$? Quite simply, it is the reduction in the relative starting stock weight (measured against the overall human capital stock) as a result of the net depreciation effect; as has already

[37] Incidentally, with this set the value 0.99 is obtained for the 'mechanical' α (cf. p. 98); cf. also Fig. 21 (broken line).

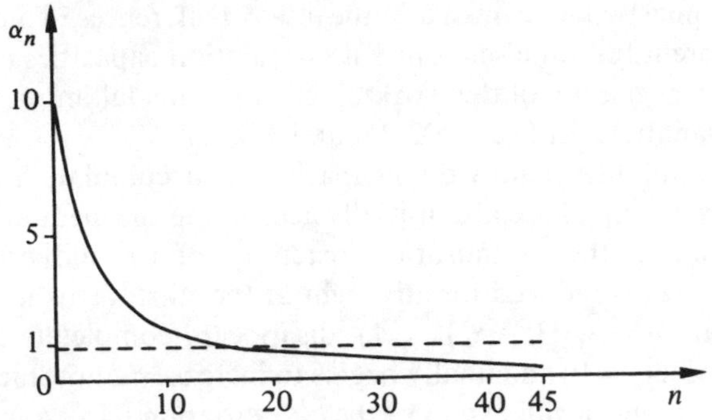

Fig. 21.

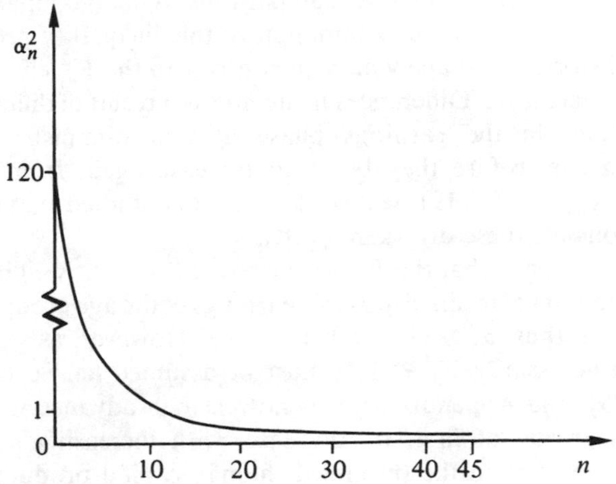

Fig. 22.

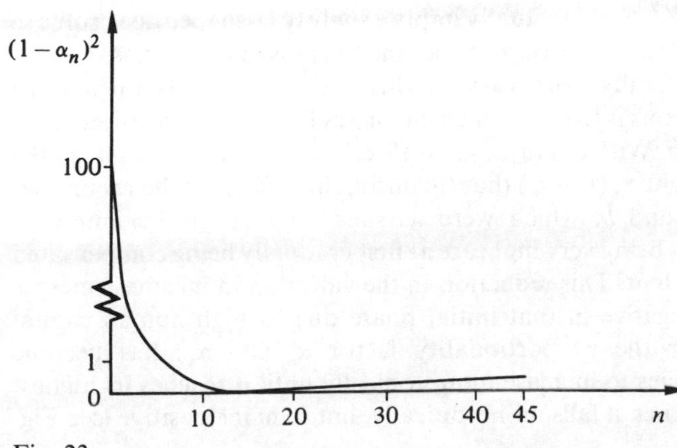

Fig. 23.

frequently been emphasised, one must assume $\delta > c$. Differences in income resulting from different full-time schooling accumulation capacities are at their greatest at the beginning of the working life and then fall monotonically – cf. the explanations in Section 2.3.4 and Fig. 18.

Variations in the (modified) individual capacities to accumulate human capital during the working phase also initially accentuate the inequality of earnings as a result of the optimisation reactions of the individuals. However, the V_b^2 effect is reduced rapidly right at the start, turns into an under-proportional impact ($(1 - \alpha_n)^2 < 1$), disappears completely for a short time ($\alpha_n = 1$ or $w_{2n} = 0$) and finally begins to increase monotonically, even if it does not exploit the full extent of the $\tilde{b}_0^{1/a}$ variation ($(1 - \alpha_n)^2$ still remains smaller than 1; cf. Fig. 23).

The 'overtaking' discovered in the comparative dynamic analysis concerning b_0 provides an intuitive explanation of this inequality profile forming almost a distorted U-shape which, in contrast to the $V_{a_1}^2$ effect, is not monotonically decreasing. Differences in income as a result of differing accumulation abilities in the earnings phase at first diminish with increasing working age, before they begin to increase again from the 'overtaking' point n_{0,b_0} (see Fig. 19). Section 2.3.4 must be studied again for the economic reasons for these divergent paths.

Also it must be mentioned that the $V_{a_1}^2$ weight exceeds the V_b^2 weight as long as the $w_{1n}\mu_{a_1}$ fraction of mean disposable earnings of the age group n is greater than one half, thus: $\alpha_n^2 > (1 - \alpha_n)^2 \Leftrightarrow \alpha_n > \frac{1}{2}$. However, as $V_{a_1}^2 < V_{b_0}^2$, and therefore necessarily $V_{a_1}^2 < V_b^2$, must be assumed (cf. Sections 3.2.2 and 3.1 (p. 99), and Appendix 3), it is not clear in advance which inequality effect is greater at first; in any case, with increasing n the inequality effect assumed from the (modified) human capital production efficiency $\tilde{b}$ dominates more and more. The paths observed so far (on consideration of $V_b^2 > V_{a_1}^2$) actually imply a slightly U-shaped age profile in the inequality within age groups of planned disposable earnings.

Whether $V_{A_n^{**}}^2$ really does vary in this manner depends on a third inequality factor; this is the one which emanates from the correlation of the variables $\tilde{a}_1$ and $\tilde{b}$. With $\text{cov}(\tilde{a}_1, \tilde{b}) > 0$ (Section 3.2.2), it follows from the profile of the weight $\alpha_n (1 - \alpha_n)$ that the inequality effects of the accumulation abilities $\tilde{a}_1$ and $\tilde{b}$, which were as such seen at the beginning of professional life as being very high, are at first gradually being compensated for to a certain extent. This reduction in the variation in incomes emerges because w_{2n} is negative in that initial phase due to high human capital investment. After the proportionality factor $\alpha_n (1 - \alpha_n)$ has become positive, it continues to increase monotonically until it reaches its highest value for $\alpha_n = \frac{1}{2}$; then it falls monotonically, but remains positive (see Fig. 24).

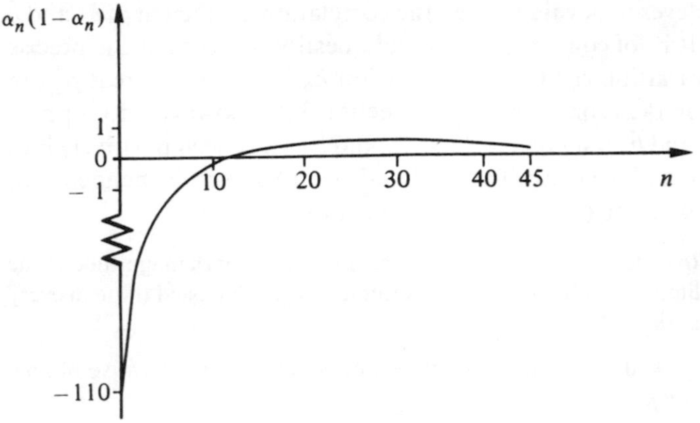

Fig. 24.

These individual preliminary observations for the purposes of interpretation permit an educated guess to be made of the age trend of the $\tilde{A}_n^{**}$ inequality, yet they do not provide precise overall statements. These can be obtained from the derivate $\partial V_{A_n^{**}}^2/\partial\alpha_n$ in combination with the property that the weight α_n is a strictly monotonically decreasing function of n. From:

$$\frac{\partial V_{A_n^{**}}^2}{\partial\alpha_n} = 2\alpha_n V_{a_1}^2 - 2(1-\alpha_n)V_b^2 + 2(1-2\alpha_n)V_{a_1}V_b\rho_{a_1b}$$

with $\rho_{a_1b} > 0$ and $V_b > V_{a_1}$ (> 0), the following condition is obtained:

$$\frac{\partial V_{A_n^{**}}^2}{\partial\alpha_n} \gtreqless 0 \Leftrightarrow \alpha_n \gtreqless \xi, \quad n = 0, \ldots, N; \tag{67}$$

where:

$$\xi := \frac{1}{1 + \dfrac{1/h_0 - \rho_{a_1b}}{h_0 - \rho_{a_1b}}} \quad \text{and} \quad h_0 := \frac{V_b}{V_{a_1}}.$$

With $V_b > V_{a_1}$, one immediately obtains: $\xi > \frac{1}{2}$. However, no precise information can be obtained *a priori* on the upper limit of ξ. The following general relationship applies:

$$\xi > x \in (\tfrac{1}{2}, \infty) \Leftrightarrow (1-x)(h_0 - \rho_{a_1b}) + x\left(\rho_{a_1b} - \frac{1}{h_0}\right) > 0.$$

By choosing the relevant combinations of h_0 and ρ_{a_1b}, the previous inequality can be fulfilled with any high value of x. Yet, it does become clear that ξ only achieves high values when the correlation coefficient of $\tilde{a}_1$ and $\tilde{b}$ approaches 1. It is, of course, an empirical question as to what the precise nature of the variation coefficient proportion h_0 is, and how great ρ_{a_1b} in fact is. The theoretical considerations in Section 3.2.2, however, do support the fact that $\tilde{a}_1$ and $\tilde{b}_0$ (and thereby also $\tilde{a}_1$ and $\tilde{b}$) are indeed positively but, by no means perfectly positively correlated (bearing the independence of the determining factor $\widetilde{QPC}$ in mind, for example).

Note: In order to give the reader an idea of the order of magnitude of the upper limit of ξ, a few numerical examples have been listed (note in every case that $h_0 > 1$):

(i) If $\rho_{a_1b} = 0$, then ξ can only take values below 1 (irrespective of how great h_0 is).

(ii) Where $\rho_{a_1b} = 0.3$, the upper limit of ξ amounts to 1.025 (this is obtained for $h_0 = 6.5$; all other h_0 values imply a smaller value for ξ than 1.025).

(iii) In the event that $\rho_{a_1b} = 0.5$ then the highest possible value of ξ is 1.08 (this is obtained for $h_0 = 3.73$).

(iv) $\rho_{a_1b} = 0.6$ implies an upper limit for ξ amounting to 1.125 (which requires that $h_0 = 3$).

(v) For $\rho_{a_1b} = 0.9$ the highest value for ξ which can be obtained amounts to 1.65 ($h_0 = 1.59$ is a condition of this).

(vi) For $\rho_{a_1b} = 0.95$ the upper limit of ξ is 2.1 (which is obtained with $h_0 = 1.38$).

(vii) For $\rho_{a_1b} = 0.99$ the maximum value which can be obtained for ξ is 4 (which requires that $h_0 = 1.15$).[38]

At the very most (ii), (iii) and (iv) in the previous note can be seen as realistic. But even if the correlation coefficient between the ability to increase productivity in the full-time schooling phase and the (modified) ability to increase productivity in the earnings phase, ρ_{a_1b}, did have the theoretically somewhat implausible value of 0.9, ξ would, at the most, reach the upper limit of 1.65. That, of course, is not sufficient to exceed the high

[38] These are purely hypothetical calculations, as it is clear that ρ_{a_1b} and h_0 are not independent of one another. The reader should, however, note that $\rho_{a_1b} = 1$ does not necessarily imply that $V_{a_1} = V_0$ (thus $h_0 = 1$). The following is known to apply (see, for example, Roussas, 1973, p. 96):

$$\rho_{a_1b} = 1 \Leftrightarrow \tilde{a}_1 = c_1 + c_2\tilde{b}, \quad c_2 > 0, \text{ with probability } 1.$$

One thereby obtains: $V_{a_1} = c_2\sigma_b/(c_1 + c_2\mu_b)$ which only corresponds to $V_b = \sigma_b/\mu_b$ when $c_1 = 0$. Where $c_1 > 0$ on the other hand, it would follow in every case that $V_{a_1} < V_b$, thus $h_0 > 1$ (with probability 1).

initial values of the weight α_n (cf. also Fig. 21) and certainly one is cautious to assume $\alpha_n > \xi$ in the initial periods. This, in connection with $\xi > \frac{1}{2}$, immediately provides the *U-shape of the $V^2_{A_n^{**}}$ profile* suggested in the previous explanations for, as long as $\alpha_n > \xi$, $V^2_{A_n^{**}}$ also falls with α_n (cf. (67)); however, as the very latest from $\alpha_n = \frac{1}{2}$ (this point occurs approximately in the middle of working life on the basis of the standard parameter set) $V^2_{A_n^{**}}$ begins to increase with the continued decrease of α_n.

> *Note*: *If* (for whatever reason at all) $\xi > \alpha_0$, then the permanent inequality within age groups $V^2_{A_n^{**}}$ would not exhibit a U-shaped age profile, but would increase from the very beginning from age group to age group. $\xi > \alpha_0$ is, however, an unrealistic assumption, as has already been explained.

The larger ξ is, the earlier the 'reversal' occurs; so the shorter is the phase where the inequality of planned disposable earnings decreases from age group to age group and, correspondingly, the longer is the phase of increasing inequality. In other words, the lowest point in the U-shaped $V^2_{A_n^{**}}$ profile is shifted towards earlier periods (or age groups). Therefore the reversal takes place *earlier* the *larger* the correlation coefficient $\rho_{a_1 b}$ is, since, where $V_b > V_{a_1}$, it follows that $\partial\xi/\partial\rho_{a_1 b} > 0$, *ceteris paribus*. In fact, the comparative dynamic analysis of a simultaneous increase in the human capital accumulation abilities in the full-time schooling phase and in the earnings phase provides an intuitive reason for this advancement: the 'overtaking' occurs at an earlier stage than with a pure increase in the accumulation ability in the earnings phase (see Appendix 2). Moreover, one can see from the following interrelation:

$$\frac{\partial\xi}{\partial h_0} > 0 \Leftrightarrow \rho_{a_1 b} < \frac{2h_0}{1 + h_0^2},$$

that the reversal mentioned takes place much earlier in the case of a sufficiently small correlation coefficient $\rho_{a_1 b}$, the more obviously the inequality in the (modified) abilities to increase productivity in the earnings phase V_b *exceeds* (*ceteris paribus*) the inequality in the capabilities of increasing productivity in the full-time schooling phase V_{a_1}.

> *Note*: What effects would the *special case* $\mu_{A_n^{**}} < 0$ have on the age profile of the inequality of planned disposable earnings within age groups? It corresponds to the logic of maximising behaviour, that negative planned disposable earnings only ever occur, if at all, right at the very beginning of working life (cf. Chapter 2). If this case applies for a sufficient number of individuals and to a sufficient extent, such that the average disposable income within these initial age groups becomes negative, then the beginning of the 'U-phase' is *delayed*; it is preceded by a short phase of

increase in $V^2_{A_n^{**}}$ (lasting until $n'(\mu_{A^{**}_{n'}} \equiv 0)$). This can be shown in line with the altered α_n profile with the aid of (67).[39]

Before we pursue the question any further as to what extent the characteristics of the $V^2_{A_n^{**}}$ profile discovered here are carried over to the $V^2_{Y_n^{**}}$ profile, the following must be stressed. In contrast to the heuristic derivations in the literature on human capital so far,[40] in this case not only is the U-shape of the $V^2_{A_n^{**}}$ profile, as such, the result of the dynamic optimising behaviour of the individuals, but is the interaction of this shape with the model parameters, and therefore both are generated *endogenously*. Simultaneously, explicit solutions for these interrelations can be obtained.

Now that the age profiles of the transitory inequality and the permanent inequality have been discussed, their combined effect on the age profile of the realised *ex post* inequality $V^2_{Y_n^{**}}$ is of interest. The following relation is obtained from (53):

$$V^2_{Y^{**}_{n+1}} - V^2_{Y^{**}_n} \gtreqless 0 \Leftrightarrow \frac{V^2_{A^{**}_{n+1}} - V^2_{A^{**}_n}}{V^2_{A^{**}_{n+1}} + 1} \gtreqless -\sigma^2_e; \quad n=0,\ldots,N-1. \tag{68}$$

Whether the U-trend of the $V^2_{A_n^{**}}$ profile is carried over to the $V^2_{Y_n^{**}}$ pattern depends significantly on the size of the uncertainty of income, σ^2_e (>0), caused by the transitory factors of change. It is clear that the realised *ex post* inequality also increases in phases of increase in the permanent inequality. If the $V^2_{A_n^{**}}$ decrease occurring in the initial phase of earnings life overrides the monotonic increase in $V^2_{C_n}$, then the age profile of $V^2_{Y_n^{**}}$ does in fact exhibit a U-trend; the 'reversal' discussed above takes place earlier, however.[41] If, on the other hand, the variance of the stochastic shocks, σ^2_e, is so great that the '$>$' condition in (68) is fulfilled even in the phase of the $V^2_{A_n^{**}}$ decrease, then the realised *ex post* inequality generally increases in a strictly monotonic manner with the working age n.

Notes: (i) Of course, the empiricists have to have the last word here. On the basis of the empirical results of Lillard and Weiss (1979, pp. 444, 450–2) and Bourguignon and Morrisson (1982, pp. 28–37 (in particular, Table 3)) a σ^2_e value amounting to 0.02 is considered to be an empirical upper limit. Where $\sigma^2_e \leqslant 0.02$ and the values from the standard parameter set (19), and in line with $V_b > V_{a_1}$ and $\rho_{a_1 b} > 0$, the U-trend is also carried over to the $V^2_{Y_n^{**}}$ profile.

(ii) The reader should note, in general, that the questions occurring in the

[39] α_n here is negative at the beginning of working life (or more precisely, for $\forall n < n'$); the following also applies in this phase: $\alpha_{n+1} - \alpha_n < 0$; i.e. α_n is decreasing (becoming 'even more negative'). α_n is not defined at n' (a pole point). Where $n > n'$ (thus where $\mu_{A^{**}_n} > 0$) α_n behaves as before again (cf. the above explanations as well as Figs. 21 and 25a, b).

[40] See, for example, Mincer (1974, pp. 32–6).

[41] From (68): if $V^2_{A^{**}_{n+1}} = V^2_{A^{**}_n}$, then $V^2_{Y^{**}_n}$ is already increasing.

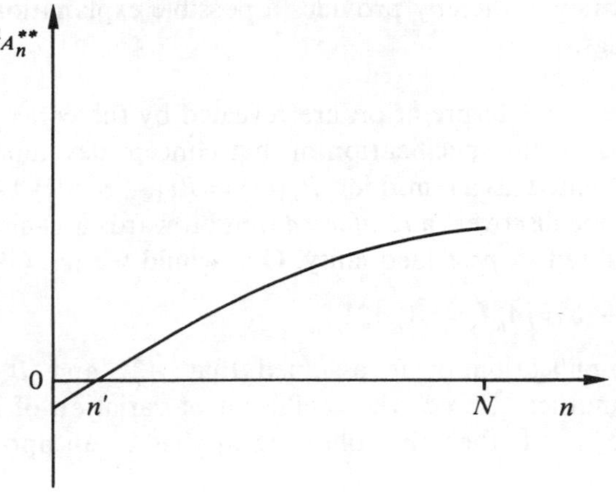

Fig. 25a.

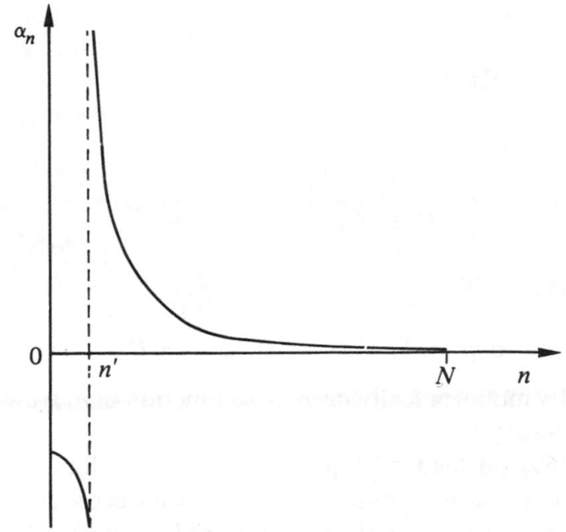

Fig. 25b.

present context are not in all cases designed to have only one, unequivocal answer. What a formal theory can achieve, is the provision of an analytical framework within which the questions of potential interest can be discussed in a logically consistent manner.

The above theoretical results relating to the age profiles of earnings inequality are *compatible* with the results of recent *empirical* examinations.[42] The present model thereby provides a possible explanation for these empirical findings.

Additional possibilities for interpretation are revealed by the concept of 'learning by observing'. If the specification of that concept developed in Section 2.3.5 is implemented (as a reminder: $R_n(v^j) = R(1 - b_3^n v^j); 0 < v^j, b_3 < 1; b_2 = 0$), then one discovers a *reinforced* trend towards a U-shaped age profile for the realised *ex post* inequality. One would see (cf. (49)):

$$\tilde{A}_n^{**}(\tilde{v}) = (1 - b_3^n \tilde{v})\tilde{A}_n^{**} =: \tilde{B}_n \tilde{A}_n^{**}.$$

For purposes of simplification, it is assumed that $\tilde{A}_n^{**}$ and $\tilde{B}_n$ are independent of one another.[43] Since the coefficient of variation of $\tilde{B}_n$ is small because of $0 < b_3 < 1$, then the following applies as an approximation:[44]

$$V^2_{A_n^{**}(v)} \simeq V^2_{B_n} + V^2_{A_n^{**}}, \quad n = 0, \ldots, N; \tag{69}$$

where

$$V^2_{B_n} := \frac{\sigma^2_{B_n}}{\mu^2_{B_n}} = \frac{b_3^{2n}\sigma_v^2}{(1 - b_3^n \mu_v)^2}.$$

Furthermore, one finds:

$$V^2_{B_{n+1}} - V^2_{B_n} = \frac{(1 - b_3^n \mu_v)^2 b_3^{2(n+1)}\sigma_v^2 - (1 - b_3^{n+1}\mu_v)^2 b_3^{2n}\sigma_v^2}{(1 - b_3^n \mu_v)^2 (1 - b_3^{n+1}\mu_v)^2} < 0, \tag{70}$$

since:

$$0 < 1 - \mu_v \leqslant 1 - b_3^n \mu_v < 1; \quad 0 < b_3 < 1; \quad n = 0, \ldots, N - 1.$$

$V^2_{B_n}$ is therefore a strictly monotonically *decreasing* function of n. However, the assertion above thereby follows.

After substituting (69) (instead of $V^2_{A_n^{**}}$) into (53), one does, in fact, recognise that now the resulting condition for an initial decrease of the realised *ex post* inequality is weaker than before (cf. (68); note (70)):

$$V^2_{Y_{n+1}^{**}(v)} - V^2_{Y_n^{**}(v)} \gtreqless 0 \Leftrightarrow \frac{V^2_{A_{n+1}^{**}} - V^2_{A_n^{**}} + V^2_{B_{n+1}} - V^2_{B_n}}{V^2_{A_{n+1}^{**}} + V^2_{B_{n+1}} + 1} \gtreqless -\sigma_e^2;$$

$$n = 0, \ldots, N - 1. \tag{71}$$

[42] Cf. Lillard and Weiss (1979, p. 443), Creedy and Hart (1979, pp. 282–3) and Bourguignon and Morrisson (1982, pp. 37–9). It is clear that in the present context, only *panel* studies permit a valid conclusion (keyword: CS-fallacy). The studies just quoted fulfil this criterion. Cf. here also Creedy and Hart (1979), Beach *et al.* (1981, pp. 79–84) and Baudelot (1983).

[43] In fact, the ability to establish one's own productivity and then communicate this as plausibly and precisely as possible, $1/\tilde{v}$, and the production efficiencies, $\tilde{a}_1$ and $\tilde{b}_0$, should be slightly positively correlated.

[44] See Goodman (1960, p. 709).

Obviously, the empiricists have the final word here too. For a sufficiently large level of income uncertainty σ_e^2, the $V_{C_n}^2$ increase can override the $V_{A_n^{**}(v)}^2$ decrease from the very outset, such that $V_{Y_{n+1}^{**}(v)}^2 - V_{Y_n^{**}(v)}^2 > 0$ for *all* values of n.

Finally, consider an interesting point. What could be said about the $V_{Y_n^{**}(v)}^2$ profile in the event that individuals do not differ in their human capital accumulation abilities a_1^j and b_0^j (so that: $V_{A_n^{**}}^2 = 0 \forall n$)? In contrast to the above (cf. Section 3.2.1), the earnings inequality within age groups is now *not* necessarily a strictly monotonically increasing function of n, since:[45]

$$V_{Y_n^{**}(v)}^2\Big|_{V_{A_n^{**}}^2=0} \simeq V_{B_n}^2 + V_{C_n}^2, \quad n = 0, \ldots, N;$$

and:

$$V_{Y_{n+1}^{**}(v)}^2 - V_{Y_n^{**}(v)}^2 = \underbrace{V_{B_{n+1}}^2 - V_{B_n}^2}_{<0[(70)]} + \underbrace{V_{C_{n+1}}^2 - V_{C_n}^2}_{>0[(65)]}; \; n=0,\ldots,N-1.$$

Even if the individuals, apart from their signalisation capability $1/\tilde{v}$, are identical, the present model generates a trend towards a U-shape in the age profile of the inequality of disposable earnings within age groups by way of a combination of the phenomena of 'learning by observing' (Section 2.3.5) and 'random walk' (Section 1.3).

This trend is, of course, all the more clearly defined, the more clearly the $V_{B_n}^2$ decrease dominates the $V_{C_n}^2$ increase within the younger age groups (see the conditions). The fact that, in the end, i.e. for sufficiently large values of n, the $V_{C_n}^2$ increase gains the upper hand, can be recognised from:

$$\lim_{n\to\infty} (V_{B_{n+1}}^2 - V_{B_n}^2) = 0, \quad \text{but} \quad \lim_{n\to\infty} (V_{C_{n+1}}^2 - V_{C_n}^2) = \infty.$$

3.4 Effects of public pricing policies: a comparative dynamic analysis of inequality

What effect would an increase in the human capital price R (thus an increase in the wage rate, or a fall in wage income tax, if you like) have on the inequalities within age groups? Would that have any effect at all? If it did, is this effect uniform or are different age groups affected in different ways by one and the same measure?

Assuming that the state subsidised the acquisition of human capital in the earnings phase, but not in the full-time schooling phase ($\hat{=}$ fall in the price of educational goods, P), what would the predicted effect on the earnings distribution between age groups look like? What would follow for

[45] This approximation is due to Goodman (1960, p. 709).

the opposite case ($\hat{=}$ (indirectly) increase in the price of educational goods, P)? If we take the case of the public sector (or the central bank) inducing an increase in the interest rate by way of some monetary policy measures, how would the inequality structure of the distribution within age groups react on the basis of the present model? Relevant questions of this type affecting the distribution will be answered in what follows within the context of an explicit comparative dynamic inequality analysis.

One can exploit the split (54) to obtain:

$$\frac{\partial V^2_{A_n^{**}}}{\partial x} = \frac{\partial V^2_{A_n^{**}}}{\partial \alpha_n} \frac{\partial \alpha_n}{\partial x}; \quad x \in \{R, P, r\}.$$

Furthermore, the following can be obtained in line with $(1 >)\ \rho_{a_1 b} > 0$, $h_0 > 1$ and $\mu_{A_n^{**}} > 0$, $n = 0, \ldots, N$ (I will go into the special case of a negative disposable average income in more detail below):

$$\frac{\partial V^2_{A_n^{**}}}{\partial \alpha_n} \gtreqless 0 \overset{(67)}{\Leftrightarrow} \alpha_n \gtreqless \xi \Leftrightarrow \frac{w_{2n}}{w_{1n}} \lesseqgtr \chi;$$

where:

$$\chi := \frac{1 - h_0 \rho_{a_1 b}}{h_0 - \rho_{a_1 b}} \frac{\sigma_{a_1}}{\sigma_b}.$$

And:

$$\frac{\partial \alpha_n}{\partial x} \gtreqless 0 \Leftrightarrow \frac{\partial w_{1n}}{\partial x} w_{2n} \gtreqless w_{1n} \frac{\partial w_{2n}}{\partial x}.$$

The following conditions are thereby finally obtained in consideration of (56):

$$\frac{\partial V^2_{Y_n^{**}}}{\partial R} > 0 \Leftrightarrow \frac{\partial w_{2n}/\partial R}{\partial w_{1n}/\partial R} \lessgtr \frac{w_{2n}}{w_{1n}} \lessgtr \chi, \quad n = 0, \ldots, N; \tag{72}$$

in all other cases $\partial V^2_{Y_n^{**}}/\partial R \leqslant 0$.

$$\frac{\partial V^2_{Y_n^{**}}}{\partial P} > 0 \Leftrightarrow \frac{\partial w_{2n}}{\partial P} \lessgtr 0 \text{ and simultaneously } \frac{w_{2n}}{w_{1n}} \lessgtr \chi; \quad n = 0, \ldots, N. \tag{73}$$

$$\frac{\partial V^2_{Y_n^{**}}}{\partial r} > 0 \Leftrightarrow \frac{w_{2n}}{w_{1n}} \lessgtr \frac{\partial w_{2n}/\partial r}{\partial w_{1n}/\partial r} \text{ and simultaneously } \frac{w_{2n}}{w_{1n}} \lessgtr \chi; \quad n = 0, \ldots, N. \tag{74}$$

Note: Note that $w_{1n} > 0$, $n = 0, \ldots, N$ and that:

$$\frac{\partial w_{1n}}{\partial R} = \frac{(1-\delta+c)^n}{\ln(1+r)} > 0, \quad n = 0, \ldots, N;$$

$$\frac{\partial w_{1n}}{\partial P} = 0, \quad n = 0, \ldots, N;$$

$$\frac{\partial w_{1n}}{\partial r} = -\frac{R(1-\delta+c)^n}{(1+r)[\ln(1+r)]^2} < 0, \quad n = 0, \ldots, N.$$

This set of conditions contains all the replies to the *fundamental question* of the present section, i.e. in what way the realised *ex post* inequality of disposable earnings within an age group n, $n = 0, \ldots, N$, is marked by variations in the instrumental parameters of the economic policymakers which are associated with the model, and thus by variations in the prices R, P or r.

Now, in order to obtain a more precise definition of the comparative dynamic inequality analysis based on (72), (73) and (74), some preliminary analytical work is required, the details of which have been placed in Appendix 4. There you will find, firstly, an analysis of the characteristics of the distributional constant χ and also examinations of the age profiles of the quotients w_{2n}/w_{1n} and $(\partial w_{2n}/\partial x)/(\partial w_{1n}/\partial x)$, $x \in \{R, r\}$, and of the age profile of $\partial w_{2n}/\partial P$. An explicit analytical treatment of these patterns (and thereby also on explicit analytical processing of (72), (73) and (74)) requires a return to the simplified formulations $\underline{w}_{1n}$ and $\underline{w}_{2n}$ (cf. (39)) developed in Section 2.3.1 for a sufficiently large earnings life span N. With the aid of this, a precise derivation of the age profiles is possible.

Equipped with the results from Appendix 4 an *explicit* comparative dynamic inequality analysis can then be carried out. First of all, a brief explanation of what this type of analysis means is included. The comparative dynamic analysis of the optimum $\underline{A}_n^{j**}$ path carried out in Sections 2.3.3 and 2.3.4 provides a solution to the problem of how the optimum programme would change as a result of a (marginal) parameter variation. This examination carried out with regard to all model parameters not only produced results on how the dynamic maximising behaviour of the individual j (characterised by a_1^j and b_0^j), and the optimum trajectory of disposable earnings resulting from this, shift with parameter variations, but it also revealed that individuals with *different* human capital accumulation abilities react in *different* ways to those variations. This immediately poses the question of which inequality effects arise from such variations in the parameters, which are at the disposal of the state in the present model as instruments which can influence the individual income streams, i.e. arise by way of variations in R, P or r. The effect of a variation in these public policy parameters on the inequalities in disposable earnings within age groups is dependent, firstly, on how the single individuals j adapt their optimal plans $\{\underline{A}_n^{j**}\}_{n=0}^{N}$ to the altered conditions and, secondly, on the characteristics of the individuals themselves – thus the characteristics of the production efficiency distributions $\tilde{a}_1$ and $\tilde{b}_0$ (or $\tilde{b}$). This *interdependence* makes a comparative dynamic inequality analysis explicit by way of the evaluation of the relationships in (72), (73) and (74).

With the results of Appendix 4 one has:

$$\frac{\partial V_{\underline{Y}_n^{**}}^2}{\partial R} > 0 \Leftrightarrow \frac{1-b_1}{a}\frac{\underline{w}_{2n}}{\underline{w}_{1n}} \lessgtr \frac{\underline{w}_{2n}}{\underline{w}_{1n}} \lessgtr \chi; \quad n = 0, \ldots, N. \tag{72a}$$

The trajectory shifts caused by a (marginal) human capital price increase therefore induce an increase in the realised *ex post* inequality within younger age groups; the relative distance between the individual income profiles increases in these groups, since, as long as $n < n_0$, it applies that:

$$\frac{1-b_1}{a}\frac{\underline{w}_{2n}}{\underline{w}_{1n}} < \frac{\underline{w}_{2n}}{\underline{w}_{1n}},$$

and $\underline{w}_{2n}/\underline{w}_{1n}$ initially lies below χ (cf. also Fig. 28).[46] If one assumes a negative value of χ (a perfectly feasible assumption, considering that $\rho_{a_1b} > 0$, $V_{b_0} > V_{a_1}$ (Section 3.2.2) and $V_b \gg V_{b_0}$ so that $h_0 \gg 1$; cf. Appendices 3 and 4) then there are reductions in inequality within the age groups n with $n_\chi < n < n_0$, before the inequalities within age group increase again for $n > n_0$.[47]

In the case of $\chi = 0$ (thus: $h_0\rho_{a_1b} = 1$), an increase in the human capital

[46] Note the theoretical parameter restrictions from Section 2.1.1. In accordance with this, $(1-b_1)/a > 1$ and $-\pi_w rq/R \ll -1$. Simultaneously, (cf. Appendix 4): $\chi > -k > -1$. It is theoretically plausible that the price ratio R/P is so small, that the price for one unit of goods and services purchased for the purposes of human capital accumulation, P, therefore so clearly exceeds the reward for the services from one unit of human capital R made available for one period, that the starting point of the $\underline{w}_{2n}/\underline{w}_{1n}$ path approaches -1 and under certain circumstances even becomes greater than -1 (because $\pi_w rq/R > 0$ it always remains negative, of course). In the case of a correspondingly small value of χ, $\underline{w}_{2n}/\underline{w}_{1n}$ could lie above χ from the very beginning; in accordance with (72a), this would mean a reduction in inequality within all $n < n_0$ age groups, no change for $n = n_0$ (this is a hypothetical provisional case, since n_0 will only coincidentally be a natural number) and an increase in inequality for all $n > n_0$. This unrealistic special case (that is, $-\pi_w rq/R > \chi$) will not be expanded any further.

[47] n_0 and n_χ are defined as follows:

$$\frac{\underline{w}_{2n_0}}{\underline{w}_{1n_0}} \equiv 0, \quad \frac{\underline{w}_{2n_\chi}}{\underline{w}_{1n_\chi}} \equiv \chi.$$

Note also that: $(1-b_1)\underline{w}_{2n}/a\underline{w}_{1n} > \underline{w}_{2n}/\underline{w}_{1n}\ \forall n > n_0$.

price leads to an increase in inequality within all age groups $n \neq n_0$. For a positive χ, the phase of the decrease in inequality occurs after n_0 and in fact between n_0 and n_χ (see (72a) and Fig. 28).

A summary of this produces the following:

$$\frac{\partial V^2_{Y^{**}_n}}{\partial R} \begin{cases} >0 \text{ for } 0 \leqslant n < \min(n_0, n_\chi), \text{ and for } n > \max(n_0, n_\chi); \\ <0 \text{ for } \min(n_0, n_\chi) < n < \max(n_0, n_\chi). \end{cases} \tag{75}$$

Note: Purely in theoretical terms, one could present the following additional case:

$$\frac{\partial V^2_{Y^{**}_n}}{\partial R} = 0 \quad \text{for } n = n_0 \text{ and } n = n_\chi.$$

However, it must be noted here that while the working age n is a natural number, in line with the assumption, n_0 and n_χ are not restricted to this range of numbers (cf. the definitions in footnote 47). Strictly speaking, the formulation $n = n_0$ or $n = n_\chi$ is, therefore, inadmissible as it is only coincidental that $n_0, n_\chi \in \mathbf{N}$. If this is, in fact, the case, then the statement that there are no changes of any kind in the inequality within the n_0 and n_χ age groups is correct. I shall not, however, be going into this special case furthermore.

An *increase* in the price R therefore results in *increases in inequality* within age groups, apart from the relatively short interim period $\min(n_0, n_\chi) <$ n $< \max(n_0, n_\chi)$. The duration of this interim period becomes *longer* (for a given χ), the *flatter* the w_{2n}/w_{1n} path in the vicinity of n_0 (see Fig. 28). It is, for example possible, to find out by way of partial differentiation of the rate of increase derived in Appendix 4[48] that, *ceteris paribus*, the length of this phase increases where there is a falling price ratio R/P[49] and a falling rate of interest r. Furthermore, it can be established that this phase is comparatively longer within economies with lower production elasticities b_1 and b_2 (therefore, for example, with minimal 'technical knowledge' of the human capital accumulation methods) and with greater learning-by-doing opportunities c;[50] thus, the number of those age groups, within which the

[48] This is expressed as follows ($c \neq \delta$):

$$\frac{w_{2n+1}}{w_{1n+1}} - \frac{w_{2n}}{w_{1n}} = \frac{b_1^{b_1/a}\left(\frac{R}{P}b_2 q\right)^{\frac{b_2}{a}}(r+\delta)^{\frac{b_2-1}{a}}(r+\delta a + c b_2 r q)r}{(1-\delta+c)^{n+1}}; \; n = 0, \ldots, N-1.$$

[49] This would require a simultaneous and relatively sharper increase in P in the case in question of an increase in R.

[50] This effect requires a certain minimum level of n, but one which can still be reached before $\min(n_0, n_\chi)$ with the model assumptions.

inequality decreases, rises. On the other hand, the duration of the reduction in inequality for a *given* slope of the $\underline{w}_{2n}/\underline{w}_{1n}$ profile is increased, the nearer χ becomes to its *extreme values*. As has already been established, it disappears altogether when χ is zero. χ approximates its upper limit where both $\rho_{a_1b} = 0$ and there is a constantly falling value of h_0 (>1). χ reaches its lower limit, irrespective of the level of the coefficient of variation ratio h_0, where $\rho_{a_1b} = 1$; it is expressed thus: $-k := -\sigma_{a_1}/\sigma_b$ (see Appendix 4) and therefore, is defined by the ratio of the standard deviations for the distributions of the human capital production efficiency during the full-time schooling phase, $\tilde{a}_1$, and the modified human capital production efficiency during the working phase, $\tilde{b} = \tilde{b}_0^{1/a}$.

Note: The characteristics of the mixed partial derivative of the second order $\partial^2 \underline{A}_n^{j**}/\partial \hat{m}\, \partial R$, calculated within the framework of the comparative dynamic analysis of a simultaneous increase in a_1^j, b_0^j and R, provide an intuitive explanation for the fact that, in the case of $\rho_{a_1b} = 1$, there is a reduction in inequality within age groups just before n_0 (to be more exact: for all values of n where $n_{-k} < n < n_0$). These characteristics imply that the turning point of this derivative is after $n_{0,R}$ but before $n_{0,p}$ (which corresponds to the n_0 in question); the positive effect of an increase in R (i.e. $\partial \underline{A}_n^{j**}/\partial R > 0$) present in this interim period is thus weakened for higher values of $\hat{m}$ ($\hat{=}$ a higher a_1^j and a higher b_0^j) or strengthened in a similar way for lower values of $\hat{m}$.

The interim phase just analysed and demarcated by n_{-k} and n_k occurs in the vicinity of n_0, an age which can be defined exactly: $n_0 = (\log rq)/\log(1 - \delta + c)$. The age groups falling into this phase, which is entered into, according to the standard parameter set (19), after approximately the first third of working life, are therefore younger, *ceteris paribus*, the smaller the rate of interest r, the greater the rate of human capital depreciation δ and the smaller the learning-by-doing efficiency c within the economy observed.[51] Finally, it can be established from the results of Appendix 4 that this interim period occurs at an earlier stage, the higher the correlation coefficient ρ_{a_1b} and the higher the coefficient of variation ratio h_0 (as with both cases, χ approaches $-k$).

Now to the effects of variation in the price of educational goods, P. With the results from Appendix 4, it follows that:

$$\frac{\partial V^2_{\underline{Y}_n^{**}}}{\partial P} > 0 \Leftrightarrow \frac{-b_2}{aP}\underline{w}_{2n} \lesseqgtr 0 \quad \text{and simultaneously} \quad \frac{\underline{w}_{2n}}{\underline{w}_{1n}} \lesseqgtr \chi; \qquad n = 0, \ldots, N. \quad (73a)$$

[51] These statements are obtained by way of partial differentiation of the n_0 equation with consideration of the theoretical parameter restrictions $r > 0$, $c > 0$, $0 < \delta < 1$ and $r + \delta > c$.

An analysis carried out in a similar way to (72a) provides the following result:

$$\frac{\partial V^2_{\underline{Y}_n^{**}}}{\partial P} \begin{cases} <0 \text{ for } 0 \leqslant n < \min(n_0, n_\chi), \text{ and for } n > \max(n_0, n_\chi); \\ >0 \text{ for } \min(n_0, n_\chi) < n < \max(n_0, n_\chi). \end{cases} \tag{76}$$

It is immediately clear that the structure of the P effect is exactly opposite to that of the R effect.

The reactions of the optimising individuals on a (marginal) *increase* in the price of educational goods P, thus leads to a *reduction* in the age group inequalities, apart from the intermediate period $\min(n_0, n_\chi) < n < \max(n_0, n_\chi)$. The direction and length of the effects of decreasing and increasing are obtained here explicitly from the model and distribution parameters as well.

With an increase in P, the number of age groups affected by an *increase* in inequality is, for example, *ceteris paribus*, all the greater, the nearer χ comes to its limits (as in the case mentioned above, the number of age groups included in the intermediate phase shrinks completely, in the event that $\chi = 0$ $(\rightarrow n_\chi = n_0)$), the smaller the price ratio R/P, the smaller the rate of interest r, the smaller the 'technical knowledge' of human capital production processes embodied in the elasticities b_1 and b_2, the smaller the human capital depreciation rate δ, and the greater the opportunities for experience c.[52] The notes on the beginning of the intermediate phase above (p. 122) also apply here.

Last but not least, to reply to the question posed at the beginning of this section; if the state *subsidised* the acquisition of human capital in the *earnings phase*, but not, however, in the full-time schooling phase (i.e. it introduced measures, which would result in the reduction of the price of educational goods, P), then this would induce an *increase* in the inequalities of disposable earnings within age groups, apart from the intermediate period mentioned.

Variations in the interest rate affect inequalities within age groups as follows. Here the results from Appendix 4 result in the following interaction:

$$\frac{\partial V^2_{\underline{Y}_n^{**}}}{\partial r} > 0 \Leftrightarrow \frac{\underline{w}_{2n}}{\underline{w}_{1n}} \lessgtr \chi$$

[52] The two effects mentioned last are dependent on the working age n. What was said in footnote 50, p. 121 applies here as well.

$$\text{and simultaneously} \begin{cases} \dfrac{\underline{w}_{2n}}{\underline{w}_{1n}} \lesseqgtr \dfrac{\underline{w}_{2n}}{\underline{w}_{1n}} \beta_n, & n \neq n_0; \\ \dfrac{\underline{w}_{2n_0}}{\underline{w}_{1n_0}} \lesseqgtr -\dfrac{\pi_w r q^2}{\underline{w}_{1n_0}}, & n = n_0; \end{cases}$$

$$n = 0, \ldots, N. \quad \text{(74a)}$$

On evaluation of the characteristics of the function β_n obtained in Appendix 4, the following is found:

$$\frac{\partial V^2_{\underline{Y}^{**}_n}}{\partial r}(\delta > c) \begin{cases} <0 & \text{for } 0 \leqslant n < n_\chi; \\ >0 & \text{for } n > n_\chi. \end{cases} \quad (77)$$

Notes: (i)

$$\frac{\partial V^2_{\underline{Y}^{**}_n}}{\partial r}(c > \delta) \begin{cases} <0 & \text{for } 0 \leqslant n < n_\chi, \quad \text{and for } n > \hat{n}; \\ >0 & \text{for } n_\chi < n < \hat{n}. \end{cases}$$

$\hat{n}$ is defined by $\beta_{\hat{n}} \equiv 1$.

(ii) For the special case $c = \delta$ the structure of the case $c > \delta$ results if $\pi_{\beta, c=\delta} > 1$ (which requires a sufficiently large ratio r/c; see Appendix 4); otherwise the one from the case $\delta > c$ results.

The comparative dynamic inequality analysis of variations in r is more complicated than that of variations in R or P. The discounting function derived from the rate of interest within the framework of the life-cycle model developed in Chapter 2, is more complex than that for the prices R and P. One is forced to make distinctions from case to case. The structures of the two cases $\delta > c$ and $c > \delta$ ($c = \delta$ can be attached to one of these two cases) only deviate from one another in one final phase beginning with n where n is very high: $n > \hat{n}$; as a reaction to an increase in the rate of interest, the relative distance between the individual trajectories widens in the case $\delta > c$ for all n from n_χ, and it becomes smaller in the case of $c > \delta$ from $\hat{n}$ ($> n_\chi$) again.[53]

Note: It must be stressed once again at this point that, with the empirical results of Carliner (1982), one must assume $\delta > c$; the case where $c > \delta$, i.e. that of an overcompensation of the human capital depreciation rate by the learning-by-doing efficiency, cannot be empirically substantiated and is consequently purely of theoretical interest.

[53] Incidentally for $\hat{n}$ one finds:

$$\hat{n} \overset{(c>\delta)}{=} n_0 + \log\left[\frac{q(\delta - c)}{1 - \pi_\beta} + 1\right] \Big/ \log(1 - \delta + c).$$

The nearer π_β (>1) comes to one, the larger $\hat{n}$ becomes. See also Appendix 4, in particular Fig. 29.

Apart from the different inequality effects from $\hat{n}$, the relative variation in earnings within the younger age groups ($n < n_\chi$) decreases in both cases with a rise in the interest rate; from n_χ on, however, the shifts in the optimal earnings profiles caused by an increase in r result in an increased inequality within age groups. The reader should again refer to Sections 2.3.3 and 2.3.4 concerning the economic motives behind these path modifications. The said reversal occurs, *ceteris paribus*, all the earlier, the smaller the distribution factor χ – thus, the larger the correlation coefficient $\rho_{a_1 b}$ and the greater the coefficient of variation ratio h_0. Furthermore, the number of age groups, within which an increase in the rate of interest results in a reduction in inequality of disposable earnings, is smaller for a negative (positive) χ, *ceteris paribus*, the smaller (greater) the price ratio R/P is and the smaller (greater) the human capital production elasticities b_1 and b_2 are.[54]

All in all, it has been established that the effects of the policy measures occurring by way of R, P and r are quite complex and *anything but uniform*. If, for the purposes of combating inequality of disposable earnings, there was an obvious opportunity to reduce the reward R, lower the rate of interest r and increase the input price P, then, in the face of the complicated time patterns of these effects, no general prognosis concerning the *overall* distribution over all individuals is possible (since all age groups are affected by the measures) without knowledge of the age structure within the economy observed and, therefore, without knowledge of the relative weights of the age groups. This is considered further later (Chapter 4). The *interaction* between the instruments for combating inequality and the other model parameters is not the same for all policy instruments either. Just to give an example: while the reductions in equality effected by a decrease in R or a rise in P were reinforced, *ceteris paribus*, by higher production elasticities b_1 and b_2, it would be exactly the opposite in the case of a decrease in r.[55]

Insights of this type would not have been possible *a priori*, given the complex interaction of the factors considered, without formalisation. Now, however, the *direction* and *length* of the changes in the inequalities within age groups caused by public policies are given, *explicitly* dependent on the model and distribution parameters.

In fact, with the preceding comparative dynamic inequality analysis of partial price variations, one of the *fundamental* aims of this study has been achieved at the first of the three distribution levels mentioned at the

[54] Cf. the slope measure in footnote 48, p. 121 and Fig. 28. n_0 remains unaffected by these variations. If $\chi = 0$, then these variations have no effect on the turning point.

[55] With the requirement of a negative χ (which is a more cautious assumption than '$\chi > 0$'). The statement refers to the number of age groups affected.

beginning of Section 3.1; namely, to demonstrate a *method* of analysing the effects of economic policy measures (here via R, P and r) on the inequality of earnings on the basis of a dynamic maximisation model embedded in a stochastic framework of the type developed in Chapter 2.

Notes: (i) It must be remembered that all statements from this section have been derived on the assumption of a sufficiently large working-life span N, as *analytical* results are only possible in this case. The qualitative agreement of all results obtained in this manner with the results obtained numerically for small values of N reveals however that greater generality results in analytical intractabilities but not in deeper insights. The assumption of a sufficiently large N has proved useful for the derivation of handy expressions; it is, however, not responsible, as such, for the results obtained.

(ii) The special case of *negative* disposable average earnings within younger age groups produces a *change in the initial phase* in the results summarised in (75), (76) and (77). The policy analysis here must be carried out with the aid of α_n and ξ, as the current relationship: $\alpha_n \gtreqless \xi \Leftrightarrow w_{2n}/w_{1n} \lesseqgtr \chi$ in the case of a 'negative start' (thus: $\mu_{A_n^{**}} < 0, n = 0, 1, \ldots$) is no longer valid.[56] According to the changed α_n profile (cf. footnote 39, p. 114 and Figs. 25a and b), the following initial-phase modifications are produced:

- The effects summarised in (75) for the (marginal) variation in R are upheld, apart from a brief initial phase; there (to be more precise, where $0 \leqslant n < n'$)[57], an increase in the reward R now results in a reduction in the inequalities within age groups.
- The P effects, which are otherwise unchanged (cf. (76)), now require an initial phase ($0 \leqslant n < n'$) in which a rise in the price of educational goods P results in an increase in the inequalities within age groups.
- The same applies for the effects caused by an increase in the rate of interest (cf. (77)); they now induce an initial phase ($0 \leqslant n < n'$) with an increase in inequality (and this is incidentally irrespective of the δ/c ratio).

(iii) Assuming that the dependence between the human capital accumulation ability in the full-time schooling phase and the human capital accumulation ability in the earnings phase (cf. also Section 3.2.2) were to

[56] ξ can be derived from the following: $\xi = 1/(1 + \chi/kh_0)$.

[57] As a reminder, n' is implicitly defined by $\mu_{A_n^{**}} \equiv 0$. The following inequality applies: $n' < \min(n_0, n_\chi)$.

For: $n' < \min(n_0, n_\chi) \Leftrightarrow -\mu_{a_1}/\mu_b < \min(0, \chi)$, since $\underline{w}_{2n'}/\underline{w}_{1n'} = -\mu_{a_1}/\mu_b$. Now $-\mu_{a_1}/\mu_b < 0$, is, of course, always true as $\mu_{a_1} > 0$ and $\mu_b > 0$; on the other hand, with $h_0 > 1$ and $0 < \rho_{a_1 b} < 1$; $-\mu_{a_1}/\mu_b < \chi$ is also fulfilled (this is seen directly when χ is expressed in the form

$$\chi = \underbrace{\frac{1/h_0 - \rho_{a_1 b}}{h_0 - \rho_{a_1 b}}}_{>-1} \frac{\mu_{a_1}}{\mu_b}\Big).$$

be defined in a concrete sense, in such a way that $\log \tilde{a}_1$ and $\log \tilde{b}_0$ were perfectly positively correlated, i.e. $\rho_{\log \tilde{a}_1, \log \tilde{b}_0} = 1$, then it is known that (with probability one) there would be a linear dependency between the two variables, or a constant elasticity function $\tilde{a}_1 = c_2 \tilde{b}_0^{1/a}$ (with $c_2 > 0$, $a > 0$) between $\tilde{a}_1$ and $\tilde{b}_0$, respectively. a $(= 1 - b_1 - b_2)$ can thus be written in the following form: $a = (d\tilde{b}_0/d\tilde{a}_1)(\tilde{a}_1/\tilde{b}_0)$, i.e. a would be the (constant) elasticity of $\tilde{b}_0$ with respect to $\tilde{a}_1$.

In this not particularly realistic but theoretically interesting case of constant elasticity, one has: $\tilde{A}_n^{**} = \tilde{b}_0^{1/a}(c_2 w_{1n} + w_{2n})$ so that, instead of (53), the following is obtained for the inequality of disposable earnings within age groups:

$$V_{Y_n^{**}}^2 = (1 + \sigma_e^2)^n V_{b_0^{1/a}}^2 + V_{C_n}^2; \quad n = 0, \ldots, N. \tag{53a}$$

None of the price instruments R, P or r now appears here. Thus, if the proportional directional change in the two variables $\tilde{a}_1$ and $\tilde{b}_0$ is the same, the economic policymaker would have the opportunity of only indirectly influencing the inequality of the accumulation abilities in the earnings phase and the elasticity a (the uncertainty in income σ_e^2 is, of course, removed completely from the sphere of influence of the state). This control is weak compared with control of R, P and r to influence the inequality, measured by $V_{Y_n^{**}}^2$, of disposable earnings within an age group n.

Incidentally, one can see immediately from (53a), in combination with (65), that, in the case of constant elasticity, the realised *ex post* inequality $V_{Y_n^{**}}^2$ is a strictly monotonically increasing function of n (→ Section 3.3).

3.5 On the correlation between abilities and earnings

An interesting question, which can be answered from the model developed in this study, is that of the correlation between the human capital accumulation abilities and earnings, and its development over the life-cycle. There is, in fact, a whole series of *empirical* studies on this question (wherein, of course, the theoretical human capital accumulation abilities $\tilde{a}_1$ and $\tilde{b}$ defined in this study do not appear as such, although partial aspects of these variables which can be measured, do occur in the empirical regression equations). However the remaining picture is not altogether clear, as the available empirical observations are *unrelated*: they always refer to certain variables and certain sections of the life-cycle, so that comparisons and theoretical explanations are made difficult. It has, for example, been established that, in early phases of the earnings life, the effect of learning ability on earnings is minimal; in later phases, on the other hand, under certain circumstances, it is considerable.[58] Furthermore, it has

[58] Cf. Conlisk (1971), Hause (1972), Griliches and Mason (1972), Bowles and Nelson (1974), Taubman and Wales (1974), Lillard (1977a) and Willis and Rosen (1979). The indicator of learning ability normally used in empirical examinations is incidentally the *measured IQ*.

been discovered that the correlation between schooling quality and earnings is not constant over the working life, but increases with working age.[59] Hause (1980, p. 1014) writes in connection with empirical results of this type: 'There seems to be no systematic attempt to develop and extend these sorts of findings within the framework of a consistent theoretical model. It may be that the increasing availability of panel data extending over significant intervals of time will encourage such a development.' The model developed in the present study represents a *first theoretical step* in this direction. It provides a framework which allows for a uniform economic interpretation of these scattered empirical observations.

On the basis of (51), the following is obtained for the correlation coefficient between *full-time schooling* human capital production efficiency and disposable earnings in the working period n;[60]

$$\rho_{a_1 Y_n^{**}} := \frac{\operatorname{cov}(\tilde{a}_1, \tilde{Y}_n^{**})}{\sigma_{n_1}\sigma_{Y_n^{**}}} = \frac{w_{1n}\sigma_{a_1}^2 + w_{2n}\operatorname{cov}(\tilde{a}_1, \tilde{b})}{\sigma_{a_1}\sigma_{Y_n^{**}}};$$

$$n = 0, \ldots, N. \qquad (78)$$

Prior to an analysis of the age profile of this correlation, a few static characteristics will be briefly mentioned.

Firstly one finds:[61] $|\rho_{a_1 Y_n^{**}}| < |\rho_{a_1 A_n^{**}}|\ \forall n \geqslant 1$. Because of the random walk process (cf. Section 1.3.1) occurring from $n = 1$, the absolute value of the correlation coefficient between the full-time schooling efficiency and disposable earnings from $n = 1$ is always *below* the absolute value of the correlation coefficient between the full-time schooling efficiency and *planned* disposable earnings; a result which was expected.

In addition, after several algebraic transformations, the following is obtained:

$$\rho_{a_1 Y_n^{**}}^2 = \frac{\sigma_{A_n^{**}}^2}{\sigma_{Y_n^{**}}^2}\left[1 - \frac{w_{2n}^2\sigma_b^2}{\sigma_{A_n^{**}}^2}(1 - \rho_{a_1 b}^2)\right]. \qquad (79)$$

It is clear from this, that the squared correlation coefficient between $\tilde{a}_1$ and $\tilde{Y}_n^{**}$ is exactly equivalent to the share of the variance of planned disposable earnings over the variance of realised disposable earnings within age group n, if the human capital accumulation abilities in the full-time schooling

[59] Cf. Solmon (1975) and Wachtel (1975).

[60] Here the (stochastic) independence of $\tilde{A}_n^{**}$ and $\tilde{C}_n$ (or $\tilde{a}_1$ and $\tilde{C}_n$ and $\tilde{b}_0$ (or $\tilde{b}$) and $\tilde{C}_n$) must be noted again. It must also be remembered: $\tilde{e}_i \sim \text{iid}(0, \sigma_e^2)$, which implies $E(\tilde{C}_n) = 1$.

[61] With $\operatorname{cov}(\tilde{a}_1, \tilde{Y}_n^{**}) = \operatorname{cov}(\tilde{a}_1, \tilde{A}_n^{**})$ (cf. conditions in footnote 60) it follows that: $\rho_{a_1 Y_n^{**}} = \rho_{a_1 A_n^{**}}\sigma_{A_n^{**}}/\sigma_{Y_n^{**}}\ \forall n$. Now: $\sigma_{Y_n^{**}} = (\sigma_{A_n^{**}}^2 + \mu_{A_n^{**}}^2\sigma_{C_n}^2 + \sigma_{A_n^{**}}^2\sigma_{C_n}^2)^{1/2}$, and $\sigma_{C_n}^2 = (1 + \sigma_e^2)^n - 1 > 0\ \forall n \geqslant 1$, thus: $(0<)\,\sigma_{A_n^{**}} < \sigma_{Y_n^{**}}\ \forall n \geqslant 1$.

phase and the earnings phase are perfectly correlated. The same result follows for the case where individuals are not differentiated in their abilities to increase productivity in the earnings phase (i.e. for the case where $\sigma_b^2 = 0$).

Consider again the question of the life-cycle development of the correlation between $\tilde{a}_1$ and $\tilde{Y}_n^{**}$. Firstly, it must be explicitly emphasised that the present model does actually generate an *age-dependent* correlation between abilities and earnings, in contrast to the standard human capital approaches.[62] The following is obtained from (78):

$$\rho_{a_1 Y_n^{**}} \gtrless 0 \Leftrightarrow -\frac{k}{\rho_{a_1 b}} \lessgtr \frac{w_{2n}}{w_{1n}}, \quad n = 0, \ldots, N. \tag{80}$$

According to this, the correlation is in general negative as a result of the dynamic maximising behaviour of the individual at the beginning of working life, but positive from an age prior to n_0.[63] In that initial phase, $\rho_{a_1 Y_n^{**}}$ therefore must in the end have *increased*. (80) still provides no explanation of the precise age profile of the correlation. The only aspect which can be recognised from (80) is that the correlation coefficient $\rho_{a_1 Y_n^{**}}$ stays positive after it has become positive for the first time.[64]

With the aid of the coefficient expressions $\underline{w}_{1n}$ and $\underline{w}_{2n}$ developed in Section 2.3.1 for a sufficiently long working lifespan N, one can obtain the following for the covariance of the ability to increase productivity in the basic education phase and disposable earnings (note (78) and Appendix 4):

$$\operatorname{cov}(\tilde{a}_1, \underline{\tilde{Y}}_{n+1}^{**}) - \operatorname{cov}(\tilde{a}_1, \underline{\tilde{Y}}_n^{**}) \gtreqless 0 \Leftrightarrow \frac{\rho_{a_1 b}}{k} \gtreqless \frac{\delta - c}{r}\frac{R}{\pi_w}; \quad n = 0, \ldots, N-1. \tag{81}$$

This covariance, in the hypothetical case of an overcompensation of the human capital depreciation rate by the learning-by-doing efficiency (i.e. $c > \delta$) is seen to be a *strictly monotonically increasing* function of working age n.[65] The same applies for $\delta = c$. On the other hand, if the rate of depreciation δ exceeds the learning-by-doing efficiency c (this is the case which can be empirically substantiated), then it depends on the relative values of the parameters occurring in the above condition, how the covariance develops over the working life.

62 Cf. Mincer (1974, 1979), Becker (1975) and Rosen (1973).

63 Note the explanations on $\rho_{a_1 b}$ (>0), $k(>0)$ and w_{2n}/w_{1n} in parts of the two previous sections and in Appendixes 3 and 4. The only point where $\rho_{a_1 Y_n^{**}}$ is not negative at the beginning of the earnings life, is if the correlation between $\tilde{a}_1$ and $\tilde{b}$ is unrealistically weak (in fact $\rho_{a_1 Y_n^{**}}$ for $\rho_{a_1 b} = 0$ would be positive from the very beginning).

64 Since: $k = 0$, $\rho_{a_1 b} > 0$ and $\underline{w}_{2n}/\underline{w}_{1n} > 0 \, \forall n > n_0$.

65 As a reminder: $\rho_{a_1 b}, k, R, r, \pi_w > 0$.

Note: The empiricists have the last word again of course. On the basis of the theoretical distribution constellation of Appendix 3 and on the basis of the parameter restrictions formulated theoretically and empirically in Section 2.1.1, the model in question, however, *also* forecasts a monotonic increase in the covariance of full-time schooling efficiency and disposable earnings for the case where $\delta > c$.[66]

In the light of the previous results, the reader should note both Fig. 18, and the economic discussion on this in Section 2.3.4, and the empirical findings quoted at the beginning (since the individual learning ability is a component of the a_1 specification; cf. (35)).

These covariance characteristics cannot be assigned directly to the *normalised* covariance, the correlation coefficient (78), since $\sigma_{Y_n^{**}}$ is age-dependent. In fact, no precisely defined predictions can be made for the age profile of $\rho_{a_1 Y_n^{**}}$ (more on this later); however, this is possible for the age profile of the correlation between full-time schooling efficiency and *planned* disposable earnings, $\rho_{a_1 A_n^{**}}$, which is why this profile should be observed first of all. With $\rho_{a_1 Y_n^{**}} = \rho_{a_1 A_n^{**}} \sigma_{A_n^{**}} / \sigma_{Y_n^{**}}$ (see footnote 61, p. 128) and $\sigma_{A_n^{**}}, \sigma_{Y_n^{**}} > 0$ the results derived from (80) are also applicable to $\rho_{a_1 A_n^{**}}$, i.e. $\rho_{a_1 A_n^{**}}$ rises at the beginning of earnings life, becomes positive (incidentally, even before n_0) and then remains positive. So how does the correlation coefficient of the ability to increase productivity in the full-time schooling period and the planned disposable earnings change in that phase of life beginning at n_0 at the very latest? As $\rho_{a_1 A_n^{**}}$ is always positive there, one can examine $\rho^2_{a_1 A_n^{**}}$ instead of $\rho_{a_1 A_n^{**}}$ to reply to this question (which is simpler from a technical point of view) and one has:

$$\rho^2_{a_1 \underline{A}_{n+1}^{**}} - \rho^2_{a_1 \underline{A}_n^{**}} < 0 \quad \forall n > n_0;^{67} \tag{82}$$

i.e. from n_0 the correlation in question falls again (and, incidentally, irrespective of whether $c \geqslant \delta$ or $\delta > c$). This bell-shaped correlation profile

[66] Under the requirements given, $\text{cov}(\tilde{a}_1, \tilde{b}) > \sigma^2_{a_1}$ and consequently $\rho_{a_1 b}/k > 1$; then, simultaneously, the following applies: $R(\delta - c)/r\pi_w < 0.1$.

Incidentally, if the human capital accumulation abilities in the full-time education phase and earnings phase were uncorrelated (an unrealistic, purely hypothetical case), then the result with $\delta > c$ would be a monotonic decrease in the covariance, $\text{cov}(\tilde{a}_1, \underline{Y}_n^{**})$, over the life-cycle.

[67] The expression in square brackets in (79) corresponds exactly to $\rho^2_{a_1 A_n^{**}}$. For the term occurring there which is dependent on n:

$$\frac{w_{2n}^2 \sigma_b^2}{\sigma^2_{A_n^{**}}} = \frac{1}{1 + \dfrac{w_{1n}}{w_{2n}} k \left(\dfrac{w_{1n}}{w_{2n}} k + 2\rho_{a_1 b} \right)}.$$

As the coefficient quotient $\underline{w}_{1n}/\underline{w}_{2n}$, irrespective of the ratio δ/c, is a strictly monotonically decreasing function of $n (n > n_0)$ (cf. Appendix 4), (and as $k > 0$, $0 < \rho_{a_1 b} < 1$ and $\underline{w}_{1n}, \underline{w}_{2n} > 0 \, \forall n > n_0$) (82) follows.

stands in complete contrast to the covariance progression obtained above;[68] hence the monotonicity of the sequence $\{\operatorname{cov}(\tilde{a}_1, \underline{\tilde{A}}_n^{**})\}_{n=0}^{N}$, which is implied by the age-independency of condition (81), does not carry over to the $\rho_{a_1\underline{A}_n^{**}}$ path.

> *Note*: This result has no economic significance as such. It is chiefly directed at statisticians and/or econometricians and tries to warn against conclusions falsely drawn from empirical findings. For the latter, as can be seen, depend on the measure which we have used to evaluate the interdependence of $\tilde{a}_1$ and $\tilde{A}_n^{**}$. Although the underlying economic mechanism is *the same* in each case, *different* measures can promote the occurrence of *different* profile results.[69]

A single precisely defined general result of the type given in (82) cannot be set up for the age profile of the correlation coefficient $\rho_{a_1Y_n^{**}}$. A sufficient condition for $\rho^2_{a_1Y_n^{**}}$ also having the path characteristic of (82), is for example:[70]

$$\frac{\sigma_e^2}{1-(1+\sigma_e^2)^{-n}} > \frac{V^2_{\underline{A}_{n+1}^{**}} - V^2_{\underline{A}_n^{**}}}{V^2_{\underline{A}_n^{**}}(1+V^2_{\underline{A}_{n+1}^{**}})} \quad \forall n > n_0.$$

But whether the variance of the stochastic shocks caused by the transitory income change factors, σ_e^2, is sufficient to satisfy this requirement is still open to debate in theoretical terms.

The correlation between the (modified) human capital production efficiency in the *earnings phase* and disposable earnings is analysed in exactly the same way. The following results are obtained:

$$\rho_{bY_n^{**}} := \frac{\operatorname{cov}(\tilde{b}, \tilde{Y}_n^{**})}{\sigma_b \sigma_{Y_n^{**}}} = \frac{w_{2n}\sigma_b^2 + w_{1n}\operatorname{cov}(\tilde{a}_1, \tilde{b})}{\sigma_b \sigma_{Y_n^{**}}}; \quad n = 0, \ldots, N. \tag{83}$$

[68] (81) applies similarly for the covariance of the full-time schooling efficiency and *planned* disposable earnings, as $\operatorname{cov}(\tilde{a}_1, \underline{\tilde{Y}}_n^{**}) = \operatorname{cov}(\tilde{a}_1, \underline{\tilde{A}}_n^{**})$, $n = 0, \ldots, N$ (note footnote 60, p. 128).

[69] The measure indicated for comparison purposes is then, of course, the correlation coefficient, as this is independent of the units of measurement of the variables in question.

[70] This condition can be derived by a series of algebraic transformations with the aid of (79) and (82). It is independent of whether N is very large or not (instead of $V^2_{\underline{A}_n^{**}}$ it could also be written as $V^2_{A_n^{**}}$); it is however more correct to use the '_' notation as n_0 explicitly refers to the context of a sufficiently long lifespace N (cf. Appendix 4).

Incidentally:

$$\frac{\sigma_e^2}{1-(1+\sigma_e^2)^{-n}} = \frac{V^2_{C_{n+1}} - V^2_{C_n}}{V^2_{C_n}}.$$

Here, the following also applies: $|\rho_{bY_n^{**}}| < |\rho_{bA_n^{**}}|\ \forall n \geqslant 1$. Furthermore, the following is obtained (with the same interpretations as above):

$$\rho^2_{bY_n^{**}} = \frac{\sigma^2_{A_n^{**}}}{\sigma^2_{Y_n^{**}}}\rho^2_{bA_n^{**}}, \tag{84}$$

with:

$$\rho^2_{bA_n^{**}} = 1 - \frac{w^2_{1n}\sigma^2_{a_1}}{\sigma^2_{A_n^{**}}}(1-\rho^2_{a_1b}).$$

The following is also obtained from (83) and (78):

$$\frac{\rho_{a_1Y_n^{**}}}{\rho_{bY_n^{**}}} = \frac{\rho_{a_1A_n^{**}}}{\rho_{bA_n^{**}}}, \quad n = 0,\dots,N; \tag{85}$$

i.e. the ratio of the correlation coefficients between human capital accumulation abilities and realised disposable earnings coincides with that between human capital accumulation abilities and planned disposable earnings.

As far as the life-cycle development of the correlation coefficient $\rho_{bY_n^{**}}$ is concerned, it must be stressed, first of all, that the model in question generates a correlation between the economic ability $\tilde{b}$ and the disposable earnings, which is, in fact, *age-dependent*:

$$\rho_{bY_n^{**}} \gtreqless 0 \Leftrightarrow -k\rho_{a_1b} \lesseqgtr \frac{w_{2n}}{w_{1n}}, \quad n = 0,\dots,N; \tag{86}$$

therefore, the correlation coefficient between $\tilde{b}$ and $\underline{\tilde{Y}}_n^{**}$ is (generally speaking) negative at the beginning of earnings life, but positive from n_0 at the latest.[71]

The same has applied for the correlation coefficient between full-time schooling efficiency and disposable earnings. Yet, there are differences between them. A direct comparison of the order of magnitude is possible (correlation coefficients are dimensionless numbers); in accordance with $0 < \rho_{a_1b} < 1$ the following is obtained from (78) and (83):

$$\rho_{a_1Y_n^{**}} \lesseqgtr \rho_{bY_n^{**}} \Leftrightarrow \frac{w_{2n}}{w_{1n}} \gtreqless k; \quad n = 0,\dots,N. \tag{87}$$

According to this, the correlation between the ability to increase productivity in the basic education phase and disposable earnings exceeds the correlation between the ability to increase productivity in the earnings

[71] The details of the time point n_0 are based on the coefficient expressions $\underline{w}_{1n}$ and $\underline{w}_{2n}$ (thus $\underline{\tilde{Y}}_n^{**}$ instead of $\tilde{Y}_n^{**}$). Note Appendix 4.

phase and disposable earnings within the younger age groups;[72] from n_k it behaves in completely the opposite manner: the correlation coefficient between $\tilde{b}$ and disposable earnings exceeds the correlation coefficient between $\tilde{a}_1$ and disposable earnings.

Furthermore, it will be shown that the age profiles of the correlations $\rho_{a_1 \underline{A}_n^{**}}$ and $\rho_{b\underline{A}_n^{**}}$ do not correspond to one another at the latest from n_0; whereas the former falls monotonically from n_0 (cf. (82)), the latter rises monotonically from n_0.

Firstly, however, the covariance relationship analogous to (81) must be provided:[73]

$$\operatorname{cov}(\tilde{b}, \underline{\tilde{Y}}_{n+1}^{**}) - \operatorname{cov}(\tilde{b}, \underline{\tilde{Y}}_n^{**}) \gtreqless 0 \Leftrightarrow \frac{1}{k\rho_{a_1 b}} \gtreqless \frac{\delta - c}{r} \frac{R}{\pi_w}; \qquad n = 0, \ldots, N-1. \quad (88)$$

From this, it can immediately be established that the covariance between the earnings phase production efficiency $\tilde{b}$ and disposable earnings in the case where $c \geqslant \delta$, is a *strictly monotonically increasing* function of working age. If one considers the theoretical and empirical parameter restrictions formulated in Section 2.1.1 as well as $0 < k, \rho_{a_1 b} < 1$, then this covariance path characteristic also applies for $\delta > c$.

Note: The *similarity* of the profiles of $\operatorname{cov}(\tilde{b}, \underline{\tilde{Y}}_n^{**})$ and $\operatorname{cov}(\tilde{a}_1, \underline{\tilde{Y}}_n^{**})$ are based on the *positive correlation* between the full-time schooling accumulation abilities and accumulation abilities in the earnings phase, $\tilde{a}_1$ and $\tilde{b}$. In fact, the differences are clearly apparent when one (unrealistically) sets up $\rho_{a_1 b} = 0$:[74] whereas $\operatorname{cov}(\tilde{b}, \underline{\tilde{Y}}_n^{**})$ also rises monotonically in this case – and this, incidentally, occurs independently of the δ/c ratio – $\operatorname{cov}(\tilde{a}_1, \underline{\tilde{Y}}_n^{**})$ only increases where $c > \delta$; it remains constant where $c = \delta$ and falls for the empirically substantiated case $\delta > c$.

Now let us return to the age profiles of the correlation coefficients. From (86), one is aware that $\rho_{b\underline{Y}_n^{**}}$ and $\rho_{b\underline{A}_n^{**}}$ rise at the beginning of earnings life. Do they continue to increase after n_0 (one can only establish from (86) that they remain positive)? A positive answer can be given to this question for the correlation coefficient between $\tilde{b}$ and *planned* disposable earnings:

[72] To be more precise: for all $n < n_k$ where n_k is implicitly defined by: $\underline{w}_{2n_k}/\underline{w}_{1n_k} \equiv k$. $n_k > n_0$ applies. Cf. also Fig. 28.

[73] (88) also applies, of course, for the covariance of $\tilde{b}$ and *planned* disposable earnings, since:

$$\operatorname{cov}(\tilde{b}, \underline{Y}_n^{**}) = \operatorname{cov}(\tilde{b}, \underline{A}_n^{**}); \quad n = 0, \ldots, N.$$

[74] Note that this requires a reformulation of the condition in (88).

$$\rho^2_{b\underline{A}^{**}_{n+1}} - \rho^2_{b\underline{A}^{**}_n} > 0 \quad \forall n > n_0.\text{[75]} \tag{89}$$

No unambiguous statement of this kind is possible for the correlation coefficients between $\tilde{b}$ and *realised* disposable earnings. In the case of a sufficiently small shock variance σ_e^2, however, the profile characteristic (89) also applies to $\rho_{b\underline{Y}^{**}_n}$.[76]

With the results obtained from (88) and from (86) and (89), the approach developed provides a theoretical explanation for the empirical observations quoted at the beginning of this section. These relate to the effect on income of both learning ability (*LA*) and schooling quality (*SQ*) increasing over the earnings life. The reader is reminded of (18): both entities are components of the production efficiency in the earnings phase.

Two results from the comparative dynamic analysis of Chapter 2 (cf. in particular, Appendix 2) reveal what is ultimately behind the correlation increases obtained. There, it was established that:

$$\frac{\partial \underline{A}_0^{j**}}{\partial b_0^j} < 0 \quad \text{and} \quad \frac{\partial(\underline{A}_{n+1}^{j**} - \underline{A}_n^{j**})}{\partial b_0^j} > 0, \quad n = 0, \ldots, N-1;$$

a higher accumulation efficiency b_0^j (and consequently, a higher (modified) accumulation efficiency b^j ($:= b_0^{j1/a}$)) causes planned disposable initial earnings to decrease and, simultaneously, the slope of the optimal income trajectory of the individual j to increase.[77] The result derived in the following section (3.6) of a *negative* correlation between initial income and income growth (cf. (93), p. 138) is based on this connection.[78] However, that provides the intuitive reason for the correlation between the economic efficiency $\tilde{b}_0$ (or $\tilde{b}$) and planned disposable earnings increasing during the life-cycle.

Notes: (i) It should briefly be noted that a very similar analysis can also be carried out on the (empirical) *regression coefficients* $\text{cov}(\tilde{a}_1, \tilde{Y}_n^{**})\sigma^2_{a_1}$

[75] As the coefficients in the area in question are positive, their squares can be applied for the purpose of an examination of the path. One then has:

$$\frac{w_{1n}^2 \sigma_{a_1}^2}{\sigma^2_{A_n^{**}}} = \frac{1}{1 + \dfrac{w_{2n}}{w_{1n}} \dfrac{1}{k}\left(\dfrac{w_{2n}}{w_{1n}} \dfrac{1}{k} + 2\rho_{a_1 b}\right)}.$$

$\underline{w}_{2n}/\underline{w}_{1n}$ is a strictly monotonically increasing function of n which is independent of the δ/c ratio (see Appendix 4). Furthermore, $\underline{w}_{2n}/\underline{w}_{1n} > 0 \, \forall n > n_0$. If one observes that $k > 0$, $0 < \rho_{a_1 b} < 1$ and notes the $\rho^2_{bA_n^{**}}$ formula in (84), then (89) follows.

[76] Cf. the σ_e^2 condition, p. 131, only now with the converse terms of inequality.

[77] These two effects have incidentally been confirmed empirically, by Lillard (1977a, pp. 45–6; 1977b). On the economic causes of these effects, the reader should consult Section 2.3.4 once again.

[78] The positive correlation between the accumulation efficiencies $\tilde{b}_0$ (or $\tilde{b}$) and $\tilde{a}_1$ are to be noted in all cases. As has already been mentioned, the learning ability *LA* is also integrated into (35) in the same effective direction, in fact, as in (18)).

and $\text{cov}(\tilde{b}, \tilde{Y}_n^{**})/\sigma_b^2$.[79] In fact, the covariance profile results (81) and (88) can be directly carried over to the regression coefficients. This can serve as an interpretation of empirical studies examining the determination of earnings, where, typically, linear regressions of $\tilde{Y}_n^{**}$ on $\tilde{a}_1$ and $\tilde{b}$ (or on empirical counterparts to these theoretical variables) are considered.
(ii) If one expands $\tilde{Y}_n^{**}$ from (51) by the learning-by-observing concept developed in Section 2.3.5, i.e. if one studies the variable $\tilde{Y}_n^{**}(\tilde{v}) := \tilde{B}_n \tilde{Y}_n^{**}$ where $\tilde{B}_n := 1 - b_3^n \tilde{v}$ instead of $\tilde{Y}_n^{**}$,[80] then one establishes that the covariances and correlation coefficients obtained as results for this variable (and $\tilde{a}_1$ or $\tilde{b}$) are always found *below* the original (thus those for $\tilde{Y}_n^{**}$ and $\tilde{a}_1$ or $\tilde{b}$). This is logical, since the individual rate of return $R_n(v^j) = R(1 - b_3^n v^j)$ is, due to the risk premium and the lack of fit between workers and jobs in every earnings period n, *smaller* than the rate R, which is the reward for the 'true' productivity of one unit of human capital; $R_n(v^j)$ only gradually approaches the value R underlying the preceding analysis in Section 3.5 (supported by the individual ability for recognising productivity and communicating this, $1/v^j$, and the on-the-job-sorting opportunities on the demand side, $1/b_3$). At the same time, one discovers that the growth rates of the correlations between $\tilde{Y}_n^{**}(\tilde{v})$ and $\tilde{a}_1$ or $\tilde{b}$ are higher in comparison; the rates of decrease, on the other hand, appear to be relatively lower.

In conclusion, two more results for the correlation between the inability to recognise productivity and communicate this, $\tilde{v}$, and disposable earnings $\tilde{Y}_n^{**}(\tilde{v})$ are introduced. Firstly, one has the following (with the requirement of a positive disposable average income within age groups):

$$\rho_{vY_n^{**}(v)} = -\frac{\sigma_v b_3^n}{\mu_{B_n} V_{Y_n^{**}(v)}} < 0; \quad n = 0, \ldots, N.$$

The sign of this correlation signifies economic intuition. Moreover, it can be established that the absolute value of $\rho_{vY_n^{**}(v)}$ is the higher, the less the on-the-job-sorting opportunities $1/b_3$, the greater the individual variation over $\tilde{v}$ and the smaller the coefficient of variation of $\tilde{Y}_n^{**}(\tilde{v})$.

Secondly, one discovers that the correlation between $\tilde{v}$ and $\tilde{Y}_n^{**}(\tilde{v})$ increases during the course of earnings life – a result which was expected.

3.6 The covariance structure of earnings

With the interpretation in Section 1.3.2, the model in question can be classed as one of the group of stochastic income determination models; in fact, $\{\tilde{Y}_n^{**}\}_{n \in \mathbb{N}}$, where $\tilde{Y}_n^{**}$ originates from (51), can be seen as that

[79] The coefficients given are the least squares estimates (*ex ante*) derived from the normal equations.
[80] Whereby, for reasons of simplification, it should be assumed again that $\tilde{B}_n$ and $\tilde{Y}_n^{**}$ are independent of one another. Note also that $b_2 = 0$ is assumed here.

stochastic process which describes the development of disposable earnings over working life.

As has been seen, the present model combines a series of factors which, according to the empirical literature, are essential to explaining the level of income inequality and the form of the distribution of earnings within an age group. These factors are: ability distributions structures of economies, life-cycle decisions and random shocks. The sources of 'randomness' in the process equation (51) are, firstly, the human capital production efficiencies $\tilde{a}_1$ and $\tilde{b}_0$ and, secondly, the random shock $\tilde{e}_i$ caused by the transitory income change factors. The type of integration of these variables into the analytical end-form (51) is derived from the general model structure designed in Chapter 1 and the economic life-cycle model formulated in Chapter 2.

In contrast to earlier stochastic models of the income determination process,[81] the present model can be identified as a *structural* model, in that it identifies the forces determining the stochastic process describing the formation of income and its evolution. In this way, the classic criticism of the lack of economic content of stochastic models is countered; the reader is reminded here of Section 1.2.3.

Consequently, the present formulation is to be considered in close relation to the recent appearances of panel studies of the covariance structure of earnings,[82] which have suffered a lack of theoretical foundation so far. In fact, the basic equation (51) generates the following *endogenous covariance structure of earnings*:

$$\begin{aligned}\operatorname{cov}(\tilde{Y}_n^{**}, \tilde{Y}_{n-\theta}^{**}) &= \operatorname{cov}(\tilde{A}_n^{**}, \tilde{A}_{n-\theta}^{**})(1+\sigma_e^2)^{n-\theta} \\ &\quad + \mu_{A_n^{**}}\mu_{A_{n-\theta}^{**}}[(1+\sigma_e^2)^{n-\theta}-1], \\ &\qquad \theta(\in \mathbf{N}) \leqslant n,\ n = 0,\ldots,N; \quad (90)\end{aligned}$$

where:

$$\begin{aligned}\operatorname{cov}(\tilde{A}_n^{**}, \tilde{A}_{n-\theta}^{**}) &= w_{1n}w_{1n-\theta}\sigma_{a_1}^2 + w_{2n}w_{2n-\theta}\sigma_b^2 \\ &\quad + (w_{1n}w_{2n-\theta} + w_{2n}w_{1n-\theta})\operatorname{cov}(\tilde{a}_1,\tilde{b}).\end{aligned}$$

With the aid of the coefficient expressions developed in Section 2.3.1 for a sufficiently long working lifespan N, the following are obtained explicitly for the terms occurring in (90):[83]

[81] Such as, for example, Gibrat (1931), Champernowne (1953), Rutherford (1955), Mandelbrot (1960, 1961), Ijiri and Simon (1977, ch. 1).

[82] Cf. Hart (1976), Hause (1977, 1980), Parsons (1978), Lillard and Willis (1978), Lillard and Weiss (1979), Bourguignon and Morrisson (1982).

[83] Instead of $\theta \in \mathbf{N}$, one could, of course, work on the basis of $\theta \in \mathbf{Z}$ from (90). However, in order not to have to distinguish between a positive and a negative θ subsequently, θ has been limited to the range of natural numbers.

$$\underline{w}_{1n-\theta}-\underline{w}_{1n}=\frac{R}{r}(1-\delta+c)^{n-\theta}[1-(1-\delta+c)^{\theta}]\lesseqgtr 0 \overset{(\theta>0)}{\Leftrightarrow} c \gtreqless \delta.$$

$$\underline{w}_{2n-\theta}-\underline{w}_{2n}=\begin{cases}\pi_w(1-\delta+c)^{n-\theta}\dfrac{(1-\delta+c)^{\theta}-1}{\delta-c}, & \text{if } c\neq\delta;\\ -\theta\pi_{w,c=\delta}, & \text{if } c=\delta;\end{cases}$$

in both cases (where $\theta > 0$; the case $\theta = 0$ is trivial):

$$\underline{w}_{2n-\theta}-\underline{w}_{2n}<0.$$

Also for $c \neq \delta$ (and $\theta > 0$), one has the following:

$$\underline{w}_{1n}\underline{w}_{2n-\theta}+\underline{w}_{2n}\underline{w}_{1n-\theta}<2\underline{w}_{1n}\underline{w}_{2n} \quad [\hat{=} \text{ ‘}\theta=0\text{’}]$$

$$\Leftrightarrow \pi_w(1-\delta+c)^n\frac{(1-\delta+c)^{\theta}-1}{\delta-c}<\underline{w}_{2n}[(1-\delta+c)^{\theta}-1]$$

$$\Leftrightarrow (1-\delta+c)^n>\frac{r}{2(r+\delta-c)};$$

the latter is, however, fulfilled for all empirically substantiated parameter sets;[84] if $c = \delta$, the condition here results in: $-\theta\pi_{w,c=\delta} < 0$, which is, however, fulfilled as well. Furthermore (irrespective of $c \gtreqless \delta$): $\mu_{\underline{A}^{**}_{n-\theta}} - \mu_{\underline{A}^{**}_{n}} < 0$; see the discussion of the life-cycle profile of planned disposable earnings in Section 2.3.2.

Ultimately: $(1+\sigma_e^2)^{n-\theta}-(1+\sigma_e^2)^n=(1+\sigma_e^2)^n[(1+\sigma_e^2)^{-\theta}-1]<0$; i.e. $(1+\sigma_e^2)^{n-\theta}$ falls monotonically with increasing θ.

If one accumulates the previous results and observes, in addition, the theoretical parameter restrictions formulated in Section 2.1.1, then one discovers two things:

$$\operatorname{cov}(\underline{\tilde{Y}}_n^{**}, \underline{\tilde{Y}}_{n-\theta}^{**})>0 \quad \forall\theta\leqslant n, \quad n=0,\ldots,N, \tag{91}$$

i.e. disposable annual incomes are *positively correlated with one another* and:

> the covariance $\operatorname{cov}(\underline{\tilde{Y}}_n^{**}, \underline{\tilde{Y}}_{n-\theta}^{**})$ is a *monotonically falling* function of θ, $\theta \leqslant n$, $n = 0, \ldots, N$, (92)

i.e. with an increasing interval between periods, the correlation between incomes becomes smaller and smaller.

These theoretical results, in particular, the predicted monotonic fall in covariance, are *compatible* with the available *empirical* results on the covariance structure of earnings.[85]

[84] The case $\delta > c$ requires a sufficiently small n; $n \leqslant 45$ (cf. (19)) is generally sufficient.
[85] See the studies cited in footnote 82, p. 136.

Furthermore in view of the previous material and on consideration of the stochastic independence of $\underline{\tilde{A}}_n^{**}$ and $\tilde{C}_n$ (apart from this it must be noted that $\tilde{C}_0 \equiv 1$):

$$\operatorname{cov}(\underline{\tilde{Y}}_0^{**}, \underline{\tilde{Y}}_{n+1}^{**} - \underline{\tilde{Y}}_n^{**}) = \operatorname{cov}(\underline{\tilde{A}}_0^{**}, \underline{\tilde{A}}_{n+1}^{**}) - \operatorname{cov}(\underline{\tilde{A}}_0^{**}, \underline{\tilde{A}}_n^{**}) < 0, \quad n = 0, \ldots, N-1, \tag{93}$$

i.e. *initial* income and income *growth* are *negatively* correlated with one another. This result has also been repeatedly confirmed empirically.[86]

Two effects, in economic terms, are contained within (93). On the one hand, there is the compensatory mechanism of the earnings phase investment, which immediately implies a trade-off between initial income and income growth in itself (see Section 2.3); on the other hand, there is the negative correlation between full-time schooling investment and further education investment in the earnings phase,[87] which is caused by the stipulated substitutional relationship between these two investment forms (see Section 2.2).

The above covariance results can be transferred directly to the *autocorrelation coefficient* $\rho_{\theta n}$, as the latter is defined as follows:

$$\rho_{\theta n} := \frac{\operatorname{cov}(\tilde{Y}_n^{**}, \tilde{Y}_{n-\theta}^{**})}{\sigma^2_{Y_n^{**}}}$$

$$= \frac{\operatorname{cov}(\tilde{A}_n^{**}, \tilde{A}_{n-\theta}^{**})(1+\sigma_e^2)^{n-\theta} + \mu_{A_n^{**}}\mu_{A_{n-\theta}^{**}}[(1+\sigma_e^2)^{n-\theta} - 1]}{\sigma^2_{A_n^{**}}(1+\sigma_e^2)^n + \mu^2_{A_n^{**}}[(1+\sigma_e^2)^n - 1]};$$

$$\theta \leqslant n, \; n = 0, \ldots, N. \tag{94}$$

Note: $0 < \rho_{\theta n} \leqslant 1 \quad \forall \theta \leqslant n; n = 0, \ldots, N.$

This does not only account for the fact that a series of the empirical studies cited refer to the autocorrelation coefficient, but also opens up an interesting perspective. The present coefficient is counted as one of the most used descriptive measures for the intertemporal *income mobility* of the individuals. By introducing $\rho_{\theta n}$, the approach developed in this work does not only provide a description, but also an economic explanation of that phenomenon, since an *endogenous* form of this measure has been dis-

[86] Cf. Hause (1980, pp. 1016–24), Bourguignon and Morrisson (1982, p. 34) and Baudelot (1983, p. 123).

[87] It applies that:

$$\operatorname{cov}[\tilde{S}^*, (s_n^* \tilde{K}_n)] < 0 \quad \text{and} \quad \operatorname{cov}(\tilde{S}^*, \tilde{D}_n^*) < 0; \quad n = 0, \ldots, N-1.$$

The positive correlation between $\tilde{a}_1$ and $\tilde{b}_0$ incidentally weakens these effects induced by way of $\tilde{b}_0$ without, however, altering anything relating to the directions of the effects.

covered with (94).[88] Specific prognoses on income mobility can be set up by way of partial differentiations of (94) with respect to the model parameters. An analytical examination of $\rho_{\theta n}$ of this type is, however, too laborious to be pursued at this point. It seems to me to be an interesting but separate project.

> *Note*: However, one result still can be mentioned. From the previous analysis, it follows, in connection with the known parameter restrictions, that:
>
> $$\rho_{\theta n}(\sigma_e^2 = 0) > \rho_{\theta n}(\sigma_e^2 > 0) \quad \forall \theta > 0.$$
>
> The existence of a transitory income component therefore results in an increase in mobility.[89] This does not only intuitively make sense, but has also been confirmed empirically.[90]

[88] On $\mathrm{cov}(\tilde{Y}_n^{**}, \tilde{Y}_{n-\theta}^{**})$ see (90); $\mu_{A_n^{**}} = w_{1n}\mu_{a_1} + w_{2n}\mu_b$; $\sigma^2_{A_n^{**}} = w_{1n}^2\sigma_{a_1}^2 + w_{2n}^2\sigma_b^2 + 2w_{1n}w_{2n}\,\mathrm{cov}(\tilde{a}_1, \tilde{b})$; w_{1n} and w_{2n} can be obtained from (38) (or (39)).

[89] The smaller $\rho_{\theta n}$, the greater the income mobility. Any evaluation of income mobility measured by $\rho_{\theta n}$ also depends on in which context one is interested in mobility: whether this measure is to be seen in relation to, e.g., 'income inequality' or 'inequality of opportunity' (how 'open' society is).

[90] Most recently by Bourguignon and Morrisson (1982, pp. 38, 46).

4 The overall distribution of earnings

The population was divided into subgroups, defined by working age, in Chapter 3, and the distribution of earnings within these age groups was there the subject of discussion. Now the question naturally arises as to the distribution over *all* working age groups, thus of the *overall* distribution of earnings within an economy.

4.1 Age distribution and inequality decomposition

In order to find the overall distribution on the basis of the previous work, the *age distribution* within the economy under observation is required.[1]

If $h(n)$ denotes the (expected) proportion of the population with a working age of n, $n = 0, \ldots N$, then it follows for the (expected) relative frequency distribution of disposable earnings within the economy that:

$$f_{Y^{**}}(y) = \sum_{n=0}^{N} h(n) f_{Y_n^{**}}(y), \tag{95}$$

where $f_{Y_n^{**}}$ originates from (52).

Before a theoretical generation of the function $h(n)$ is tackled, it must be noted that my model does not contain any 'vintage' effects, or anything similar; thus the implementation of a calendar time value t has been omitted. Consequently, a stationary economy has been implicitly assumed. It would be possible to substantiate this approach by way of the empirical fact that the distribution of earnings has proven extremely stable over time. However it must be emphasised once again that the distribution derivation and inequality analyses in Chapters 3, 4 and 5 are *not* dependent on a stationarity assumption, and therefore are independent of whether that state of the economy exists or not. No explicit consideration of t will take

[1] As a reminder, by 'age' I mean 'working age' in all cases.

place at this point for reasons of consistency, which is why the function h has been made dependent only on n.[2]

A stable age distribution is not generally accessible to any simple parameterisation. For the present purposes (of illustration), it is however sufficient to generate a hypothetical age structure, which is dependent on several parameters which can be demographically interpreted in an explicit way. This can occur in the following manner.[3] Let $l(n)$ denote the probability of survival from the time of entry into the market ($\hat{=}\ n = 0$) to working age n. This probability would apply to the same extent for all individuals,[4] so that it can be used in the case of a sufficiently large population (and under certain requirements of independence) as a measure for the (expected) relative frequency (keywords: Law of Large Numbers). $l(n)$ would be independent of the calendar time t and would assume the following form:

$$l(n) = (1 + \eta_2)^{-n}; \quad \eta_2 > 0; \quad n = 0, \ldots, N. \tag{96}$$

This represents a useful approximation for the majority of the populations in accordance with existing life tables. $1/\eta_2$ is thereby a value which can be seen as related to general life expectancy.

If the number of 'births' (or entries into the market) at time t amounts to $GB_0(1 + \eta_1)^t$ where GB_0 is the number of births at $t = 0$ and η_1 denotes the geometric rate of increase in births per time unit (generally per year),[5] then one has to go back n years in order to find out the (expected) number of

[2] See also footnote 72, p. 63. Of course, $h(n, t)$ would provide another possibility for involving the calendar time effect explicitly.

[3] The instructions which follow for obtaining a stable age distribution (therefore one independent of t) can be found in similar forms in many places in the mathematical demography literature. Cf., e.g., Keyfitz (1977, ch. 4.1). The origins go back to Leonhard Euler.

[4] This assumption is problematic to a certain extent within the context of the present model, since individuals of the same working-age can also be of a different *physical* age; the individual lengths of basic education S^j are, of course, endogenous (the physical age of the initial education decision and, thus, the physical age at economic birth should be approximately the same for all individuals – cf. also Fig. 7). The same problem occurred with the definition of the working lifespan N; cf. the explanations on this, p. 61. With the results of Mincer quoted there, physical differences in age of up to five years are justifiable and as long as individual differences in full-time schooling are limited to this range, the postulate in question of the same probability of survival is acceptable. The question of whether they are in fact limited to this range is however an empirical one.

Note that S^j denotes the length of *full-time* schooling of the individual j and this is meant literally; in accordance with the definition, any way of earning money, however small (odd-jobs, etc.) is characterised as entry into the earnings phase (see Section 2.1.1).

[5] With the aid of η_1, different hypothetical steady growth population structures can be described. η_1 is a geometric rate of increase, i.e. the number of births increases every year by the ratio $(1 + \eta_1)$.

$\eta_1 = 0$ means the same as a constant birth rate; $\eta_1 > 0 \mathrel{\hat{=}}$ increase in number of births; $\eta_1 < 0 \mathrel{\hat{=}}$ decrease in number of births ($\eta_1 = -1 \mathrel{\hat{=}}$ no births).

n-year-olds living at l. The number of births amounted to $GB_0(1 + \eta_1)^{t-n}$ at that time; since the proportion of those born and anticipated to be still alive in t follows $l(n)$, the (expected) absolute number of n-year-olds must, at time t, be: $GB_0(1 + \eta_1)^{t-n}l(n)$. If one sums over all n, the result is the total population under consideration at time t. For the desired (expected) *proportion* of n-year-olds in the total population at time t, the following is obtained:

$$\frac{GB_0(1 + \eta_1)^{t-n}l(n)}{\sum\limits_n GB_0(1 + \eta_1)^{t-n}l(n)} = \frac{(1 + \eta_1)^{-n}l(n)}{\sum\limits_n (1 + \eta_1)^{-n}l(n)} = h(n);$$

Thus:

$$h(n) = \gamma_3(1 + \gamma)^{-n}, \quad n = 0, \ldots, N; \tag{97}$$

where:

$$\gamma := \eta_1 + \eta_2; \quad \eta_1 > -1, \eta_2 > 0;^6$$

$$\gamma_3 := \frac{1}{\sum\limits_{n=0}^{N} (1 + \gamma)^{-n}}$$

$$= \begin{cases} \dfrac{1}{N + 1}, & \text{if } \gamma = 0; \\[2ex] \dfrac{\gamma}{1 + \gamma - (1 + \gamma)^{-N}}, & \text{if } \gamma \neq 0; \\[2ex] \dfrac{\gamma}{1 + \gamma}, & \text{if } \gamma > 0 \text{ and } N = \infty. \end{cases}$$

The conditions of a large population, a survival function which is independent of calendar time and a constant birth rate are thus sufficient for the existence of a stable age distribution of the type $h(n)$.

> *Notes*: (i) The latter two conditions stated above are equivalent to the assumption that birth and death rates have remained the same over a long period.[7]
> (ii) Note that a stable age distribution is, in fact, compatible with a

[6] The present definition of γ neglects (for the purposes of the present study) the term $\eta_1\eta_2((1 + \eta_1)(1 + \eta_2) = 1 + \eta_1 + \eta_2 + \eta_1\eta_2)$ since the empirical findings provide the result: $|\eta_1\eta_2| \ll 1$.

The parameter restrictions $\eta_1 > -1$ and $\eta_2 > 0$ are justified by the content: $\eta_1 = -1$ implies a complete absence of births and $\eta_2 = 0$ would correspond to the case of immortality; both are unrealistic.

[7] Cf. Keyfitz (1977, pp. 79, 113).

stationary population (where the number of births = the number of deaths) but this is not a requirement.
(iii) Interpretations relating to (97):

$\eta_1 \triangleq$ growth rate of births (in the present context, entries into the market)
$\eta_2 \triangleq$ death rate
$\gamma_3 \triangleq$ births per capita of the population (or entries into the market per capita of the earning population), since γ_3 can be rewritten as:

$$\gamma_3 = \frac{GB_0(1+\eta_1)^t}{\sum_n GB_0(1+\eta_1)^{t-n} l(n)}$$

$h(n) \triangleq$ proportion of n-year-olds in the working population; relative frequency function of working age.[8]

(iv) The function developed in (97) generates the special case of a uniform distribution for $y = 0: h(n) = 1/(N+1); n = 0, \ldots, N$. The assumption of this type of uniform age distribution, frequently encountered in theoretical analyses of income distribution would allow a considerable analytical simplification. However it is unrealistic and furthermore produces no parameters which can be interpreted demographically. $\gamma = 0$ will not, therefore, be studied in any greater detail below.
(v) In the *Statistisches Jahrbuch 1984* (pp. 70–8), the following figures which have not changed for about 10 years are given for Germany:

$$\eta_1 \simeq 0 \quad \text{and} \quad \eta_2 \simeq 0.01 \text{ (thus } \gamma \simeq 0.01).$$

What effects do variations in the demographic parameters η_1 and η_2 have on the age distribution? Since $h = h[n; \gamma(\eta_1, \eta_2)]$, it follows, where $\gamma = \eta_1 + \eta_2$, that:

$$\frac{\partial h}{\partial \eta_1} = \frac{\partial h}{\partial \gamma}\frac{\partial \gamma}{\partial \eta_1} = \frac{\partial h}{\partial \gamma} \quad \text{and} \quad \frac{\partial h}{\partial \eta_2} = \frac{\partial h}{\partial \gamma}\frac{\partial \gamma}{\partial \eta_2} = \frac{\partial h}{\partial \gamma}.$$

Because $h(n) > 0, n = 0, \ldots, N$, to evaluate the sign we can make use of the logarithmic derivative, which also is more convenient in this case, and one obtains:

$$\frac{\partial \ln h}{\partial \gamma} = \frac{\partial[\ln \gamma_3 - n\ln(1+\gamma)]}{\partial \gamma} = \frac{DA - n}{1+\gamma},$$

[8] The fact that $h(n)$ is a valid relative frequency function can be seen from the following:

$$h(n) > 0, n = 0, \ldots, N \text{ (since: } \gamma_3 > 0;\ 1+\gamma > 0\text{), and: } \sum_{n=0}^{N} h(n) = 1.$$

where:

$$DA := \sum_{n=0}^{N} nh(n) = \text{average working age in the working population under observation.}$$

Thus $\left(\text{as a reminder: } \frac{\partial \ln h}{\partial \gamma} = \frac{1}{h}\frac{\partial h}{\partial \gamma}\right)$:

$$\frac{\partial h}{\partial \eta_1} = \frac{\partial h}{\partial \eta_2} \begin{cases} >0 & \text{where } 0 \leqslant n < DA; \\ <0 & \text{where } n > DA. \end{cases} \quad (98)$$

Therefore, if, for example, the birth growth rate η_1 falls and/or the life expectancy increases (i.e. the death rate η_2 falls), then the proportion of the population in the younger working age groups diminishes and that in the older ones increases; the dividing line between these effects is the average age DA.[9]

Finally, a further fundamental remark can be made on the age distribution (97). If one bases the above derivation on the more realistic case of a logistic increase in the population instead of a geometric increase in the population,[10] then the number of parameters which can be interpreted is increased by one (namely that of the upper limit of the population size), thereby destroying, however, the closed solvability of the model structure formulated below. The price for this is too high. The present section is not concerned with implementing the 'most realistic' age distribution, but with developing a functional relationship between demographic parameters and the income distribution, to enable it, amongst other things, to show *interdependencies* between the *policy analysis* of Chapter 3 (Section 3.4) and the *demographic aspects* in an explicit analytical way.[11]

As detailed in Section 3.1, the shape of the income distribution as such (the one from f_{Y**} of (95)), plays only a subordinate role in distribution policy terms. On the other hand, the relative disparity, the *inequality* of earnings, is of crucial significance. The inequality value used in this study is the squared coefficient of variation and the reader is reminded at this point

[9] Note that the critical point, DA, varies with η_1 and η_2; one finds that $\partial DA/\partial \eta_1 = \partial DA/\partial \eta_2 < 0$. Incidentally, if $\eta_1 + \eta_2 > 0$ and $N = \infty$, then $DA = 1/(\eta_1 + \eta_2)$.

[10] For the working population at time t, the result was: $GB_0(1 + \eta_1)^t/\gamma_3$.

[11] Incidentally, the variability of the hypothetical age structures which can be illustrated by way of (97) should not be underestimated. $h(n)$ does not, necessarily, have to be a strictly monotonically falling function of n, as one is typically familiar with from relative frequency functions of geometric distributions; in fact one has: $h(n + 1) - h(n) = [(-\gamma)/(1 + \gamma)]h(n) > 0$, if $-1 < \gamma < 0$. The criticism that $h(n)$ decreased too rapidly for higher values of n, can be effectively countered by the choice of a correspondingly small value of γ (cf. also Table 4.1 in Keyfitz, 1977, p. 80).

of the discussion relating to this in Section 3.1. The question which occurs naturally is the one concerning the *overall* inequality of disposable earnings.

How will the realised *ex post* inequality of disposable earnings within the observed economy, $V^2_{Y^{**}}$, be characterised by the inequality within age groups $V^2_{Y^{**}_n}$, $n = 0, \ldots, N$, analysed in Chapter 3? Can $V^2_{Y^{**}}$ be built up, with the aid of the function $h(n)$ obtained above, from the analytical components developed in Chapter 3? Since the squared coefficient of variation is a member of the generalised entropy family, it can be decomposed in such a way that this is possible.[12] The following decomposition expression is obtained:

$$V^2_{Y^{**}} := \frac{\sigma^2_{Y^{**}}}{\mu^2_{Y^{**}}} = \sum_{n=0}^{N} \Xi(n) V^2_{Y^{**}_n} + V^2_{BT}, \tag{99}$$

where:

$$\Xi(n) := h(n)\frac{\mu^2_{Y^{**}_n}}{\mu^2_{Y^{**}}},$$

$$V^2_{BT} := \frac{\sum_{n=0}^{N} h(n)(\mu_{Y^{**}_n} - \mu_{Y^{**}})^2}{\mu^2_{Y^{**}}},$$

$$\mu_{Y^{**}} := \sum_{n=0}^{N} h(n)\mu_{Y^{**}_n},$$

$$\mu_{Y^{**}_n} = \mu_{A^{**}_n} = w_{1n}\mu_{a_1} + w_{2n}\mu_b \quad \text{(cf. (51) and the note on p. 108).}$$

Note: The decomposition in (99) is based on the variance decomposition theorem from mathematical statistics.

The first summand in (99) reflects the contribution of the inequalities within age groups to the overall inequality, whereas the second summand V^2_{BT} reflects the contribution of the inequality *between* age groups.[13] The latter arises from the differing average incomes of the individual age groups, reflecting, if you like, the pure working age effect. With $V^2_{Y^{**}_n}$ from (53) and $h(n)$ from (97) the overall inequality $V^2_{Y^{**}}$ can be determined explicitly and in full.

The decomposition notation (99) is accessible, but for present analytical purposes is still too intricate. Having carried out some algebraic reformulations, one obtains the following form instead of (99):[14]

[12] See Theil (1967, ch. 4) and Shorrocks (1980).
[13] Note, in connection with this, Theil (1967, p. 125) or Shorrocks (1980, pp. 624–5).
[14] As a reminder: $\sigma^2_{Y^{**}_n} = \sigma^2_{A^{**}_n} + \mu^2_{A^{**}_n}\sigma^2_{C_n} + \sigma^2_{A^{**}_n}\sigma^2_{C_n}$; $\sigma^2_{C_n} = (1 + \sigma^2_e)^n - 1$; and $\mu_{Y^{**}_n} = \mu_{A^{**}_n}$.

$$V_{Y^{**}}^2 = \frac{1}{\mu_{Y^{**}}^2} \sum_{n=0}^{N} h(n)(1+\sigma_e^2)^n(\mu_{A_n^{**}}^2 + \sigma_{A_n^{**}}^2) - 1. \tag{99a}$$

If one also notes that with $\mu_{Y_n^{**}} = \mu_{A_n^{**}}$ one also has $\mu_{Y^{**}} = \mu_{A^{**}} := \Sigma_{n=0}^{N} h(n)\mu_{A_n^{**}}$ and if one uses the following approximation, which is sufficient for the present purpose:[15] $(1+\sigma_e^2)^n \simeq 1 + n\ln(1+\sigma_e^2) \simeq 1+\sigma_e^2 n$, then $V_{Y^{**}}^2$ can be rewritten further:

$$V_{Y^{**}}^2 = V_{A^{**}}^2 + \sigma_e^2 \frac{\sum_{n=0}^{N} h(n)n(\mu_{A_n^{**}}^2 + \sigma_{A_n^{**}}^2)}{\mu_{A^{**}}^2}, \tag{100}$$

where:

$$V_{A^{**}}^2 := \frac{1}{\mu_{A^{**}}^2} \sum_{n=0}^{N} h(n)(\mu_{A_n^{**}}^2 + \sigma_{A_n^{**}}^2) - 1. \tag{101}$$

As expected, the realised *ex post* inequality of disposale earnings $V_{Y^{**}}^2$, exceeds the planed *ex ante* inequality, $V_{A^{**}}^2$, if there are transitory influences on income; in fact it is the case that $V_{Y^{**}}^2 \geqslant V_{A^{**}}^2 \Leftrightarrow \sigma_e^2 \geqslant 0$. In addition, one has $\partial V_{Y^{**}}^2/\partial\sigma_e^2 > 0$; therefore the higher the uncertainty of income caused by transitory factors, σ_e^2, the greater the inequality of disposable earnings within the economy under observation.

Equation (101) for the *permanent* inequality of disposable earnings provides the key to the inequality analyses in Sections 4.3 and 4.4. The reader will not be surprised by the statement that an analytical evaluation of the comparative static information[16] contained in $V_{A^{**}}^2$ would run into difficulties; with the aid of the expressions derived in Section 2.3.1 it is, however, possible to develop a manageable analytical form for $V_{A^{**}}^2$: more on this later.

The question, which naturally arises by limiting ourselves to the permanent inequality, is that concerning the transferability of the $V_{A^{**}}^2$ results to the realised *ex post* inequality $V_{Y^{**}}^2$. In an analogous situation in Chapter 3, this caused no problems; recall (56). In the present case of (99) (or (100)), the response is less clear. To come straight to the point, however: there will be *no qualitative* changes to the results found in Section 4.3 and

[15] With $\sigma_e^2 < 0.02$ (cf. Lillard and Weiss (1979, pp. 444, 450–2); according to Bourguignon and Morrisson (1982, pp. 32, 36) with even $\sigma_e^2 < 0.01$) and $n = 0, \ldots, N$ (= 45), this approximation is well supported. Cf. also Bronstein and Semendjajew (1979, pp. 85, 153).

[16] One could also refer to comparative *dynamic* information since the change in $V_{A^{**}}^2$ caused by a parameter variation is, of course, based on the induced shifts of the individual income *trajectories* (cf. Sections 2.3 and 3.4). $V_{A^{**}}^2$ itself however is independent of n, (n has been 'summed out') and, in this (rather technical) sense, a partial derivative of $V_{A^{**}}^2$ with respect to a model parameter is, correspondingly, a comparative static exercise. This note is, incidentally, applicable in the same way to Appendix 1 (S^*) and Chapter 5 ($V_{w^*}^2$).

4.4 due to the inclusion of stochastic shocks (i.e. by letting $\sigma_e^2 > 0$). The directions of the effects, which we found out, remain the same: only the extent of the effects changes; there is a *strengthening* of the effects.

In fact, one can see from the general V_{Y**}^2 equation (99), that neither the weights $\Xi(n)$, nor the inter-age group component V_{BT}^2 are dependent on σ_e^2. The shock variance affects only the within-age group components $V_{Y_n^{**}}^2$ (cf. (53)); therefore deviating effects can only manifest themselves there. With the use of (56), it is possible to recognise immediately that the introduction of transitory influences on income – therefore the incorporation of the random component $\tilde{C}_n$ – does not result in any change in the signs, but merely leads to stronger effects (in $V_{Y_n^{**}}^2$ compared with $V_{A_n^{**}}^2$; $n = 0, \ldots, N$).[17] Furthermore, one discovers that the strengthening factor $(1 + \sigma_e^2)^n$ increases monotonically with working age n and, apart from σ_e^2, is not dependent on any model parameter. Thus, the repetition of the directional effects found below for $\sigma_e^2 = 0$ (or for V_{A**}^2) and the asserted strengthening of the generated effects in the aggregate follow as consequences in connection with the results of the comparative dynamic inequality analysis of Chapter 3. This is because the now ($\sigma_e^2 > 0$) relatively higher weighted inequality effects within the older age groups exhibit the *same* direction in every case as that of the inequality effect for $\sigma_e^2 = 0$ within the population as a whole.[18]

Now let us return to the equation defining permanent inequality. As has already been mentioned, an explicit analytical treatment of the questions of interest concerning inequality in Sections 4.3 and 4.4 is made possible by reverting to the coefficients $\underline{w}_{1n}$ and $\underline{w}_{2n}$ developed in Section 2.3.1 for a sufficiently long earning lifespan N. With their aid, the solution of V_{A**}^2 can be provided in a closed form so that the interdependence between *income inequality*, on the one hand, and *public policy parameters*, *structural parameters*, *demographic parameters*, *distribution parameters* and *optimising behaviour*, on the other hand, can be shown in an explicit manner.

> *Note*: As in previous chapters, a numerical analysis based on the standard parameter set (19) and the theoretical parameter restrictions of the model was carried out. This led to the conclusion that the inclusion of the end-of-horizon effect causes no qualitative change in the results obtained

[17] Note that the relationship (56) is also valid for the structural parameters (c, δ, b_1, b_2), as none of these parameters are incorporated in $V_{C_n}^2$, $n = 0, \ldots, N$.

[18] See, in particular, Section 3.4 and (anticipating) Section 4.3. This argument is not applicable for the special case of a variation in r where $c > \delta$ because of the negative effect from $\hat{n}$. With the empirically substantiated assumption $\gamma > c - \delta$ (Appendix 5), however, it is ensured that V_{A**}^2 and V_{Y**}^2 move in the same direction and that there is a strengthened effect for V_{Y**}^2. The same applies for the effects of the structural parameters (c, δ, b_1 and b_2).

> analytically for a sufficiently large value of N. The inequality results of Sections 4.3 and 4.4, as with the results of Section 4.2, remain unaffected. However, when referring to a sufficiently large value for N in the context of an approximation, the symbol _ is retained correctly. The reader is already familiar with this notation.

The reader will find analytical details in Appendix 5.

The approximate expression finally obtained for the inequality of the planned disposable earnings within the economy under observation is as follows:

$$V_{\underline{A}^{**}}^2 = u^2 V_{a_1}^2 + (1-u)^2 V_b^2 + 2u(1-u) V_{a_1} V_b \rho_{a_1 b}, \tag{102}$$

where:

$$u := \frac{z_1 \mu_{a_1}}{\mu_{\underline{A}^{**}}}, \quad \mu_{\underline{A}^{**}} = z_1 \mu_{a_1} + z_2 \mu_b,$$

$$z_1 := \frac{\gamma}{\gamma + \delta - c} \frac{R}{r}, \quad z_2 := \frac{r - \gamma}{(\gamma + \delta - c)(r + \delta - c)} \pi_w.$$

This structure, reflecting the permanent overall inequality, now allows an explicit analysis of the questions of interest concerning inequality.

Since:

$$V_{\underline{A}^{**}}^2(x) = V_{\underline{A}^{**}}^2[u(x)], \quad x \in \{R, P, r; c, \delta, b_1, b_2; \gamma\};$$

it follows that:

$$\frac{\partial V_{\underline{A}^{**}}^2}{\partial x} = \frac{\partial V_{\underline{A}^{**}}^2}{\partial u} \frac{\partial u}{\partial x}.$$

With the theoretical parameter restrictions given in Section 2.1.1 and Appendix 5, which, it is known, can all be empirically substantiated, we have $z_1 > 0$ and $z_2 > 0 \Leftrightarrow r > \gamma$. The latter condition is typically fulfilled.[19] Also, if one remembers note (iii) p. 92, it follows that $\mu_{\underline{A}^{**}}$ is positive, i.e. that the disposable average income is positive within the economy being observed. This is not exactly a surprising piece of information, but it is a condition which is necessary for the subsequent reformulations. If one also notes that $h_0 > 1$ (cf. Section 3.2.2 and Appendix 3), then the following conditions result:

[19] I am not aware of any contradictory empirical findings. In Germany, for example, the real interest rate (obtained by averaging over the term structure of all interest rates and assuming no risk of default) has been at 6% for a considerable length of time; γ, the sum of the birth growth rate and the death rate has been at approximately 1%.

Incidentally; the condition $r > \gamma$ is sufficient but not necessary for $\mu_{\underline{A}^{**}}$ to be positive.

$$\frac{\partial V_{A^{**}}^2}{\partial x} \begin{Bmatrix} >0, \text{ if } \frac{z_2}{z_1} \lessgtr \chi \text{ and simultaneously } \frac{\partial z_1}{\partial x} z_2 \gtrless z_1 \frac{\partial z_2}{\partial x}; \\ = 0, \text{ if } \frac{z_2}{z_1} = \chi \text{ and/or } \qquad \frac{\partial z_1}{\partial x} z_2 = z_1 \frac{\partial z_2}{\partial x}; \\ < 0, \text{ if } \frac{z_2}{z_1} \lessgtr \chi \text{ and simultaneously } \frac{\partial z_1}{\partial x} z_2 \lessgtr z_1 \frac{\partial z_2}{\partial x}. \end{Bmatrix} \tag{103}$$

With the information given above, a positive quotient z_2/z_1 must be assumed. On the other hand, it is known from Chapter 3 that $\chi \leqslant 0$ is a reasonable parameter value.[20] This implies: $z_2/z_1 > \chi$, so that (103) can be reduced to:

$$\frac{\partial V_{A^{**}}^2}{\partial x} \gtreqqless 0 \Leftrightarrow \frac{\partial z_1}{\partial x} z_2 \gtreqqless z_1 \frac{\partial z_2}{\partial x}. \tag{104}$$

This is the key relationship in the inequality analysis carried out in Sections 4.3 and 4.4.

Note: Out of theoretical interest, the consequences of the unusual condition $z_2/z_1 \leqslant \chi$ will also be examined at the relevant points.

4.2 Positive skewness and constant variance

The overall distribution of disposable earnings generated by the model in question is *positively skewed* because 'A positive correlation between means and variances of subsets of the distribution leads to positive skewness in the aggregate' (Mincer, 1974, p. 38). This statement is based on a formula for the aggregate skewness of an overall distribution created out of several subdistributions developed by Baten (1935). In the present case, those subsets correspond to the working age groups. Under the presumption of positively skewed distributions within age groups, the condition:

$$\frac{\sum_n h(n)\mu_{Y_n^{**}}\sigma_{Y_n^{**}}^2}{\sum_n h(n)\mu_{Y_n^{**}}} > \sum_n h(n)\sigma_{Y_n^{**}}^2 \tag{105}$$

is sufficient for a positive skewness in the total distribution as well. Now the characteristic of positive skewness of the distribution within age groups is ensured with the results of Sections 3.1 and 3.2, and (105) is evidently fulfilled, if the $\sigma_{Y_n^{**}}^2$'s and the $\mu_{Y_n^{**}}$'s are positively correlated with one

[20] With this, one is definitely on the safe side; cf. also p. 120 and Appendix 3. See p. 118 concerning the definition of χ.

another. But, this is, in fact, the case for long stretches of working life as we know from the two previous chapters, as there both $\sigma^2_{Y_n^{**}}$ and $\mu_{Y_n^{**}}$ increase with n.

Note: The positive skewness of the overall distribution can be proven in a purely technical manner with the following formula (derived in Appendix 5 and in the next paragraph):

$$\sum_n h(n)\mu_{\underline{Y}_n^{**}} = \mu_{Y^{**}} = \mu_{\underline{A}^{**}} \quad \text{and} \quad \sum_n h(n)\sigma^2_{\underline{Y}_n^{**}},$$

and:

$$\mu_{\underline{Y}_n^{**}} = \mu_{\underline{A}_n^{**}} = \underline{w}_{1n}\mu_{a_1} + \underline{w}_{2n}\mu_b \quad \text{(where } \underline{w}_{1n}, \underline{w}_{2n} \text{ are from (39))}$$

and:

$$\sigma^2_{\underline{Y}_n^{**}} = \sigma^2_{\underline{A}_n^{**}}(1+\sigma_e^2)^n + \mu^2_{\underline{A}_n^{**}}[(1+\sigma_e^2)^n - 1]$$

being incorporated either in (105) or in the general expression for the overall skewness (see Baten 1935, p. 97):

$$\gamma_1(\tilde{Y}^{**}) = \frac{1}{\sigma^3_{Y^{**}}}\left\{\sum_n h(n)\sigma^3_{Y_n^{**}}\gamma_1(\tilde{Y}_n^{**}) + \sum_n h(n)(\mu_{Y_n^{**}} - \mu_{Y^{**}})[3\sigma^2_{Y_n^{**}} + (\mu_{Y_n^{**}} - \mu_{Y^{**}})^2]\right\}. \tag{106}$$

With the theoretical parameter restrictions of the model and $\gamma_1(\tilde{Y}_n^{**}) > 0$ $\forall n$, $\gamma_1(\tilde{Y}^{**}) > 0$ is the result.

Furthermore the approach in question generates a *constant overall variance* of disposable earnings. This will not surprise the reader after studying Sections 1.2.1, 1.3.1, 1.4.1 and 4.1. In fact, both the absolute variance $\sigma^2_{Y^{**}}$ and the relative variance $V^2_{Y^{**}}$ are independent of the age parameter n:

$$\begin{aligned}\sigma^2_{Y^{**}} &= \sum_n h(n)\sigma^2_{Y_n^{**}} + \sum_n h(n)(\mu_{Y_n^{**}} - \mu_{Y^{**}})^2 \\ &= \sum_n h(n)(1+\sigma_e^2)^n(\mu^2_{A_n^{**}} + \sigma^2_{A_n^{**}}) - \mu^2_{A^{**}};\end{aligned}$$

$$V^2_{Y^{**}} = \frac{\sigma^2_{Y^{**}}}{\mu^2_{A^{**}}} \quad \text{(see (99) or (99a)).} \tag{107}$$

In the case of a sufficiently long working lifespace N, closed forms can be derived for the expressions appearing in $\sigma^2_{Y^{**}}$ or $V^2_{Y^{**}}$ in the style of Appendix 5. $\mu_{A^{**}}$ is already available (cf. Appendix 5) and under the additional condition (see Appendix 5, concerning the remaining restrictions) that $\gamma > \sigma_e^2$, the following is obtained:[21]

$$\sum_n h(n)(1+\sigma_e^2)^n(\mu_{\underline{A}_n^{**}}^2 + \sigma_{\underline{A}_n^{**}}^2) = \begin{cases} \text{(I)}, & \text{if } c \neq \delta; \\ \text{(II)}, & \text{if } c = \delta; \end{cases}$$

with:

$$\begin{aligned}
\text{(I)} = {} & \frac{\gamma}{1+\gamma-(1+\sigma_e^2)(1-\delta+c)^2}\frac{R^2}{r^2}(\mu_{a_1}^2+\sigma_{a_1}^2) \\
& + \left[\frac{\gamma}{1+\gamma-(1+\sigma_e^2)(1-\delta+c)^2} + \frac{\gamma}{\gamma-\sigma_e^2}(rq)^2\right. \\
& \left. - 2\frac{\gamma}{\gamma-\sigma_e^2+(1+\sigma_e^2)(\delta-c)}rq\right]\frac{\pi_w^2}{(c-\delta)^2}(\mu_b^2+\sigma_b^2) \\
& + 2\left[\frac{\gamma}{1+\gamma-(1+\sigma_e^2)(1-\delta+c)^2}\right. \\
& \left. - \frac{\gamma}{\gamma-\sigma_e^2+(1+\sigma_e^2)(\delta-c)}rq\right] \\
& \cdot \frac{R}{r}\frac{\pi_w}{c-\delta}[\mu_{a_1}\mu_b + \operatorname{cov}(\tilde{a}_1,\tilde{b})];
\end{aligned}$$

$$\begin{aligned}
\text{(II)} = {} & \frac{\gamma}{\gamma-\sigma_e^2}\frac{R^2}{r^2}(\mu_{a_1}^2+\sigma_{a_1}^2) \\
& + \left[\frac{\gamma(1+\sigma_e^2)(2+\gamma+\sigma_e^2)}{(\gamma-\sigma_e^2)^3} + \frac{\gamma}{\gamma-\sigma_e^2}\frac{1}{r^2} - \frac{2}{r}\frac{\gamma(1+\sigma_e^2)}{(\gamma-\sigma_e^2)^2}\right] \\
& \cdot \pi_{w,c=\delta}^2(\mu_b^2+\sigma_b^2) \\
& + 2\left[\frac{\gamma(1+\sigma_e^2)}{(\gamma-\sigma_e^2)^2} - \frac{\gamma}{\gamma-\sigma_e^2}\frac{1}{r}\right]\frac{R}{r}\pi_{w,c=\delta}[\mu_{a_1}\mu_b + \operatorname{cov}(\tilde{a}_1,\tilde{b})].
\end{aligned}$$

Technically speaking, the independence of the total variance from n results from a 'summing out' of the working age. As far as the content is concerned, this result is based on the constancy of the demographic parameters and, therefore, on the *stability of the age distribution*.

[21] In contrast to the other theoretical parameter restrictions cited in Appendix 5, the condition $\gamma > \sigma_e^2$ cannot necessarily be empirically substantiated. If the shock variance σ_e^2 within an economy should exceed the sum of the birth growth rate and the death rate, γ, then a closed form solution of the type below is not possible.

The copyright for the structure which causes that, belongs to Rutherford (1955) as far as the purely stochastic part of the model is concerned, cf. Section 1.2.1. The only aspect common to the model developed in this study and to the purely descriptive, economically bare approach of Rutherford is at this point.

> *Note*: The Rutherford model structure is included in this model as a special case. The values occurring in (99) (or (99a)) $\mu_{A_n^{**}}$ and $\sigma^2_{A_n^{**}}$ occur in Rutherford's model only in the form of constants; they are not generated from economic considerations; rather they are set randomly. With $\mu_{A_n^{**}} =: \mu_\tau$ and $\sigma^2_{A_n^{**}} =: \sigma^2_\tau$, V^2_{Rd} is obtained for the coefficient of variation corresponding to the Rutherford model structure:
>
> $$\begin{aligned} V^2_{Rd} &:= V^2_{Y^{**}}\big|_{\mu_{A_n^{**}}=\mu_\tau,\sigma^2_{A_n^{**}}=\sigma^2_\tau} \\ &= (1+V^2_\tau)\sum_n h(n)(1+\sigma^2_e)^n - 1 \\ &= \frac{\gamma}{\gamma-\sigma^2_e}V^2_\tau + \frac{\sigma^2_e}{\gamma-\sigma^2_e};^{22} \quad \gamma = \eta_1 + \eta_2 \text{ (Section 4.1).} \end{aligned}$$
>
> Descriptive variance expressions of this type can be found in Rutherford (1955, pp. 282, 285).[23]

The distribution characteristics obtained in this section (positive skewness and constant (relative) variance of the overall distribution) are some of the most familiar and stable empirical facts of the earnings distribution.[24] Every theoretical model of the distribution of earnings should therefore satisfy this test.

4.3 Inequality effects of public pricing policies

Equipped with the results of Section 4.1, in particular with (104), the effects of the policy instruments R, P and r on permanent overall inequality (and thereby also on the realised *ex post* inequality)[25] of disposable earnings within the economy under observation can be explicitly determined.

With the use of the coefficients z_1 and z_2 and in accordance with the theoretical parameter restrictions of the model, the following is obtained:

$$\frac{\partial V^2_{\underline{A}^{**}}}{\partial R} > 0. \tag{108}$$

[22] The last step requires a sufficiently large value of N and that $\gamma > \sigma^2_e$ (> 0).
[23] Note that his model (in contrast to this one) is formulated in continuous time and in log values.
[24] Cf., e.g. Lydall (1968, ch. 3), Thatcher (1968, 1976), Göseke and Bedau (1974, section 5), Phelps Brown (1977, ch. 9.1) and Blinder (1980, section 6.4).
[25] The reader is reminded of the explanations in Section 4.1.

Since:

$$\frac{\partial z_1}{\partial R} z_2 < z_1 \frac{\partial z_2}{\partial R} \Leftrightarrow 1 < \frac{1 - b_1}{a};$$

the latter, however, is fulfilled as: $a := 1 - b_1 - b_2$, $b_1 > 0$, $b_2 > 0$ and $b_1 + b_2 < 1$.

Furthermore:

$$\frac{\partial V^2_{\underline{A}**}}{\partial P} < 0. \tag{109}$$

Since:

$$\frac{\partial z_1}{\partial P} = 0, \quad \frac{\partial z_2}{\partial P} = -\frac{b_2}{aP} z_2 < 0 \quad \text{and} \quad z_1 > 0,$$

it follows that:

$$\frac{\partial z_1}{\partial P} z_2 > z_1 \frac{\partial z_2}{\partial P},$$

which, together with (104), implies the result (109).

The fact that total inequality of disposable earnings changes as in (108) and (109) as a result of the reactions of maximising individuals to a (marginal) increase in the reward R or the price of educational goods P, is not surprising when one visualises the results of the comparative dynamic inequality analysis of Section 3.4 (in particular (75) and (76)).

Note: Even the reversals of effect within younger age groups caused by possible 'negative starts' penetrate the $V^2_{\underline{A}**}$ structure: *ceteris paribus*, a high average modified human capital production efficiency μ_b (→ or negative start becomes more probable, as $w_{2n} < 0$ for small values of n) causes the coefficient of variation ratio h_0 to decrease, which, in turn, increases χ (see Appendix 4). If a sufficiently small correlation coefficient $\rho_{a_1 b}$ occurs, in addition to the reduced h_0, such that $h_0 \rho_{a_1 b} < 1$, then χ becomes positive, with the consequence, in the extreme case of a very high value of γ (which realistically remains smaller than r – cf. also footnote 19, p. 148) that the relation $z_2/z_1 < \chi$ can arise; as the following would continue to apply: $z_2 \partial z_1/\partial R < z_1 \partial z_2/\partial R$ and $z_2 \partial z_1/\partial P > z_1 \partial z_2/\partial P$, this would indicate a reversal in the policy effects obtained in (108) and (109). This is, however, compatible with the results in note (ii), p. 126, as the reversals of effect established within young age groups penetrate through to the total distribution if the relative weight of those age groups is correspondingly high; as seen in Section 4.1, a very high value of γ implies a very high share of the population in young age groups.

Precise prognoses were clearly not possible solely on the basis of (75) and (76) without knowledge of the *age structure* of the economy under observation. The explanations in the above note have emphasised this. In fact, in the model discussed here, the overall effect of policy measures affecting prices, and motivated by a distributional concern, depends on the *interaction* of policy parameters, structural parameters, demographic parameters and distribution parameters; this interrelation results from the dynamic optimising behaviour of the individuals. This interaction has been made explicit and been reduced by way of the complex set of conditions (103) and the exploitation of the available empirical and theoretical information on the relation (104). For a further discussion of the shifts of the individual trajectories, which cause the changes in earnings inequality, and of their economic incentives, the reader again is referred to Section 2.3. As was seen in Chapter 3 (in Section 3.4), different age groups are affected in different ways by one and the same measure relating to pricing policy. Nevertheless, the following *unambiguous* results are obtained for the population as a whole, on the basis of available empirical findings and the theoretical knowledge of the previous chapters: an *increase* in the wage rate R results in an *increase* in overall inequality, whereas an increase in the price of educational goods P (therefore, the *more costly* acquisition of human capital in the earnings phase) leads to a *decrease* in overall inequality.

Note: There may be economies where $z_2/z_1 < \chi$, so that under certain circumstances reversals of effect may occur (cf. the previous note). In this respect, the direction of the overall effect of a distribution-related pricing policy measure may, in the final analysis, be an empirical question as well. In this kind of situation, it is the job of the theorist to reveal the interdependencies of the factors involved and determine precise conditions for a possible reversal in the effect. This has been done in (103) (with z_1 and z_2 from (102) and χ from Section 3.4). What the empirical information actually available implies for the overall effects, taking into account the theoretical results obtained, can be seen from the results (108) and (109).

At this point, an additional interesting aspect must be pointed out. On the basis of the result (108), one would recommend the policy of a decrease in R for the purpose of decreasing the inequality of incomes. If the equation for disposable average income within the population is inspected, then it is seen that (in accordance with $z_1 > 0$ and $z_2 > 0$): $\partial\mu_{\underline{A}^{**}}/\partial R > 0$; the lower the wage rate, the smaller the average income. If the policy of a reduction in reward was put at the top of the list and R was allowed to approach zero, then, ultimately: $A_n^{j**} = 0 \,\forall j, \forall n$ (see (38) or (39)). Therefore it is reasonable for the recommended policy to be equipped with a lower limit located, for example, at the level of the bread line.[26]

Note: The positivity of the covariance terms, thus the *positive correlation* between the two human capital accumulation abilities $\tilde{a}_1$ and $\tilde{b}$, is chiefly responsible for the fact that the percentage $\sigma^2_{\underline{A}^{**}}$ change caused by a variation in R exceeds the percentage change in $\mu^2_{\underline{A}^{**}}$, despite $\sigma^2_{\underline{A}^{**}}$ and $\mu^2_{\underline{A}^{**}}$ varying in the same direction (so that the $V^2_{\underline{A}^{**}} = \sigma^2_{\underline{A}^{**}}/\mu^2_{\underline{A}^{**}}$ change runs in line with the $\sigma^2_{\underline{A}^{**}}$ change).

The same applies for the price instrument P.

It should be noted at this point that the model developed here predicts a basic *policy conflict* between the *level of per capita income* and the *level of income inequality* and, therefore, provides a possible explanation for this known[27] problem.

As is to be expected from the experiences in Chapters 2 and 3, the policy analysis of the third instrument associated with the model, the interest rate r, is the most complex in technical terms.

The following is ultimately obtained:

$$\frac{\partial z_1}{\partial r} z_2 < z_1 \frac{\partial z_2}{\partial r}.$$

Since:

$$\frac{\partial z_1}{\partial r} = -\frac{1}{r} z_1;$$

$$\frac{\partial z_2}{\partial r} = \Delta_2 z_2 + \pi_w q^2 \quad \text{(see Appendix 4 on the definition of } \Delta_2\text{)}.$$

One thereby has (note that: $z_1 > 0, z_2 > 0$):

$$\frac{\partial z_1}{\partial r} z_2 < z_1 \frac{\partial z_2}{\partial r} \Leftrightarrow \frac{\partial z_1/\partial r}{z_1} < \frac{\partial z_2/\partial r}{z_2}$$

$$\Leftrightarrow -r\Delta_2 - \frac{r(\gamma + \delta - c)}{(r - \gamma)(r + \delta - c)} < 1;$$

for $\gamma = 0$ follows the relationship: $\pi_\beta - (\delta - c)q < 1$, $\pi_\beta := r\Delta_2$, $q := 1/(r + \delta - c)$ known from Appendix 4 (footnote 15), and this

26 In connection with this, it should be noted that the objective of the present study is to provide information on the basis of *positive* analysis; income inequality is considered without any explicit reference to welfare theory. Concrete policy recommendations are, however, dependent on the prevailing economic policy aims and the values of society, which would lead into the area of normative analysis.

27 See, for example, the empirical material in Blinder (1980).

is fulfilled for the empirically relevant case $\delta > c$. γ is, however, positive (cf. also Appendix 5) which together with $r + \delta > c$, $\gamma + \delta > c$ and $r > \gamma$ (note the admission of $c > \delta$) implies the following inequalities:

$$\frac{r(\gamma + |\delta - c|)}{r - \gamma} > |\delta - c| \quad \text{and} \quad \frac{r(\gamma + \delta - c)}{r - \gamma} > 0;$$

thus, in fact:

$$-r\Delta_2 - \frac{r(\gamma + \delta - c)}{(r - \gamma)(r + \delta - c)} = \pi_\beta - \frac{r(\gamma + \delta - c)}{r - \gamma} q < 1.$$

By applying (104) one obtains the following:

$$\frac{\partial V^2_{\underline{A}^{**}}}{\partial r} > 0. \tag{110}$$

The modifications to the intertemporal decision-making of the individuals caused by a (marginal) *increase in the interest rate* lead to an *increase in the inequality* of the overall distribution of disposable earnings.

This result could not be ascertained solely on the basis of the comparative dynamic inequality analysis of Section 3.4, since the trade-off between the negative and positive effects in (77) could not be predicted.

The conditions (77) however permit, for example, the presumption that the increase in inequality, obtained in (110), for the hypothetical case of an exceptionally high proportion of the population in the young working age groups, reverts, *ceteris paribus*, to a decrease in inequality. This is, in fact, the case for a sufficiently large value of γ, which corresponds to a high percentage in younger age groups.[28] This type of high value for γ (in particular, therefore, $\gamma > r$) cannot, of course, be empirically substantiated. However, $\gamma < r$ can be supported and (110) reveals what sort of interest effect this has in the present model.

[28] For $z_2/z_1 > \chi$ ultimately turns into $z_2/z_1 < \chi$; on the other hand, it still is true that: $z_2 \partial z_1/\partial r < z_1 \partial z_2/\partial r$. Cf. (103). The requirement is of course that $\mu_{\underline{A}^{**}} > 0$.

Note that for the hypothetical case $\gamma > r$, the coefficient z_2 is negative, so that:

$$\frac{\partial z_1}{\partial r} z_2 < z_1 \frac{\partial z_2}{\partial r} \Leftrightarrow \frac{\partial z_1/\partial r}{z_1} > \frac{\partial z_2/\partial r}{z_2} \Leftrightarrow \pi_\beta + \frac{r(\gamma + \delta - c)}{\gamma - r} q > 1,$$

which is, however, fulfilled with the known theoretical parameter restrictions and $\gamma > r$, since then:

$$\frac{r(\gamma + \delta - c)}{\gamma - r} q > 0$$

(and from Appendix 4 it is known that $\pi_\beta > 1$).

Here, the advantage of a closed $V_{\underline{A}^{**}}^2$ solution comes to light again: the dependence on the *age structure* of the working population of the inequality effect of a variation in a policy parameter can be determined explicitly.

4.4 Further results

The fact that we have been successful in deriving $V_{\underline{A}^{**}}^2$ in a closed form, has not only made an explicit policy analysis possible, but also allows an explicit analysis of the remaining inequality questions of interest in the present context; questions which concern the interdependencies between the overall inequality of disposable earnings, on the one hand, and the distribution parameters, the structural parameters, the demographic parameters and the life-cycle decisions of the optimising individual, on the other.

4.4.1 *Optimising behaviour and inequality*

Here a brief response is to be provided to the question of how changes in the distribution charactertistics of $\tilde{a}_1$ and $\tilde{b}$ (described by the distribution measures V_{a_1}, V_b and $\rho_{a_1 b}$) affect income inequality.

With $z_1 > 0$ and $z_2 > 0$, $z_2 \mu_b / z_1 \mu_{a_1} > 0$, so that $0 < u < 1$. The following is therefore obtained directly from (102) in accordance with $\rho_{a_1 b} > 0$ and note (iii), p. 92. Thus (*ceteris paribus*):

$$\frac{\partial V_{\underline{A}^{**}}^2}{\partial V_{a_1}} = 2u^2 V_{a_1} + 2u(1-u) V_b \rho_{a_1 b} > 0; \tag{111}$$

$$\frac{\partial V_{\underline{A}^{**}}^2}{\partial V_b} = 2(1-u)^2 V_b + 2u(1-u) V_{a_1} \rho_{a_1 b} > 0. \tag{112}$$

Therefore, a *more homogeneous* population as regards the human capital accumulation abilities $\tilde{a}_1$ and $\tilde{b}$ results in a *reduction* in inequality in the aggregate distribution of earnings.

Moreover:

$$\frac{\partial V_{\underline{A}^{**}}^2}{\partial \rho_{a_1 b}} = 2u(1-u) V_{a_1} V_b > 0; \tag{113}$$

therefore, the *less correlation* between the human capital production efficiency in the full-time schooling phase, $\tilde{a}_1$, and the (modified) human capital production efficiency in the earnings phase, $\tilde{b}$, the *less* inequality (*ceteris paribus*) is there in the overall distribution of disposable earnings.

Now to an interesting aspect: if one compares the *endogenous* structure here with that of a 'mechanical' model, one discovers that the weighting factor u

resulting from the maximising process of the individuals lies *below* the factor u_{ME} originating from the purely 'descriptive' model:

$$u := \frac{z_1\mu_{a_1}}{z_1\mu_{a_1} + z_2\mu_b} \quad \text{(see (102))}, \quad u_{ME} := \frac{\mu_{a_1}}{\mu_{a_1} + \mu_{bo}};$$

$$u < u_{ME} \Leftrightarrow \frac{z_2\mu_b}{z_1\mu_{a_1}} > \frac{\mu_{bo}}{\mu_{a_1}}$$

$$\Leftrightarrow z_2 > \frac{\mu_{bo}}{\mu_b} z_1 = \frac{\mu_{bo}}{\mu_{bo}^{1/a}} z_1,$$

which is, however, fulfilled with the known theoretical parameter restrictions (including $r > \gamma$).

What implications does this discovery have for the picture of overall inequality developed in this study? Before this question is answered, it must be remembered that the present approach sees income inequality neither as an isolated result of individual choices nor as an isolated result of individual endowments and abilities; rather it is considered to be the result of a simultaneous interaction of the factors mentioned; equation (102) is the explicit expression of this interaction. Of course, the question emerges here of how this picture of inequality differs from a situation where the individuals are *not* optimising. This type of situation is illustrated by way of a 'mechanical' model. This remains restricted to the original forms of the initial distributions (thus to $\tilde{a}_1$ and $\tilde{b}_0$), as it ignores any optimising reactions of individuals to their individual circumstances; the specification of relative income variation then occurs in a purely 'descriptive' manner.

A comparison of u and u_{ME} is aimed directly at the question of the optimising effect. Since $\mu_{\underline{A}^{**}} > 0$ and $h_0 > 1$ (and therefore $V_b > V_{a_1}$), the following inequality applies when $z_2/z_1 > \chi$ (cf. p. 149): $\partial V^2_{\underline{A}^{**}}/\partial u < 0$, so that from $u < u_{ME}$ it follows that:

$$V^2_{\underline{A}^{**}}(u) > V^2_{\underline{A}^{**}}(u_{ME}) =: V^2_{AME}. \text{[29]} \tag{114}$$

According to this, mechanical models *underestimate* the inequality effects generated altogether by the basic variables $\tilde{a}_1$ and $\tilde{b}_0$. The influence of learning ability (and thereby also of basic genetic endowment, family background and cultural factors), of the DF factor, but also of the leadership and organisational abilities, of the willingness to take risks, of examination results and of school quality (cf. (35) and (18)) on the overall inequality of disposable earnings is strengthened by the optimising reactions of the individuals. In this sense, a part of the existing inequality of

[29] Here, the fact operating in the same direction has been omitted, that: $V_b = V_{bo}^{1/a} > V_{bo}$ (p. 98).

earnings can be seen as *self-generated*. Mechanical approaches consider this phenomenon, in particular, unworthy of mention. An assessment of the inequality situation within the economy on the basis of a mechanical model would not meet the actual inequality effect of the factors incorporated in $\tilde{a}_1$ and $\tilde{b}_0$.

4.4.2 *Variations in structural parameters*

The parameters c, δ, b_1 and b_2, which are assumed to be the same for all individuals, reflect *structural* characteristics of the economy under observation (cf. Section 2.1.1).

For the learning-by-doing opportunities within an economy, reflected by the parameter c, the following is found in accordance with the theoretical parameter restrictions of the model (including $r > \gamma$):

$$\frac{\partial V^2_{\underline{A}^{**}}}{\partial c} > 0. \tag{115}$$

Since:

$$\frac{\partial z_1}{\partial c} = \frac{z_1}{\gamma + \delta - c};$$

$$\frac{\partial z_2}{\partial c} = \left[\frac{b_2}{a} q + \frac{b_2 - 1 - \delta a/r}{(r + \delta a)/(rq) + cb_2} + \frac{r + \gamma + 2(\delta - c)}{(\gamma + \delta - c)(r + \delta - c)}\right] z_2.$$

Therefore:

$$\frac{\partial z_1}{\partial c} z_2 < z_1 \frac{\partial z_2}{\partial c}$$

$$\Leftrightarrow \underbrace{\frac{\gamma + \delta - c}{r + \delta - c}}_{>0} \Bigg[\underbrace{\frac{b_2}{a}}_{>0} + 1 - \underbrace{\frac{1 - b_2/(1 + \delta a/r)}{1 + cb_2/[(1 + \delta a/r)(r + \delta - c)]}}_{<1}\Bigg] > 0,$$

which is however fulfilled. Together with (104), the result is (115).

An *improvement* in the possibility of increasing the human capital stock by practical job experience induces *additional* inequalities in the overall distribution of disposable earnings. A higher value of c causes the gap between the optimal plans of the individuals to become more extreme in comparison.

Note: It must be noted that the average disposable income of the population $\mu_{\underline{A}^{**}}$ also increases with the learning-by-doing efficiency c.

In the same way, the effect of a variation in δ on overall inequality can be ascertained. One obtains:

$$\frac{\partial V^2_{\underline{A}^{**}}}{\partial \delta} < 0. \tag{116}$$

A *higher* human capital depreciation rate δ, caused, for example, by more rapid technical change therefore leads to a *reduction* in the overall inequality of disposable earnings within the economy under observation.

Note: The per capita income then decreases as well, however, since: $\partial \mu_{\underline{A}^{**}}/\partial \delta < 0$.

Finally, one also has:

$$\frac{\partial V^2_{\underline{A}^{**}}}{\partial b_1} > 0; \quad \frac{\partial V^2_{\underline{A}^{**}}}{\partial b_2} > 0.\text{[30]} \tag{117}$$

Economies with *higher* input production elasticities therefore exhibit *higher* income disparities.

4.4.3 *Inequality effects of demographic factors*

The structure of the model developed in this study permits an explicit examination of *demographic* inequality effects as well, in connection with the closed $V^2_{\underline{A}^{**}}$ solution.

One obtains the following relationship:

$$\frac{\partial V^2_{\underline{A}^{**}}}{\partial \gamma} < 0; \quad \gamma = \eta_1 + \eta_2. \tag{118}$$

Since:

$$\frac{\partial z_1}{\partial \gamma} = \frac{R}{r} \frac{\delta - c}{(\gamma + \delta - c)^2}; \quad \frac{\partial z_2}{\partial \gamma} = \frac{-\pi_w}{(\gamma + \delta - c)^2}.$$

Therefore:

$$\frac{\partial z_1}{\partial \gamma} z_2 > z_1 \frac{\partial z_2}{\partial \gamma} \Leftrightarrow \frac{r(\gamma + \delta - c)}{\gamma(r - \gamma)} > 0,$$

[30] This follows via (104):

$$\partial z_1/\partial b_1 = \partial z_1/\partial b_2 = 0, \quad \partial z_2/\partial b_1 > 0, \quad \partial z_2/\partial b_2 > 0.$$

Additional effects (with the same sign; see also Appendix 3):

$$\partial V_b/\partial b_1 > 0, \quad \partial V_b/\partial b_2 > 0; \quad \partial(V_b \rho_{a_1 b})/\partial b_1 > 0, \quad \partial(V_b \rho_{a_1 b})/\partial b_2 > 0.$$

which is, however, fulfilled with the theoretical parameter restrictions of the model (including $r > \gamma > 0$).[31] With the application of (104), (118) then follows.

The overall inequality in disposable earnings consequently *increases* with a falling γ ($<r$), and thus with a *decreasing* birth rate η_1 and/or *falling* death rate η_2. If one observes two economies, identical apart from their age structures, the one with a larger share of the population in older working age groups exhibits a relatively higher earnings inequality.

Notes: (i) Empirical confirmations of the prognosis $\partial V^2_{Y^{**}}/\partial\gamma < 0$ (the $V^2_{\underline{A}^{**}}$ results can be carried over to $V^2_{\underline{Y}^{**}}$; see Section 4.1) can be found in Danziger, Haveman and Smolensky (1977) and in Blinder (1980).[32]
(ii) If in a hypothetical economy $\gamma > r$ ($\hat{=}$ extremely high percentage of young age groups), so that ultimately $z_2/z_1 < \chi$, then the effects are reversed. Thus: $\partial V^2_{\underline{A}^{**}}/\partial\gamma > 0$ as, in the same way as before: $z_2\partial z_1/\partial\gamma > z_1\partial z_2/\partial\gamma$.[33] Cf. (103). The requirement is of course that: $\mu_{\underline{A}^{**}} > 0$. This result is compatible with the U-shape of the $V^2_{A_n^{**}}$ profile established in Section 3.3.
(iii) With the known restrictions and $r > \gamma > 0$ one finds that: $\partial\mu_{\underline{A}^{**}}/\partial\gamma < 0$. This is a result which was only to be expected, when one considers that the proportion of the population in the younger age groups decreases with a reduction in γ and $\partial\mu_{\underline{A}_n^{**}}$ is a monotonically increasing function of n (cf. Sections 4.1 and 2.3.2).

The discoveries made on the basis of (118) are all in favour, in terms of distribution policy, of not making observations of inequality on the basis of the current distribution, i.e. the overall distribution of annual income dealt with in this chapter, but on the basis of the *lifetime* income distribution (cf. Chapter 5 with regard to this). In almost all advanced industrialised nations, it has been possible to observe two things in the past thirty years: firstly, the life expectancy of the individuals has risen because of medical progress (falling η_2) and, secondly, the birth rate (η_1) has clearly fallen ('prosperity factor' and the 'pill'). These two purely demographic effects induce increases in inequality in accordance with (118); these are increases

[31] The reader is reminded that the theoretical parameter restrictions of the model (the same applies for the relationship $0 < \gamma < r$) are in all cases empirically substantiated.

[32] Strictly speaking, these should be referred to as 'indirect' confirmations, as the studies cited refer to income and not exclusively to earnings.

[33] For $\gamma > r$: $z_2 < 0$; so that:

$$\frac{\partial z_1}{\partial\gamma} z_2 > z_1 \frac{\partial z_2}{\partial\gamma} \Leftrightarrow \frac{r(\gamma + \delta - c)}{\gamma(r - \gamma)} < 0,$$

which is fulfilled where $\gamma > r$. Note that $\gamma > r$ cannot be supported empirically. The case under analysis here is of theoretical interest only.

which have nothing to do with the inequality relevant in the normative sense (that is the one whose roots in the present model lie in $\tilde{a}_0$, $\tilde{a}_1$ and $\tilde{b}_0$).

Now, the observation that the influence of the age distribution on the income distribution distorts the picture of inequality, is not a new idea in itself: 'The superimposition of different age structures on populations of otherwise like characteristics will in general be non-neutral in respect of income distribution' (Cowell, 1973, p. 1). But what does this 'non-neutrality' look like exactly? The present model is in a position, with the aid of the analytical structure formulated in the previous chapters, to provide an *explicit reason and direction* for this distortion. The trials carried out so far to identify the interaction between income and age distribution by means of numerical simulation (Cowell, 1973) or graphical processes (Beach, Card and Flatters, 1981, pp. 84–9) can at best be described as vague.

5 The distribution of lifetime earnings

On the basis of one and the same basic economic model, namely the one contained in Chapter 2, a third distribution level can also be explicitly analysed: that of *lifetime* earnings.

In fact an examination of the lifetime earnings distribution suggests itself – Chapter 2 is after all concerned with a *life-cycle* model. The aim of every individual was to maximise the present value of his disposable annual earnings, therefore his disposable lifetime earnings, and the question obviously occurs as to the distribution of this target value. Simultaneously, by way of concentration on lifetime income, the distortion effect induced by the age structure of the population is eliminated (cf. Section 4.4.3).

In contrast to the two previous chapters, the present chapter will no longer restrict itself to snapshots of the distribution situation, but will use the total earnings phase of the economic subjects as the basis for considering inequality issues. This method of observation is of great normative significance. The range of questions treated here can be found in the general outline in the introduction of this book.[1]

5.1 The basic set-up

In accordance with the economic model drafted in Chapter 2, every individual j behaves as though he wanted to maximise the value W^j of his disposable annual earnings discounted from the time of his economic birth. In order to obtain the optimal value of his disposable lifetime earnings so defined, the individual must solve a two-stage optimisation problem whose structure the reader may like to visualise with the help of Fig. 7. The end-value resulting from this is:

[1] Beyond the scope of the issues treated here, the present model can provide new insights in, for example, the theory of optimal taxation or the theory of social security. This is however reserved for future projects.

$$W^{j*} = V^{j**}(1+r)^{-S^{j*}}$$
$$= (1+\mathrm{r})^{-S^{j*}} \sum_{n=0}^{N} A_n^{j**}(1+r)^{-n}, \qquad (119)$$

with A_n^{j**} from (38) and S^{j*} from (36).[2]

Notes: (i) The stochastic shocks caused by the transitory income change factors are intentionally suppressed in this chapter. The overall 'transitory' character of the shock process defined in Section 1.3 should not only be expressed by $E(\tilde{C}_n^j) = 1$ (cf. p. 17), but also by the fact that the present value of the transitory income components is equal to zero, so that the purely random income elements so defined neutralise one another over the life-cycle. Consequently, those stochastic shocks from the current life-view of earnings are ignored and attention is focused on W^j. Purists may however insert the term 'expected lifetime earnings' instead of 'lifetime earnings' in each case (on consideration of assumption 7, Section 2.1.1).
(ii) Optimal lifetime disposable earnings of the individual j, W^{j*}, represent, if you will, the optimum *human capital* of the individual j.
(iii) If one calculates the present value V^{j**} based on the point of entry into the labour market, by inserting (38), then an interesting discovery is made; one finds that:

$$V^{j**} = \sum_{n=0}^{N} A_{-n}^{j**}(1+r)^{-n} = \frac{R\Pi_N}{\ln(1+r)} a_1^j.$$

If one studies the optimal individual lifetime earnings from the aspect of the initial working period ($\hat{=}\ n = 0$), then the human capital production efficiency in the earnings phase ($= b_0^j$) is without influence; if the individuals do not differ in their human capital production efficiencies in the full-time schooling phase, a_1^j, then there would be no individual variations of V^{j**} either. Behind this surprising result lies the presumed substitutional relationship between human capital investment in the full-time schooling phase and in the earnings phase (Section 2.2); S^{j*} is the regulator compensating b_0^j, causing V^{j**} to be independent of b_0^j.

An evaluation of inequality based on measured V^{j**} values, which is a practice which is widely applied, ignores, however, an important aspect: how long has the individual j had to subject himself to full-time schooling and thereby wait for the beginning of his income flow to reach the value $V^{j**} = V^{j*}(S^{j*})$? This only affects the target value W^{j*}.

As well, it thereby becomes clear at what point the benefit of a higher value of b_0^j, questioned in the note on p. 84, occurs. As has been seen in the comparative dynamic analysis of Section 2.3.4, individuals with higher

[2] As a reminder: the person index j was omitted from Chapter 2 for the purposes of clarification. It is admitted to the equations quoted by way of the 'individual' parameters a_0^j, a_1^j and b_0^j (or b^j).

values of b_0^j exhibit shorter full-time schooling phases, because human capital accumulation during the earnings phase is more profitable for them, in comparison. If the individuals only differ in their production efficiencies b_0^j, then the value V^{j**} is the same for all of them; for those individuals who are equipped with a higher value of b_0^j, the income flow begins *earlier* however. Therefore, the individuals with a higher human capital production efficiency in the earnings phase are in a better position, *ceteris paribus*, than those with a lower value, owing to the opportunity they have of earning a fixed rate of interest r on the capital market (assumption 4, Section 2.1.1).

The reader will find an analytical proof that $\partial W^{j*}/\partial b_0^j > 0$ in Appendix 6.

If one now considers the population as a whole and varies the individual parameters according to the characteristics of each individual, one obtains the following (using the notation which is, by now, familiar to the reader):

$$\tilde{W}^* = \tilde{V}^{**}(1+r)^{-\tilde{S}^*}. \tag{120}$$

Owing to the technical difficulties caused by the complicated non-linear term $(1+r)^{-\tilde{S}^*}$ (cf. (36)), an explicit distribution or inequality analysis in the style of the two previous chapters is not possible on the basis of (120). With the aid of the approximation obtained from the Taylor series expansion: $(1+r)^{-S} \doteqdot 1 - \ln(1+r)S$, it is however possible to circumvent these problems.

Notes: (i) The quantitative requirement of $\ln(1+r)\cdot S$ being as small as possible is fulfilled here. The relative error of this approximation, in accordance with the calculation carried out on the basis of the standard parameter set, amounts to less than 6% (see also Bronstein and Semendjajew, 1979, p. 153 and p. 85). The qualitative results derived in the following sections are all unaffected by this approximation.
(ii) An inherent price of this linearisation as to the content is the drop-out of $\tilde{a}_1$ (cf. (121)). This is, however, accepted since, as one will see subsequently, the consequences for interpretation are minimal for the lifetime earnings distribution analysed here.

Thus (as an approximation): $\tilde{W}^* = \tilde{V}^{**}[1 - \ln(1+\mathrm{r})\tilde{\mathrm{S}}^*]$, which can be transformed with the aid of (38) and (36) into:

$$\tilde{W}^* = d_2\tilde{a}_0 + d_3\tilde{b}, \tag{121}$$

where:

$$d_2 := R\Pi_N \quad \text{and} \quad d_3 := \sum_{n=0}^{N} \hat{M}_n(1+r)^{-n}.$$

This is the key equation with which the present chapter is concerned.

The inequality of disposable lifetime earnings, measured by the squared coefficients of variation, results in the following:

$$V_{W^*}^2 := \frac{\sigma_{W^*}^2}{\mu_{W^*}^2} = \rho^2 V_{a_0}^2 + (1-p)^2 V_b^2 + 2p(1-p) V_{a_0} V_b \rho_{a_0 b}, \quad (122)$$

with

$$p := \frac{d_2 \mu_{a_0}}{\mu_{W^*}} = \frac{\mu_{a_0}}{\mu_{a_0} + d\mu_b},$$

$$d := \frac{\sum_{n=0}^{N} \hat{M}_n (1+r)^{-n}}{R\Pi_N}.$$

Before a closer examination is made of this closed form solution, a few remarks are inserted on the distribution of the variable $\tilde{a}_0$ and on the constant d.

As is already known from Section 2.2, $\tilde{a}_0$ represents the basic stock of human capital at the beginning of the economic planning horizon. Significant determining factors of $\tilde{a}_0$ include the inherited characteristics, the family background and the cultural influences; with (34) one therefore has, in general:

$$\begin{aligned}\tilde{a}_0 &= a_0(\tilde{G}, \tilde{HO}, \tilde{CU}) \\ &= a_0(\tilde{G}_1, \tilde{G}_2, \ldots, \tilde{HO}_1, \tilde{HO}_2, \ldots, \tilde{CU}_1, \tilde{CU}_2, \ldots). \quad (123)\end{aligned}$$

The distribution of the basic stock of human capital consequently depends on the distributions and the type of interaction of the individual components making up the three factor clusters $\tilde{G}$, $\tilde{HO}$ and $\tilde{CU}$ (see footnote 34, p. 36). The present study has already dealt with this topic in a different context and a similar analysis to the one in Section 3.2.2 can be applied to (123). In accordance with this, the $\tilde{a}_0$ distribution displays a positive skewness and a positive kurtosis, the variable $\tilde{a}_0$ is positively correlated with the human capital production efficiency $\tilde{b}_0$ (and thereby also with $\tilde{b} := \tilde{b}_0^{1/a}$) and, according to all theoretical knowledge:[3] $V_{b_0} > V_{a_0}$ (and therefore: $V_b > V_{a_0}$).

The coefficients d_2 and d_3 occurring in the constant d are familiar from Chapter 2. d_3, the numerator of d, denotes the discounted sum of the total

[3] The argument formulated in Section 3.2.2 relating to this, of a larger number of factors (with the same direction of interaction) is, of course, of a more indirect nature in the present case, since the determining factors of $\tilde{a}_0$ are only indirectly applied to $\tilde{b}_0$ by way of $\tilde{LA}$ and $\tilde{DF}$ (cf. (63), (64) and (18a)). This does not, however, alter the outcome of the argument.
For the sake of formal completeness, it is noted that the stock value $\tilde{a}_0$ (as with the production efficiency $\tilde{b}_0$) is a positive variable.

net increases in earnings $\hat{M}_n$ (cf. (38) on the formal definition of $\hat{M}_n$), whereas d_2, the denominator of d, corresponds to the shadow price of an additional disposable unit of human capital from period 0 (therefore, from the beginning of working life): $R\Pi_N = \psi_0$ (cf. (25)). The constant d can therefore be interpreted as a 'human capital growth value in human capital price units'. It can immediately be concluded from the positive nature of d_2 and d_3 that d is also positive and that p lies between 0 and 1 (since $\mu_{ao}, \mu_b > 0$). Numerical calculations based on the standard parameter set have also resulted in: $d_3 \gg d_2$ and consequently $d \gg 1$; only for a completely unrealistic case can d fall below 1.

If a long earnings lifespan N is assumed (the reader is reminded of Section 2.3.1 in connection with this), then d can be approximated by the following:

$$d_1 := \left(\frac{b_1}{r+\delta}\right)^{\frac{b_1}{a}} \left(\frac{R}{P}\frac{b_2}{r+\delta-c}\right)^{\frac{b_2}{a}} \frac{a}{r}, \quad a := 1 - b_1 - b_2, \tag{124}$$

I will revert to this subsequently whenever the constant d is no longer analytically tractable.[4]

Notes: It must be expressly emphasised at this point, that all qualitative results obtained analytically in this chapter on the basis of d_1 correspond to those obtained numerically on the basis of d. Even the quantitative approximation bias introduced by the application of d_1 (instead of d) is minimal, as the explanations on p. 68 clearly indicate. Any use of d_1 has no effect otherwise on the validity of note (i) p. 165. However, any reference below to d_1 will be identified by the '_' sign in the correct manner: $V^2_{\underline{W}*}$.

We now return to (122). With the previous explanations, it immediately follows, *ceteris paribus*, that:

$$\frac{\partial V^2_{W*}}{\partial V_{ao}} > 0, \quad \frac{\partial V^2_{W*}}{\partial V_b} > 0 \quad \text{and} \quad \frac{\partial V^2_{W*}}{\partial \rho_{aob}} > 0; \tag{125}$$

a *reduction* in lifetime earnings inequality is thus brought about, *ceteris paribus*, not only by a *more homogeneous* population with regard to the human capital basic stock $\tilde{a}_0$ and the human capital accumulation ability $\tilde{b}$ but also by a *lower* correlation between initial and growth endowment.

Now, how does the inequality of lifetime disposable earnings react to variations in the instrumental parameters of the economic policymaker associated with the model? What effects do the structural parameters have?

[4] An analytical evaluation of the partial derivatives $\partial d/\partial R$ and $\partial d/\partial P$ is, for example, still possible; the partial derivative $\partial d/\partial r$ and an anlytical analysis of the interaction with the remaining model parameters, on the other hand, cause the problems known from Chapter 2. In this case, d_1 can be of further use.

In order to be able to respond to questions of this type in an analytical fashion, the derivation is required of the conditions which permit the basic interdependencies between lifetime earnings inequality, on the one hand, and public policy parameters, structural parameters, distribution parameters and the underlying rational economic behaviour of the individuals, on the other, to be rendered explicit. Here, analogies to the two previous chapters gleam through; there also, this kind of explicit condition is required to uncover these interdependent structures.

In this case this can be put into practice as follows. Formally, one has:

$$V_{W^*}^2(x) = V_{W^*}^2[p(x)], \qquad x \in \{\underbrace{R, P, r}_{\text{policy parameters}};\ \overbrace{c, \delta, b_1, b_2}^{\text{structural parameters}}\};$$

such that:

$$\frac{\partial V_{W^*}^2}{\partial x} = \frac{\partial V_{W^*}^2}{\partial p}\frac{\partial p}{\partial x}.$$

Now, in accordance with $(1 >)\ \rho_{a_0 b} > 0$, $V_b > V_{a_0}$ and $d > 0$:

$$\frac{\partial V_{W^*}^2}{\partial p} \gtreqless 0 \Leftrightarrow d \lesseqgtr \chi_W, \tag{126}$$

where

$$\chi_W := \frac{1 - h_W \rho_{a_0 b}}{h_W - \rho_{a_0 b}} \frac{\sigma_{a_0}}{\sigma_b}, \quad h_W := \frac{V_b}{V_{a_0}}.$$

Furthermore:

$$\frac{\partial p}{\partial x} \gtreqless 0 \Leftrightarrow \frac{\partial d}{\partial x} \lesseqgtr 0. \tag{127}$$

Therefore, the following conditions are obtained:

$$\frac{\partial V_{W^*}^2}{\partial x} \begin{cases} >0, & \text{if } d \lessgtr \chi_W \text{ and simultaneously } \dfrac{\partial d}{\partial x} \lessgtr 0; \\ =0, & \text{if } d = \chi_W \text{ and/or } \dfrac{\partial d}{\partial x} = 0; \\ <0, & \text{if } d \lessgtr \chi_W \text{ and simultaneously } \dfrac{\partial d}{\partial x} \gtrless 0. \end{cases} \tag{128}$$

The results developed in Appendix 4 relating to χ can also be applied in the same way to the distribution constant χ_W. According to this, χ_W is always smaller than one, where $h_w > 1$ and $\sigma_b > \sigma_{a_0}$. In fact, χ_W is only positive when, *ceteris paribus*, the correlation coefficient ρ_{a_0b} assumes sufficiently small values,[5] and, from a theoretical point of view, one is on the safe side when $\chi_W \leqslant 0$ is assumed. On the other hand, the human capital growth value d is positive in any case and, as has been mentioned above, is only not significantly above 1 for parameter values which cannot be empirically substantiated. Both together imply that $d > \chi_W$, so that (128) can be reduced to:

$$\frac{\partial V_{W^*}^2}{\partial x} \gtreqless 0 \Leftrightarrow \frac{\partial d}{\partial x} \gtreqless 0. \tag{129}$$

This is the key relationship which the results derived below and in Section 5.2 are based on.

The question posed above on the inequality effects of the structural parameters of the model (the question on the effects of the policy parameters will be treated separately in the next section) can now be answered explicitly. In accordance with the theoretical parameter restrictions formulated in Section 2.1.1, the following is now obtained for the learning-by-doing opportunities, reflected by c, within an economy:

$$\frac{\partial V_{\underline{W}^*}^2}{\partial c} > 0; \tag{130}$$

since:

$$\frac{\partial d_1}{\partial c} > 0.$$

Better learning-by-doing opportunities therefore result in a *larger* lifetime earnings inequality.

What is behind this result? The reader will remember that the learning-by-doing parameter c is a fixed given structural characteristic which is the same for all individuals in the economy under observation, but the amount of human capital produced in period n 'at the same time' by way of the learning-by-doing effect (thus by the accumulation of practical job experience) can vary from individual to individual, since: $c(1 - s_n^j)K_n^j$, $n = 0, \ldots, N$; cf. Section 2.1.1. From the comparative static analysis of optimal lifetime earnings it is known that a higher c is of benefit to all individuals $\partial \underline{W}^{j*}/\partial c > 0\, \forall j$ (see Appendix 6). Those individuals, however, who are equipped with a better human capital basic stock a_0^j and/or higher human capital accumulation ability b_0^j and, thereby, also have, *ceteris paribus*, higher lifetime earnings at their disposal (cf. Appendix 6: (III) and (IV)), can adapt their plans to changing surroundings, so that they finally

[5] The precise condition is as follows (in accordance with the fact that $h_W > 1$): $\chi_W > 0 \Leftrightarrow \rho_{a_0b} < 1/h_W$.

end up with even higher lifetime earnings in comparison. The c effect on optimum human wealth is connected to the levels of a_0^j and b_0^j: in a wider sense, more capable individuals can make larger profits from a value of c which has increased and therefore exploit the new situation more effectively than those who are less capable: $\partial^2 \underline{W}^{j^*}/\partial a_0^j \partial c > 0, \partial^2 \underline{W}^{j^*}/\partial b_0^j \partial c > 0$. This provides an intuitive argument for the inequality effect obtained in (130) in connection with the comparative dynamic analysis of $\underline{A}_n^{j^{**}}$ relating to c (Section 2.3.4).

Furthermore, one has:

$$\frac{\partial V^2_{\underline{W}^*}}{\partial \delta} < 0; \tag{131}$$

since:

$$\frac{\partial \mathrm{d}_1}{\partial \delta} < 0.$$

A *higher* depreciation rate δ, caused for example by more rapid technical change within the economy under observation, results in a *reduction* in lifetime earnings inequality. The reasons for this are similar to those for the c effect. Those individuals who are more capable in a wider sense (therefore, those individuals who have higher values of a_0^j and/or b_0^j) are made to feel the effects of a higher human capital rate of decline δ more strongly than the less capable.

Last but not least, one obtains the following (mindful of the influences on the distribution parameters):

$$\frac{\partial V^2_{\underline{W}^*}}{\partial b_1} > 0; \quad \frac{\partial V^2_{\underline{W}^*}}{\partial b_2} > 0. \tag{132}$$

Higher input elasticities in human capital production consequently induce a *higher* inequality in lifetime disposable earnings.

5.2 Conflicts of public pricing policies

As detailed in Section 2.1.1, the human capital price R, the price of educational goods P and the interest rate r are termed 'policy parameters' since these prices represent those model parameters which the state can influence in the most direct fashion. Inequality effects of state measures are thus analysed within the framework of the present approach via these three quantities.

The objective outlined in the introduction of deriving analytically useful relationships between the distribution (or the inequality) of earnings and policy parameters, in order to obtain the most precise information possible on the consequences of distributional interventions, has been achieved with the closed form solution developed in Section 5.1 for the present third level of distribution as well. The question of the reaction of lifetime earnings inequality to variations in the instrumental parameters of the economic policymaker associated with the model can thus be explicitly answered.

In accordance with the theoretical parameter restrictions now familiar to the reader, the following result is obtained from (129):

$$\frac{\partial V_{W*}^2}{\partial R} > 0; \tag{133}$$

since:

$$\frac{\partial d}{\partial R} = \frac{b_2}{aR} d > 0.$$

An *increase* in the wage rate R thus results in an *increase* in lifetime earnings inequality. The adaptation reactions of the optimising individuals behind this effect (mindful of the relation $d > \chi_W$) to the changed price situation and the individual trajectory shifts resulting from this, are known to the reader from Section 2.3.

If one observes the inequality derived in Appendix 6: $\partial W^{j^*}/\partial R > 0 \, \forall j$, which implies that a higher human capital price increases the human capital of any individual, then the following mixed comparative static results: $\partial^2 W^{j^*}/\partial a_0^j \partial R > 0$ and $\partial^2 W^{j^*}/\partial b_0^j \partial R > 0$, provide an intuitive explanation for the inequality effect (133): the new situation of a higher wage rate R for all individuals is certainly advantageous; those individuals, however, who have a better human capital basic endowment a_0^j and/or higher human capital production efficiency b_0^j (note that $\tilde{a}_0$ and $\tilde{b}_0$ are positively correlated), and thereby have higher lifetime earnings (see Appendix 6), can benefit more from this change in situation with a corresponding modification in their optimal investment plans. This however results in a wider relative gap in individual lifetime earnings, compared to the original situation.

The two results below can be interpreted in a similar way. One finds:

$$\frac{\partial V_{W*}^2}{\partial P} < 0; \tag{134}$$

since:

$$\frac{\partial d}{\partial P} = -\frac{b_2}{aP} d < 0.$$

A *higher* price for human capital investment goods, P, accordingly induces a *reduction* in lifetime earnings inequality.

It is known that an increase in P corresponds to an indirect subsidy of human capital accumulation in the full-time schooling phase, for an increase in the price of educational goods causes investment in the earnings phase to become more expensive.[6] The present model predicts a reduction in the relative dispersion of human wealth in the event of such an (indirect) promotion of basic education. If the state introduces measures, on the other hand, which result in a fall in P, i.e. if it is subsidising the acquisition of human capital in the *working phase*, then this entails an *increase* in lifetime earnings inequality, according to (134).

Finally, for the third policy instrument, the following is obtained:

$$\frac{\partial V^2_{\underline{W}^*}}{\partial r} < 0; \tag{135}$$

since:

$$\frac{\partial \mathrm{d}_1}{\partial \mathrm{r}} < 0.$$

An *increase* in the interest rate r consequently instigates a *reduction* in the inequality of human capital.

Note: There is empirical confirmation of this model prediction; see Lillard (1977b, pp. 588–92). The other model prognoses ((125), (130)–(134)) have not been examined in the empirical literature published so far.

An intuitive argument for this effect can be developed once again on the basis of some comparative static results. On the one hand $\partial \underline{W}^{j^*}/\partial r < 0\, \forall j$ (cf. Appendix 6) implies that a higher interest rate lowers the human wealth of any individual; on the other hand one obtains: $\partial^2 \underline{W}^{j^*}/\partial a_0^j \partial r < 0$ and $\partial^2 \underline{W}^{j^*}/\partial b_0^j \partial r < 0$, i.e. the negative effect of an increase in interest rate has a stronger effect for the more capable individuals (in the wider sense) than for those less capable in comparison (thus for those who have a better basic endowment a_0^j and/or larger accumulation ability b_0^j; note here again the positive correlation between $\tilde{a}_0$ and $\tilde{b}_0$). The relative distance between individual human wealth is reduced; inequality decreases.

Note: The effect obtained in (135) also makes sense from another position. Reference has already been made in the comparative dynamic analysis in Section 2.3.3 to the 'horizon-reducing' effect of an increase in interest rate. The income flow over later periods with an increasing interest rate is always allotted less significance (cf. (119)). The widening gap between individual trajectories, increasing towards the

[6] The reader is reminded of the substitutional relationship between investment in full-time schooling and on-the-job training.

end of working life, is now of less importance in comparison; consequently, $V^2_{\underline{W}^*}$ falls.

The present model structure reveals a *policy conflict* which has already been encountered in a similar form in Section 4.3. The policy effects resulting from the intertemporal optimising reactions of the individuals with a given distribution constellation (summarised in the characteristics of the distribution constant χ_W) are of two types.

Firstly, one has the inequality results (133), (134) and (135). On the other hand, one finds with the help of the relations (V), (VI) and (VII) from Appendix 6 applicable to all individuals, that the following applies for the average lifetime earnings within the economy under observation:

$$\frac{\partial \mu_{W^*}}{\partial R} > 0, \quad \frac{\partial \mu_{W^*}}{\partial P} < 0 \quad \text{and} \quad \frac{\partial \mu_{\underline{W}^*}}{\partial r} < 0. \tag{136}$$

The present approach therefore implies an *incompatibility* (given the instrumental parameters the model offers to the policymaker) of the two social objectives of a higher per capita human wealth (in a wider sense, of a *higher living standard* in general) and of a *lower level of inequality in the distribution of human wealth.*

Moreover, the result (135), together with the results of the policy analysis of Chapter 4 leads to one of the key points of this study.

Now, it must be agreed that the main argument in terms of distribution policy for any influencing of the prices R, P and r by the state is based on the desire to achieve a more even distribution of earnings. This criterion is, however, more *ambiguous* than it seems at first glance; in particular, it must be explained what precisely is meant by a 'more even distribution of earnings'.

Empirical information on inequality of earnings is usually presented on the basis of the *current* earnings distribution.[7] This, however, means in the context of the life-cycle model developed in this study that there would be income inequality even if the income profiles of the individuals were identical; the current earnings distribution would show inequality because the type and extent of individual human capital investment in the course of the working-life change, and indiviuals of different working ages typically exhibit different earnings levels (cf. Chapter 2).[8] Also, for the case where the

[7] The current earnings distribution corresponds to the distribution of periodic earnings (in general, annual earnings) over all individuals living within the economy under observation at the time (→ Chapter 4).

[8] V^2_{BT} in (99) is positive. The age-dependence of earnings has been empirically established as well and it is regarded as an indisputable fact today (see the references cited in footnote 76, p. 69).

individual income flows have the same present value (based on the time of entry onto the labour market, i.e. in terms of the initial period ($\hat{=} n = 0$)), but where the trajectories have different growth rates, there is no inequality of human wealth (viewed from the initial period); on the other hand, for the current earnings distribution there would be positive disparities. And finally: what would happen to the unequalising influence of the initial endowment of human capital $\tilde{a}_0$, if we restrict ourselves to the discussion of the current earnings distribution in the context of the present model?

For all these reasons the current, or periodic, concept of inequality seems to be too shortsighted for the evaluation of distributional policy measures. The present approach rather suggests a *lifetime concept* of inequality, in order to filter out the 'long-term' differences between individuals.[9] According to this, a society in question is to be considered as a completely egalitarian one, if the human wealth of each individual is the same (thus: $W^{j^*} = W \, \forall j$) – even if such a view can be accompanied by considerable inequalities in the current earnings distribution.

> *Note*: Reference to this type of point occurs without any normative intentions; after all, a purely positive analysis is being carried out. The extent to which lifetime earnings is used as a reference value, in distribution policy terms, for the evaluation of earnings inequality is also dependent on the question of interest. Inequality, in terms of a lifetime, is, for example, useful when it is concerned with the inequality of *opportunities* in a lifetime; the inequality of lifetime earnings can hardly be very suitable for the measurement of *poverty*, however. An examination at this point of the normative, social significance of the lifetime earnings distribution would be interesting, but would constitute an independent research project.

As, in reality, policy measures aimed at achieving a more equal distribution of earnings are generally directed at the *current* distribution (often, simply for the lack of empirical information on the lifetime earnings distribution), the crucial question now emerges as to whether the decisions made on this basis are *generally compatible* with those which would have been made on the basis of the lifetime earnings distribution. The answer to this is *no*. For there can be situations where a certain policy measure, in distribution policy terms, reduces inequality in the lifetime earnings distribution but at the same time alters the allocation plans of the maximising individuals in such a way that inequality in the current earnings distribution increases.

The present model does, in fact, contain an explicit example of such a situation: an increase in the interest rate reduces inequality in human

[9] Cross-sectional measurements are not capable of this.
Incidentally, the reader is reminded of the assumption of a perfect capital market.

capital (cf. (135)); on the other hand, it was established in Chapter 4 that an increase in the interest rate increases inequality in the current earnings distribution (cf. (110)). An interest rate policy, motivated by distributional considerations, which is tailored to the periodic concept of inequality, thereby results in a *systematic increase* in lifetime earnings inequality.

The policy instruments R and P, however, have been proved to be compatible with both inequality concepts.

Notes: (i) The incompatibility in the case of the instrument r and the compatibility in the case of the instruments R and P are *robust* against empirically observable variations of the model parameters since:

- there are identical parameter conditions for a hypothetical inversion of effects in (108)–(110) and (133)–(135),[10] and
- the results (108)–(110) remain valid for any change in the age structure in the empirically relevant region $0 < \gamma < r$.[11]

(ii) If the sum of the birth growth rate and the death rate, γ, exceeds the interest rate r in a hypothetical economy (without, however, violating the assumption of positive average disposable earnings within the economy) such that $z_2 < 0$ and, finally, $z_2/z_1 < \chi$, then all three distribution policy instruments are compatible with both inequality concepts. Therefore, if there is an economy with an extremely high proportion of young age groups, then the policy effects relating to the inequality of current earnings and the inequality of lifetime earnings are shown to be in the same direction, (in particular, the sign in (110) changes given the present empirically not observable conditions).

(iii) The fact that the above incompatibility affects the interest rate, but not the prices R and P, originates from the structure of the control problem of Chapter 2 and from the relationships of the distribution parameters. Just from the first factor mentioned, it is clear that the discounting function assumed by r is more complex than the function of the prices R and P. Whereas R and P enter the objective functional of the control problem (and finally also the optimal trajectories $\{A_n^{j**}\}_{n \in \mathbf{N}}, j \in \mathbf{J}$) in a simple, multiplicative manner, r is related to working age n (and thereby to the age structure within an economy) in a non-linear way.

The essence of the above analysis is that reallocation reactions of optimising individuals and the fact that not all individuals within a population are of the same age, can destroy simple relationships between

[10] Namely (mindful of the theoretical restrictions: $\rho_{a_0b} > 0; \rho_{a_1b} > 0; h_W > 1; h_0 > 1; R, P, b_1, b_2, r, \delta, c > 0; b_1 + b_2 < 1; r + \delta > c; 0 < \delta < 1$); ρ_{a_0b} (or ρ_{a_1b}) is close to 0, h_W (or h_0) is approximately equal to 1, $P \gg R$, b_1 and b_2 are small, r large, δ large and c small. These hypothetical conditions are required in order to generate the relationships $z_2/z_1 < \chi$ and $d < \chi_W$ and thereby the reversals of effect mentioned.

[11] See Section 4.3. (133)–(135) are independent of γ.

the inequality of current earnings, the inequality of lifetime earnings and public policy.

In order to illustrate the reallocation mechanism of the individual investment plans, at least one choice variable is required (the present model has three: $\{s_n^j\}$, $\{D_n^j\}$ and S^j). An addition of further choice variables would not remove any of the above-mentioned influences and it is these influences which are responsible for the characteristic results of Sections 4.3 and 5.2. What is making the model tick is the complicated reaction of earnings inequality to a variation in the policy parameters, when the *reallocation effects* of maximising individuals, the existence of an *age distribution* and the *heterogeneous nature* of the population over and above the age differences, are explicitly taken into account – influential factors which all appear in a more general model as well.

One of the objectives expressed for this study was to provide a *method* for analysing the effects of policy measures on the inequality of earnings and to do this within the context of a dynamic micro-economic investment model of the type developed in Chapter 2. At the same time, by way of an explicit distinction between three levels (namely, that of the distribution within an age group, that of the distribution over all age groups and that of the lifetime earnings distribution) connections between *age structure*, *inequality* and *public pricing policy* are to be demonstrated.

The specific model and the specific analytical approach served primarily to provide illustrations and explanations of that method in these terms. The specific results of the present section are therefore intended not so much to assert empirical truths, but rather to *warn* economic policymakers practising in this sphere. For, from the above results, it does not only follow that there can be *inconsistencies* (with regard to R, P and r) in the social aims of a higher standard of living and a lower inequality in lifetime earnings, but it has also been shown that there can be a *policy conflict*, under certain circumstances, between a reduction in current earnings inequality and a reduction in lifetime earnings inequality. This conflict only arises in certain cases. It is the task of economic theory to develop models which illustrate such cases.

5.3 Inequality of lifetime earnings versus inequality of annual earnings

According to an opinion frequently expressed in discussions on distribution policy, inequality of lifetime earnings is *always less* than that of annual earnings. The empirical findings available on this topic also seem to confirm this view.[12] However, it is difficult to shake off the impression that

[12] Cf. Lillard (1977a, 1977b), Blinder (1980), Irvine (1980) and Blomquist (1981).

the results of these studies are more dependent on the assumptions made than the actual given empirical cases.[13] In fact, the following analysis will show that it is in no way clear, *a priori*, whether inequality in the current earnings distribution exceeds that in the lifetime earnings distribution or not. Thanks to the closed form solutions developed in Sections 4.1 and 5.1, the interdependencies of the factors involved can be traced explicitly and precise conditions for a positive or negative answer to the question posed can be provided.

Whether lifetime earnings inequality is below or above annual earnings inequality is dependent on the extent to which differences in individual earnings trajectories are compensated for by the summation relating to W^{j^*} (cf. (119)), or how large the remaining 'long-term' differences in the $\tilde{W}^*$ distribution are compared with the overall variability in the current earnings distribution. The reader must first of all understand that the $\tilde{W}^*$ inequality can also exceed the annual earnings inequality, and this occurs earlier, the stronger the variation in individual characteristics (not dependent on *n*) becomes, compared to the pure age variation of earnings.[14]

If one sets aside any potential differences in the coefficients of variation V_{a_1} and V_{a_0} and the correlation coefficients $\rho_{a_1 b}$ and $\rho_{a_0 b}$, then one finds, in accordance with the known theoretical parameter restrictions of the model and the relationships developed in Sections 4.1 and 5.1,[15] that:

$$
\begin{aligned}
V^2_{\underline{W}^*} \lesseqqgtr V^2_{\underline{A}^{**}} &\Leftrightarrow p \gtreqqless u \\
&\Leftrightarrow d_1 \lesseqqgtr \frac{z_2}{z_1}\frac{\mu_{a_0}}{\mu_{a_1}} \\
&\Leftrightarrow \frac{r(r-\gamma)(r+\delta a+cb_2 rq)}{\gamma a(r+\delta)} \gtreqqless \frac{\mu_{a_1}}{\mu_{a_0}}.
\end{aligned}
\tag{137}
$$

The quotient μ_{a_1}/μ_{a_0} (> 0) is smaller than 1, whenever the average initial human capital stock of the population exceeds the average basic education efficiency; this should, however, be the case as a rule.[16] Whether the left-hand side of the final condition above is greater than 1 cannot be determined *a priori*; it depends on the specific parameter constellation in the economy under observation.[17]

[13] Cf., for example, Lillard (1977a, pp. 49–50).

[14] Extreme example: the individual earnings profiles run horizontally; thus no income change occurs with working age.

[15] In particular, therefore, in accordance with: $0 < u < 1, z_2/z_1 > \chi; 0 < p < 1$ and $d > \chi_W$.

[16] On the basis of the standard parameter set, a quotient value of below 0.5 is obtained.

[17] The empirically supported standard parameter set (19) provides the following value when $\gamma = 0.01$ (p. 143): $r(r-\gamma)(r+\delta a+cb_2 rq)/\gamma a(r+\delta) = 0.59 < 1$.

The result of partial differentiation of this expression is that the inequality $V^2_{\underline{W}*} < V^2_{\underline{A}**}$ is *violated* all the earlier, such that annual earnings are distributed at least *as evenly* as lifetime earnings, the larger γ is (= sum of birth growth rate and death rate), the *larger*, thereby, the proportion of the population in younger age groups,[18] the *smaller* the interest rate r, the *worse* the learning-by-doing opportunities within the economy (the smaller, therefore, c), the *more rapid* the decline in productivity caused by ageing (the larger, therefore, δ) and the *smaller* the human capital production elasticities b_1 and b_2; in addition, the *larger* the average full-time schooling efficiency μ_{a_1} and the *smaller* the average human capital basic stock μ_{ao}.

> *Note*: The statements relating to γ, r, μ_{a_1} and μ_{ao} could have been derived from the results already available.[19] The remaining statements were not clear from the outset, as the signs of the effects in (115)–(117) and (130)–(132) coincide respectively. Note also that the two prices R and P have no effect in this instance.

Even when one considers that, in general, $\rho_{aob} < \rho_{a_1b}$,[20] which interacts with the suppressed $\sigma^2_e > 0$ in the direction: '$V^2_{\underline{W}*} < V^2_{\underline{Y}**}$',[21] it is *not clear, in theoretical terms*, whether the question posed at the beginning of this section should be answered positively or negatively. Under the requirements just derived from the final condition in (137), the non-compensated 'long-term' differences (mindful of the divergences caused by $\tilde{S}^*$) prove to be considerable and, under certain circumstances, even dominating.

One should approach this result with the necessary caution owing to the simplifying assumption of the underlying life-cycle model (see Chapter 2); however it does suggest a basic reflection of the widely held view, that the inequality of human capital is always less than that of current earnings (thus than that of earnings in cross-sectional analyses).

5.4 Decomposition analysis of lifetime earnings inequality

The additive structure of the $\tilde{W}^*$ equation (121) developed in Section 5.1 allows the level of lifetime earnings inequality to be observed at a more disaggregate level than before; it permits a *decomposition analysis* of

[18] Note in this instance that γ must realistically remain smaller than r.

[19] Cf. (118) ($V^2_{\underline{W}*}$ is not dependent on γ), (110) and (135), as well as (111) and (125).

[20] In contrast to $\tilde{a}_0$ and $\tilde{b}_0$, $\tilde{a}_1$ and $\tilde{b}$ are, in their content, related variables: both $\tilde{a}_1$ and $\tilde{b}$ $(:= \tilde{b}_0^{1/a})$ denote human capital production efficiencies. $\tilde{a}_0$, on the other hand, embodies the basic stock of human capital at the beginning of economic life.

Whether V_{a_1} is larger or smaller than V_{ao} cannot be judged in theoretical terms.

[21] Cf. (100), (102) and (122).

inequality.[22] This type of analysis has significant consequences, since in terms of distribution policy and, in particular, social policy, it is in general not the extent of inequality which is important, but the *causes* of inequality and the *relative significance* of these causes.

As a reminder:

$$\tilde{W}^* = \tilde{W}_1 + \tilde{W}_2,$$

where:

$$\tilde{W}_1 := d_2\tilde{a}_0 \quad \text{and} \quad \tilde{W}_2 := d_3\tilde{b}.$$

$\tilde{W}^*$ represents the distribution of optimal disposable lifetime earnings within an economy; in short: the distribution of optimal human wealth.

The terms of the sum, $\tilde{W}_1$ and $\tilde{W}_2$, generated by the structure of the key equation (121), are open to a convenient and at the same time informative interpretation. $\tilde{W}_1$ represents the distribution of the *initial component*, since it concerns the basic stock of productive capacity at the beginning of the economic planning horizon, $\tilde{a}_0$, weighted with the proportionality factor d_2 originating from the optimising process. $\tilde{W}_2$ represents the distribution of the *growth component*, since, in this instance, one is confronted with the accumulation efficiency $\tilde{b}$ $(:= \tilde{b}_0^{1/a})$ weighted with the proportionality factor d_3 originating from the optimising process, in which the permanent income change factors relevant for the growth of individual earnings are incorporated (see Chapter 2).

What share of the overall inequality in human wealth is allocated to the initial component and what is allocated to the growth component? The *relative inequality contributions* of these components are normally determined from the following:

$$RU_1 := \frac{\text{cov}(\tilde{W}_1, \tilde{W}^*)}{\sigma^2_{W^*}}; \quad RU_2 := \frac{\text{cov}(\tilde{W}_2, \tilde{W}^*)}{\sigma^2_{W^*}}. \qquad (138)$$

Notes: (i) RU_1 and RU_2 are based on the so-called 'natural' decomposition which assigns to each component half of the common interaction term $2p(1-p)V_{a_0}V_b\rho_{a_0b}$ (from (122)).[23]

(ii) One of the main attractions of these *relative* measures consists of the fact that they are independent of the choice of the inequality index under certain mild requirements (therefore, they are independent of whether the inequality is measured, for example, by the square of the coefficient of variation or not).[24]

(iii) To limit oneself to $\tilde{a}_0$ instead of $\tilde{W}_1$ and to $\tilde{b}_0$ instead of $\tilde{W}_2$ would be ignoring the maximising effects.

[22] A formal piece of literature has been produced on this topic; see Shorrocks (1982) and the approaches there. [23] Cf. Shorrocks (1982, pp. 194–5).

[24] See Shorrocks (1982, pp. 204–5).

If one applies the appropriate variance and covariance expressions to (138), the following is obtained after some algebraic reformulations:[25]

$$RU_1 = \frac{1}{1+\Omega}, \quad RU_2 = \frac{\Omega}{1+\Omega}; \tag{139}$$

with:

$$\Omega := \frac{\operatorname{cov}(\tilde{W}_2, \tilde{W}^*)}{\operatorname{cov}(\tilde{W}_1, \tilde{W}^*)} = \frac{d/k_W + \rho_{a_0b}}{k_W/d + \rho_{a_0b}},$$

$$d := d_3/d_2, \quad k_W := \sigma_{a_0}/\sigma_b.$$

The proportionality factor ratio d is a quantity which has already been analysed in Section 5.1; in accordance with that, it is realistic to assume $d > 1$. The ratio of the standard deviations, k_W (> 0), is, in contrast to that, below 1; on the one hand, the cause of this is within the structure of the variables $\tilde{a}_0$ and $\tilde{b}_0$ themselves,[26] but, on the other hand, it is also, however, in the fact that $a < 1$.

With the relationship arising from this, $d/k_W > 1$, one obtains the following straightaway (in accordance with $\rho_{a_0b} > 0$):

$$RU_2 > RU_1; \tag{140}$$

i.e. the initial component is *below* the growth component in its relative significance for lifetime earnings inequality.

As long as $\sigma_{b_0} > \sigma_{a_0}$, a mechanical model, i.e. a model which ignores all optimising effects of any kind, is also capable of achieving this result. Taking into account the individual optimising reactions, however, leads to a *strengthening* of that trend.[27] The intertemporal maximising behaviour of the individuals accordingly induces a weakening of the influence of the initial stock variable $\tilde{a}_0$ and an increase in the influence of the accumulation variable $\tilde{b}_0$. Consequently, a policy aimed at a reduction in lifetime earnings inequality must chiefly ensure a *reduction* in the relative inequality contribution of the *growth component*.

Before an examination is undertaken of where approaches could be made to this within the framework of the present model, the question of what *overall* influence the intertemporal optimising behaviour of the individuals has on the inequality of human wealth is examined briefly. If one compares

[25] $\operatorname{cov}(\tilde{W}_1, \tilde{W}^*) = d_2^2\sigma_{a_0}^2 + d_2 d_3 \operatorname{cov}(\tilde{a}_0, \tilde{b})$; $\operatorname{cov}(\tilde{W}_2, \tilde{W}^*) = d_3^2\sigma_b^2 + d_2 d_3 \operatorname{cov}(\tilde{a}_0, \tilde{b})$.

[26] See (123) and (18a).

[27] One gets: $\Omega_{ME} := (\sigma_{b_0}/\sigma_{a_0} + \rho_{a_0b_0})/(\sigma_{a_0}/\sigma_{b_0} + \rho_{a_0b_0})$. Now: $\sigma_{a_0}/\sigma_{b_0} > \sigma_{a_0}/\sigma_b$, since $\sigma_b = \sigma_{b_0^{1/a}} > \sigma_{b_0}$ (because $a < 1$), and thereby: $(1 <) 1/(\sigma_{a_0}/\sigma_{b_0}) < d/k_W$; with $\rho_{a_0b_0} \geqslant \rho_{a_0b}$ (similar argument as on p. 218), it therefore follows that: $\Omega_{ME} < \Omega$. This means however that: $RU_1 < RU_{1,ME}$ and $RU_2 > RU_{2,ME}$.

the weighting factor p originating from the optimising process with the factor p_{ME} resulting from the mechanical descriptive model, then one discovers that $p < p_{ME}$;

since:

$$p := \frac{\mu_{ao}}{\mu_{a_0} + d\mu_b} \quad \text{(cf. (122))}, \quad p_{ME} := \frac{\mu_{ao}}{\mu_{a_0} + \mu_{b_0}};$$

thus: $p < p_{ME} \Leftrightarrow d > \mu_{b_0}/\mu_b$, which is however satisfied since it is known that $d > 1$, and at the same time $\mu_b = \mu_{b0}^{1/a} > \mu_{b_0}$ (> 0) (as a reminder: $a < 1$).

However, this implies that:

$$V_{W^*}^2(p) > V_{W^*}^2(p_{ME}) =: V_{WME}^2, \tag{141}$$

for, since $d > \chi_W$, then: $\partial V_{W^*}^2/\partial p < 0$ (see (126)). As in the previous chapter, one also notes here an *increase*, caused by the optimising reactions of the individuals, of the inequality effect resulting overall from the basic individual variables.

Let us return to the policy recommendations developed from the above decomposition analysis to concentrate primarily on RU_2. What measures can cause a weakening in the relative inequality contribution of the growth component? How does public policy (working through the prices R, P and r) affect the proportional component contributions? How are these inequality contributions affected by variations of the structural features (reflected by c, δ, b_1 and b_2) and by changes in the distribution properties of $\tilde{a}_0$ and $\tilde{b}$ (characterised by k_W and ρ_{aob})?

The closed forms of RU_1 and RU_2 permit these questions to be answered analytically. Using (139), it is first possible to obtain the following, *ceteris paribus*, for the distribution characteristics of the basic variables summarised in k_W and ρ_{aob}:

$$\frac{\partial RU_1}{\partial k_W} > 0, \quad \frac{\partial RU_2}{\partial k_W} < 0; \tag{142}$$

and

$$\frac{\partial RU_1}{\partial \rho_{aob}} > 0, \quad \frac{\partial RU_2}{\partial \rho_{aob}} < 0.\text{[28]} \tag{143}$$

[28] Since: $\partial RU_1/\partial \Omega < 0$, $\partial RU_2/\partial \Omega > 0$; and, *ceteris paribus*: $\partial \Omega/\partial k_W < 0$ and $\partial \Omega/\partial \rho_{aob} < 0$ (since $0 < k_W < d$).

Note: The fact that the partial derivatives of RU_1 and RU_2 always have opposite signs, is based on the fact that: $RU_1 + RU_2 = 1$.

According to (143), a *stronger* correlation between initial and growth variables generates an *increase* in the decomposition share RU_1 and a *reduction* in the relative inequality contribution of the growth component RU_2, which is a result in line with (140).

Note: Note that the *absolute* inequality contribution of the growth component, AU_2, and that of the initial component, AU_1, *increases* in the event of a stronger correlation between start and growth:

$$AU_1 := \frac{\operatorname{cov}(\tilde{W}_1, \tilde{W}^*)}{\mu_{W^*}^2}, \quad AU_2 := \frac{\operatorname{cov}(\tilde{W}_2, \tilde{W}^*)}{\mu_{W^*}^2},^{29} \tag{144}$$

and

$$\frac{\partial AU_1}{\partial \rho_{aob}} = \frac{\partial AU_2}{\partial \rho_{aob}} = p(1-p)V_{ao}V_b > 0,$$

since $V_{ao} > 0$, $V_b > 0$ and $0 < p < 1$. This is a 'decomposition confirmation' of the result obtained in (125) concerning ρ_{aob}: because $AU_1 + AU_2 = V_{W^*}^2$.

The result (142) is also obvious: a *larger* value of k_W, i.e. an increase in σ_{ao} and/or a decrease in σ_b, *increases, ceteris paribus*, the relative inequality contribution of the initial component and *decreases* that of the growth component.

In view of the distributional target derived above, (142) and (143) force us to watch for influences which increase the correlation coefficient ρ_{aob} and the dispersion ratio k_W. Now it can be established from (123) and (18a) (in combination with (63) and (64)) that the variables $\tilde{G}$, $\tilde{HO}$ and $\tilde{CU}$ determining the human capital basic stock $\tilde{a}_0$ are also indirectly involved in the human capital accumulation efficiency $\tilde{b}_0$ (and thereby also in $\tilde{b}_0^{1/a} =: \tilde{b}$) by way of the learning ability $\tilde{LA}$ and the *DF* factor $\tilde{DF}$; consequently, no clear predictions relating to ρ_{aob} and k_W are possible as regards either the inherited characteristics $\tilde{G}$, the family background $\tilde{HO}$ or the cultural influences $\tilde{CU}$. In the three additional variables occurring in $\tilde{b}_0$, $\tilde{QPC}(\underline{\tilde{a}}, \underline{\tilde{b}}, \underline{\tilde{c}})$, $\tilde{CR}$ and $\tilde{SQ}$, one does, however, discover the factor cluster required for the purposes of clear predictions, since, firstly, none of these variables occurs in $\tilde{a}_0$ and, secondly, $\tilde{QPC}$, $\tilde{CR}$ and $\tilde{SQ}$ are (stochastically) independent of $\tilde{G}$, $\tilde{HO}$ and $\tilde{CU}$ by construction; in accordance with note (i), p. 37 this independence can also be justified with regard to its contents. Measures which induce a *reduction in the relative variation* in the *leadership*

[29] Cf. Shorrocks (1982, p. 195) on these definitions.

and organisation abilities of the individuals, in the *willingness to take risks*, in the *ability to assume responsibility*, in the *standard of the examination results* as well as in the *quality of the education establishments*, lead to an increase in both ρ_{aob} and k_W and thus to the distributionally desired change in RU_2.

Moreover, how does the relative inequality contribution of the growth component react to the instrumental parameters of economic policymakers associated with the model? What effects do the structural parameters have? A response to these questions requires, first of all, several formal steps. The interdependent model structure behind the results developed below, in particular the role of the maximising behaviour of the individuals, must be fairly familiar to the reader by now and therefore no longer requires any special emphasis.

Generally one has the following (cf. (139)):

$$RU_2 = RU_2\{\Omega[d(x)]\}, \quad x \in \{R, P, r; c, \delta, b_1, b_2\};$$

so that:

$$\frac{\partial RU_2}{\partial x} = \frac{\partial RU_2}{\partial \Omega}\frac{\partial \Omega}{\partial d}\frac{\partial d}{\partial x};$$

since:

$$\frac{\partial RU_2}{\partial \Omega} > 0 \quad \text{and} \quad \frac{\partial \Omega}{\partial d} > 0,$$

it follows that:

$$\frac{\partial RU_2}{\partial x} \gtreqless 0 \Leftrightarrow \frac{\partial d}{\partial x} \gtreqless 0. \tag{145}$$

An analytical evaluation of the productivity growth value d has already been carried out in the previous sections of this chapter.[30] With those results, the following price and structural effects are obtained:

$$\frac{\partial RU_2}{\partial R} > 0, \quad \frac{\partial RU_2}{\partial P} < 0, \quad \frac{\partial RU_2}{\partial r} < 0; \tag{146}$$

$$\frac{\partial RU_2}{\partial c} > 0, \quad \frac{\partial RU_2}{\partial \delta} < 0, \quad \frac{\partial RU_2}{\partial b_1} > 0, \quad \frac{\partial RU_2}{\partial b_2} > 0. \tag{147}$$

Note: Accordingly one obtains the opposite signs for the decomposition share with the initial component RU_1.

[30] Not least with the aid of d_1, which was always called upon when d could no longer be handled analytically – see Section 5.1.

A *lower* wage rate R, a *higher* price for educational goods P, a *higher* interest rate r, *worse* opportunities for human capital accumulation by practical job experience c, a *higher* human capital depreciation rate δ and *lower* input production elasticities b_1 and b_2 accordingly decrease the relative inequality contribution of the growth component. As long as $d/k_W > 1$, therefore as long as the relative inequality contribution of the growth component exceeds that of the initial component (cf. (140)), these measures, which alter the price and structural parameters in the indicated directions, generate a modification of the proportional inequality contributions RU_1 and RU_2 which is consistent with the policy recommendation derived above.

In conclusion, it must be pointed out that the signs obtained in (146) and (147) in the present decomposition analysis of lifetime earnings inequality, which involve a desired weakening of the relative inequality contribution of the growth component, are *compatible* with those which follow the general aim of a reduction in the inequality of human wealth and which were derived in Sections 5.1 and 5.2. In fact, the conditions occurring in (145) and (129) correspond to one another.[31]

5.5 On the functional form of the lifetime earnings distribution

A determination of the functional type of the lifetime earnings distribution is of both theoretical interest and practical significance. The theoretical attraction of this task comes, on the one hand, from the fact that the theoretical literature on the subject has so far not had anything to say on the functional form of the distribution of human wealth and, on the other, from the hope that it will be possible to explicitly combine the *parameters* of that distribution with the *economic factors* of the model developed in this study; this would permit responses to be made to a series of new questions which have not so far been dealt with (see Section 5.6 on this as well).

In practical terms, knowledge of the functional type of the distribution is a crucial requirement for a *sound* analysis of *empirical data* on the distribution of lifetime earnings and therefore, for example, for an estimation of population characteristics of interest. Furthermore, *simulation experiments* are made possible.

Let us make a brief recapitulation:

$$\tilde{W}^* = \tilde{W}_1 + \tilde{W}_2;$$

$$\tilde{W}_1 := d_2\tilde{a}_0, \quad d_2 := R\Pi_N;$$

[31] The reader may have the 'intuitive' idea that in the case where $RU_2 > RU_1$ the directions of change in RU_2 and $V^2_{W^*}$ must *always* be the same. The fact that this is not the case can be established, for example, from (143) and (125).

$$\tilde{W}_2 := d_3\tilde{b}, \quad d_3 := \sum_{n=0}^{N} \hat{M}_n(1+r)^{-n}, \quad \tilde{b} := \tilde{b}_0^{1/a}.$$

For the notation and interpretation, please refer to the previous sections, 5.1 and 5.4.

With the analysis in Section 3.2.2 and the explanations relating to $\tilde{a}_0$ in Section 5.1, the assumption of a *joint log-normal distribution* for both the variables $\tilde{a}_0$ and $\tilde{b}_0$ is obvious. With $d_2 > 0$ and $d_3 > 0$, it follows that $\tilde{W}_1$ and $\tilde{W}_2$ are also jointly log-normally distributed,[32] so that the variable $\tilde{W}^*$, which represents the distribution of optimal human wealth within the economy under observation, is found to be the *sum* of two *stochastically dependent, non-identically log-normally distributed* variables.

The density function of $\tilde{W}^*$ is then formally represented as:

$$f_{W^*}(w) = \int_0^w f_{W_1,W_2}(w_1, w - w_1)dw_1; \tag{148}$$

where:

$$f_{W_1,W_2}(w_1,w_2) = \frac{1}{2\pi\sigma_1\sigma_2\sqrt{1-\rho^2}}\frac{1}{w_1w_2} \cdot \exp\left\{-\frac{1}{2(1-\rho^2)}\left[\left(\frac{\log w_1 - \mu_1}{\sigma_1}\right)^2 - 2\rho\frac{\log w_1 - \mu_1}{\sigma_1}\frac{\log w_2 - \mu_2}{\sigma_2} + \left(\frac{\log w_2 - \mu_2}{\sigma_2}\right)^2\right]\right\};$$

$$0 < w_1, w_2 < \infty; \sigma_1, \sigma_2 > 0; \ -1 < \rho < 1;$$

and where:

$$\mu_1 := \log(R\Pi_N) + \mu_{\log ao}, \quad \sigma_1^2 := \sigma_{\log ao}^2;$$

$$\mu_2 := \log\left(\sum_{n=0}^{N} \hat{M}_n(1+r)^{-n}\right) + \frac{1}{a}\mu_{\log bo}, \quad \sigma_2^2 := \frac{1}{a^2}\sigma_{\log bo}^2;$$

$$\rho^2 := \rho_{\log W_1, \log W_2}^2 = \left[\frac{\text{cov}(\log \tilde{W}_1, \log \tilde{W}_2)}{\sigma_1\sigma_2}\right]^2.$$

Notes: (i) w, w_1 and w_2 denote the values assumed by $\tilde{W}^*$, $\tilde{W}_1$ and $\tilde{W}_2$ ('realisations').

[32] See theorem 2.1 in Aitchison and Brown (1957, p. 11).

(ii) $f_{W_1,W_2}(w_1, w_2) \equiv 0$, if $w_1 \leqslant 0$ and/or $w_2 \leqslant 0$.
(iii) For the marginal distributions in the two-dimensional distribution of the vector $(\tilde{W}_1, \tilde{W}_2)$:

$$\tilde{W}_1 \sim \Lambda(\mu_1, \sigma_1^2) \quad \text{and} \quad \tilde{W}_2 \sim \Lambda(\mu_2, \sigma_2^2).$$

The density function f_{W^*} specified in this way, which can be interpreted under the assumptions formulated in Section 1.3.2 as (expected) relative frequency distribution, is difficult to handle analytically. The theoretical statistics literature known to me has not been able to develop an explicit formula for a density of this type, i.e. to obtain the precise solution of (148) in a closed form, and neither have I.

For the case where the first three theoretical moments of the variable $\tilde{W}^*$ can be determined explicitly, an *approximate form* $\hat{f}_{W^*}$ can be obtained for the complicated theoretical density function f_{W^*}. This fact is due to the approach devised by Karl Pearson[33] and the further development of this by Müller and Vahl (1976). According to this, the member of the Pearson distribution family to be used for an approximation to f_{W^*} is derived from the value of a criterion κ, where:

$$\kappa := \frac{\beta_1(\beta_2 + 3)^2}{4(4\beta_2 - 3\beta_1)(2\beta_2 - 3\beta_1 - 6)}, \tag{149}$$

with:

$$\beta_1 := \mu_3^2/\mu_2^3, \quad \beta_2 := \mu_4/\mu_2^2; \quad \mu_k := E[\tilde{W}^* - E(\tilde{W}^*)]^k.$$[34]

For the calculation of this criterion, the fourth moment of the $\tilde{W}^*$ distribution is apparently also required. Müller and Vahl (1976) have, however, found a formula for β_2 which does not include μ_4, provided that the left boundary of the $\tilde{W}^*$ distribution is known in addition to the first three moments. If this point is denoted as w_0, then β_2 is determined from:[35]

[33] See the presentations in Elderton and Johnson (1969, chapters 4–5) and Solomon and Stephens (1978).

[34] β_1 and β_2 are two parameters known from mathematical statistics, which may serve to characterise the form of a distribution. '$\sqrt{\beta_1}$' is, for example, a common measure of *skewness* and '$\beta_2 - 3$' is a common measure of *kurtosis*. (The reader has already encountered these measurements, although in a different notation: $\sqrt{\beta_1} = \gamma_1$ and $\beta_2 - 3 = \gamma_2$.)

Incidentally the present β_1 and β_2 must not be confused with β_n from Section 3.4.

[35] Note, in this case, the following *limiting conditions* for $\sqrt{\beta_1}$ and $\sigma_{W^*}/(\mu_{W^*} - w_0)$ ($\beta_2 < 1$ is not defined; cf., for example, Kendall and Stuart, 1977, p. 88):

$$\textit{Lower bound}: \sqrt{\beta_1} = \frac{\left(\dfrac{\sigma_{W^*}}{\mu_{W^*} - w_0}\right)^2 - 1}{\dfrac{\sigma_{W^*}}{\mu_{W^*} - w_0}};$$

$$\beta_2 = \frac{3\left[\frac{\sigma_{W^*}}{\mu_{W^*} - w_0}\sqrt{\beta_1}\left(1 + \frac{\sigma_{W^*}}{\mu_{W^*} - w_0}\sqrt{\beta_1}\right) + \beta_1 + 2\right]}{4\frac{\sigma^2_{W^*}}{(\mu_{W^*} - w_0)^2} - \frac{\sigma_{W^*}}{\mu_{W^*} - w_0}\sqrt{\beta_1} + 2}. \qquad (150)$$

This supplementary information is, in fact, available in the present case; the $\tilde{W}^*$ distribution begins where $w_0 = 0$.

What are those first three theoretical moments of the variable $\tilde{W}^*$? The following is obtained:

$$E(\tilde{W}_1^k) = \exp\{k\mu_1 + \tfrac{1}{2}k^2\sigma_1^2\}, \quad E(\tilde{W}_2^k) = \exp\{k\mu_2 + \tfrac{1}{2}k^2\sigma_2^2\};$$
$$E(\tilde{W}_1^{k_1}\tilde{W}_2^{k_2}) = \exp\{k_1\mu_1 + k_2\mu_2 + \tfrac{1}{2}(k_1^2\sigma_1^2 + k_2^2\sigma_2^2 + 2k_1k_2\rho\sigma_1\sigma_2)\}.$$ [36]

Thence it follows that:

$$\mu_{W^*} := E(\tilde{W}^*) = E(\tilde{W}_1) + E(\tilde{W}_2) = e^{\mu_1 + \frac{1}{2}\sigma_1^2} + e^{\mu_2 + \frac{1}{2}\sigma_2^2}. \qquad (151)$$

$$\begin{aligned}\sigma^2_{W^*} &:= \mu_2(\tilde{W}^*) = \mathrm{var}(\tilde{W}^*) = \mathrm{var}(\tilde{W}_1) + \mathrm{var}(\tilde{W}_2) + 2\,\mathrm{cov}(\tilde{W}_1, \tilde{W}_2)\\ &= e^{2\mu_1 + \sigma_1^2}(e^{\sigma_1^2} - 1) + e^{2\mu_2 + \sigma_2^2}(e^{\sigma_2^2} - 1)\\ &\quad + 2e^{\mu_1 + \frac{1}{2}\sigma_1^2}e^{\mu_2 + \frac{1}{2}\sigma_2^2}(e^{\rho\sigma_1\sigma_2} - 1). \end{aligned} \qquad (152)$$

Note: $\mathrm{Cov}(\tilde{a}_0, \tilde{b}_0) > 0$ for the economic reasons explained in Section 5.1 (or 3.2.2).

From Lemma 1 in Roussas (1973, p. 121), $\mathrm{cov}(\tilde{a}_0, \tilde{b}_0^{1/a}) > 0$ and $\mathrm{cov}(\tilde{W}_1, \tilde{W}_2) > 0$; the latter implies $\rho > 0$.

$$\mu_3(\tilde{W}^*) = E(\tilde{W}^{*3}) - 3E(\tilde{W}^*)E(\tilde{W}^{*2}) + 2[E(\tilde{W}^*)]^3; \qquad (153)$$

$$\textit{Upper bound}: \sqrt{\beta_1} = \begin{cases} \dfrac{4\frac{\sigma_{W^*}}{\mu_{W^*} - w_0}}{1 - \left(\frac{\sigma_{W^*}}{\mu_{W^*} - w_0}\right)^2} & \text{where } \dfrac{\sigma_{W^*}}{\mu_{W^*} - w_0} \leqslant \sqrt{\tfrac{1}{2}};\\[2ex] 4\dfrac{\sigma_{W^*}}{\mu_{W^*} - w_0} + 2\dfrac{\mu_{W^*} - w_0}{\sigma_{W^*}} & \text{where } \dfrac{\sigma_{W^*}}{\mu_{W^*} - w_0} > \sqrt{\tfrac{1}{2}}. \end{cases}$$

Cf. Müller and Vahl (1976, p. 192).

36 Since $\tilde{W}_1 =: e^{\tilde{\Phi}_1}$ and $\tilde{W}_2 =: e^{\tilde{\Phi}_2}$; $(\tilde{\Phi}_1, \tilde{\Phi}_2)$ is bivariate normally distributed (note that this is only another way of expressing the joint log-normal distribution of the variables $\tilde{W}_1$ and $\tilde{W}_2$). Thus $E(\tilde{W}_1^k) = E(e^{k\tilde{\Phi}_1})$ = moment generating function of $\tilde{\Phi}_1$; $E(\tilde{W}_2^k) = E(e^{k\tilde{\Phi}_2})$ = moment generating function of $\tilde{\Phi}_2$; $E(\tilde{W}_1^{k_1}\tilde{W}_2^{k_2}) = E(e^{k_1\tilde{\Phi}_1 + k_2\tilde{\Phi}_2})$ = moment generating function of $(\tilde{\Phi}_1, \tilde{\Phi}_2)$. See, for example, Hogg and Craig (1978, pp. 119–20) on these moment generating functions.

$E(\tilde{W}^*)$ is taken from (151);

$E(\tilde{W}^{*2}) = \mu_2(\tilde{W}^*) + \mu_{W^*}^2$, see (151) and (152);

and finally:

$$\begin{aligned} E(\tilde{W}^{*3}) &= E(\tilde{W}_1^3) + 3E(\tilde{W}_1^2 \tilde{W}_2) + 3E(\tilde{W}_1 \tilde{W}_2^2) + E(\tilde{W}_2^3) \\ &= e^{3\mu_1 + \frac{9}{2}\sigma_1^2} + 3\exp\{2\mu_1 + \mu_2 + \tfrac{1}{2}(4\sigma_1^2 + 4\rho\sigma_1\sigma_2 + \sigma_2^2)\} \\ &\quad + 3\exp\{\mu_1 + 2\mu_2 + \tfrac{1}{2}(\sigma_1^2 + 4\rho\sigma_1\sigma_2 + 4\sigma_2^2)\} \\ &\quad + e^{3\mu_2 + \frac{9}{2}\sigma_2^2}. \end{aligned}$$

Equipped with the explicit results (151), (152) and (153), we are now in a position to calculate the Pearson criterion in a recursive way:

(i) Firstly, the distribution parameters $\mu_1, \mu_2, \sigma_1, \sigma_2$ and ρ are determined on the basis of empirically substantiated parameter sets, where (cf. (148)):

$$\mu_1 = \mu_1(\mu_{\log a_0}; R, r, \delta, c, N),$$

$$\mu_2 = \mu_2(\mu_{\log b_0}; R, P, r, \delta, c, b_1, b_2, N),$$

$$\sigma_1 = \sigma_1(\sigma_{\log a_0}),$$

$$\sigma_2 = \sigma_2(\sigma_{\log b_0}; b_1, b_2),$$

$$\rho = \rho\left[\sigma_{\log a_0}, \sigma_{\log b_0}, \operatorname{cov}\left(\log \tilde{a}_0, \frac{1}{a}\log \tilde{b}_0\right); b_1, b_2\right].$$

Note: The numerical fixing of the prices R and P and the characteristics of the population $\sigma_{\log a_0}, \sigma_{\log b_0}$ and ρ is subject to a certain randomness for the simple reason that there is only unreliable or no empirical information at all.

- From the reduced forms of the decision equations of Chapter 2 it can be established that only the price ratio R/P is decisive, so that for the purposes of this study $R = 1$ will be fixed and only P will be varied.
- Economic reasons are responsible for the condition $\rho > 0$ (see the note on p. 187).
- According to all the theoretical sources, the relative dispersion of $\tilde{b}_0$ exceeds that of $\tilde{a}_0$, so that $\sigma_{\log b_0} > \sigma_{\log a_0}$.
- There are no further *a priori* restrictions at this point.

(ii) Now (151), (152) and (153) are evaluated.

(iii) β_1 can thereby be obtained.

(iv) With $w_0 = 0$ and $\sigma_{W^*}/\mu_{W^*} = \sqrt{(152)}/(151) = V_{W^*}$, a value for β_2 is obtained (in accordance with the boundary conditions listed in footnote 35, pp. 186–7):

$$\beta_2 = \frac{3(V_{W*}\sqrt{\beta_1} + V_{W*}^2\beta_1 + \beta_1 + 2)}{4V_{W*}^2 - V_{W*}\sqrt{\beta_1} + 2}. \tag{150a}$$

(v) Finally, κ is obtained by substituting β_1 and β_2 in (149).

In this manner, extensive calculations of κ were done on the basis of realistic (empirically substantiated) values of the model parameters. Whilst these calculations were in progress, the measures $\gamma_1 = \sqrt{\beta_1}$ and $\gamma_2 = \beta_2 - 3$ where also obtained.[37]

It has turned out that the measures γ_1 and γ_2 *always* assume *positive* values *irrespective* of the levels of μ_1, μ_2, σ_1 and σ_2 chosen within the restrictions listed in footnote 37 and that the value of κ is always *larger than 1* (and $< \infty$), *as long as* $\rho \geqslant 0$. For the economic reasons already presented there is no doubt that $\tilde{W}_1$ and $\tilde{W}_2$ are indeed positively correlated, therefore ρ is in fact larger than 0. Consequently, the $\tilde{W}^*$ distribution has a *positive skewness* ($\gamma_1 > 0$) and a *positive kurtosis* ($\gamma_2 > 0$).

With $1 < \kappa < \infty$, however, the member of the Pearson system for the approximation to the theoretical density f_{W*} has been found; $\tilde{W}^*$ has a *Pearson Type VI distribution*.[38] The density function of this distribution is given by:[39]

$$\hat{f}_{W*}(w) = v_0 w^{m_2}(v_3 + w)^{-m_1}; \quad 0 \leqslant w < \infty, m_1 > m_2 + 1 > 0. \tag{154}$$

The parameters occurring in this can be calculated from known quantities as follows:

$$v_0 := v_3^{m_1 - m_2 - 1} \frac{\Gamma(m_1)}{\Gamma(m_1 - m_2 - 1)\Gamma(m_2 + 1)},$$

$$v_3 := \tfrac{1}{2}\sigma_{W*}[\beta_1(v_4 + 2)^2 + 16(v_4 + 1)]^{\frac{1}{2}},$$

37 The basic set underlying these calculations was as ever the empirically supported reference specification (19); cf. the discussion in Section 2.1.1. Moreover, arbitrary values of parameters were admitted but, with the restriction, of course, that the resultant parameter constellations did not contradict the known theoretical parameter restrictions of the model and did not violate the boundary conditions listed in footnote 35, pp. 186–7. The theoretical restrictions under consideration in this instance are:

$$R > 0;\ P > 0;\ r > 0;\ c > 0;\ N > 0;\ b_1 > 0,\ b_2 > 0,\ b_1 + b_2 < 1;$$
$$0 < \delta < 1;\ r + \delta > c;$$
$$\mu_{\log ao} > 0;\ \mu_{\log bo} > 0;$$
$$\sigma_{\log ao} > 0,\ \sigma_{\log bo} > 0,\ \sigma_{\log bo} > \sigma_{\log ao}.$$

38 Cf. Elderton and Johnson (1969, pp. 41 and 49).

39 Cf. Elderton and Johnson (1969, p. 67) and Kendall and Stuart (1977, pp. 159–63) in connection with Müller and Vahl (1976, p. 193).

$$v_4 := \frac{2(1 + V_{W^*}^2)}{V_{W^*}(2V_{W^*} - \sqrt{\beta_1})} - 2,$$

$$m_1 := m_2 - v_4 + 2,$$

$$m_2 := \frac{V_{W^*}\sqrt{\beta_1}(3 - V_{W^*}^2) - 6V_{W^*}^2 + 2}{V_{W^*}\sqrt{\beta_1}(V_{W^*}^2 - 1) + 4V_{W^*}^2}. \tag{155}$$

With $v_1 := m_1 - m_2 - 1$, $v_2 := m_2 + 1$, $\Upsilon = 1/v_3$ and $B(\cdot\,,\cdot) =$ the beta function, (154) can be rewritten as:

$$\hat{f}_{W^*}(w) = \frac{\Upsilon^{v_2}}{B(v_1, v_2)} \frac{w^{v_2 - 1}}{(1 + \Upsilon w)^{v_1 + v_2}}; 0 \leqslant w < \infty;\ \Upsilon, v_1, v_2 > 0.\text{[40]} \tag{154a}$$

It can thus be seen that the Pearson type VI distribution is equivalent to the *generalised F distribution* or to the *generalised beta distribution of the second kind*.

(154a) contains a series of distributions as special cases, as for example:

- (154a) = density function of the beta distribution of the second kind, if $\Upsilon = 1$;[41]
- (154a) = density function of the Pareto distribution of the second kind, or the Lomax distribution, if $v_2 = 1$;
  (154a) = density function of the F distribution if $v_1 = l_1/2$, $v_2 = l_2/2$, $\Upsilon = l_2/l_1$ and $l_1, l_2 \in \mathbf{N}$;

to name but a few of the most important.[42]

The density function (154a) also possesses, *inter alia*, the following characteristics:

- $\hat{f}_{W^*}$ has only one modal value; therefore the $\tilde{W}^*$ distribution is *uni-modal*;

  w_{mode} is given by:

$$w_{\text{mode}} = \begin{cases} v_3 \dfrac{v_2 - 1}{v_1 + 1} & \text{where } v_2 > 1; \\ 0 & \text{otherwise.[43]} \end{cases} \tag{156}$$

[40] $\hat{f}_{W^*}(w) \equiv 0$ where $w \leqslant 0$.

$$B(v_1, v_2) := \int_0^1 x^{v_1 - 1}(1 - x)^{v_2 - 1} dx;\ v_1, v_2 > 0.$$

It is the case that: $B(v_1, v_2) = \Gamma(v_1)\Gamma(v_2)/\Gamma(v_1 + v_2)$, where Γ = gamma function; see, for example, Fisz (1976, p. 186).

[41] Cf. Kendall and Stuart (1977, p. 163).

[42] For further special cases, see, for example, McDonald (1984, pp. 648–9).

[43] If $v_2 < 1$, so: $\lim_{w \to 0} \hat{f}_{W^*}(w) = \infty$.

– $\hat{f}_{W^*}$ is J-shaped if $v_2 \leqslant 1$.
– $\hat{f}_{W^*}$ is bell-shaped if $v_2 > 1$.

With (154a) (or (154)) and the relationships listed under (155), not only has it been possible to provide an approximate *type of distribution* for the lifetime earnings distribution, but also an explicit connection has been established between the parameters of (154a) and the economic parameters of the micro-model developed in this study, and thereby an *economic endogenisation of the distribution parameters* has been achieved.[44]

However, it remains difficult to determine analytically, for example, partial effects on the density function $\hat{f}_{W^*}(w)$ or on the distribution parameters Υ, v_1 and v_2; in most cases the signs of the derivatives must be evaluated numerically (although not the derivatives themselves of course). Without the explicit structure obtained above, it would not be possible to make an examination of this kind at all – an examination which can provide entirely new insights. See Section 5.6 on this.

5.6 Inequality and form of distribution: quantitative sensitivity analysis

In what follows, results of a quantitative sensitivity analysis will be presented; these were obtained on the basis of an expanded standard parameter set.

This reference specification can be partially supported by estimated parameters by which means the empirically relevant area is directly referred to (cf. the discussion relating to (19) in Section 2.1.1):

$$r = 0.06;\ \delta = 0.04;\ c = 0.02;\ b_1 = 0.4;\ b_2 = 0.2;\ N = 45.$$

For the remaining parameters, there is no reliable empirical information; their values were fixed in such a way that they both harmonise with the theoretical considerations of the previous sections and generate model values which are, in terms of the order of magnitude, compatible with existing evidence on the lifetime earnings distribution:[45]

$$R = 1 \text{ (normalised)}, \quad P = 1;$$

$$\mu_{\log ao} = 0.1, \quad \mu_{\log bo} = 0.01;$$

$$\sigma^2_{\log ao} = 0.04, \quad \sigma^2_{\log bo} = 0.06; \quad \rho^2 = 0.2.$$

44 The distribution parameters in (154a) (or (154)) can be traced back via (155) to $\sigma_{W^*} = \sqrt{(152)}$, $V_{W^*} = \sqrt{(152)}/(151)$ and $\beta_1 = (153)^2/(152)^3$; (151), (152) and (153) are explicit functions of $\mu_1, \mu_2, \sigma_1, \sigma_2$ and ρ, which conversely themselves are functions of the model parameters (see (148)).

45 The latter are the empirical results of Lillard on the coefficient of variation and on the skewness of the lifetime earnings distribution (1977a, p. 50; 1977b, p. 613). On the theoretical restrictions of the model see footnote 37, p. 189; in addition $\rho > 0$.

Of course, this second group of parameter values is not the only one which meets the specified criteria. The results, derived from Table 2 below, have proved however to be extremely *robust* with respect to variations in these values.[46] On the basis of those results, the specification introduced can therefore be considered to be representative and be accepted; what follows below is not an arbitrary numerical exercise.

The target measures subjected to sensitivity analysis are the following:

$V^2_{W*} = \frac{\sigma^2_{W*}}{\mu^2_{W*}}$: the measure used in this study for the *inequality* of human capital;

$\gamma_1(\tilde{W}^*) = \sqrt{\beta_1(\tilde{W}^*)}$: measure of the *skewness* of the lifetime earnings distribution;

$\gamma_2(\tilde{W}^*) = \beta_2(\tilde{W}^*) - 3$: measure of the *kurtosis* of the lifetime earnings distribution;

Υ, v_1, v_2: the *distribution parameters* of the density function (154a).

The previous section should be consulted for explicit equations for these six values.

With the partly empirically and partly theoretically supported benchmark parameter specification above, one can obtain the absolute levels of the target measures:

$$V^2_{W*} = 0.43;\ \gamma_1(\tilde{W}^*) = 2.32;\ \gamma_2(\tilde{W}^*) = 12.31;$$

$$\Upsilon = 0.0015;\ v_1 = 7.33;\ v_2 = 4.85.$$

These values not only confirm the *positive skewness* ($\gamma_1 > 0$) and the *positive kurtosis* ($\gamma_2 > 0$) (see Section 5.5) but also enable a *bell shape* to be seen ($v_2 > 1$) in the $\tilde{W}^*$ distribution curve.[47]

An interesting question emerges at this point: in what way is the *form*, characterised by skewness and kurtosis, of the distribution of human wealth influenced by the intertemporal *optimising behaviour* of the individuals? A response to this question is to be found, as always, in comparison with a model which does not assume any maximising behaviour. In the case in question, the mechanical descriptive model is obtained by setting $d_2 = d_3 = a = 1$ in (121), which cuts off all optimising effects.[48]

With the same assumption of a joint log-normal distribution of the basic variables $\tilde{a}_0$ and $\tilde{b}_0$, it is hardly surprising to discover that the human

[46] Of course, only those parameter constellations were examined which do not contradict the theoretical restrictions listed in footnote 37, p. 189.

[47] Furthermore, the relative frequency distribution $\tilde{f}_{W*}(W)$, $0 \leqslant w < \infty$, could be given explicitly with the values obtained for Υ, v_1 and v_2 as $0 \leqslant w < \infty$. However, this will not be undertaken; the present section concentrates exclusively on an examination of the sensitivity of the target measures.

[48] Cf. also Section 5.4.

wealth distribution is here also positively skewed and exhibits a positive kurtosis. However, it can further be established that:[49]

$$(0<)\gamma_{1,ME} < \gamma_1(\tilde{W}^*) \quad \text{and} \quad (0<)\gamma_{2,ME} < \gamma_2(\tilde{W}^*),$$

i.e. the optimising behaviour of the individuals, the reaction to their individual circumstances and the economic features given for them, results in both an *increase in the positive skewness* and an *increase in the positive kurtosis* of the lifetime earnings distribution.

If one proceeded on the basis of the mechanical descriptive model, and the optimising reactions of the individuals were ignored, then this would result in an *underestimation* of the distortion effects of the human capital basic stock $\tilde{a}_0 = a_0(\tilde{G}, \tilde{HO}, \tilde{CU})$ and the human capital accumulation efficiency $\tilde{b}_0 = b_0[LA(\tilde{G}, \tilde{HO}, \tilde{CU}); DF(\tilde{HO}, \tilde{CU}); QPC(\underline{\tilde{a}}, \underline{\tilde{b}}, \underline{\tilde{c}}); \tilde{CR}; \tilde{SQ}]$.

But now to the core question of the current section: how sensitive are the target measures to changes in the model parameters? The information needed to be able to answer this question is contained in Table 2.[50]

First of all, the inequality of human wealth $V^2_{\tilde{W}^*}$ will be considered. The *qualitative* $V^2_{\tilde{W}^*}$ sensitivities were analytically obtained (apart from $x = N$) in Sections 5.1 and 5.2 and have already been discussed in great detail.[51] Table 2 now provides insights into the *quantitative extent* of the target measure variations (in the vicinity of the reference specification). This reveals remarkable implications of the model which are not obvious from the purely analytical sections. Lifetime earnings inequality reacts in a quite

[49] $\tilde{W}_{ME} = \tilde{a}_0 + \tilde{b}_0$ ($ME \mathrel{\hat{=}}$ 'mechanical').
With $\mu_1 = \mu_{\log a_0} = 0.1$; $\mu_2 = \mu_{\log b_0} = 0.01$; $\sigma_1^2 = \sigma^2_{\log a_0} = 0.04$; $\sigma_2^2 = \sigma^2_{\log b_0} = 0.06$ and $\rho^2 = 0.2$ (for comparison purposes), one has, for example:

$$\gamma_{1,ME} := \gamma_1(\tilde{W}_{ME}) = 0.26 \quad \text{and} \quad \gamma_{2,ME} := \gamma_2(\tilde{W}_{ME}) = 0.03.$$

[50] The information on sensitivities is presented in the form of *elasticities*:

$$\frac{\partial y}{\partial x}\frac{x}{y}; \quad y \in \{V^2_{\tilde{W}^*}, \gamma_1(\tilde{W}^*), \gamma_2(\tilde{W}^*), v_1, v_2, \Upsilon\},$$
$$x \in \{R, P, r, \delta, c, b_1, b_2, N, \sigma_{\log a_0}, \sigma_{\log b_0}, \rho\}.$$

$(\partial y/\partial x)\,x/y$ denotes the elasticity of y with respect to x and gives (approximately) the percentage change in y resulting from a 1% increase in x, *ceteris paribus*.

Elasticities are more useful for the purpose of *comparative* evaluation of the quantitative effects than pure derivatives, since elasticities are independent of the units of the variables y and x; elasticities are dimensionless numbers. Note that elasticities are always *point* elasticities.

[51] Incidentally, with the log-normal distribution of the variables $\tilde{a}_0$ and $\tilde{b}_0$ the following applies:

$$V^2_{a_0} = \exp\{\sigma^2_{\log a_0}\} - 1 = e^{\sigma_1^2} - 1;$$

$$V^2_b = \exp\left\{\frac{1}{a^2}\sigma^2_{\log b_0}\right\} - 1 = e^{\sigma_2^2} - 1;$$

$$\rho_{a_0 b} = \frac{e^{\rho\sigma_1\sigma_2} - 1}{V_{a_0} V_b}.$$

Table 2. *Quantitative* ceteris paribus *sensitivities*

$\left(\text{Elasticities } \frac{\partial y}{\partial x}\frac{x}{y}\right)$

y \ x:	R	P	r	δ	c
$V^2_{W^*}$	0.025	-0.025	-0.068	-0.023	0.0022
$\gamma_1(\tilde{W}^*)$	0.0021	-0.0021	-0.0057	-0.0019	0.00018
$\gamma_2(\tilde{W}^*)$	0.00066	-0.00066	-0.0018	-0.0006	0.00006
v_1	0.0039	-0.0039	-0.01	-0.0036	0.00033
v_2	-0.049	0.049	0.133	0.045	-0.0042
Υ	-1.52	0.54	2.076	0.94	-0.27

y \ x:	b_1	b_2	N	$\sigma_{\log a_0}$	$\sigma_{\log b_0}$	ρ
$V^2_{W^*}$	2.61	1.28	0.037	0.0057	2.43	0.0075
$\gamma_1(\tilde{W}^*)$	1.56	0.77	0.0031	-0.009	1.53	-0.0035
$\gamma_2(\tilde{W}^*)$	3.79	1.86	0.00097	-0.012	3.75	-0.011
v_1	-1.39	-0.7	0.0058	0.0069	-1.4	0.0068
v_2	-2.72	-1.34	-0.073	-0.019	-2.4	-0.022
Υ	-4.42	-1.96	-0.89	-0.028	-1.16	-0.029

Reference specification: $R = 1$; $P = 1$; $r = 0.06$; $\delta = 0.04$; $c = 0.02$; $b_1 = 0.4$; $b_2 = 0.2$; $N = 45$; $\mu_{\log a_0} = 0.1$; $\mu_{\log b_0} = 0.01$; $\sigma_{\log a_0} = 0.2$; $\sigma_{\log b_0} = 0.25$; $\rho = 0.45$.

inelastic way to changes in the policy parameters R, P and r. Yet, there are clear differences: the (absolute) interest elasticity of the $\tilde{W}^*$ inequality is more than double the size of the (absolute) R and P elasticities. In accordance with this, the *interest rate r* represents a far more *effective* instrument for combating inequality of human wealth than the wage rate R or the price of educational goods.[52]

Also, variations in the human capital depreciation rate δ or the learning-by-doing efficiency c have no considerable influence on $V^2_{W^*}$. $V^2_{W^*}$, on the other hand, responds markedly *elastically* to changes in the two technical production parameters b_1 and b_2 and to variations in the $\tilde{b}_0$

[52] According to Table 2, an increase in the interest rate by 1% would lead to a reduction in the inequality by 0.068%; on the other hand, a 1% increase in the price of training or a 1% decrease in the wage rate would result in a fall in inequality of only 0.025%. In all three cases the effects are minimal however.

The fact that the (absolute) R and P elasticities of the $\tilde{W}^*$ inequality are identical lies, incidentally, in the fact that $R = P$ in the reference specification; see (133) and (134) on this.

inequality measured by $\sigma_{\log bo}$.[53] If one attempts to achieve a reduction in lifetime earnings inequality, then, consequently, a reduction in the production elasticities of the 'human capital' and 'purchased goods' factors, for example, by a reduction of technical knowledge about learning methods (individuals with a high livel of b_0^j profit comparatively more from this knowledge than those with a lower level), or a decrease in the relative dispersion of the human capital accumulation efficiency $\tilde{b}_0$ is *considerably more effective* than policy measures affecting the prices R, P and r (which have just been discussed). The problem for the state lies, of course, in the fact that it is not able to influence these variables and, in particular, the basic factors which apply to $\tilde{b}_0$ (cf. (18a)), as directly as the prices R, P and r, which can be controlled by means of taxes, contributions and transfer policies. Reductions in inequalities in learning ability, the DF factor, the willingness to take risks, the ability to assume responsibility and the quality of educational establishments, to name but a few of the basic factors, would be very worthwhile, however, in the light of the results here.

Moreover, the relative lack of significance of the $\tilde{a}_0$ inequality is striking.[54] An *equalisation* of the human capital basic stock, the individual initial opportunities at the beginning of economic life, would accordingly, *ceteris paribus*, only contribute *slightly* to diminishing lifetime earnings inequality. The same applies for a decrease of the correlation between initial and growth variables measured by ρ.

Finally, it can be seen from Table 2 that a reduction in the earnings lifespan N – a very current topic – is a measure for combating inequality of human wealth which certainly merits consideration compared to the policy instruments R, P and r. Compared with a change in b_1, b_2 or $\sigma_{\log bo}$, implemented in whatever manner, a variation in N is clearly revealed as being fairly ineffective.

Skewness and kurtosis of the lifetime earnings distribution are almost completely *rigid* with respect to changes in the policy parameters R, P and r (the interest rate r is again the most effective instrument in comparison). On the other hand, skewness and kurtosis react in an extremely *elastic* way to variations in b_1 and $\sigma_{\log bo}$ which again emphasises the importance attached to these factors. Incidentally, the directions of change of $\gamma_1(\tilde{W}^*)$ and $\gamma_2(\tilde{W}^*)$ are the same for each model parameter. Apart from $x = \sigma_{\log ao}$ and $x = \rho$, these also show the same changes in direction as $V_{W^*}^2$.

> *Note*: The fact that the $\sigma_{\log ao}$ elasticity and the ρ elasticity of the skewness and kurtosis are negative arises from the dominance of the $\tilde{b}_0$ inequality strengthened by $0 < a < 1$, thus from the dominance of the growth component (cf. the decomposition analysis in Section 5.4).

53 $\sigma_{\log bo}$, just like the squared coefficient of variation, is a measure of the *relative* dispersion.
54 This will not however surprise the attentive reader of Section 5.4.

> The relativising effect of a larger $\tilde{a}_0$ inequality or a greater correlation between initial and growth variables results in a reduction in the asymmetry and in the peakedness of the lifetime earnings distribution.

The characteristics of the density function (154a) derived in Section 5.5 permit even more detailed statements to be made in connection with Table 2 on the change in shape of the human wealth distribution curve. If, for example, the inequality of the human capital accumulation efficiency $\tilde{b}_0$ was above the current value of the reference specification by 33% (thus $\sigma_{\log b_0} = 0.33$ instead of 0.25), then the $\tilde{W}^*$ distribution would change to a Pareto distribution of the second kind, provided that the function $v_2(\sigma_{\log b_0})$ exhibited the same elasticity in that region as in Table 2.[55] Conversely, the lifetime earnings distribution becomes more and more *bell-shaped*, the higher v_2, and therefore the higher the price of educational goods P, the interest rate r and the rate of depreciation δ, or the lower, for example, the human capital price R, the learning-by-doing rate c, the production elasticities b_1 and b_2, the earnings lifespan N and the inequality $\sigma_{\log b_0}$. The intuitive idea – 'the more bell-shaped, the more equal and less positively skewed and less peaked', with regard to the model parameters just listed – is confirmed by the sensitivity results of Table 2.[56]

On the basis of the reference specification, the density function $\hat{f}_{W^*}$ with a falling v_2 generally approximates the *Pareto distribution of the second kind*, and with an increasing Υ, *the beta distribution of the second kind*. The parameter variations which generate these v_2 or Υ shifts and the extent to which they do so can be seen from Table 2.[57] However, the following interesting observation should be noted. As is known from Appendix 6, individual human capital W^{j*} increases with a rising level of R, c, b_1 and b_2 and with falling P, r and δ (this applies for all j). From Table 2 it is clear that these parameter movements all lead to a reduction in v_2. However, this means that the $\tilde{W}^*$ distribution within an economy with a *high level of human wealth* shifts towards the *Pareto* distribution. Thus, what has been frequently observed for the current earnings distribution (i.e., for the distribution of annual earnings) – namely, that the upper end of that distribution approximately satisfies the Pareto law – is also to be expected for the distribution of lifetime earnings.

[55] For an increase in $\sigma_{\log b_0}$ of 33% would result in a reduction of v_2 by $(2.4 \times 33)\% = 79.2\%$; on the basis of the reference set this would mean a fall in v_2 from 4.85 to 1, with the consequence that the density function (154a) would assume the form of a Pareto density of the second kind. This is of course just an experimental idea since the stability of the elasticity is not guaranteed. In the face of the relative robustness of the elasticities which has been established, this type of experiment can however be supported.

[56] See the previous note on the exceptions $\sigma_{\log a_0}$ and ρ.

[57] It is clear that the density $\hat{f}_{W^*}$ cannot approximate both types of distribution simultaneously. A glance at Table 2 shows that it does not do this anyway: the elasticities of v_2 and Υ have the same signs.

Selected results

(1) Generation of an explicit decision equation for the optimum length of full-time schooling.

(2) Derivation of a closed form expression for the optimal path of individual earnings.
   - The theoretical earnings path exhibits a concave life-cycle profile.
   - Explicit comparative dynamic results (Figs. 9–19).

(3) The theoretical (i.e. generated by the model) distribution of earnings within age groups is positively skewed and has positive kurtosis.
   - The transitory shock process affecting all earnings results, in isolation, in asymmetry: the distribution of earnings within an age group consisting of identical individuals is positively skewed.
   - The earnings within an age group consisting of identical individuals are asymptotically log-normally distributed.
   - The within age group distribution of the planned (or expected optimal) earnings also displays a positive skewness and positive kurtosis, as:
     (a) the distributions of the full-time schooling and earnings phase human capital accumulation abilities are positively skewed and exhibit positive kurtosis,
     (b) the full-time schooling and earnings phase human capital accumulation abilities are positively correlated with each other, and
     (c) there are decreasing returns to scale in human capital production.
   - Even if both the permanent and the transitory earnings component within an age group are symmetrically distributed, the distribution of earnings within age groups can be positively skewed.

(4) Representation of a closed expression for the inequality of earnings within age groups. From this it can be explicitly seen how the interaction of ability distributions, economic structures, life-cycle

decisions and random shocks is transformed into income inequality.

(5) Models which ignore the reaction of individuals to their individual abilities ('optimising behaviour'), underestimate the inequality effect resulting from variation in these aptitudes.

(6) The greater the uncertainty about income, the larger the earnings inequality.

(7) The transitory inequality within age groups caused by the random income change factors is a strictly monotonically increasing function of working age.

(8) The age profile of the permanent inequality of earnings, resulting from the dynamic optimising behaviour of the individuals, is U-shaped.
  - The turning point (= the lowest point of the U-shaped profile) appears earlier, the greater the correlation between the full-time schooling and earnings phase human capital accumulation abilities.

(9) The intertemporal effects on the inequalities within age groups resulting from the instrumental parameters of economic policymakers associated with the model have proven to be complex and anything but uniform. Different age levels can be affected differently by one and the same distribution policy measure. The interaction of the instruments for combating inequality with the other model parameters is not the same for all instruments.

  Thanks to the closed form solution of the present model, the direction and length of the changes in inequalities within age groups induced by public policy, can be obtained dependent explicitly on model and distribution parameters.
  - An increase in interest rate leads to a decrease in inequality within the younger age groups and to a rise in inequality within the older age groups.
  - If the state subsidises the acquisition of human capital in the earnings phase ($\hat{=}$ fall in the price of educational goods), then this induces an increase in the inequalities of earnings within age groups with the exception of a short interim period. Within that interim period, there is a reduction in the age group inequalities.

(10) The model framework developed permits an economic interpretation of the widely discussed and empirically observed life-cycle profile of the correlation between abilities and earnings.
  - This correlation is shown (with the exception of certain special cases) to be a strictly monotonically increasing function of working age.

(11) Derivation of an endogeneous variance–covariance structure of earnings.
  - Annual earnings are positively correlated with each other.

- With increasing intervals between the periods, the correlation between earnings becomes less and less.
- Initial earnings and earnings growth are negatively correlated with each other.

(12) Derivation of a functional relationship between the earnings distribution and the age distribution within an economy. Explicit analytical representation of the interdependence between the overall inequality of earnings, on the one hand, and state distribution policy, individual optimising behaviour, structural parameters, distribution parameters and demographic aspects, on the other.
- An increase in the wage rate results in a rise in the overall inequality of earnings.
- An increase in the expense of acquiring human capital in the earnings phase results in a reduction of earnings inequality within an economy.
- The modifications of the intertemporal choice activities of individuals caused by an increase in the interest rate effect an increase in inequality in the overall distribution.
- The influence of the basic individual variables on total inequality of earnings is strengthened by the optimising reactions of the individuals. In this sense, a part of the existing earnings inequality can be considered to have been self-generated.
- An improvement in the general opportunities of increasing the human capital stock by way of practical job experience (learning-by-doing), causes additional inequalities in the overall distribution of earnings to occur.
- A higher human capital depreciation rate leads to a reduction in the overall inequality of earnings.
- Economies with higher input production elasticities exhibit greater earnings inequality.
- The lower the correlation between the full-time schooling human capital production efficiency and the working phase human capital production efficiency, the less the overall inequality becomes.
- If the birth rate of the population falls, then the overall inequality of earnings increases.
- If the death rate of the population falls, then the earnings inequality within the economy goes up.
- The higher the uncertainty of earnings caused by the transitory factors, the greater the total inequality of earnings within an economy.

(13) The model developed predicts a basic policy conflict between the level of per capita earnings and the level of earnings inequality; according to

which, the social aims of higher per capita earnings and lower earnings inequality are not generally compatible with each other.

(14) The overall distribution of earnings generated by the present model is positively skewed.

(15) The present approach generates a constant (relative) variance of the overall distribution of earnings.

(16) Derivation of a closed form solution for the inequality of lifetime earnings.

(17) The inequality of lifetime earnings can be broken down, according to the present model structure, into an initial component and a growth component.
- If the correlation between these components falls, then lifetime earnings inequality decreases.
- The relative contribution to inequality of the initial component lies below that of the growth component.
  - Allowing for the optimising reactions of individuals results in an increase in this trend.

(18) The present approach implies an incompatibility between the social aims of a higher standard of living and a lower inequality in lifetime earnings with respect to the instrumental parameters of economic policymakers associated with the model.

(19) The policy decisions made on the basis of the current earnings distribution are not generally compatible with those which would have been made on the basis of the lifetime earnings distribution. There may be situations where a specific distributional policy action reduces the inequality of lifetime earnings but at the same time changes the allocation plans of maximising individuals to such an extent that the inequality of annual earnings increases.

(20) Derivation of an analytical relationship between the inequality of lifetime earnings and the inequality of current earnings.

Thanks to the closed form solutions, the interdependencies of the factors involved can be shown explicitly and precise conditions are provided for when each form of inequality dominates.

(21) The lifetime earnings distribution has the functional form of a Pearson Type VI distribution.
- By producing an explicit connection between the parameters of the density function of this distribution and the economic parameters of the micro-model developed in this study, it is possible to create an economic endogenisation of the distribution parameters obtained.

(22) The intertemporal optimising behaviour of the individuals leads both to an increase in the positive skewness and to an increase in the positive kurtosis of the lifetime earnings distribution.

(23) Quantitative sensitivity results on the inequality and the distributional form of lifetime earnings (Table 2).

Last but not least, the reader is reminded once again of the price of the above results: the assumptions of the underlying micro-model (see the discussion in Sections 1.3, 1.4, 2.1 and 2.2).

Appendix 1 Comparative static analysis of the optimal length of basic education

The variable referenced in the analysis below is $\underline{S}^*$ from (40).

Notes: (i) In this context, please refer again to the explanations on p. 62. (ii) In the following, the theoretical parameter restrictions of the model should be noted in each case (see the list on p. 39).

$$\frac{\partial \underline{S}^*}{\partial a_0} = \frac{-1}{a_1} < 0. \qquad [\alpha]$$

$$\frac{\partial \underline{S}^*}{\partial a_1} = \frac{1}{a_1^2}\left[a_0 + \frac{a(r+\delta)}{b_1 r}T\right] > 0. \qquad [\beta]$$

$$\frac{\partial^2 \underline{S}^*}{\partial a_0 \partial a_1} = \frac{1}{a_1^2} > 0. \qquad [\gamma]$$

$$\frac{\partial \underline{S}^*}{\partial b_0} = -\frac{r+\delta}{a_1 b_1 r b_0}T < 0. \qquad [\delta]$$

$$\frac{\partial \underline{S}^*}{\partial \delta} = \frac{b_1 + b_2(1+cq)}{a_1 b_1 r}T = \frac{I^*}{a_1 r R} > 0. \qquad [\varepsilon]$$

Note: $I^* = R(sK)^* + PD^*$, with $(sK)^*$ from (45) and D^* from (46).

$$\frac{\partial \underline{S}^*}{\partial c} = \frac{(r+\delta)b_2 q}{a_1 b_1 r}T < 0. \qquad [\zeta]$$

Notes: (i) For $b_2 = 0$, i.e. in the case of a lack of purchased inputs: $\partial \underline{S}^*/\partial c = 0$.

(ii) $$\left.\frac{\partial \underline{S}^*}{\partial c}\right|_{\delta = c} = \frac{T}{a_1 r} > 0.$$

(iii) $$\left|\frac{\partial \underline{S}^*}{\partial c}\right| < \frac{\partial \underline{S}^*}{\partial \delta}.$$

$$\frac{\partial \underline{S}^*}{\partial R} = -\frac{(r+\delta)b_2}{a_1 b_1 r R} T < 0. \qquad [\eta]$$

$$\frac{\partial \underline{S}^*}{\partial P} = \frac{(r+\delta)b_2}{a_1 b_1 r P} T > 0. \qquad [\theta]$$

Note: If *R and P* were changed by the same percentage in each case, then the optimal length of full-time schooling $\underline{S}^*$ would remain unaffected.

$$\frac{\partial \underline{S}^*}{\partial r} = \frac{1}{r^2}\left[(r + \delta a + cb_2 rq)\frac{T}{a_1 b_1} - 1\right] \gtreqless 0$$

$$\Leftrightarrow a_1 \lesseqgtr (r + \delta a + cb_2 rq)\frac{T}{b_1}. \qquad [\iota]$$

Notes:

(i) $\frac{\partial \underline{S}^*}{\partial r} = -\frac{\underline{A}_0^{**}}{a_1 r R}$; $\underline{A}_0^{**} = R\underline{K}_0^* - I^*$. Hence:

$$\frac{\partial \underline{S}^*}{\partial r} \gtreqless 0 \Leftrightarrow \underline{A}_0^{**} \lesseqgtr 0.^{1}$$

(ii) $\frac{\partial \underline{S}^*}{\partial r} < \frac{\partial \underline{S}^*}{\partial \delta}$.

[1] Incidentally, result formulations of this type are permitted for continuity reasons for a sufficiently small range around $\underline{S}^*$.
$[\underline{A}_0^{**} = R(a_0 + a_1\underline{S}^*) - I^*]$.

Appendix 2 Comparative dynamic analysis of the optimal age–earnings profile

The reference equation in the following analysis is equation (39). As always, the theoretical parameter restrictions of the model should be noted (see the list on p. 39).[2]

The human capital price *R*

$$\frac{\partial \underline{A}_n^{**}}{\partial R} = \frac{(1-\delta+c)^n}{r}a_1 + T\frac{1-b_1}{b_1 a}\left(\frac{r+\delta a}{rq} + cb_2\right)$$
$$\cdot\frac{(1-\delta+c)^n - rq}{c-\delta}; \quad n = 0,\ldots,N. \qquad [\kappa]$$

Notes:

(i) $$\frac{\partial \underline{A}_n^{**}}{\partial R} = \underbrace{\frac{1-b_1}{aR}}_{>0}\underline{A}_n^{**} - \underbrace{\frac{a_1 b_2}{ar}(1-\delta+c)^n}_{>0}; \quad n = 0,\ldots,N.$$

Positive disposable earnings $\underline{A}_n^{**}$ are consequently a necessary but not sufficient condition for $\partial\underline{A}_n^{**}/\partial R$ to be positive.[3]

(ii) $$n_{0,R} < \frac{\log r - \log(r+\delta-c)}{\log(1-\delta+c)}, \quad \text{as} \quad \frac{a_1}{r}(1-\delta+c)^n > 0.$$

Note, that $[(1-\delta+c)^n - rq]/(c-\delta)$ is a strictly monotonically increasing function of n (irrespective of $c \gtrless \delta$), and that:

$$\frac{(1-\delta+c)^n - rq}{c-\delta} \lesseqgtr 0 \Leftrightarrow n \lesseqgtr \frac{\log r - \log(r+\delta-c)}{\log(1-\delta+c)}.$$

[2] Subsequently $c \neq \delta$ is assumed. The theoretically interesting special case $c = \delta$, which cannot, however, be empirically supported, will only be dealt with sporadically.
[3] Such statements are permitted, for continuity reasons, for a sufficiently small range around $\underline{A}_n^{**}$.

With the values from the standard parameter set (19), one has the following:

$$\frac{\log r - \log(r + \delta - c)}{\log(1 - \delta + c)} \simeq 14.2.$$

(iii) Since the production efficiency a_1 cannot be observed directly, the sign conditions for the derivatives should be given here for a better understanding for the optimal initial stock, $\underline{K}_0^*$ (i.e., after multiplication by R, for the potential initial earnings):

$$\underline{K}_0^* = a_0 + a_1 \underline{S}^* = \frac{a_1}{r} - \frac{a(r+\delta)}{b_1 r} T \quad (>0).$$

At the same time the prior knowledge that $\underline{K}_0^* > 0$ is thereby exploited. One obtains:

$$\frac{\partial \underline{A}_n^{**}}{\partial R} \gtreqless 0 \Leftrightarrow \underline{K}_0^{**} \gtreqless \frac{T}{b_1}\left[\frac{1-b_1}{a(c-\delta)}\left(\frac{r+\delta a}{rq} + cb_2\right)\right.$$

$$\left.\cdot \left(\frac{rq}{(1-\delta+c)^n} - 1\right) - \frac{a}{r}(r+\delta)\right]; \quad n = 0, \ldots, N.$$

Both for $\delta > c$ and for $c > \delta$ the right-hand side of the $\underline{K}_0^*$ condition achieves its maximum in the initial period ($n = 0$) and then falls *monotonically* with increasing n.

(iv) For $b_2 = 0$, therefore for the case where the purchased inputs do not enter human capital production, it follows that:

$$\frac{\partial \underline{A}_n^{**}}{\partial R} = \frac{1}{R}\underline{A}_n^{**}; \quad n = 0, \ldots, N.$$

Here, the condition $\underline{A}_n^{**} > 0$ is thus necessary and sufficient for $\partial \underline{A}_n^{**}/\partial R$ to be positive.

$$\frac{\partial(\underline{A}_{n+1}^{**} - \underline{A}_n^{**})}{\partial R} = [\;](1-\delta+c)^n$$

$$+ \frac{R}{b_1}(1-\delta+c)^n\left(\frac{r+\delta a}{rq} + cb_2\right)\frac{\partial T}{\partial R},$$

$$n = 0, \ldots, N-1. \quad [\lambda]$$

where '[ ]' denotes the square bracket expression from (41). The positive nature of the constant '[ ]' is clearly apparent where $c > \delta$; however, this is not the case for the realistic case where $\delta > c$. This is discussed in detail in Section 2.3.2; according to this, also in the case where $\delta > c$, it is to be derived from '[ ]' > 0. With this, however, it follows instantly that

$\partial(\underline{A}^{**}_{n+1} - \underline{A}^{**}_n)/\partial R$ is *positive* ($n = 0, \ldots, N-1$), since all other terms in the above equation (including $\partial T/\partial R$) are also positive.[4]

The price of educational goods P

$$\frac{\partial \underline{A}^{**}_n}{\partial P} = -T\frac{Rb_2}{Pb_1 a}\left(\frac{r+\delta a}{rq} + cb_2\right)\frac{(1-\delta+c)^n - rq}{c-\delta};$$

$$n = 0, \ldots, N. \qquad [\mu]$$

Notes:

(i) $$\frac{\partial \underline{A}^{**}_n}{\partial P} = \underbrace{\frac{a_1 Rb_2}{Par}(1-\delta+c)^n}_{>0} - \underbrace{\frac{b_2}{Pa}}_{>0}\underline{A}^{**}_n; \quad n = 0, \ldots, N.$$

(ii) $$\frac{\partial \underline{A}^{**}_n}{\partial P}\begin{cases} >0 & \text{where } 0 \leqslant n < n_{0,P}; \\ <0 & \text{where } n > n_{0,P}; \end{cases}$$

$$\text{with: } n_{0,P} := \frac{\log r - \log(r+\delta-c)}{\log(1-\delta+c)}.$$[5]

The sign of the change in the profile caused by a variation in P is therefore solely dependent on the parameters r, δ and c.

$$\frac{\partial(\underline{A}^{**}_{n+1} - \underline{A}^{**}_n)}{\partial P} = -T\frac{Rb_2}{Pb_1 a}\left(\frac{r+\delta a}{rq} + cb_2\right)(1-\delta+c)^n < 0;$$

$$n = 0, \ldots, N-1. \qquad [\nu]$$

Joint variations of R and P

$$\underline{A}^{**}_n = \underline{A}^{**}_n[R(m), P(m)], \quad n = 0, \ldots, N;$$

$m \mathrel{\hat{=}}$ policy influence, macro-influence

$$\frac{d\underline{A}^{**}_n}{dm} = \frac{\partial \underline{A}^{**}_n}{\partial R}\frac{dR}{dm} + \frac{\partial \underline{A}^{**}_n}{\partial P}\frac{dP}{dm}, \quad n = 0, \ldots, N.$$

Assuming that the prices R and P (which incidentally are measured in the same units, say \$/unit) increase by one unit and thus by the *same absolute*

[4] It is clear that '[ ]' > 0 is a sufficient condition but not, however, a necessary condition for $\partial(\underline{A}^{**}_{n+1} - \underline{A}^{**}_n)/\partial R$ to be positive.

[5] Theoretically, one could also mention the case: $\partial \underline{A}^{**}_n/\partial P = 0$ for $n = n_{0,P}$. It should, however, be noted here that it is assumed $n \in \mathbf{N}$. On the other hand, $n_{0,P}$ is not restricted to this range of numbers. The notation '$n = n_{0,P}$' is therefore only correct when $n_{0,P} \in \mathbf{N}$, which will only occur by chance. This special case will be ignored hereafter. With (19), for example, $n_{0,P} \cong 14.2$; the sign reversal therefore occurring between $n = 14$ and $n = 15$.

amount. How, then, would the optimal age profile of disposable earnings change?

Thus, if (for the purposes of this study): $dR/dm = dP/dm = 1$, it follows that:

$$\frac{d\underline{A}_n^{**}}{dm} = \left(1 + \frac{b_2}{a}\frac{P-R}{P}\right)\frac{1}{R}\underline{A}_n^{**} - \frac{a_1 b_2}{ar}\frac{P-R}{P}(1-\delta+c)^n; \qquad n = 0,\ldots,N.$$

$$\frac{d\underline{A}_n^{**}}{dm} \gtreqless 0 \Leftrightarrow \underline{K}_0^* \gtreqless \frac{T}{b_1}\left[\left(1 + \frac{b_2}{a}\frac{P-R}{P}\right) \cdot \left(\frac{r+\delta a}{rq} + cb_2\right)\frac{\dfrac{rq}{(1-\delta+c)^n} - 1}{c-\delta} - \frac{a}{r}(r+\delta)\right]; \qquad n = 0,\ldots,N. \quad [\xi]$$

There are three cases:

(a) $R = P$

Here one has:

$$\frac{d\underline{A}_n^{**}}{dm} \gtreqless 0 \Leftrightarrow \underline{A}_n^{**} \gtreqless 0; \quad n = 0,\ldots,N.$$

(b) $R > P$

In contrast to (a), $d\underline{A}_n^{**}/dm$ for $\underline{A}_n^{**} = 0$ is positive. Where $\underline{A}_n^{**} > 0$, $n = 0,\ldots,N$, which for example applies in the case of the standard parameter set (19), $d\underline{A}_n^{**}/dm$ is positive for *all* values of n, as long as $R/P \leqslant (h1 - b_1)/b_2$ (sufficient).

In the case of $R/P > (1 - b_1)/b_2$ (>1, since $b_1 + b_2 < 1$) the same derivative can be negative as well, if b_0 ($\underline{A}_n^{**}$, respectively) is sufficiently large; this change in sign only then takes place *after* $n_{0,P}$.

(c) $R < P$

For $\underline{A}_n^{**} = 0$, $d\underline{A}_n^{**}/dm$ is negative (in contrast to (a) and (b)). The same applies for negative disposable earnings $\underline{A}_n^{**}$. In the case where $\underline{A}_n^{**} > 0$, $n = 0,\ldots,N$, $d\underline{A}_n^{**}/dm$ is positive from a point before $n_{0,P}$ (note that $\underline{K}_0^* > 0$).

If one compares the above $\underline{K}_0^*$ condition for $d\underline{A}_n^{**}/dm$ with the one relating to $\partial \underline{A}_n^{**}/\partial R$ (see note (iii), p. 205), it is clear that the present point of reversal of the sign (if there is one) occurs even *before* $n_{0,P}$.[6]

Now assuming R and P increase by the *same percentage*, the price ratio R/P would thus remain constant. What significance does this have for the optimal plan $\{\underline{A}_n^{**}\}$?

If $R/P = \text{constant} =: \kappa_0$, then $P = R/\kappa_0 = P(R)$; with $R = R(m)$, $P = P[R(m)]$ therefore. Thus:

$$\frac{d\underline{A}_n^{**}}{dm} = \frac{\partial \underline{A}_n^{**}}{\partial R}\frac{dR}{dm} + \frac{\partial \underline{A}_n^{**}}{\partial P}\frac{dP}{dR}\frac{dR}{dm}; \quad n = 0, \ldots, N.$$

With $dP/dR = 1/\kappa_0 = P/R$ and the assumption $dR/dm = 1$, it follows that $d\underline{A}_n^{**}/dm = (1/R)\underline{A}_n^{**}$, $n = 0, \ldots, N$ so that:

$$\frac{d\underline{A}_n^{**}}{dm} \gtreqless 0 \Leftrightarrow \underline{A}_n^{**} \gtreqless 0; \quad n = 0, \ldots, N. \qquad [o]$$

Notes: (i) If $R = P$, then an increase in the two prices by the same absolute amount corresponds to an increase by the same percentage. This is the reason for the agreement between the result derived above in (a) and this one.

(ii) $$\left.\frac{\partial \underline{A}_n^{**}}{\partial R}\right|_{R/P=\text{const.}} \gtrless \left.\frac{\partial \underline{A}_n^{**}}{\partial P}\right|_{R/P=\text{const.}} \Leftrightarrow R \lesseqgtr P; \quad n = 0, \ldots, N.$$

The interest rate r

After lengthy (but elementary) algebraic reformulations, the following is obtained:

$$\frac{\partial \underline{A}_n^{**}}{\partial r} = -\frac{R}{r^2}(1 - \delta + c)^n a_1 + T\frac{R}{b_1}\left\{\left[1 + \frac{\delta a}{r^2}(c - \delta) - \frac{1 + cb_2 q}{a(r + \delta)}\left(\frac{r + \delta a}{rq} + cb_2\right)\right]\frac{(1 - \delta + c)^n - rq}{c - \delta} + q^2\left(\frac{r + \delta a}{rq} + cb_2\right)\right\}; \quad n = 0, \ldots, N. \qquad [\pi]$$

With the help of the equation for $\underline{K}_0^*$, the following is eventually obtained:

$$\frac{\partial \underline{A}_n^{**}}{\partial r} \gtreqless 0 \Leftrightarrow \underline{K}_0^* \lesseqgtr \frac{Tr}{b_1}\left\{\left[\frac{(1 + cb_2 q)(r + \delta - cb_1)}{a(r + \delta)} - 1\right]\right.$$

[6] Since:

$$\frac{1 - b_1}{a} > 1 + \frac{b_2}{a}\frac{P - R}{P} = \frac{1 - b_1}{a} - \frac{Rb_2}{Pa}.$$

$$\cdot \frac{\frac{rq}{(1-\delta+c)^n}-1}{c-\delta}+\frac{1}{r}[b_1+b_2(1+cq)]\Bigg\};$$

$$n = 0,\ldots,N.$$

Independently of whether $\delta \gtrless c$, the right-hand side of the $\underline{K}_0^*$ condition achieves its maximum in the initial period (n = 0) and then falls *monotonically* with increasing *n*.

Notes: (i) For the initial period, one has, in particular:

$$\frac{\partial \underline{A}_0^{**}}{\partial r} \gtreqless 0 \Leftrightarrow \underline{A}_o^{**} \lesseqgtr \underbrace{\frac{TrqR}{b_1}}_{>0}\underbrace{\left[\frac{(1+cb_2q)(r+\delta-cb_1)}{a(r+\delta)}-1\right]}_{>0}.^{7}$$

(ii) For the point defined by $n_0 := [\log r - \log(r+\delta-c)]/\log(1-\delta+c)$ the following is obtained:

$$\frac{\partial \underline{A}_{no}^{**}}{\partial r} \gtreqless 0 \Leftrightarrow \underline{A}_0^{**} \lesseqgtr 0.$$

Therefore, if initial disposable earnings $\underline{A}_0^{**}$ are positive, then the derivative $\partial\underline{A}_n^{**}/\partial r$ takes the negative sign from n_0 at the very latest. If $\underline{A}_0^{**}$ is larger than the limit given in (i), then no change in sign takes place at all; then: $\partial\underline{A}_n^{**}/\partial r < 0\,\forall n$. In the case of negative initial disposable earnings $\underline{A}_0^{**}$, $\partial\underline{A}_n^{**}/\partial r$ is (at first) positive; a change in sign occurs if at all only after n_0.

$$\frac{\partial[Q^* - c(sK)^*]}{\partial r} = \underbrace{\frac{T}{b_1}}_{>0}\underbrace{\left[1-\frac{(1+cb_2q)(r+\delta-cb_1)}{a(r+\delta)}\right]}_{<0 \text{ (cf. footnote 7)}} < 0.$$

The following is obtained for the slope of the optimum age–earnings profile:

7

$$\frac{(1+cb_2q)(r+\delta-cb_1)}{a(r+\delta)}-1 = \left[\frac{b_1}{q}+b_2(r+\delta)+cb_2q(r+\delta-cb_1)\right]$$

$$\cdot\frac{1}{a(r+\delta)} > 0,$$

since $r+\delta > c > 0$ and $0 < b_1, b_2 < 1$.

It is apparent from (i) that a positive $\underline{A}_0^{**}$ is compatible with $\partial\underline{A}_0^{**}/\partial r > 0$.

8 For the case which can be empirically substantiated, $\delta > c$, this type of change is more probable than where $c > \delta$. For

$$\left[\frac{rq}{(1-\delta+c)^n}-1\right]\Big/(c-\delta)$$

with n increasing and $\delta > c$ converges to $-\infty$; for $c > \delta$, it only converges to $-1/(c-\delta)$. Note that $\underline{K}_0^* > 0$.

$$\frac{\partial(\underline{A}^{**}_{n+1} - \underline{A}^{**}_{n})}{\partial r} = (1 - \delta + c)^n R \left\{ \frac{\delta - c}{r^2} a_1 + \frac{T}{b_1} \left[1 + \frac{\delta a}{r^2}(c - \delta) - \frac{1 + cb_2 q}{a(r + \delta)} \left(\frac{r + \delta a}{rq} + cb_2 \right) \right] \right\};$$

$$n = 0, \ldots, N - 1. \quad [\rho]$$

With the theoretical parameter restrictions formulated in Section 2.1.1 (see the list on p. 39), the expression in square brackets is negative. It is, therefore, instantly clear that where $c > \delta$ the optimum trajectory occurring after an increase in r is flatter than the original one, i.e.:

$$\frac{\partial(\underline{A}^{**}_{n+1} - \underline{A}^{**}_{n})}{\partial r} < 0; \quad n = 0, \ldots, N - 1.$$

The situation for the case $\delta > c$, which can be substantiated empirically, is less obvious. Here, the following condition is established:

$$\frac{\partial(\underline{A}^{**}_{n+1} - \underline{A}^{**}_{n})}{\partial r} \lesseqgtr 0$$

$$\Leftrightarrow \underline{A}^{**}_0 \lesseqgtr \frac{TrR}{b_1(\delta - c)} \left[\frac{(1 + cb_2 q)(r + \delta - cb_1)}{a(r + \delta)} - 1 \right] \quad (>0);$$

$$n = 0, \ldots, N - 1.$$

As long as the initial disposable earnings $\underline{A}^{**}_0$ are below the limit given, an increase in the interest rate also results in a reduction in earnings growth in the present case. Here, the empiricists are allowed the final say. On the basis of (19), a reduction in the slope of the $\underline{A}^{**}_n$ profile does in fact take place after an increase in the interest rate.

> *Note*: At the end of the R, P and r analyses, it is noted that the special case $c = \delta$ does not promote the discovery of any new knowledge. The results obtained previously are produced in a similar manner for this case as well.[9]

The learning-by-doing rate c

$$\frac{\partial \underline{A}^{**}_n}{\partial c} = \underbrace{R(1 - \delta + c)^n}_{>0} \underbrace{\frac{\partial \underline{K}^*_0}{\partial c}}_{<0} + \underbrace{R\underline{K}^*_0}_{>0} \underbrace{n(1 - \delta + c)^{n-1}}_{\geqslant 0}$$

[9] Instead of the term $[rq/(1 - \delta + c)^n - 1]/(c - \delta)$, for example, $1/r - n$ now appears. Also $n_{0,c=\delta} = 1/r$.

$$+ R\underbrace{\frac{(1-\delta+c)^n-1}{c-\delta}}_{\geqslant 0,\ \text{increases with } n}\frac{\partial[Q^*-c(sK)^*]}{\partial c}$$

$$+ \underbrace{R[Q^*-c(sK)^*]}_{>0}\underbrace{\frac{\partial\left[\frac{(1-\delta+c)^n-1}{c-\delta}\right]}{\partial c}}_{\geqslant 0,\ \text{increases with } n} - \underbrace{\frac{\partial I^*}{\partial c}}_{>0};$$

$$n=0,\ldots,N. \quad [\sigma]$$

Details:

$$\frac{\partial \underline{K}_0^*}{\partial c} = -\frac{(r+\delta)b_2 q}{b_1 r}T < 0.$$

$$\frac{\partial[Q^*-c(sK)^*]}{\partial c} = T\left[\frac{b_2 q}{a}\left(\frac{r+\delta}{b_1}-c\right)-1\right];$$

the sign of this derivative is indeterminate in theoretical terms. With the values of the standard parameter set (19),

$$T\left[\frac{b_2 q}{a}\left(\frac{r+\delta}{b_1}-c\right)-1\right] > 0;$$

therefore, on the basis of that empirically supported case, a higher learning-by-doing rate results in an increase in the amount of net production.

$$Q^*-c(sK)^* = T\left(\frac{r+\delta}{b_1}-c\right) > 0,$$

since: $T > 0$, $r+\delta > c$ and $0 < b_1 < 1$.

$$\frac{\partial\left[\frac{(1-\delta+c)^n-1}{c-\delta}\right]}{\partial c} = \frac{1+(1-\delta+c)^{n-1}[(c-\delta)(n-1)-1]}{(c-\delta)^2}$$

$$\begin{cases} =0 & \text{where } n=0 \text{ and } n=1; \\ >0 & \text{where } 2\leqslant n\leqslant N. \end{cases}$$

$$\frac{(1-\delta+c)^{n+1}-1}{c-\delta} - \frac{(1-\delta+c)^n-1}{c-\delta} = (1-\delta+c)^n > 0;$$

$$n=0,\ldots,N-1.$$

$$\frac{\partial\left[\frac{(1-\delta+c)^{n+1}-1}{c-\delta}\right]}{\partial c}-\frac{\partial\left[\frac{(1-\delta+c)^{n}-1}{c-\delta}\right]}{\partial c}$$

$$= n(1-\delta+c)^{n-1} > 0; \quad n = 1,\ldots,N-1.$$

$$\frac{\partial I^*}{\partial c} = T\frac{Rb_2q^2}{b_1a}(r+\delta-cb_1) > 0.$$

Notes:

(i) $\frac{\partial \underline{A}_0^{**}}{\partial c} = R\frac{\partial \underline{K}_0^*}{\partial c} - \frac{\partial I^*}{\partial c} < 0.$

(ii) $\frac{\partial(\underline{A}_{n+1}^{**} - \underline{A}_n^{**})}{\partial c} > 0; \quad n = 0,\ldots,N-1.$

(iii) $\frac{\partial \underline{W}^*}{\partial c} > 0;$ see Appendix 6.

The special case where $c = \delta$ results in the following:[10]

$$\left.\frac{\partial \underline{A}_n^{**}}{\partial c}\right|_{c=\delta} = \underbrace{\frac{TR}{a(r+c)}}_{>0}\underbrace{[r(a+1)+c(1-b_1)]}_{>0}\left(\frac{1}{r}-n\right); n = 0,\ldots,N.$$

Consequently:

$$\left.\frac{\partial \underline{A}_n^{**}}{\partial c}\right|_{c=\delta} \begin{cases} >0 \text{ where } 0 \leqslant n < \frac{1}{r}; \\ <0 \text{ where } n > \frac{1}{r}. \end{cases} \qquad [\tau]$$

Also one has:

$$\left.\frac{\partial(\underline{A}_{n+1}^{**} - \underline{A}_n^{**})}{\partial c}\right|_{c=\delta} = -\frac{TR}{a(r+c)}[r(a+1)+c(1-b_1)] < 0;$$

$$n = 0,\ldots,N-1. \quad [\upsilon]$$

Notes:

(i) $\left.\frac{\partial[Q^* - c(sK)^*]}{\partial c}\right|_{c=\delta} = \frac{-T}{a(r+c)}[r(a+1)+c(1-b_1)] < 0.$

[10] Note, that in this case, a marginal variation in c also implies an identical marginal variation in δ.

(ii) $\left.\dfrac{\partial \underline{W}^*}{\partial c}\right|_{c=\delta} < 0.$

The full-time schooling production efficiency a_1

$$\frac{\partial \underline{A}_n^{**}}{\partial a_1} = \frac{R}{r}(1-\delta+c)^n > 0; \quad n = 0, \ldots, N. \qquad [\phi]$$

$$\frac{\partial(\underline{A}_{n+1}^{**} - \underline{A}_n^{**})}{\partial a_1} = (c-\delta)\frac{R}{r}(1-\delta+c)^n \begin{cases} <0, & \text{if } \delta > c; \\ =0, & \text{if } c = \delta; \\ >0, & \text{if } c > \delta; \end{cases}$$

$$n = 0, \ldots, N-1. \qquad [\chi]$$

The working phase production efficiency b_0

$$\frac{\partial \underline{A}_n^{**}}{\partial b_0} = \frac{1}{a}\underline{w}_{2n} b_0^{\frac{b_1+b_2}{a}}; \quad n = 0, \ldots, N.$$

$$\frac{\partial \underline{A}_n^{**}}{\partial b_0} \begin{cases} <0 & \text{where } 0 \leqslant n < n_{0,b_0}; \\ >0 & \text{where } n > n_{0,b_0}; \end{cases} \qquad [\psi]$$

where:

$$n_{0,b_0} = \begin{cases} \dfrac{\log r - \log(r+\delta-c)}{\log(1-\delta+c)}, & \text{if } c \neq \delta; \\ \dfrac{1}{r}, & \text{if } c = \delta. \end{cases}$$

In the unsolved form (see text):

$$\frac{\partial \underline{A}_n^{**}}{\partial b_0} = \underbrace{R(1-\delta+c)^n}_{>0} \underbrace{\frac{\partial \underline{K}_0^*}{\partial b_0}}_{<0}$$

$$+ R \underbrace{\frac{(1-\delta+c)^n - 1}{c-\delta}}_{\geqslant 0, \text{ increases with } n} \underbrace{\frac{\partial[Q^* - c(sK)^*]}{\partial b_0}}_{>0} - \underbrace{\frac{\partial I^*}{\partial b_0}}_{>0}; \quad n = 0, \ldots, N.$$

$$\frac{\partial(\underline{A}_{n+1}^{**} - \underline{A}_n^{**})}{\partial b_0} = \frac{1}{a} b_0^{\frac{b_1+b_1}{a}} \pi_w (1-\delta+c)^n > 0; \quad n = 0, \ldots, N-1. \qquad [\omega]$$

Joint variations of a_1 and b_0

Because of the possibility of different orders of magnitude an examination is undertaken to discover what effects a simultaneous variation of a_1 and b_0 by the same *percentage* has on the optimal $\underline{A}_n^{**}$ profile.

$\underline{A}_n^{**} = \underline{A}_n^{**}[a_1(\hat{m}), b_0(\hat{m})], \quad n = 0, \ldots, N;$

$\hat{m} \mathrel{\hat{=}}$ policy effect; LA, DF.

Thus, if: $a_1/b_0 = \text{constant} = \kappa_1$, then $b_0 = a_1/\kappa_1 = b_0(a_1)$; with $a_1 = a_1(\hat{m})$, $b_0 = b_0[a_1(\hat{m})]$ so that:

$$\frac{d\underline{A}_n^{**}}{d\hat{m}} = \frac{\partial \underline{A}_n^{**}}{\partial a_1}\frac{da_1}{d\hat{m}} + \frac{\partial \underline{A}_n^{**}}{\partial b_0}\frac{db_0}{da_1}\frac{da_1}{d\hat{m}}; \quad n = 0, \ldots, N.$$

With $db_0/da_1 = 1/\kappa_1 = b_0/a_1$ and the assumption $da_1/d\hat{m} = 1$, it follows that:

$$\frac{d\underline{A}_n^{**}}{d\hat{m}} = \frac{R}{r}(1 - \delta + c)^n + \frac{\underline{w}_{2n}}{aa_1} b_0^{1/a}; \quad n = 0, \ldots, N. \qquad [\Gamma]$$

It can be established at once from this that the point of change of the sign (if there is one) shifts to an *earlier* period than n_{0,b_0}, since $d\underline{A}_n^{**}/d\hat{m}$ is already positive at n_{0,b_0}.[11]

In particular, for the initial period, the following is obtained:

$$\frac{d\underline{A}_0^{**}}{d\hat{m}} = \frac{R}{r} - \frac{qb_0^{1/a}}{aa_1}\pi_w,$$

which is an indeterminate expression in theoretical terms. If it is positive then it follows, in connection with the next result, that: $d\underline{A}_n^{**}/d\hat{m} > 0$, $n = 0, \ldots, N$; thus no change of sign takes place at all here; the a_1 effect dominates the b_0 effect, if you like (cf. also Figs. 18 and 19). If $d\underline{A}_0^{**}/d\hat{m} < 0$ then there is an 'overtaking' which occurs before n_{0,b_0}.

$$\frac{d(\underline{A}_{n+1}^{**} - \underline{A}_n^{**})}{d\hat{m}} = \frac{R}{a_1}(1 - \delta + c)^n \cdot \left[\frac{c - \delta}{r}a_1 + \left(\frac{r + \delta a}{rq} + cb_2\right)\frac{T}{b_1}\frac{1}{a}\right] > 0; \quad n = 0, \ldots, N - 1. \qquad [\Theta]$$

11 The same can also be shown for a variation of a_1 and $b := b_0^{1/a}$ (a fixed). As a reminder: $R, r, a, a_1, b_0 > 0$; $(1 - \delta + c)^n > 0$, $n = 0, \ldots, N$; and:

$$\underline{w}_{2n} \begin{cases} < 0 & \text{where } 0 \leqslant n < n_{0,b_0}; \\ \geqslant 0 & \text{where } n \geqslant n_{0,b_0}. \end{cases}$$

The reader will discover from the discussion relating to (41) that this also applies for $\delta > c$.[12]

Interaction effects

The interrelations between the public policy parameters (R, P, r) and the human capital accumulation capabilities (a_1, b_0) are as follows:

$$\frac{\partial^2 \underline{A}_n^{**}}{\partial a_1\, \partial R} = \frac{(1-\delta+c)^n}{r} > 0; \quad n = 0, \ldots, N. \qquad [\Delta]$$

$$\frac{\partial^2 \underline{A}_n^{**}}{\partial a_1\, \partial P} = 0, \quad n = 0, \ldots, N; \qquad [\Lambda]$$

the effect of variations in the price of educational goods P on the optimal earnings profile thereby remains unaffected by the level of the full-time schooling production efficiency a_1.

$$\frac{\partial^2 \underline{A}_n^{**}}{\partial a_1\, \partial r} = -\frac{R}{r^2}(1-\delta+c)^n < 0; \quad n = 0, \ldots, N. \qquad [\Xi]$$

$$\frac{\partial^2 \underline{A}_n^{**}}{\partial b_0\, \partial R} = \frac{1-b_1}{Ra^2} \underline{w}_{2n} b_0^{\frac{b_1+b_2}{a}}, \quad n = 0, \ldots, N;$$

thus:

$$\frac{\partial^2 \underline{A}_n^{**}}{\partial b_0\, \partial R} \begin{cases} <0 & \text{where } 0 \leqslant n < n_0; \\ >0 & \text{where } n > n_0; \end{cases} \qquad [\Pi]$$

with:

$$n_0 = \begin{cases} [\log r - \log(r+\delta-c)]/\log(1-\delta+c), & \text{if } c \neq \delta; \\ 1/r, & \text{if } c = \delta. \end{cases}$$

Note: As a reminder: $n_{0,R} < n_0$.

$$\frac{\partial^2 \underline{A}_n^{**}}{\partial b_0\, \partial P} = \frac{-b_2}{Pa^2} \underline{w}_{2n} b_0^{\frac{b_1+b_2}{a}}, \quad n = 0, \ldots, N;$$

consequently:

$$\frac{\partial^2 \underline{A}_n^{**}}{\partial b_0\, \partial P} \begin{cases} >0 & \text{where } 0 \leqslant n < n_0; \\ <0 & \text{where } n > n_0. \end{cases} \qquad [\Sigma]$$

[12] The expression '[ ]' occurring in (41) differs from the square brackets employed here only by a multiplication of the second main summand by the factor $1/a$. The second main summand is, however, positive for both $c > \delta$ and for $\delta > c$ and $a = 1 - b_1 - b_2$ is between 0 and 1 (cf. Section 2.1.1; $0 < a < 1 \Rightarrow 1/a > 1$). '[ ]' >0 is, consequently, sufficient for the expression in square brackets to be positive in the present case.

$$\frac{\partial^2 \underline{A}_n^{**}}{\partial b_0\, \partial r} = \frac{TR}{ab_0 b_1}\left\{\left[1 + \frac{\delta a}{r^2}(c-\delta) - \frac{1+cb_2 q}{a(r+\delta)}\left(\frac{r+\delta a}{rq} + cb_2\right)\right]\right.$$
$$\left.\cdot \frac{(1-\delta+c)^n - rq}{c-\delta} + q^2\left(\frac{r+\delta a}{rq} + cb_2\right)\right\}; \quad n = 0, \ldots, N. \qquad [\Upsilon]$$

The expression in the square brackets within the curly brackets is known to be negative. Therefore, it becomes clear that $\partial^2 \underline{A}_n^{**}/\partial b_0\, \partial r$ is initially positive. $[(1-\delta+c)^n - rq]/(c-\delta)$ increases monotonically with n and is positive from n_0. A change in sign of the derivative $\partial^2 \underline{A}_n^{**}/\partial b_0\, \partial r$ (from positive to negative) is, therefore, possible; if at all, it takes place after n_0.

With $a_1 = a_1(\hat{m})$ and $b_0 = b_0(\hat{m})$ and if $a_1/b_0 =: \kappa_1$ (cf. p. 214), then $b_0 = a_1(\hat{m})/\kappa_1 = b_0[a_1(\hat{m})]$ and, formally, one has the following:

$$\frac{\partial^2 \underline{A}_n^{**}}{\partial \hat{m}\, \partial x} = \frac{\partial^2 \underline{A}_n^{**}}{\partial a_1\, \partial x}\frac{da_1}{d\hat{m}} + \frac{\partial^2 \underline{A}_n^{**}}{\partial b_0\, \partial x}\frac{db_0}{da_1}\frac{da_1}{d\hat{m}}, \quad x \in \{R, P, r\};$$
$$n = 0, \ldots, N.$$

Where $db_0/da_1 = 1/\kappa_1 = b_0/a_1$ and $da_1/d\hat{m} = 1$, it follows that:

$$\frac{\partial^2 \underline{A}_n^{**}}{\partial \hat{m}\, \partial R} = \frac{(1-\delta+c)^n}{r} + \frac{1-b_1}{Ra^2 a_1}\underline{w}_{2n} b_0^{1/a}; \quad n = 0, \ldots, N. \qquad [\Phi]$$

Note: Here, it is possible to draw conclusions both from the $d\underline{A}_n^{**}/d\hat{m}$ analysis and from the analysis of $1/a_1 \cdot \partial \underline{A}_n^{**}/\partial R$ (noting $a_1 > 0$ and $1/a > 1$). For example, one discovers that a possible turning point of $\partial^2 \underline{A}_n^{**}/\partial \hat{m}\, \partial R$ (from negative to positive) comes after $n_{0,R}$ but prior to n_0.

For $x = P$:

$$\frac{\partial^2 \underline{A}_n^{**}}{\partial \hat{m}\, \partial P} = \frac{-b_2}{Pa^2 a_1}\underline{w}_{2n} b_0^{1/a}, \quad n = 0, \ldots, N;$$

thus:

$$\frac{\partial^2 \underline{A}_n^{**}}{\partial \hat{m}\, \partial P}\begin{cases} >0 & \text{where } 0 \leqslant n < n_0; \\ <0 & \text{where } n > n_0. \end{cases} \qquad [\Psi]$$

For $x = r$:

$$\frac{\partial^2 \underline{A}_n^{**}}{\partial \hat{m}\, \partial r} = -\frac{R}{r^2}(1-\delta+c)^n + \underbrace{\frac{\partial^2 \underline{A}_n^{**}}{\partial b_0\, \partial r}}_{\text{see above}}\frac{b_0}{a_1}; \quad n = 0, \ldots, N. \qquad [\Omega]$$

Appendix 3 The distribution factors V_{a_1}, V_b and $\rho_{a_1 b}$: an illustration

The purpose of the following analysis is to illustrate the integration of the factors determining earnings listed in Chapter 2 into the recurring distribution factors V_{a_1}, V_b and $\rho_{a_1 b}$ on the basis of (35) and (18) and Section 3.2.2. This also serves as a motivation for, and as a more precise explanation of many of the relations employed in the text.

The following multiplicative component interaction is presumed in line with the discoveries from Section 3.2.2:

$$\tilde{a}_1 = \widetilde{LA} \cdot \widetilde{DF};$$

$$\tilde{b}_0 = \widetilde{LA} \cdot \widetilde{DF} \cdot \widetilde{RE}, \quad \widetilde{RE} := \widetilde{QPC}(\underline{a}, \underline{b}, \underline{c}) \cdot \widetilde{CR} \cdot \widetilde{SQ}.$$

All the variables listed are positive variables (this can always be achieved by means of a corresponding normalising procedure). $\tilde{a}_1$ and $\widetilde{RE}$ are assumed independent of one another (this can be substantiated by note (i) p. 37).

Primarily for analytical convenience (but see also Section 3.2.2), it is assumed that the variables $\tilde{a}_1$ and $\tilde{b}_0$ are jointly log-normally distributed with parameters $\mu_{\log a_1}$, $\mu_{\log bo}$, $\sigma^2_{\log a_1}$, $\sigma^2_{\log bo}$ and $\sigma_{12} := \mathrm{cov}(\log \tilde{a}_1, \log \tilde{b}_0)$.

We then have (note Aitchison and Brown, 1957, ch. 2):

$$V^2_{a_1} = \exp\{\sigma^2_{\log a_1}\} - 1;$$

$$V_{a_1} = (\exp\{\sigma^2_{\log a_1}\} - 1)^{\frac{1}{2}} > 0, \quad \text{since } \sigma^2_{\log a_1} > 0.$$

$$V^2_{bo} = \exp\{\sigma^2_{\log bo}\} - 1.$$

$$\mathrm{cov}(\tilde{a}_1, \tilde{b}_0) = E[(\tilde{a}_1 - \mu_{a_1})(\tilde{a}_1 \widetilde{RE} - \mu_{a_1}\mu_{RE})] = \mu_{RE}\sigma^2_{a_1} > 0.$$

$$\rho_{a_1 bo} = \mu_{RE}\sigma_{a_1}/\sigma_{bo}; \quad \sigma_{bo} = (\mu^2_{a_1}\sigma^2_{RE} + \mu^2_{RE}\sigma^2_{a_1} + \sigma^2_{a_1}\sigma^2_{RE})^{\frac{1}{2}}.$$

$$\sigma^2_{\log a_1} = \sigma^2_{\log LA} + \sigma^2_{\log DF} + 2\underbrace{\mathrm{cov}(\log \widetilde{LA}, \log \widetilde{DF})}_{>0};$$

$\sigma^2_{\log b_0} = \sigma^2_{\log a_1} + \sigma^2_{\log RE}$; thus

$V^2_{b_0} > V^2_{a_1}$, $\gamma_1(\tilde{b}_0) > \gamma_1(\tilde{a}_1) > 0$ and $\gamma_2(\tilde{b}_0) > \gamma_2(\tilde{a}_1) > 0$.

Because:

$$\mu_{\log a_1} = \mu_{\log LA} + \mu_{\log DF} \quad \text{and} \quad \mu_{\log b_0} = \mu_{\log a_1} + \mu_{\log RE}$$

we also get:

$$\sigma^2_{b_0} > \sigma^2_{a_1}.$$

Note: It cannot be ruled out that $\sigma^2_{b_0} > \sigma^2_{a_1}$ still applies even when $RE^j < 1\,\forall j$, i.e. $\mu_{\log RE} < 0$, since $\sigma^2_{\log b_0} > \sigma^2_{\log a_1}$.

For the 'modified' human capital production efficiency during the earnings activity phase, one has the following:

$$\tilde{b} := \tilde{b}_0^{1/a} = (\widetilde{LA} \cdot \widetilde{DF} \cdot \widetilde{RE})^{1/a} = \tilde{a}_1^{1/a} \widetilde{RE}^{1/a}.$$

$$V_b^2 := V^2_{b_0^{1/a}} = \exp\left\{\frac{1}{a^2}\sigma^2_{\log b_0}\right\} - 1.$$

$$\operatorname{cov}(\tilde{a}_1, \tilde{b}) = \mu_{a_1}\mu_b(e^{\sigma_{12,a}} - 1);$$

$$\sigma_{12,a} := \operatorname{cov}\left(\log \tilde{a}_1, \frac{1}{a}\log \tilde{b}_0\right) = \frac{1}{a}\sigma^2_{\log a_1}.\text{[13]}$$

Therefore (as a reminder: $a = 1 - b_1 - b_2$, $0 < a < 1$):

$$\rho_{a_1 b} = \frac{\operatorname{cov}(\tilde{a}_1, \tilde{b})}{\sigma_{a_1}\sigma_b} = \frac{\exp\left\{\frac{1}{a}\sigma^2_{\log a_1}\right\} - 1}{V_{a_1} V_b} > 0.$$

Notes:

(i) $\partial\rho_{a_1 b}/\partial\sigma^2_{\log RE} < 0$.

$\partial\rho_{a_1 b}/\partial\sigma^2_{\log a_1}$ is indeterminate; this partial derivative becomes negative for a sufficiently small value of a, *ceteris paribus*. $\partial\rho_{a_1 b}/\partial a$ is also indeterminate, since both $\operatorname{cov}(\tilde{a}_1, \tilde{b})$ and σ_b fall with increasing a, i.e. with a falling scale elasticity $b_1 + b_2$.

For a sufficiently large $\sigma^2_{\log RE}$, $\partial\rho_{a_1 b}/\partial a$ is positive, *ceteris paribus*, so that, for example:

$$\rho_{a_1 b} < \rho_{a_1 b_0}, \quad \text{since } 0 < a < 1.$$

(ii) The correlation coefficient between the human capital accumulation abilities $\tilde{a}_1$ and $\tilde{b}$ can also be presented in the following form:

[13] Since $\tilde{a}_1$ and $\widetilde{RE}$ (and consequently also $\log \tilde{a}_1$ and $\log \widetilde{RE}$) are stochastically independent by assumption.

$$\rho_{a_1 b} = \frac{(V_{a_1}^2 + 1)^{1/a} - 1}{V_{a_1}[(V_{a_1}^2 + 1)^{1/a^2}(V_{RE}^2 + 1)^{1/a^2} - 1]^{\frac{1}{2}}}.$$

In particular, one has therefore:

$$\rho_{a_1 b_0} = V_{a_1}/V_{b_0}; \quad V_{b_0} = (V_{a_1}^2 + V_{RE}^2 + V_{a_1}^2 V_{RE}^2)^{\frac{1}{2}}.$$

Where $0 < a < 1$, $\sigma_{\log b}^2 = 1/a^2 \cdot \sigma_{\log b_0}^2 > \sigma_{\log b_0}^2$, so that:

$$V_b^2 > V_{b_0}^2, \quad \gamma_1(\tilde{b}) > \gamma_1(\tilde{b}_0) \quad \text{and} \quad \gamma_2(\tilde{b}) > \gamma_2(\tilde{b}_0).$$

Moreover:

$$\sigma_b^2 > \sigma_{b_0}^2 \quad \text{and} \quad \mu_b > \mu_{b_0},$$

since:

$$\mu_{\log b} = 1/a \cdot \mu_{\log b_0} > \mu_{\log b_0}.$$

On consideration of the above, the following is finally obtained:

$$h_0 := V_b/V_{a_1} > 1 \quad \text{and} \quad k := \sigma_{a_1}/\sigma_b < 1;$$

but also:

$$h_0 \rho_{a_1 b} = \frac{\exp\left\{\dfrac{1}{a}\sigma_{\log a_1}^2\right\} - 1}{\exp\{\sigma_{\log a_1}^2\} - 1} > 1,$$

so that (see Appendix 4):

$$\chi < 0 \quad (\text{or } \xi > 1).$$

Furthermore, the question of how V_{a_1}, V_b and $\rho_{a_1 b}$, the basic elements of the decomposition (54) are related to one another, can now be examined.

The above analysis results in the following:

$$V_{a_1}^2 = \exp\{\sigma_{\log LA}^2 + \sigma_{\log DF}^2 + 2\,\text{cov}(\log \tilde{LA}, \log \tilde{DF})\} - 1;$$

$$V_b^2 = \exp\left\{\frac{1}{a^2}[\sigma_{\log LA}^2 + \sigma_{\log DF}^2 + 2\,\text{cov}(\log \tilde{LA}, \log \tilde{DF}) + \sigma_{\log RE}^2]\right\} - 1;$$

$$\rho_{a_1 b} = \frac{(V_{a_1}^2 + 1)^{1/a} - 1}{V_{a_1} V_b}.$$

Thus, the stronger the (relative) variation in the learning ability and the *DF* factor within the population, the greater the $\tilde{a}_1$ inequality (measured by the square of the coefficient of variation). These variations on their part are stronger, the greater the individual differences in the genetic endowment, the family background and the cultural factors (cf. (63) and (64)). The $\tilde{a}_1$ inequality also increases with the covariance cov(log $\tilde{LA}$, log $\tilde{DF}$); consequently, the more the variation of the family background and the variation of the cultural factors exceeds that of the genetic components, the greater this covariance contribution; on the other hand, if the variation in the genetic factors plays a comparatively larger role, then this contribution is reduced (without, however, disappearing).

What has been said up to now also applies qualitatively for the $\tilde{b}$ inequality, which incidentally exceeds the $\tilde{a}_1$ inequality the more, the smaller a is, and therefore the greater the scale elasticity $b_1 + b_2$, and the larger the (relative) $\tilde{RE}$ dispersion. The latter becomes all the more significant, the stronger the distinctions between individuals in their leadership and organisational abilities, their willingness to take risks, their capability of assuming responsibility, the (relative) standard of their examination results and the quality of their educational institutions. With an increasing inequality in $\tilde{RE}$, the relative effect of the inequalities in $\tilde{LA}$ and $\tilde{DF}$ on the $\tilde{b}$ inequality diminishes. This relationship is achieved in the above analysis by $\partial\rho_{a_1 b}/\partial\sigma^2_{\log RE} < 0$. A larger (relative) variation in $\tilde{RE}$ therefore results in an increase in the $\tilde{b}$ inequality, but at the same time in a weakening in the correlation between the two basic variables $\tilde{a}_1$ and $\tilde{b}_0$ (or $\tilde{b}$).

Last but not least, it must be mentioned that, in the case of a sufficiently large scale elasticity in human capital production, $b_1 + b_2$, a lower log $\tilde{LA}$ variation, log $\tilde{DF}$ variation or covariance between these two factors continues to induce a reduction in the $\tilde{a}_1$ and $\tilde{b}$ inequalities; the correlation between $\tilde{a}_1$ and $\tilde{b}$, however, is increased (see note (i), p. 218).

Appendix 4 Technical details for Section 3.4

Characterisation of the distribution factor χ

$$\chi := \frac{1 - h_0 \rho_{a_1 b}}{h_0 - \rho_{a_1 b}} k,$$

where:

$$0 < \rho_{a_1 b} < 1; \quad h_0 := V_b / V_{a_1} > 1; \quad 0 < k := \sigma_{a_1} / \sigma_b < 1.$$ [14]

It applies that:

$$-k < \chi < k;$$

since:

$$\chi > -k \Leftrightarrow (1 + h_0)(1 - \rho_{a_1 b}) > 0$$

and

$$\chi < k \Leftrightarrow (1 - h_0)(1 + \rho_{a_1 b}) < 0,$$

which are both satisfied.

Also, one has, *ceteris paribus*:

$$\frac{\partial \chi}{\partial \rho_{a_1 b}} = \frac{1 - h_0^2}{(h_0 - \rho_{a_1 b})^2} k < 0;$$

$$\frac{\partial \chi}{\partial h_0} = \frac{\rho_{a_1 b}^2 - 1}{(h_0 - \rho_{a_1 b})^2} k < 0;$$

and

$$\frac{\partial \chi}{\partial k} = \frac{1 - h_0 \rho_{a_1 b}}{h_0 - \rho_{a_1 b}} < 0 \Leftrightarrow h_0 \rho_{a_1 b} > 1.$$

[14] The reasons for these inequalities are given in Section 3.2.2. Cf. also Appendix 3.

Finally:

$$\chi \leqslant 0 \Leftrightarrow h_0 \rho_{a_1 b} \geqslant 1.$$

Analysis of the coefficient paths $\left\{\dfrac{\underline{w}_{2n}}{\underline{w}_{1n}}\right\}_{n=0}^{N}$ **and** $\left\{\dfrac{\partial \underline{w}_{2n}/\partial x}{\partial \underline{w}_{1n}/\partial x}\right\}_{n=0}^{N}$, $x \in \{R, P, r\}$

Preliminary note: It should be remembered that, with the empirical results of Carliner (1982), it must be assumed that $\delta > c$. For purely theoretical interest, the case $\delta \leqslant c$ will also be discussed. The illustrations, however, refer to the realistic constellation $\delta > c$ in all cases.

The following applies (cf. (39) and Figs. 26 and 27):

$$\underline{w}_{1n} = \frac{R}{r}(1 - \delta + c)^n > 0, \quad n = 0, \ldots, N;$$

$$\underline{w}_{1n+1} - \underline{w}_{1n} = \underline{w}_{1n}(c - \delta)\begin{cases} <0 & \text{where } \delta > c, \\ \geqslant 0 & \text{where } \delta \leqslant c, \end{cases} \quad n = 0, \ldots, N - 1.$$

$$\underline{w}_{2n} = \left\{\begin{array}{ll} \pi_w \dfrac{(1 - \delta + c)^n - rq}{c - \delta} & \text{where } c \neq \delta, \\ \pi_{w,c=\delta}\left(n - \dfrac{1}{r}\right) & \text{where } c = \delta, \end{array}\right\} \quad n = 0, \ldots, N;$$

$$\underline{w}_{2n+1} - \underline{w}_{2n} = \left\{\begin{array}{lll} \pi_w(1 - \delta + c)^n & >0 & \text{where } c \neq \delta, \\ \pi_{w,c=\delta} & >0 & \text{where } c = \delta, \end{array}\right\}$$

$$n = 0, \ldots, N - 1.$$

Notes:

(i) $$n_0 = \begin{cases} [\log rq]/\log(1 - \delta + c) & \text{where } c \neq \delta; \\ 1/r & \text{where } c = \delta. \end{cases}$$

(ii) $$\underline{w}_{2\infty} = \begin{cases} \pi_w \dfrac{rq}{\delta - c}, & \text{if } \delta > c; \\ \infty, & \text{if } \delta \leqslant c. \end{cases}$$

It thereby follows for the quotient $\underline{w}_{2n}/\underline{w}_{1n}$ that:

$$\frac{\underline{w}_{2n}}{\underline{w}_{1n}} = \left\{\begin{array}{ll} \dfrac{\pi_w r}{R} \dfrac{1 - rq/(1 - \delta + c)^n}{c - \delta} & \text{where } c \neq \delta, \\ \dfrac{-\pi_{w,c=\delta}}{R} + \dfrac{r\pi_{w,c=\delta}}{R} n & \text{where } c = \delta, \end{array}\right\} \quad n = 0, \ldots, N;$$

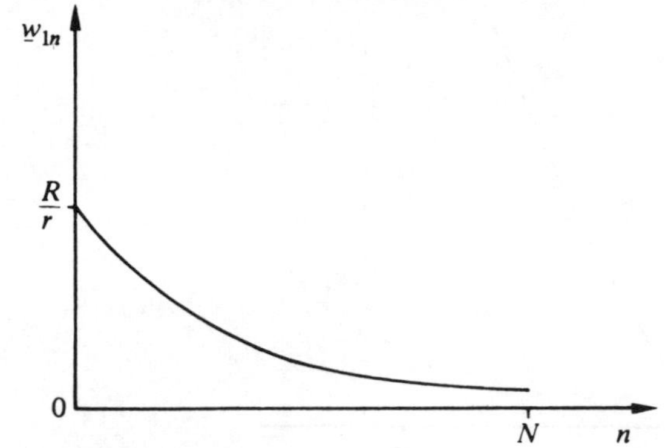

Fig. 26.

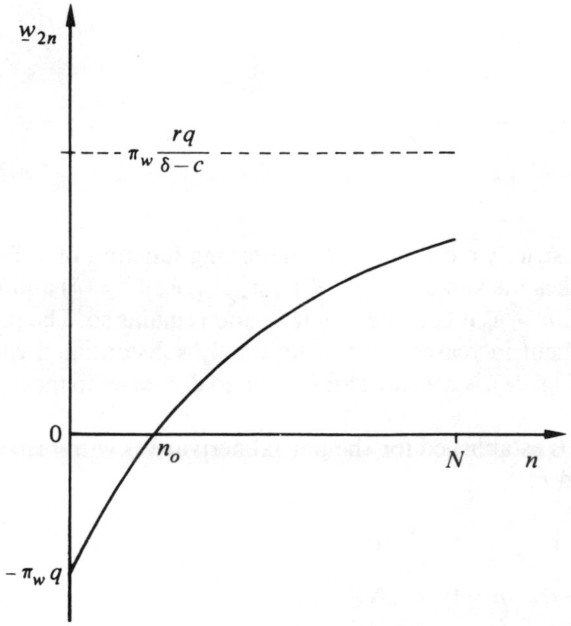

Fig. 27.

$$\frac{\underline{w}_{2n+1}}{\underline{w}_{1n+1}} - \frac{\underline{w}_{2n}}{\underline{w}_{1n}} = \begin{cases} \dfrac{\pi_w r^2 q}{R}(1 - \delta + c)^{-n-1} & >0 \quad \text{where } c \neq \delta, \\ \dfrac{r\pi_{w,c=\delta}}{R} & >0 \quad \text{where } c = \delta, \end{cases}$$

$$n = 0, \ldots, N - 1.$$

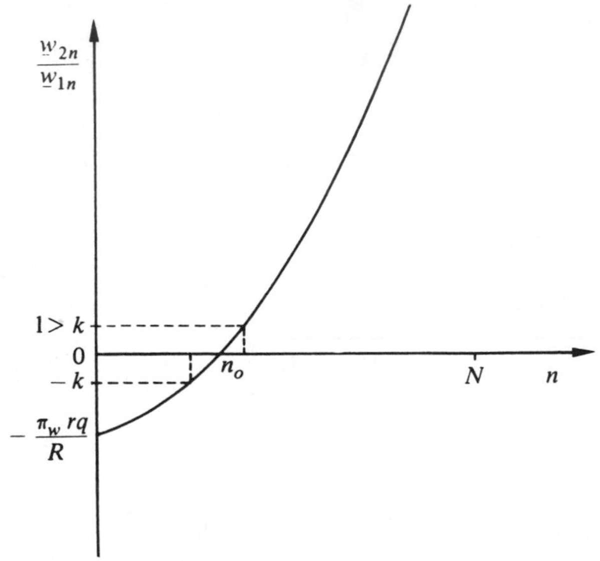

Fig. 28.

$\underline{w}_{2n}/\underline{w}_{1n}$ is therefore a strictly monotonically increasing function of n. For $n = 0$, the quotient takes the value $-\pi_w rq/R$ $(-\pi_{w,c=\delta}/R$, if $c = \delta)$ and is, therefore, negative; for $n > n_0$ it becomes positive and remains so. The rate of growth of the quotient increases in the empirically substantiated case where $\delta > c$ (see also Fig. 28), is constant for $\delta = c$ and decreases in the case where $c > \delta$.

Also, the following is established for the partial derivatives with respect to the prices R, P and r:

For R:

$$\frac{\partial \underline{w}_{1n}}{\partial R} = \frac{\underline{w}_{1n}}{R} > 0; \quad n = 0, \ldots, N.$$

$$\frac{\partial \underline{w}_{2n}}{\partial R} = \frac{1 - b_1}{aR} \underline{w}_{2n}; \quad n = 0, \ldots, N.$$

Hence:

$$\frac{\partial \underline{w}_{2n}/\partial R}{\partial \underline{w}_{1n}/\partial R} = \frac{1 - b_1}{a} \frac{\underline{w}_{2n}}{\underline{w}_{1n}}; \quad n = 0, \ldots, N.$$

Note: $(1 - b_1)/a > 1$, since: $0 < a := 1 - b_1 - b_2 < 1 - b_1$.

For P:

$$\frac{\partial \underline{w}_{1n}}{\partial P} = 0; \quad n = 0, \dots, N.$$

$$\frac{\partial \underline{w}_{2n}}{\partial P} = \frac{-b_2}{aP} \underline{w}_{2n} \gtrless 0 \Leftrightarrow \underline{w}_{2n} \lessgtr 0, \quad n = 0, \dots, N;$$

$\partial \underline{w}_{2n}/\partial P$ is therefore positive at first, but negative for $n > n_0$.

For r:

$$\frac{\partial \underline{w}_{1n}}{\partial r} = -\frac{\underline{w}_{1n}}{r} < 0; \quad n = 0, \dots, N.$$

Subsequently let us assume the realistic constellation $c \neq \delta$ (for the special case $c = \delta$, see note on pp. 227–8).

$$\frac{\partial \underline{w}_{2n}}{\partial r} = b_1^{1/a} \left(\frac{b_2 q}{P}\right)^{\frac{b_2}{a}} \left(\frac{R}{b_1}\right)^{\frac{1-b_1}{a}} (r + \delta)^{\frac{b_2 - 1}{a}}$$

$$\cdot \left[\frac{(1 - \delta + c)^n - rq}{c - \delta} \Delta_1 + q^2 \left(\frac{r + \delta a}{rq} + cb_2\right)\right],$$

$$n = 0, \dots, N;$$

where:

$$\Delta_1 := 1 + \frac{\delta a}{r^2}(c - \delta) - \frac{1 + cb_2 q}{a(r + \delta)} \left(\frac{r + \delta a}{rq} + cb_2\right).$$

Note: With the theoretical parameter restrictions $r + \delta > c$, $b_1 > 0$, $b_2 > 0$ and $b_1 + b_2 < 1$, it applies that: $\Delta_1 < 0$.

After some algebraic reformulations, the following is obtained:

$$\frac{\partial \underline{w}_{2n}}{\partial r} = \pi_w q^2 + \pi_w \Delta_2 \frac{(1 - \delta + c)^n - rq}{c - \delta}, \quad n = 0, \dots, N;$$

where:

$$\Delta_2 := \Delta_1 \left(\frac{r + \delta a}{rq} + cb_2\right)^{-1}.$$

Or:

$$\frac{\partial \underline{w}_{2n}}{\partial r} = \underline{w}_{2n} \left[\frac{q^2(c - \delta)}{(1 - \delta + c)^n - rq} + \Delta_2\right], \quad n = 0, \dots, N;\ n \neq n_0.$$

Thus:

$$\frac{\partial \underline{w}_{2n}/\partial r}{\partial \underline{w}_{1n}/\partial r} = \frac{\underline{w}_{2n}}{\underline{w}_{1n}} \beta_n, \quad n = 0, \ldots, N; n \neq n_0;$$

where:

$$\beta_n := \frac{rq^2(\delta - c)}{(1 - \delta + c)^n - rq} - r\Delta_2.$$

The function β_n is not defined for $n = n_0$; it has a pole there. With the aid of the above formulae, which are applicable for *all* values of n, the following is obtained for this point:

$$\frac{\partial \underline{w}_{2n_0}/\partial r}{\partial \underline{w}_{1n_0}/\partial r} = -\frac{\pi_w rq^2}{\underline{w}_{1n_0}} < 0.$$

The function β_n turns out to be a (type of) hyperbola[15] and has the following characteristics, *inter alia* (see also Fig. 29):

$$\beta_0 = rq + \pi_\beta, \quad \text{where: } \pi_\beta := -r\Delta_2.$$

With the theoretical parameter restrictions formulated in Section 2.1.1 and $c \neq \delta$, it follows that:

$$\pi_\beta > 1$$

$$\beta_{n+1} - \beta_n = \frac{rq^2(\delta - c)^2(1 - \delta + c)^n}{[(1 - \delta + c)^{n+1} - rq][(1 - \delta + c)^n - rq]} > 0$$

$$\Leftrightarrow (1 - \delta + c)^{n+1} \gtrless rq \quad \text{and} \quad (1 - \delta + c)^n \gtrless rq$$

$$\Leftrightarrow n + 1 < n_0 \quad \text{or} \quad n > n_0;$$

therefore, so long as the pole value n_0 is not crossed by the difference $\beta_{n+1} - \beta_n$, this difference is positive and β_n is, thereby, a strictly monotoni-

[15] A 'type of' hyperbola, since in the present case of $c \neq \delta$:

$$\lim_{n \to \infty} \beta_n \neq \lim_{n \to -\infty} \beta_n.$$

Proof:

$$\lim_{n \to \infty} \beta_n = \begin{cases} \pi_\beta - (\delta - c)q, & \text{if } \delta > c; \\ \pi_\beta, & \text{if } c > \delta; \end{cases}$$

where:

$$\pi_\beta := -r\Delta_2.$$

With the theoretical parameter restrictions from Section 2.1.1 and $\delta > c$ it applies incidentally that: $\pi_\beta - (\delta - c)q < 1$.

$$\lim_{n \to -\infty} \beta_n = \begin{cases} \pi_\beta, & \text{if } \delta > c; \\ \pi_\beta + (c - \delta)q, & \text{if } c > \delta. \end{cases}$$

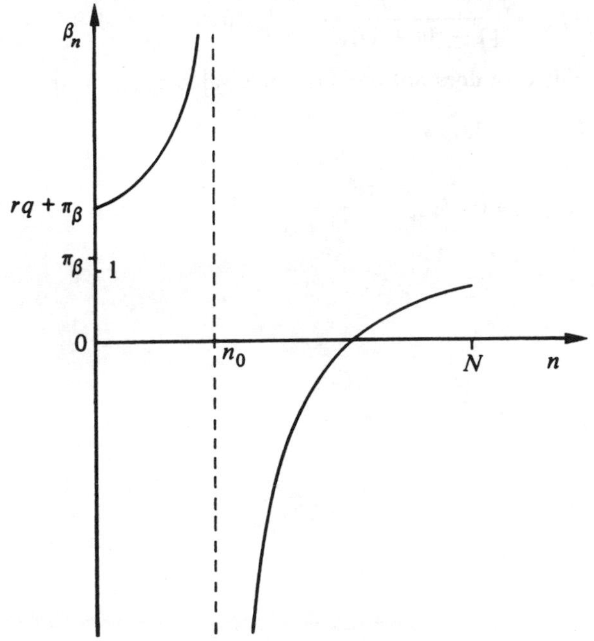

Fig. 29.

cally increasing function of n. An asymptote leads through the point n_0 parallel to the β_n axis, and has the equation: $n_0 = \lim_{\beta_n \to \pm\infty} n$. From this one obtains, for example, the following: $\beta_n > 1 \, \forall n < n_0$; for $n > n_0$, β_n is initially negative; it increases strictly monotonically, eventually becoming positive again, but it has an upper limit ($\beta_\infty < 1$ if $\delta > c$; $\beta_\infty = \pi_\beta$ (>1) if $c > \delta$).

Note: For the special case where $c = \delta$, one obtains the following:

$$\frac{\partial \underline{w}_{2n}/\partial r}{\partial \underline{w}_{1n}/\partial r} = \frac{\underline{w}_{2n}}{\underline{w}_{1n}} \beta_{n,c=\delta}, \quad n = 0, \ldots, N;\ n \neq n_0;$$

$$\beta_{n,c=\delta} := \pi_{\beta,c=\delta} + \frac{1}{1 - rn}.$$

$$\frac{\partial \underline{w}_{2n_0}/\partial r}{\partial \underline{w}_{1n_0}/\partial r} = -\frac{\pi_{w,c=\delta}}{R} < 0.$$

$$\beta_{0,c=\delta} = 1 + \pi_{\beta,c=\delta}.$$

$$\pi_{\beta,c=\delta} = \frac{r + cb_2}{a(r + c)} - \frac{r}{r + c(1 - b_1)} > 0; \quad \pi_{\beta,c=\delta} > 1, \text{ if } r \geqslant 2c.$$

$$\beta_{n+1} - \beta_n \overset{(c=\delta)}{=} \frac{r}{[1 - r(n+1)](1 - rn)} > 0,$$

so long as this difference does not cross the pole value $n_{0,c=\delta} = 1/r$.

$$\lim_{n \to \pm\infty} \beta_{n,c=\delta} = \pi_{\beta,c=\delta}.$$

$$\hat{n}_{c=\delta}: \quad \beta_{\hat{n},c=\delta} \equiv 1 \Rightarrow \hat{n}_{c=\delta} \overset{(r \geqslant 2c)}{=} \frac{\pi_{\beta,c=\delta}}{(\pi_{\beta,c=\delta} - 1)r}.$$

Appendix 5 Technical details for Section 4.1

$$\mu_{A^{**}} = \sum_{n=0}^{N} h(n)\mu_{A^{**}}$$

$$= \gamma_3 \sum_{n=0}^{N} (1+\gamma)^{-n}(w_{1n}\mu_{a_1} + w_{2n}\mu_b);$$

for a sufficiently large value of N, this can be approximated with the aid of $\underline{w}_{1n}$ and $\underline{w}_{2n}$ from (39), on the conditions that $\gamma > 0$ and $\gamma + \delta > c$, by means of: $\mu_{\underline{A}^{**}} := \Sigma_{n=0}^{\infty} h(n)\mu_{\underline{A}_n^{**}}$;

(I) $c \neq \delta$:

$$\mu_{\underline{A}^{**}} = \frac{\gamma}{\gamma+\delta-c}\frac{R}{r}\mu_{a_1} + \frac{r-\gamma}{(\gamma+\delta-c)(r+\delta-c)}\pi_w\mu_b;$$

(II) $c = \delta$:

$$\mu_{\underline{A}^{**}} = \frac{R}{r}\mu_{a_1} + \frac{r-\gamma}{r\gamma}\pi_{w,c=\delta}\mu_b.$$

Note: Refer to the note on p. 65 in connection with this.

Furthermore, the following expression occurs in (101):

$$\sum_{n=0}^{N} h(n)(\mu^2_{A_n^{**}} + \sigma^2_{A_n^{**}})$$

which provides the following more detailed expression:

$$\gamma_3 \sum_{n=0}^{N} (1+\gamma)^{-n}[w^2_{1n}(\mu^2_{a_1} + \sigma^2_{a_1}) + w^2_{2n}(\mu^2_b + \sigma^2_b) + 2w_{1n}w_{2n}(\mu_{a_1}\mu_b + \operatorname{cov}(\tilde{a}_1, \tilde{b}))].$$

In the case of a sufficiently large value of N, this expression can be approximated by substituting the coefficients $\underline{w}_{1n}$ and w_{2n} from (39) and on condition that $\gamma > 0$, $\gamma + \delta > c$ and $(1 - \delta + c)^2 < 1 + \gamma$, by:

$$\sum_{n=0}^{\infty} h(n)(\mu^2_{\underline{A}_n^{**}} + \sigma^2_{\underline{A}_n^{**}}) = \begin{cases} \text{(I)}, & \text{if } c \neq \delta; \\ \text{(II)}, & \text{if } c = \delta; \end{cases}$$

where:

$c \neq \delta$:

$$\begin{aligned}
\text{(I)} = {} & \frac{\gamma}{1 + \gamma - (1 - \delta + c)^2} \frac{R^2}{r^2} (\mu^2_{a_1} + \sigma^2_{a_1}) \\
& + \left[\frac{\gamma}{1 + \gamma - (1 - \delta + c)^2} + (rq)^2 - 2\frac{\gamma}{\gamma + \delta - c} rq\right] \\
& \cdot \frac{\pi_w^2}{(c - \delta)^2} (\mu_b^2 + \sigma_b^2) \\
& + 2\left[\frac{\gamma}{1 + \gamma - (1 - \delta + c)^2} - \frac{\gamma}{\gamma + \delta - c} rq\right] \frac{R}{r} \frac{\pi_w}{c - \delta} \\
& \cdot [\mu_{a_1}\mu_b + \operatorname{cov}(\tilde{a}_1, \tilde{b})];
\end{aligned}$$

$c = \delta$:

$$\begin{aligned}
\text{(II)} = {} & \frac{R^2}{r^2} (\mu^2_{a_1} + \sigma^2_{a_1}) + \left[\frac{2 + \gamma}{\gamma^2} + \frac{1}{r^2} - \frac{2}{r\gamma}\right] \pi^2_{w,c=\delta} (\mu_b^2 + \sigma_b^2) \\
& + 2\frac{r - \gamma}{r\gamma} \frac{R}{r} \pi_{w,c=\delta} [\mu_{a_1}\mu_b + \operatorname{cov}(\tilde{a}_1, \tilde{b})].
\end{aligned}$$

The theoretical parameter restrictions required for these formulae, $\gamma > 0$, $\gamma + \delta > c$ and $(1 - \delta + c)^2 < 1 + \gamma$, are all, incidentally, empirically substantiated: from the empirical results of Carliner (1982) it is known that $\delta > c$, and according to the *Statistische Jahrbücher*, γ has a positive value even for Germany (cf. p. 143; cf. also the empirical findings quoted in Keyfitz (1977; in particular, ch. 4), according to which γ exhibits only positive values). In general, one has:

$$\gamma < 0 \Leftrightarrow (0<)\eta_2 < -\eta_1,$$

i.e. the *fall* in the birth rate ($\hat{=}$ negative η_1), would have to exceed the death rate (η_2) in absolute terms for γ to become negative. I am not aware of any country with that type of situation.

As $\delta > c$ is the empirically relevant case attention will be focused below on the more general case where $c \neq \delta$. The special case where $c = \delta$ is of only theoretical interest – see note (i), p. 232.

If one applies the expressions developed above to (101), $V^2_{\underline{A}^{**}}$ thus obtained still proves very unwieldy for analytical purposes. The terms resulting from partial differentiation are complicated and render an analytical evaluation of the derivatives impossible as a general rule. The latter, however, is one of the explicit objectives of this study (cf. Introduction). But, progress is possible. From the empirical studies quoted at the end of Section 2.1.1 it follows that the parameters δ and c differ in value but are very close (according to the standard parameter set, which has comparatively the best empirical support, the difference amounts to: $\delta - c = 0.02$). The error generated by the approximation: $(1 - \delta + c)^2 \simeq 1 - 2(\delta - c)$ can consequently be ignored (it is below 1% at $\delta - c = 0.02$; cf. also Bronstein and Semendjajew, 1979, pp. 85 and 153). Thus:

$$\frac{\gamma}{1 + \gamma - (1 - \delta + c)^2} \simeq \frac{\gamma}{\gamma + 2(\delta - c)}.$$

At the same time, the following applies approximately for closely related parameters δ and c (i.e. for small differences $\delta - c$):

$$\left(\frac{\gamma}{\gamma + \delta - c}\right)^2 = \frac{\gamma}{\gamma + 2(\delta - c) + \dfrac{(\delta - c)^2}{\gamma}} \simeq \frac{\gamma}{\gamma + 2(\delta - c)}.$$

This discovery signifies great progress for the analytical tractability of $V^2_{\underline{A}^{**}}$, since now it is possible to identify a corresponding coefficient structure in $\mu^2_{\underline{A}^{**}}$ and $\Sigma_n h(n)(\mu^2_{\underline{A}^{**}_n} + \sigma^2_{\underline{A}^{**}_n})$:

$$\mu^2_{\underline{A}^{**}} = z_1^2 \mu^2_{a_1} + z_2^2 \mu^2_b + 2 z_1 z_2 \mu_{a_1} \mu_b;$$

$$\sum_n h(n)(\mu^2_{\underline{A}^{**}_n} + \sigma^2_{\underline{A}^{**}_n}) \simeq z_1^2(\mu^2_{a_1} + \sigma^2_{a_1}) + z_2^2(\mu^2_b + \sigma^2_b) + 2 z_1 z_2 [\mu_{a_1}\mu_b + \operatorname{cov}(\tilde{a}_1, \tilde{b})];$$

where:

$$z_1 := \frac{\gamma}{\gamma + \delta - c} \frac{R}{r},$$

$$z_2 := \frac{r - \gamma}{(\gamma + \delta - c)(r + \delta - c)} \pi_w \left[\overset{(c \neq \delta)}{=} \left(\frac{\gamma}{\gamma + \delta - c} - rq\right) \frac{\pi_w}{c - \delta}\right].$$

If these expressions are applied to the general equation (101), (102) is obtained.

Notes: (i) The special case where $c = \delta$ does not produce any new aspects. Technical simplifications are obtained, but there are no qualitative changes to the results found in Sections 4.2, 4.3 and 4.4.

In this case, an approximation also results in the discovery of a coefficient structure, which then permits an explicit analysis to be undertaken; where $c = \delta$:

$$z_1 = \frac{R}{r} \quad \text{and} \quad z_2 = \frac{r - \gamma}{r\gamma} \pi_{w,c=\delta}.$$

(ii) In the case where $r = \gamma$, it follows, in accordance with (102), that: $V^2_{\underline{A}^{**}} = V^2_{a_1}$. Thus, if the interest rate is equal to the sum of the birth growth rate and the death rate, then the inequality of planned disposable earnings is identical to that of the full-time schooling production efficiencies; the influence of the working phase production efficiencies $\tilde{b}$ drops out. This result is indeed interesting, but really just a mathematical nicety.

Appendix 6 Comparative static analysis of optimal lifetime earnings

For the optimal lifetime disposable earnings of the individual j, $j \in J$, the following applies (cf. Section 5.1):

$$W^{j*} = V^{j**}[1 - \ln(1+r)S^{j*}]$$
$$= d_2 a_0^j + d_3 b^j; \tag{I}$$

see (121) concerning d_2 and d_3; $b^j := b_0^{j^{1/a}}$.

(I) can be approximated by the following, for a sufficiently large N:

$$\underline{W}^{j*} = \frac{R(1+r)}{r+\delta-c}(a_0^j + d_1 b^j), \tag{II}$$

with d_1 obtained from (124).

(II) is always employed when (I) can no longer be handled analytically. Refer to the note on p. 167 again.

One can thereby obtain the following comparative static results, in accordance with the theoretical parameter restrictions of the model:

$$\frac{\partial W^{j*}}{\partial a_0^j} = d_2 > 0. \tag{III}$$

$$\frac{\partial W^{j*}}{\partial b_0^j} = \frac{d_3}{a} b_0^{j^{\frac{b_1+b_2}{a}}} > 0. \tag{IV}$$

$$\frac{\partial W^{j*}}{\partial R} = \Pi_N a_0^j + \frac{1-b_1}{aR} d_3 b^j > 0. \tag{V}$$

$$\frac{\partial W^{j*}}{\partial P} = -\frac{b_2 d_3}{aP} b^j < 0. \tag{VI}$$

$$\frac{\partial \underline{W}^{j*}}{\partial r} < 0; \tag{VII}$$

since:

$$\frac{\partial\left[\dfrac{R(1+r)}{r+\delta-c}\right]}{\partial r} = -\frac{R(1-\delta+c)}{(r+\delta-c)^2} < 0, \quad \text{and} \quad \frac{\partial d_1}{\partial r} < 0;$$

simultaneously (as a reminder): $a_0^j, b^j, d_1 > 0$.

In a similar way the following are obtained:

$$\frac{\partial \underline{W}^{j*}}{\partial \delta} < 0. \qquad \text{(VIII)}$$

$$\frac{\partial \underline{W}^{j*}}{\partial c} > 0. \qquad \text{(IX)}$$

$$\frac{\partial \underline{W}^{j*}}{\partial b_1} > 0; \quad \frac{\partial \underline{W}^{j*}}{\partial b_2} > 0. \qquad \text{(X)}$$

Note: The empirical findings available on individual lifetime earnings are compatible with the above model predictions. (III), (IV) and (VII) were confirmed by the empirical studies of Lillard (1977a, pp. 46–8; 1977b); also (VII) by Parsons (1978, p. 558).[16] No empirical studies exist as yet on the remaining predictions.

[16] Note that the studies quoted refer to a 'representative individual' (Lillard, 1977a, p. 46).

References

Abbreviations

AER	*American Economic Review*
EJ	*Economic Journal*
Em	*Econometrica*
IER	*International Economic Review*
JASA	*Journal of the American Statistical Association*
JHR	*Journal of Human Resources*
JPE	*Journal of Political Economy*
QJE	*Quarterly Journal of Economics*
RES	*Review of Economic Studies*
REStat	*Review of Economics and Statistics*
RIW	*Review of Income and Wealth*

Abraham, K.G., and Medoff, J.L. (1983). Length of service and the operation of internal labor markets. *NBER Working Paper*, No. 1085.

Aitchison, J., and Brown, J.A.C. (1957). *The Lognormal Distribution*. Cambridge University Press, Cambridge.

Arrow, K.J. (1962). The economic implications of learning by doing. *RES*, 29: 155–73.

Atkinson, A.B. (1975). *The Economics of Inequality*. Oxford University Press, Oxford.

Atkinson, A.B., ed. (1976). *The Personal Distribution of Incomes*. London.

Atkinson, A.B., and Cowell, F.A., eds. (1983). *Panel Data on Incomes*. London.

Atkinson, A.B., and Harrison, A.J. (1978). *Distribution of Personal Wealth in Britain*. Cambridge University Press, Cambridge.

Atkinson, A.B., Maynard, A.K., and Trinder, C.G. (1983). *Parents and Children*. London.

Barge, M., and Payen, J.F. (1982). Niveau et évolution des salaires individuels. *Annales de l'INSEE*, No. 45.

Baten, W.D. (1935). A formula for finding the skewness of the combination of two or more samples. *JASA*, 30: 95–8.

Baudelot, C. (1983). The individual evolution of earnings in France: 1970–1975. In Atkinson, A.B., and Cowell, F.A., eds. *Panel Data on Incomes*, ch. 3. London.
Beach, C.M., Card, D.E., and Flatters, F. (1981). *Distribution of Income and Wealth in Ontario: Theory and Evidence*. Toronto.
Becker, G.S. (1975). *Human Capital*. University of Chicago Press, Chicago.
(1976). *The Economic Approach to Human Behavior*. Chicago.
Behrman, J.R., and Birdsall, N. (1983). The quality of schooling: quantity alone is misleading. *AER*, 73: 928–46.
Ben-Porath, Y. (1967). The production of human capital and the life cycle of earnings. *JPE*, 75: 352–65.
Blinder, A.S. (1974). *Toward an Economic Theory of Income Distribution*. MIT Press, Cambridge, Massachusetts.
(1980). The level and distribution of economic well-being. In Feldstein, M., ed. *The American Economy in Transition*, ch. 6. University of Chicago Press, Chicago.
Blinder, A.S., and Weiss, Y. (1976). Human capital and labor supply: a synthesis. *JPE*, 84: 449–72.
Block, N., and Dworkin, G., eds. (1976). *The IQ Controversy*. London.
Blomquist, N.S. (1981). A comparison of distribution of annual and lifetime income: Sweden around 1970. *RIW*, 27: 243–64.
Boissevain, C.H. (1939). Distribution of abilities depending upon two or more independent factors. *Metron*, 13: 49–58.
Bourguignon, F., and Morrisson, C. (1982). Earnings mobility over the life-cycle: a 30-years panel sample of French 'cadres'. Ecole Normale Supérieure, CNRS, Paris. Document No. 54.
Bowles, S. (1972). Schooling and inequality from generation to generation. *JPE*, 80: 219–51.
(1973). Understanding unequal economic opportunity. *AER Papers and Proceedings*, 63: 346–56.
Bowles, S., and Nelson, V.I. (1974). The 'inheritance of *IQ*' and the intergenerational reproduction of economic inequality. *REStat*, 56: 39–51.
Bronstein, I.N., and Semendjajew, K.A. (1979). *Taschenbuch der Mathematik*. Thun.
Brown, J.A.C. (1976). The mathematical and statistical theory of income distribution. In Atkinson, A.B., ed. *The Personal Distribution of Incomes*, ch. 3. London.
Brown, J.N. (1980). How close to an auction is the labor market? *NBER Working Paper*, No. 603.
Bryson, A.E. Jr., and Ho, Y.C. (1969). *Applied Optimal Control*. Ginn, Waltham.
Burt, C. (1943). Ability and income. *British Journal of Educational Psychology*, 13: 83–98.
Carliner, G. (1982). The wages of older men. *JHR*, 17: 25–38.
Carter, C.O. (1976). The genetic basis of inequality. In Atkinson, A.B., ed. *The Personal Distribution of Incomes*, ch. 4. London.
Champernowne, D.G. (1953). A model of income distribution. *EJ*, 63: 318–51.
(1973). *The Distribution of Income between Persons*. Cambridge.
(1978). The place of stochastic models of income distribution amongst other

models of it. In Griliches, Z., et al., eds. *Income Distribution and Economic Inequality*, ch. B.2. Frankfurt.
Cliff, A.D., and Ord, J.K. (1973). *Spatial Autocorrelation*. London.
Conlisk, J. (1971). A bit of evidence on the income–education–ability interrelation. *JHR*, 6: 358–62.
Cornford, T. (1980). A life-cycle model of career experience: the American academic labour force. *CLE/LSE Discussion Paper*, No. 68.
Cowell, F.A. (1973). *Age Structure and the Size Distribution of Incomes*. Cambridge.
(1977). *Measuring Inequality*. Philip Allan, Oxford.
Cox, D.R., and Miller, H.D. (1965). *The Theory of Stochastic Processes*. London.
Creedy, J. (1978). A note on the analysis of changes in earnings. *EJ*, 88: 126–33.
Creedy, J., and Hart, P.E. (1979). Age and the distribution of earnings. *EJ*, 89: 280–93.
Dagum, C. (1977). A new model of personal income distribution: specification and estimation. *Economie Appliquée*, 30: 413–37.
Danziger, S., Haveman, R., and Smolensky, E. (1977). The measurement and trend of inequality: comment. *AER*, 67: 505–12.
Eckaus, R.S. (1963). Investment in human capital: a comment. *JPE*, 71: 501–5.
Eden, B. (1980). Stochastic dominance in human capital. *JPE*, 88: 135–45.
Eicker, F. (1964). Über den Zentralen Grenzwertsatz für abhängige Zufallsvariable. *Zeitschrift für Wahrscheinlichkeitstheorie*, 3: 193–203.
Elderton, W.P., and Johnson, N.L. (1969). *Systems of Frequency Curves*. Cambridge.
Fase, M.M.G. (1970). *An Econometric Model of Age–Income Profiles*. Rotterdam University Press.
Feller, W. (1968). *An Introduction to Probability Theory and Its Applications*, vol. I. John Wiley, New York.
Fisher, I. (1930). *The Theory of Interest*. New York.
Fisz, M. (1976). *Wahrscheinlichkeitsrechnung und Mathematische Statistik*. Berlin.
Friedman, M. (1957). *A Theory of the Consumption Function*. Princeton.
Fuller, W.C., Manski, C.F., and Wise, D.A. (1982). New evidence on the economic determinants of postsecondary schooling choices. *JHR*, 17: 477–98.
Galton, F. (1879). The geometric mean in vital and social statistics. *Proceedings of the Royal Society*, 29: 365–6.
Ghiselli, E.E. (1969). Managerial talent. In Wolfle, D., ed. *The Discovery of a Talent*. Cambridge, Massachusetts.
Gibrat, R. (1930). Une loi des répartitions économiques: l'effet proportionnel. *Bulletin Statistique Générale Francais*, 19: 469.
(1931). *Les inégalités économiques*. Sirey, Paris.
Gnedenko, B.V., and Kolmogorow, A.N. (1968). *Limit Distributions for Sums of Independent Random Variables*. Addison-Wesley, Reading, Mass.
Göseke, G., and Bedau, K.D. (1974). *Verteilung und Schichtung der Einkommen der privaten Haushalte in der BRD 1950–1975*. DIW, Berlin.
Goldberger, A.S. (1978). The genetic determination of income: comment. *AER*, 68: 960–9.
(1979). Heritability. *Economica*, 46: 327–47.
Goodman, L.A. (1960). On the exact variance of products. *JASA*, 55: 708–13.

Granovetter, M.S. (1974). *Getting a Job: A Study of Contacts and Careers.* Harvard University Press, Cambridge, Mass.

Griliches, Z. (1977a). Estimating the returns to schooling: some econometric problems. *Em*, 45: 1–22.

(1977b). The distribution of earnings and human wealth in a life-cycle context: comment. In Juster, F.T., ed. *The Distribution of Economic Well-Being*, 618–20. NBER, Cambridge, Mass.

(1979). Sibling models and data in economics: beginnings of a survey. *JPE*, 87: 37–64.

Griliches, Z., and Mason, W.M. (1972). Education, income, and ability. *JPE*, 80: 74–103.

Gustafsson, B. (1980). Income and family background. In Klevmarken, N.A., and Lybeck, J.A., eds. *The Statics and Dynamics of Income*, ch. 8. Tieto Ltd., Clevedon.

Haldane, J.B.S. (1942). Moments of the distributions of powers and products of normal variates. *Biometrika*, 32: 226–42.

Haley, W.J. (1973). Human capital: the choice between investment and income. *AER*, 63: 929–44.

(1976). Estimation of the earnings profile from optimal human capital accumulation. *Em*, 44: 1223–38.

Hanushek, E.A., and Quigley, J.M. (1978). Implicit investment profiles and intertemporal adjustments of relative wages. *AER*, 68: 67–79.

Harris, M., and Holmström, B. (1982). A theory of wage dynamics. *RES*, 49: 315–33.

Harrison, A.J. (1981). Earnings by size: a tale of two distributions. *RES*, 48: 621–31.

Hart, P.E. (1976). The dynamics of earnings, 1963–1973. *EJ*, 86: 551–65.

Hartog, J. (1976). Ability and age–income profiles. *RIW*, 22: 61–74.

Hause, J.C. (1972). Earnings profile: ability and schooling. *JPE*, 80: 108–38.

(1977). The covariance structure of earnings and the on-the-job training hypothesis. *Annals of Economic and Social Measurement*, 6: 335–65.

(1980). The fine structure of earnings and the on-the-job training hypothesis. *Em*, 48: 1013–29.

Heckman, J.J. (1976). A life-cycle model of earnings, learning, and consumption. *JPE*, 84: 11–44.

Hirshleifer, J. (1970). Investment, interest and capital. Englewood Cliffs.

Hogg, R.V., and Craig, A.T. (1978). *Introduction to Mathematical Statistics.* Macmillan Publishing Co., New York.

Houthakker, H.S. (1974). The size distribution of labour incomes derived from the distribution of aptitudes. In Sellekaerts, W., ed. *Econometrics and Economic Theory*, ch. 9. London.

Ijiri, Y., and Simon, H.A. (1977). *Skew distributions and the sizes of business firms.* North-Holland, Amsterdam.

Intriligator, M.D. (1971). *Mathematical Optimization and Economic Theory.* Prentice-Hall, Englewood Cliffs, N.J.

Irvine, I. (1980). The distribution of income and wealth in Canada in a life-cycle framework. *Canadian Journal of Economics*, 13: 455–74.

Ishikawa, T. (1975). A note on the optimal spacing properties in a simple Jevonian model of educational investment. *QJE*, 89: 633–42.
Jevons, W.S. (1871). *The Theory of Political Economy*. Macmillan, London.
Johnson, T., and Hebein, F.J. (1974). Investments in human capital and growth in personal income 1956–1966. *AER*, 64: 604–15.
Kalecki, M. (1945). On the Gibrat distribution. *Em*, 13: 161–70.
Kamien, M.I. and Schwartz, N.L. (1981). *Dynamic Optimization: The Calculus of Variations and Optimal Control in Economics and Management*. North-Holland, New York.
Kapteyn, J.C. (1903). *Skew Frequency Curves in Biology and Statistics*. Nordhoff, Groningen.
Kendall, M., and Stuart, A. (1977). *The Advanced Theory of Statistics*, vol. 1: Distribution Theory. C. Griffin, London.
Keyfitz, N. (1977). *Applied Mathematical Demography*. J. Wiley, New York.
Killingsworth, M.R. (1982). 'Learning by doing' and 'Investment in training': a synthesis of two 'rival' models of the life cycle. *RES*, 49: 263–71.
Klevmarken, N.A. (1981). On the stability of age–earnings profiles. *Working Paper* No. 1981-07-14, University of Gothenburg.
Lazear, E. (1976). Age, experience, and wage growth. *AER*, 66: 548–58.
Lee, J.K. (1981). Distributional implications of imperfect capital markets. *NBER Working Paper* No. 663.
Levhari, D., and Weiss, Y. (1974). The effect of risk on the investment in human capital. *AER*, 64: 950–63.
Lichtenberg, F.R. (1981). Training, tenure, and productivity. *NBER Working Paper* No. 671.
Lillard, L.A. (1977a). Inequality: earnings vs. human wealth. *AER*, 67: 42–53.
(1977b). The distribution of earnings and human wealth in a life-cycle context. In Juster, F.T., ed. *The Distribution of Economic Well-Being*, ch. 14. NBER, Cambridge, Mass.
Lillard, L.A., and Weiss, Y. (1979). Components of variation in panel earnings data: American scientists 1960–70. *Em*, 47: 437–54.
Lillard, L.A., and Willis, R.J. (1978). Dynamic aspects of earning mobility. *Em*, 46: 985–1012.
Lomnicki, Z.A. (1967). On the distribution of products of random variables. *Journal of the Royal Statistical Society, Series B*, 29: 513–24.
Lydall, H. (1968). *The Structure of Earnings*. Oxford.
(1976). Theories of the distribution of earnings. In Atkinson, A.B., ed. *The Personal Distribution of Incomes*, ch. 1. London.
Mandelbrot, B. (1960). The Pareto–Lévy Law and the distribution of income. *IER*, 1: 79–106.
(1961). Stable Paretian random functions and the multiplicative variation of income. *Em*, 29: 517–43.
Mayer, K.U., and Papastefanou, G. (1983). Arbeitseinkommen im Lebensverlauf: Probleme der retrospektiven Erfassung und empirische Materialien. In Schmähl, W., ed. *Ansätze der Lebenseinkommensanalyse*, 101–22. J.C.B. Mohr, Tübingen.

McAlister, D. (1879). The law of the geometric mean. *Proceedings of the Royal Society*, 29: 367.
McCabe, P.J. (1983). Optimal leisure–effort choice with endogenously determined earnings. *Journal of Labor Economics*, 1. 308–29.
McDonald, J.B. (1984). Some generalized functions for the size distribution of income. *Em*, 52: 647–63.
McDonald, J.B., and Ransom, M.R. (1979). Functional forms, estimation techniques and the distribution of income. *Em*, 47: 1513–25.
Meade, J.E. (1973). The inheritance of inequalities. *Proceedings of the British Academy*, 59: 355–81.
Mincer, J. (1958). Investment in human capital and personal income distribution. *JPE*, 66: 281–302.
(1970). The distribution of labor incomes: a survey. *Journal of Economic Literature*, 8: 1–26.
(1974). *Schooling, Experience and Earnings*. NBER, New York.
(1979). Human capital and earnings. In Windham, D., ed. *Economic Dimensions of Education*. National Academy of Education.
Mincer, J., and Ofek, H. (1982). Interrupted work careers: depreciation and restoration of human capital. *JHR*, 17: 3–24.
Moss, M. (1978). Income distribution issues viewed in a lifetime income perspective. *RIW*, 24: 119–36.
Müller, P.H., and Vahl, H. (1976). Pearson's system of frequency curves whose left boundary and first three moments are known. *Biometrika*, 63: 191–4.
Osberg, L. (1977). Stochastic process models and the distribution of earnings. *RIW*, 23: 205–15.
(1981). *Economic Inequality in Canada*. Toronto.
Parsons, D.O. (1978). The autocorrelation of earnings, human wealth inequality, and income contingent loans. *QJE*, 92: 551–69.
Phelps Brown, E.H. (1977). *The Inequality of Pay*. Oxford.
Pissarides, C.A. (1982). From school to university: the demand for post-compulsory education in Britain. *EJ*, 92: 654–67.
Psacharopoulos, G., and Layard, R. (1979). Human capital and earnings: British evidence and a critique. *RES*, 46: 485–503.
Reijn, H.v., and Theeuwes, J. (1981). Optimum accumulation of human capital. Discussion Paper No. 8112/G, Erasmus University Rotterdam, Institute for Economic Research.
Ricardo, D. (1821). *The Principles of Political Economy and Taxation*. Dent, London.
Riley, J.G. (1976). Information, screening and human capital. *AER* Papers and Proceedings, 66: 254–60.
(1979). Testing the educational screening hypothesis. *JPE*, 87: 227–52.
Rizzuto, R., and Wachtel, P. (1980). Further evidence on the returns to school quality. *JHR*, 15: 240–54.
Rosen, S. (1973). Income generating functions and capital accumulation. Discussion Paper No. 306, Harvard Institute of Economic Research.
(1976). A theory of life earnings. *JPE*, 84: 45–67.

(1977). Human capital: a survey of empirical research. In Ehrenberg, R.G., ed. *Research in Labor Economics*, vol. I, 3–39. JAI Press, Greenwich.
Ross, S., Taubman, P., and Wachter, M. (1981). Learning by observing and the distribution of wages. In Rosen, S., ed. *Studies in Labor Markets*, ch. 11. University of Chicago Press, Chicago.
Roussas, G.G. (1973). *A First Course in Mathematical Statistics*. Reading.
Roy, A.D. (1950). The distribution of earnings and of individual output. *EJ*, 60: 489–505.
Rutherford, R.S.G. (1955). Income distributions: a new model. *Em*, 23: 277–94.
Ryan, J. (1972). *IQ* – the illusion of objectivity. In Richardson, K., and Spears, D., eds. *Race and Intelligence*, 36–55. Baltimore.
Ryder, H.E., Stafford, F.P., and Stephan, P.E. (1976). Labor, leisure and training over the life cycle. *IER*, 17: 651–74.
Sahota, G.S. (1978). Theories of personal income distribution: a survey. *Journal of Economic Literature*, 16: 1–55.
Samuelson, P.A. (1965). Proof that properly anticipated prices fluctuate randomly. *Industrial Management Review*, 6: 41–9.
Sattinger, M. (1980). *Capital and the Distribution of Labor Earnings*. North-Holland, Amsterdam.
Schmähl, W., and Göbel, D. (1983). Lebenseinkommensverläufe aus Längsschnittsdaten der Rentenversicherungsträger. In Schmähl, W., ed. *Ansätze der Lebenseinkommensanalyse*, 126–72. Tübingen.
Schönfeld, P. (1971). A useful Central Limit theorem for *m*-dependent variables. *Metrika*, 17: 116–28.
Schumpeter, J. (1916). Das Grundprinzip der Verteilungstheorie. *Archiv für Sozialwissenschaft und Sozialpolitik*, 42: 1–88.
Seiler, E. (1982). Piece rate vs. time rate: the effect of incentives on earnings. *NBER Working Paper*, No. 879.
Shorrocks, A.F. (1976a). Income Mobility and the Markov Assumption. *EJ*, 86: 566–78.
(1976b). The mathematical and statistical theory of income distribution: comment. In Atkinson, A.B., ed. *The Personal Distribution of Incomes*, 88–92. London.
(1980). The class of additively decomposable inequality measures. *Em*, 48: 613–25.
(1982). Inequality decomposition by factor components. *Em*, 50: 193–211.
Smith, A. (1776). *An Inquiry into the Nature and Causes of the Wealth of Nations*. London.
Solmon, L. (1975). The definition and impact of college quality. *Explorations in Economic Research*, 2. NBER.
Solmon, L.C., and Wachtel, P. (1975). The effects on income of type of college attended. *Sociology of Education*, 48, 75–90.
Solomon, H., and Stephens, M.A. (1978). Approximations to density functions using Pearson curves. *JASA*, 73: 153–60.
Springer, M.D. (1979). *The Algebra of Random Variables*. J. Wiley, New York.
Statistisches Jahrbuch 1984. Statistisches Bundesamt, Wiesbaden.

Steindl, J. (1965). *Random Processes and the Growth of Firms*. London.
Stigler, G.J. (1962). Information in the labor market. *JPE*, 70: 94–105.
Taubman, P.J. (1975). *Sources of Inequality in Earnings*. Amsterdam.
(1976). The determinants of earnings: genetics, family, and other environments. *AER*, 66: 858–70.
Taubman, P.J., and Wales, T. (1974). *Higher Education and Earnings*. New York.
Thatcher, A.R. (1968). The distribution of earnings of employees in Great Britain. *Journal of the Royal Statistical Society Series A*, 131: 133–80.
(1976). The New Earnings Survey and the distribution of earnings. In Atkinson, A.B., ed. *The Personal Distribution of Incomes*, ch. 8. London.
Theil, H. (1967). *Economics and Information Theory*. Amsterdam.
Thurow, L.C. (1970). Comment. In Hansen, W.L., ed. *Education, income, and human capital*, 151–4. NBER, New York.
(1975). *Generating Inequality*. Basic Books, New York.
Tinbergen, J. (1956). On the theory of income distribution. *Weltwirtschaftliches Archiv* 77, II: 155–75.
Tukey, J.W. (1958). The propagation of errors, fluctuations and tolerances. Technical Report, No. 10, Statistical Techniques Research Group, Princeton University.
Tyler, L.E. (1965). *The Psychology of Human Differences*. New York.
Vartia, P.L.I., and Vartia, Y.O. (1980). Description of the income distribution by the scaled *F* distribution model. In Klevmarken, N.A., and Lybeck, J.A., eds. *The Statics and Dynamics of Income*, ch. 2. Clevedon.
Vaughan, R.N. (1975). A study of the distribution of wealth. Ph.D. thesis, University of Cambridge.
Wachtel, P. (1975). The effect of school quality on achievement, attainment levels, and lifetime earnings. *Explorations in Economic Research*, 2: 502–36. NBER.
Waldman, M. (1984). Worker allocation, hierarchies and the wage distribution. *RES*, 51: 95–109.
Wallace, T.D., and Ihnen, L.A. (1975). Full-time schooling in life cycle models of human capital accumulation. *JPE*, 83: 137–55.
Weisbrod, B.A., and Karpoff, P. (1968). Monetary returns to college education, student ability, and college quality. *REStat*, 50: 491–7.
Weiss, Y. (1971). Ability and the investment in schooling: a theoretical note on J. Mincer's 'Distribution of labor incomes'. *Journal of Economic Literature*, 9: 459–61.
Welch, F. (1970). Education in production. *JPE*, 78: 35–59.
(1975). Human capital theory: education, discrimination, and life cycles. *AER Papers and Proceedings*, 65: 63–73.
Willis, R.J., and Rosen, S. (1979). Education and self-selection. *JPE*, 87: 7–36.
Wise, D.A. (1975). Academic achievement and job performance. *AER*, 65: 350–66.
Wood, A. (1978). *A Theory of Pay*. Cambridge University Press, Cambridge.

Index

Selected notation

a_0	Basic stock of human capital at the beginning of the planning horizon ($a_0 = K_0(0)$; cf. (34))
a_1	Human capital production efficiency during the full-time schooling phase (cf. (35))
A	Expected disposable earnings (cf. (9a): A_n^j; (14): A_n; (30): A_n^*; (38): A_n^{**}; (39): $\underline{A}_n^{**}$; (51) and/or(62): $\tilde{A}_n^{**}$)
b	Modified working phase production efficiency ($b := b_0^{1/a}$)
b_0	Human capital production efficiency during the working phase (cf. (18))
b_1, b_2	Human capital production elasticities
b_3	On-the-job-sorting parameter (see Section 2.3.5)
c	Learning-by-doing rate
C	Random income component (see Section 1.3.2)
CR	Class-rank variable
CU	Cultural influences
D	Amount of educational goods and services purchased
DF	Lydall's *D*-factor (see p. 37)
e	Stochastic shock; random income variation (cf. (7))
G	Genetic endowment
$h(n)$	Age distribution (cf. (97))
HO	Family background
I	Human capital investment costs; costs of education
j	Personal index: individual j
K	Human capital stock
$l(n)$	Probability of survival (cf.(96))
LA	Learning ability
n	Working age, earning age; earnings period
N	Length of working life; earnings lifespan
P	Price of educational goods; price per unit of *D*
Q	Human capital production function; (explicitly) produced human capital (cf. (15))
QPC	Personality and character traits (see p. 37)
r	Rate of interest

R	Human capital price; wage rate
s	(Re)invested fraction of human capital stock (sK denotes the amount of human capital diverted from the existing stock for Q production)
S	Length of full-time schooling
SQ	Schooling quality
V	Value of disposable periodic earnings discounted from the point of entry into the labour market (cf. (17); Fig. 7)
W	Value of disposable periodic earnings discounted from the point of economic birth; disposable lifetime earnings; human wealth (cf. Fig. 7)
Y	Disposable earnings
δ	Human capital depreciation rate
η_1	Birth growth rate; rate of increaase in births
η_2	Death rate
v	Inability to recognise productivity and communicate this (see Section 2.3.5)
ψ	Human capital shadow price (cf. (25))

***

a	$(:=1-b_1-b_2)$
d	$(:=d_3/d_2)$
d_1	(cf. (124))
d_2, d_3	(see definition p. 165)
h_0	$(:=V_b/V_{a_1})$
h_w	$(:=V_b/V_{a_0})$
k	$(:=\sigma_{a_1}/\sigma_b)$
k_w	$(:=\sigma_{a_0}/\sigma_b)$
M_n	(see definition p. 47)
$\hat{M}_n$	(see definition p. 63)
p	(see definition p. 166)
q	$(:=1/(r+\delta-c))$
q_i	(see definition p. 47)
RU_1, RU_2	(cf. (138))
T	(see definition p. 68)
u	(see definition p. 148)
υ_1, υ_2	(see definitions p. 190)
w_{1n}, w_{2n}	(see definitions p. 62)
$\underline{w}_{1n}$, $\underline{w}_{2n}$	(see definitions p. 68)
$\tilde{W}_1$, $\tilde{W}_2$	(see definitions p. 179)
$\tilde{X}_t^j$	$(:=\log \tilde{Y}_t^j)$
z_1, z_2	(see definitions p. 148)
α_n	(see definition p. 97)
β_1, β_2	(see definitions p. 186)

β_n	(see definition p. 226)
γ	$(:=n_1+n_2)$
γ_3	(see definition p. 142)
Δ_1, Δ_2	(see definitions p. 225)
κ	(cf. (149))
ξ	(see definition p. 111)
π_w	(see definition p. 68)
$\pi_{w,c=\delta}$	(see definition p. 68)
π_β	(see definition p. 226, footnote 15)
Π_N	(see definition p. 61)
Υ	(see definition p. 190)
χ	(see definition p. 118)
χ_w	(see definition p. 168)
Ω	(see definition p. 180)

***

$\tilde{}$	normally identifies a random variable (e.g. $\tilde{X}$)
$\sim$	is distributed as
$\sim$asy	is asymptotically distributed as
$E(\tilde{X})$, μ_X	expected value or mean value of random variable $\tilde{X}$
var $(\tilde{X})$, $\sigma^2{}_X$	variance of random variable $\tilde{X}$
$V_X^2 := \sigma_X^2/\mu_X^2$	squared coefficient of variation of $\tilde{X}$

$$\gamma_1(\tilde{X}) := \frac{E[(\tilde{X}-\mu_X)^3]}{\sigma_X^3}$$ Measure of skewness of the distribution of $\tilde{X}$

$$\gamma_2(\tilde{X}) := \frac{E[(\tilde{X}-\mu_X)^4]}{\sigma_X^4} - 3$$ Measure of kurtosis of the distribution of $\tilde{X}$

***

f_X	Density function or (expected) relative frequency function of $\tilde{X}$
F_X	Distribution function of $\tilde{X}$
$N(\mu, \sigma^2)$	Normal distribution (with parameters μ and σ^2)
$\Lambda(\mu, \sigma^2)$	Log-normal distribution (with parameters μ and σ^2)
$_{iid}(\mu, \sigma^2)$	Independently and identically distributed (with parameters μ and σ^2)
cov $(\tilde{X}, \tilde{Y})$	covariance of $\tilde{X}$ and $\tilde{Y}$

$$\rho_{XY} := \frac{\text{cov}(\tilde{X}, \tilde{Y})}{\sigma_X \sigma_Y}$$ correlation coefficient of $\tilde{X}$ and $\tilde{Y}$